Transforming Urban Education

Joseph Kretovics
University of North Carolina–Chapel Hill

Edward J. Nussel
University of Toledo

Allyn and Bacon
Boston • London • Toronto • Sydney • Tokyo • Singapore

Series Editor: Virginia Lanigan
Editorial Assistant: Nicole DePalma
Cover Administrator: Linda Dickinson
Manufacturing Buyer: Megan Cochran
Production Coordinator: Sheryl Avruch
Editorial-Production Service: Spectrum Publisher Services
Cover Designer: Suzanne Harbison

Copyright © 1994 by Allyn and Bacon
A Division of Simon & Schuster, Inc.
160 Gould Street
Needham Heights, Massachusetts 02194

Library of Congress Cataloging-in-Publication Data
Kretovics, Joseph.
    Transforming urban education / by Joseph Kretovics, Edward
J. Nussel.
      p. cm.
    Includes bibliographical references and index.
    ISBN 0-205-14568-X
    1. Education, Urban—United States. 2. Educational change—United
States. 3. Educational equalization—United States. 4. Education-
Social aspects—United States. I. Title.
LC5131.K74   1994
370.19′348′0973—dc20   93-16023
                                          CIP

Printed in the United States of America
10 9 8 7 6 5 4 3 2 1   98 97 96 95 94 93

To Lorraine, Mary Lou, Erika, David, and Elaine, whose love and encouragement provided the necessary support in the completion of this project

Contents

Part III Transforming Urban Schools 301

Preface

This book is about urban schools: their development, their problems, and their prospects. Obviously, schools are inextricably linked to the communities they serve through social, political, economic, and cultural interests. Therefore, to better comprehend urban schooling, the sociocultural relationships that transpire within the school as well as within the community must be linked to the broader political and economic issues of society-at-large. In a recent forum on "Race, Poverty, and the American City," Ann Markusen lamented the fact that social policy has been divorced from economic policy and economic decisions have been made that undermine urban programs (Markusen, 1993). The editors believe that urban education has been totally ignored by both social and economic policy, which has exacerbated many of the problems in urban schools that reflect the trauma of inner-city life. In this text, we attempt to provide selections that examine these issues from historical and contemporary perspectives.

In our examination of urban schools during a period of many years, we have found that the more things change, the more they remain the same, or, perhaps, grow worse. At the same time problems and issues that influence urban schools are being renamed, reviewed, or restructured, the underlying despair of poverty and disabling effects of educational and social disadvantages remain constant. How is it that even after the political and social movements following the Great Society the structure of society still places certain adults and children at educational, social, and economic disadvantages based on their class, race, gender, ethnicity, and exceptionality?

For example, Kozol (1967) provided a devastating critique of the condition of urban schools in his book *Death at an Early Age*. More than two decades later, in *Savage Inequalities* (1991), Kozol demonstrates that the dismal political, social, and economic conditions of urban communities continue to deteriorate. The impact of these conditions on schools and communities is profound and impedes the hopes of millions of Americans for equality of educational opportunity. Although schools historically raise the possibilities for hope as they relate to the communities they serve, the degree to which these communities are able to influence the schools must also be understood.

Unfortunately, the community influence on schools often reflects the economic depression of inner cities and the milieu of hopelessness and despair. To begin to realize the possibility for transforming urban education, we must first examine the historical nature of the problems of urban education and the communities in which these schools exist. Second, we must critically examine the present context in which education takes place to illuminate both the problems and the possibilities for change. Finally, educators must have a vision for change and the ability and conviction to act on that vision. We must develop a framework that takes seriously issues of class, race, gender, and ethnicity, as well as educational structures, in the difficult process of transforming urban schools.

To understand the problems and possibilities for change in urban education, issue-specific articles have been selected for their importance in illuminating the unfulfilled promise of equal educational opportunity. These articles broadly represent many of the issues that have confounded educators for the past 50 years. As the political pendulum sways back and forth, it appears that those interested in improving the quality of life in the city have failed to learn the lessons of history. Thus, they are destined to repeat the mistakes of the past. This was never more evident than in the social and economic policies that created the conditions for the urban uprisings of 1992.

While the impetus for this book did not develop during the urban uprisings of 1992, its purpose reflects a comparison of governmental responses to recent urban uprisings and the urban problems of the 1960s. It was during the 1960s that the social programs of the Great Society attempted to improve life in the cities. This effort was often directed at schools in an attempt to improve equality of educational opportunity. It maintained that education could compensate for some of the more deleterious effects of living in urban poverty. Teacher education also benefited from federal largess as monies were made available to prepare teachers to work in urban settings.

However, this period was punctuated by the urban riots of 1967. Following those uprisings, the bipartisan Kerner Commission studied the circumstances of the riots and concluded: "Our nation is moving toward two societies, one black, one white—separate and unequal" (1968, p. 1). Within that report, a number of suggestions for improving the urban condition were offered and more than 30 pages of recommendations regarding education were delineated. Few of the recommendations that were implemented have had lasting effects (Head Start is an exception). However, most of the recommendations were never truly implemented.

Today, the problems sound similar, although the demographics may be different. Whatever progress occurred during the 1970s regressed or disappeared during the 1980s. Federal aid to the cities has been cut and the government's role in ensuring equality of educational opportunity has been devastated. Schools and teachers have come under attack, particularly in the area of multicultural education. Cultural elitists have attempted to canonize Western European culture while launching a direct assault on what they construe to be "political correctness." At the highest levels of educational policy, we have moved from deficiency theory to theories of difference back to deficiency theory. As a result, urban development and education have been abandoned for privatization, marketplace rhetoric, and the cheery notion of choice, as if most of the people living in poverty have a choice.

So 25 years later, history repeats itself with the urban riots of 1992. Although those disruptions were more localized, they remind us that the social problems identified in the 1960s have not been addressed adequately. Moreover, governmental response has changed dramatically. Rather than establishing a bipartisan commission to study the issues and make recommendations, the Bush administration responded with economic quick fixes and appeals to the private sector. Perhaps the most incredible of these responses was the suggestion that Los Angeles sell its assets, in particular its airport, to subsidize the rebuilding of the south-central portion of the city (Hatfield and Waugh, 1992). As Giroux has stated: "It is quite remarkable that as the fires were burning in this long suffering city, the nation's highest elected public official refused to address the smoldering, social, economic, and cultural conditions that fueled the uprising" (Giroux, in press). Avoiding any inquiry into the causes of these urban uprisings, the Bush administration suggested the application of a Band-Aid to a severed artery and left our urban centers to bleed.

Irrespective of the many social, economic, and political problems that face urban communities, the schools exist for the purpose of educating all children. Teachers are part of the neverending struggle to create conditions in which learning takes place and provide the best educational opportunities possible in a given situation. They become the major vehicle available for children of the inner city to achieve even the slimmest hope of upward social mobility. When teachers and schools succeed, in light of overwhelming odds, few people seem to notice. Often their successes are questioned on ethical or moral grounds. When they fail, social critics and politicians are quick to offer their often overly simplistic recommendations for educational reform.

Unfortunately, many educational reforms fail to grasp the fact that the inequalities of life in the city have spawned a sense of powerlessness, alienation, and frustration that often impede the efforts of even the most gifted teacher. The social, economic, and political problems of the city also find their way into the schools. Children are not able to leave hunger, child abuse, drug and alcohol addiction, poverty, and racism at the door when they enter the classroom. Further, social issues such as one-parent families, AIDS, and homelessness exacerbate the situation. Finally, the complexities of change encouraged by advanced technology and new images of success depicted by mass media create apparitions that challenge the urban educator's ability to succeed.

Teachers are no longer teaching the bright, white, and polite students in bastions of cultural homogeneity for which they were trained. Many teachers find themselves ill-prepared to comprehend the multiple cultures that students bring to the classroom, let alone bring dignity and respect for those cultures. They are taught subject matter but not what to do when the subject does not pertain to the life experiences of the students. Teacher education programs rarely prepare teachers to make education meaningful to diverse groups of students, nor do they provide teachers with the knowledge and skills necessary to help students access the dominant culture without asking them to sacrifice their culture integrity.

With this collection, the editors hope to revive interest in the study of urban education and describe a number of issues that have challenged educators in their attempts to provide equality of educational opportunity. We have included authors who have made important contributions, both past and present, in order to reveal that conditions in urban society have not improved but, in many instances, deteriorated. The pervasive governmental belief that urban communities and schools should "do more with less" has obviously contributed to problems urban educators will face into the next century.

However, the editors are optimistic that a new age of hope is rising to replace the age of austerity. This confidence is a product of a renewed interest in the political, economic, and educational climate demonstrated by the 1992 Presidential election and a commitment to change from the new administration. If this commitment is sincere, informed, and lasting, we believe that equality of educational opportunity can become a reality. However, leadership must be provided by educators, parents, and community leaders, as well as local, state, and federal officials in addressing the enormous barriers to urban education reform. We trust that this collection provides some measure of assistance.

REFERENCES

Hatfield, L.D., and Waugh, D. (1992, May 24). "Right Wing's Smart Bombs." *The San Francisco Examiner,* pp. A–10.

Giroux, H.A. (in press). *The Politics of Difference and Mulitculturalism in the Era of the Los Angeles Uprising.*

Kozol, J. (1967). *Death at an Early Age.* Boston: Houghton Mifflin Co.

Kozol, J. (1991). *Savage Inequalities.* New York: Crown Publisher, Inc.

Markusen, A. (1993, February 12–13). "Race, Poverty, and the American City: The Kerner Commission Report in Retrospective." As reported in the *Chapel Hill Herald* on February 14, 1993, pp. 1–2. (Ann Markusen is Director of the Project on Regional and Industrial Economics at Rutgers University.)

Report of the National Advisory Commission on Civil Disorders (1968). New York: Bantam Books. Copyright, 1968, The New York Times Company.

ACKNOWLEDGMENTS

The authors would like to thank Valerie Iatridi and Laura Jenkins for their clerical and editorial assistance in this project. Kathy Hytten and Brian McCadden assisted in the search for articles and provided comments and editing on original material for which we are grateful. The insightful comments from Christine Sleeter, William Armaline, and Kathy Farber kept us honest and ultimately led to a better inclusion of articles. Finally, critical reviews from Vivian Ikpa, Mary Harris, Jayminn Sanford, and Karen Wesson were helpful as we put together the final manuscript. Finally, thanks go to Paula, Henry, and Peter.

Introduction: School Reform and Transforming Urban Education

DEFINING THE SCHOOL REFORM MOVEMENT

The 1980s have been called the decade of the school reform report because of the proliferation of reports and criticisms concerning public education (Kretovics, Farber, and Armaline, 1991). School reform reports served to spotlight the nature and function of public schooling and attempted to delineate a specific relationship between schooling and broader social, economic, political, and cultural interests. Many of the reports argued in favor of a wide range of additive reforms such as increased testing, more homework, a longer school year, a longer school day, and the internalization of an extensive list of cultural facts. Others suggested a plethora of technical solutions for the challenges facing public schools, ranging from the addition or reduction of certain educational requirements for teachers, to restructuring the school day or school year, to the addition of specific course requirements to the public school curriculum. For the most part, the reform efforts have been driven by what Barth (1986) called *the perseverance of list logic* and what Giroux (1988) has called *the ideology of the quick fix.*

Born out of the domestic recession of the early 1980s and fueled by an international economic crisis and escalating competition, these reports decried the condi-

1

tion of public education in the United States. Moreover, they attempted to identify a causal relationship between a failing economy and what they believed to be declining educational performance and standards. In this assault on public education, poorly performing schools were blamed for a faltering domestic economy and the decline in the ability of U.S. business and industry to compete in foreign markets. The solution to the lack of economic competitiveness by the United States was to focus on school reform. The focus was to implement the techniques and skills used by fledgling businesses and the free market economy, such as choice, vouchers, total quality management, magnet schools, and a list of other "quick fixes." The theory was that what is good for General Motors is good for the United States, even if GM was losing its share of the automobile market. However, the premises and assumptions that buttress many of the proposed solutions that call for school reform may not be correct and, consequently, may be inadequate. For example, if there is a faltering economy and a decline in the competitiveness of U.S. businesses and industries in a world market, it may, as Berliner (1992) argues, have more to do with "poor business management and faulty economic policies, but it is certainly not due to the lack of a technically skilled workforce" (p. 32).

Drawing on the work of Carson, Huelskamp, and Woodall (1991) from the Sandia National Laboratories and other educators, such as Kerr and Kozol, Berliner (1992) points to hard data that illuminate the untenable assumptions on which much of the school reform movement is based. He suggests that not only is much of the school reform movement wrongheaded, but also that some of these reform efforts are "thinly disguised elitist attempts to get rid of public education, to protect the privilege such individuals have already bestowed upon their children" (Berliner, 1992, p. 55). Coming from a radical social theorist, these claims might be summarily dismissed; but Berliner is identified as a respected, traditional educational psychologist. He also draws on the work of the systems analysis department of a national laboratory that was under the authorization of the Reagan and Bush administrations.

For more than 20 years, a variety of educational and social theorists have presented compelling arguments that illuminated the reproduction of social, cultural, and economic inequalities through the organization and structure of the schooling process. Educators from diverse cultural and ideological backgrounds (i.e., Coleman, Anyon, Giroux, Arnot, Clark, McRobbie, Illich, Bowles, Gintis, and Apple), drawing on the earlier works of other scholars (i.e., Dewey, Baldwin, and Arendt), have pointed to the political and ideological nature of schooling and the ways in which schools often underserve nonmajority students and, through hegemonic practices, reproduce the status quo. The arguments have often been ignored, dismissed, or co-opted in order to blame the victims of educational inequalities. Thus, schools in general, and urban schools and their communities in particular, are blamed for the broader social and economic problems that inform and structure their existence.

Public schooling has long been a scapegoat for societal ills. After all, when the Soviet Union beat the United States into the space race with Sputnik, poor schooling was blamed rather than poor vision and judgment on the part of government, business, and industry. Government, the business community, and the media industry have a long history of denouncing schools when things are not going well and giving themselves the credit when things are going well (Berliner, 1992; Spring, 1972). Once again, schooling is being blamed for problems over which it has no control. Poor schooling is being blamed for a lack of economic competitiveness in world markets without evidence to suggest that schools are doing that poorly at what they were designed to do or that there is indeed a correlation between schooling and economic growth. Berliner (1992) is worth quoting at length on this issue; he writes

> *From 1983 on this nation has been told relentlessly by its leaders that we are a nation at risk, that our schools and our teachers have failed us. But the truth, I think, is that those leaders have failed the schools and the teachers of America. Rather than lead us to ruin, the vast majority of teachers have run a system that is remarkably good for the relatively advantaged children of America. The teachers in the schools with the least support, serving the children who need the most help, are having a harder time. Those schools may be failing, but the causes for that are outside the school building. Those causes are in the exacerbation of social inequities within our society over the last few decades. (p. 50)*

The report from the Sandia National Laboratories, if it is publicly released and given the attention of its more conservative contemporaries such as *The Nation at Risk,* has the potential to shift the terrain of debate over the problems that face public schools and educational reform in the United States. The report concludes that whereas serious problems do exist in the American education system, much of the current reform agenda is misguided. It further states, "Progress will only be made by focusing on real, not perceived, problems" (p. 175). One of the four major issues cited that impede educational improvement is the "preoccupation with (the) link to economic competitiveness" (p. 173). One of the five primary challenges facing education today is "improving the performance of minority and urban students" (p. 171).

Clearly, then, many problems need to be addressed, particularly in urban schools. However, educators and policymakers must do their homework before embarking on school reform efforts. Kerr (as quoted in Berliner, 1992) has written: "Seldom in the course of policymaking in the US have so many firm convictions held by so many been based on so little convincing proof" (p. 55). The historical, political, cultural, and economic foundations of educational problems must be critically examined before anyone attempts to establish policy. Unfortunately, to this point, this has not been the case. The roots of the problems of public schooling have been mystified while the purposes for public education have been politically twisted to support a narrowly defined political, economic, and ideological agenda.

THE POLITICS OF SCHOOLING
AND SCHOOL REFORM

Through the recent school reform movement, the problems of urban education and the general purposes of public schooling have been systematically removed from the terrain of public debate. In fact, most of the widely publicized school reform efforts have created an education climate antithetical to moral referents such as social justice and initiatives of equity that are valued in a democratic society. For the most part, school reform has attempted to shield its ideological and political agenda behind a rhetoric of crisis and a claim to objectivity. However, school reform and the schooling process are always structured on norms and values that embody specific political, social, cultural, and ideologic interests (Freire, 1985, Giroux, 1983).

As such, school reform needs to be understood as it embodies a complex web of relations that involve the production and reproduction of knowledge, culture, ideology, and relationships of power. These relationships legitimate or marginalize certain lived experiences. This suggests that schooling exists in complex relationships with the larger social order on two interrelated levels. First, schools are political institutions that exist in relationships of power and control with other social institutions and the society as a whole. Schools are political sites not simply because they contain a political message or deal with political or social topics, but because they are part of the productive process that exists within social, political, and economic interrelationships with society. These interrelationships both limit and enable the possibilities for change.

Second, schools are political in that the nature of teaching constitutes a political act because it always involves selections and choices from a larger universe of knowledge, culture, and social relations. Unfortunately, within the present organization and structure, these choices generally occur within power relationships of domination and subordination. As such, teaching must be viewed as a political act because it is produced in a cultural and ideological dimension situated within social and political interrelations among teacher, student, and society. Within schools, teachers exercise forms of authority that work both on and with students in a context that is modified by the teachers' creative interaction with, and dependence on, the larger society.

There is a need to understand and exploit the contradictions and problems inherent in the struggle over the terrain on which dominant ideologies and cultures are legitimated. For urban school reform, this points to the necessity of developing a more critical and comprehensive discourse in which the political and ideological nature of schooling can be understood and the production and legitimation of certain forms of knowledge and culture can be challenged.

In general, the reform movement has ignored the social construction of knowledge and classroom relationships within the context of power and privilege. These social constructs are mediated by students and teachers to serve particular interests in a setting influenced by issues of race, class, gender, and ethnicity. A structured silence exists within the boundaries erected by the recent educational reform movement concerning the links between schooling and the development of civic courage, educational equity, and a democratic society (Apple, 1982; Aronowitz and Giroux, 1985; Levin, 1987; Sizer, 1984, 1986). Consequently, traditional efforts at school reform have yielded solutions and results that are, at best, misguided and monocultural and, at worst, elitist, creating the potential to destroy the system of public education in the United States.

THE PROBLEMS OF URBAN SCHOOL REFORM

School reform needs to become more focused on those areas where the educational problems are most acute, such as urban centers. Urban school reform must establish a vision of the purpose of public education and conceptualization of what schools ought to look like. Unfortunately, much of the school reform movement has been based on an underdeveloped notion of the relationship between culture and school success and a set of faulty assumptions concerning the organization and structure of schooling and its relationship to larger economic issues. This error fails to identify the purpose of schooling to educate children to become mature, responsible citizens able to act within a democratic society (Apple, 1982; Aronowitz and Giroux, 1985; Levin, 1987; Sizer, 1986).

More specifically, schools have been traditionally structured for children to succeed or fail based on their class, race, gender, and ethnic positioning. The schooling process devalues the knowledge, culture, and experiences many children bring to the classroom and, consequently, places certain children at an educational disadvantage. These children often come from economically depressed families and neighborhoods where social, cultural, and economic differences are translated into education deficiencies and disadvantages by the public schools. These educational disadvantages are exacerbated by school structures such as large classes, less experienced teachers, tracking, sterile and often biased course content, differentiated curriculum, poorly equipped classrooms, outdated teaching practices, and poor professional development in areas of cultural diversity.

Poor and minority students are told that they have equality of educational opportunity, but the system is rigged against them. It is analogous to saying that everyone has equal access to the finish line in a race, but poor and minority students must start 150 meters from the finish line while white, middle-class students start with only 50 meters to travel. They have equality of access to the race without the hope of equality in the outcome. In the race for positive educational outcomes, poor and minority students are either losing or not finishing because of the barriers they must face. As such, they are blamed for the poverty into which they were born, underserved by the vehicle that claims to offer hope of mobility, and then blamed again for their lack of success in a system that is structured to virtually ensure their failure.

Thus, the immediacy of the real problems of public schooling is most prominent at urban institutions in which improvements and reforms in education need to be more focused. These problems become even more ideologically confounding, as can be seen by recent research that suggests that the poor, minority, and underserved student population is rapidly replacing the previously privileged white, middle-class majority nationwide and has already done so in urban areas (Levin, 1986, 1987; Raywid, 1987; Sizer, 1984). The implications of this demographic shift should not send fear into the hearts of the previous majority, unless they are to admit that schooling is structured to ensure their success at the expense of poor and minority students. Instead these data should imply that we must radically transform a system of public schooling that presently underserves poor and minority students into a system that will meet diverse needs of all students and develop a system for them to become active participants in a democratic society.

By focusing their efforts within a framework that assumes cultural deficiency or deprivation and the extrinsic motivation of economic success linked to educational attainment, the reform movement blames the victims of the structural inequalities in both schools and society-at-large. Furthermore, by operating within a set of assumptions that take for granted what Sizer (1986) calls the "fundamentally flawed" structure and organization of schooling, recent reform efforts provide cosmetic solutions that fail to get at the root of the problems associated with urban schools and poor and minority students (Sleeter and Grant, 1986; Levin, 1986, 1987; Raywid, 1987; Sizer, 1984). The reason for the ineffectiveness of school reform movements with reference to urban schools and poor and minority students can be attributed, in part, to their lack of historical understanding, the organizational and cultural assumptions that inform their framework, the focus of the purpose of public schooling on economic attainment rather than on democratic empowerment, and a failure to create a vision for transformation. Thus, a framework needs to be developed that can address the needs and interests of a democratic society, urban schools, and this new student population (Raywid, 1987; Sizer, 1984).

An example of the need for a more critical examination of the issue of school reform in urban areas is most visible in the areas of school dropouts and suspensions. The dropout and suspension rates for poor and minority students in urban centers remain very high, and standardized test scores and academic achievement remain well below average (Fine, 1991). In fact, the most important factors in dropout and test score prediction are still race and socioeconomic background (Coleman et al., 1966; Rumberger, 1983). Lewis (1985) has written that the recent reform movement, "in many instances, changed the rules for millions of minority and disadvantaged students. But it didn't change a system that was already practically incapable of motivating them" (pp. 251–252). In fact, few research or intervention models have successfully addressed the dropout or suspension problems associated with poor and minority students in urban schools (Stedman, 1987).

Previously held beliefs that dropouts lack the academic or psychological skills necessary for school success and are in need of remediation have not been substantiated in the research. Many dropouts are "academically above average, keenly aware of the contradiction between their academic learning and lived experience, critical of the meritocratic ideology promoted in their schools, and cognizant of race/class/gender discrimination both in schools and in the labor force" (Fine and Rosenburg, 1983, p. 159). Much of the research regarding high school dropouts has indicated that many of the problems are located within the organization and structure of schools, the availability and commitment of teachers because of large classes and overcrowded schools, and the content of the curriculum. For example, complaints about the organization and staffing of schools, dissatisfaction with teachers and the school environment, dislike of school in general, and boredom and lack of interest are among the most widely reported causes of dropping out (Duncan, 1980; Ekstrom, Goertz, Pollack, and Rock, 1985; Fine, 1983, 1986; Fine and Rosenburg, 1983). The dominant stance of blaming the victims, thus categorizing dropouts as being poorly motivated and helpless; having low scholastic aptitude, IQ scores, and reading levels; or portraying dropouts as losers ignores the economic and cultural differences of poor and minority students by imposing a supposedly common culture of schooling that translates cultural differences into cultural disadvantages or deficiencies.

Far from being helpless, many dropouts see through the false promise of social and economic mobility through schooling. This promise can best be summed up as an unspoken, tacit agreement between teachers and students in which teachers will give students knowledge if the students will give teachers respect, obedience, and control of the classroom. Implicit in this agreement is the assumption that school knowledge has some inherent worth that can be translated into social and economic success with relationship to the wider society. Recent research suggests a different relationship between education and economic development than recent reform efforts have suggested. For example, research indicates that class, race, and gender remain better predictors of economic success than education levels (Fine and Rosenburg, 1983; Kretovics, 1986). Furthermore, the socioeconomic status of one's family directly correlates with the quality and quantity of education to which one has access (Anyon, 1980; Coleman et al., 1966; Keddie, 1971).

For the majority of dropouts, poverty, unequal access to educational outcomes, and discrimination are at the core of most education problems, particularly in urban schools, not the reverse as the reform movement suggests. Public education policy must be transformed to reflect the democratic purpose of public education, to develop the critical and conceptual skills necessary to cope with the changing nature of work and the economy, and to ensure that all people have equal access to educational outcomes.

TRANSFORMING URBAN SCHOOLS

Schooling in any society is linked to political, social, economic, and cultural structures that reflect to some degree the dominant views of what the society is and what it should be. More specifically, education is an introduction to a particular way of life. All educators make choices, either explicitly or implicitly, concerning the form and content of the schooling process that create a vision of what is and what should be. These choices involve the selection of content, teaching strategies, and modes of evaluation. They also include which classroom social relationships are acceptable and how the school will be organized and structured. The decisions educators make with regard to the form and content of the schooling process are formed either implicitly or explicitly by what they perceive as the purpose of schooling. Consequently, educators and policymakers need to make clear the purpose for public schooling in a democratic society and the interest such schooling should ultimately serve. This purpose and its outcomes should apply equally to all students and schools, even though the process by which they are attained might differ.

The school reform movement has done little to provide an accurate analysis of the production of inequality in the public schools or the larger social order. Furthermore, the ideology that influences this movement has often prevented the realization of any notion of an egalitarian ideal, the elimination of inequality, or the improvement of those who are least well-off. As suggested earlier, educators must begin to reclaim the terrain of public school reform by focusing on the democratic purpose of public schooling and the problems of urban schools that often inhibit action toward this ideal.

In this book, the authors attempt to provide a series of readings that they believe will begin to restructure the debate about urban school reform and the purpose of education for poor and minority students. It is designed to serve as an introduction to the many problems and possibilities for improving the conditions that influence the education of urban youth. The problems that face urban education are not new. However, first, they must be understood within their historical and societal contexts. Second, these problems must be critically examined as they are found in the school setting. Finally, a vision for change must be presented that provides the guideposts for transforming urban education.

An examination of readings, past and present, reveals that many of the earlier concerns about the urban scene persist today. For example, how can equality of educational opportunity be provided for all children in the face of the reality of social and economic discrimination based on race, social class, gender, and ethnic differences? Thus, in Part I of this book, the authors present readings that examine the changing urban scene. Chapter 1 begins with an examination of the concept of equality of educational opportunity and how this concept has been confounded in the dismal panorama of urban schools. Chapters 2 and 3 then move through an overview of the organizational and structural problems facing urban society to an illumination of the enormous economic and social problems facing individuals and families in urban centers. Chapter 4 concludes with an examination of bureaucracy as it structures barriers to school reform for poor and minority children.

From a more critical perspective, the readings might suggest to some that the urban scene has, in fact, changed during the past few decades, but that the schools have not adjusted to these changes. In a historical sense, we should learn from the past to improve the future. How does this apply to urban education? Although there is consensus that urban schools need to be improved, there is little agreement on the causes of the problems or how the improvements should be made. A panorama of viewpoints and the potential solutions that they offer are presented.

It can definitely be said that the problems in the urban school environment are linked very clearly to the changing urban scene. No matter where one looks, the schools are plagued with problems associated with dropouts, truancy, discipline, and poor academic achievement. In Part II of this book, the authors have selected readings that focus more specifically on a number of teaching-learning problems that face urban teachers and students. Chapter 5 begins by examining the relationship among testing, tracking, expectations, and dropping out. Because the problems associated with public schooling are perceived to be severe, several alternatives have emerged. Chapter 6 describes several of these alternatives. Part II closes with an examination of equality of educational opportunity as it relates to issues of class, race, gender, and ethnicity in Chapter 7.

Do the causes of these problems rest with the structure of schools, the curriculum, the instructional strategies, the home environment, or the attitudes and expectations of teachers? There seem to be far more questions than answers. As a result of reading the selections in Parts I and II, readers will be able to (1) understand the basis for the study of urban education, (2) become familiar with conceptual frameworks used to examine urban education, (3) understand the origins of current problems in urban education, (4) have a better understanding of the complexities of urban schools and the students they serve, (5) be able to identify a number of the particular problems that face urban educators, (6) be able to identify how different concept frameworks articulate the problems and solutions in urban education and, (7) begin to develop a framework that they can use to approach the complexities of urban education.

Part III presents a number of perspectives concerning what needs to be done to improve the quality of urban education. The problems that face urban education in the twenty-first century present one of the greatest challenges to education in the United States since Sputnik. The decade of the 1980s once again illuminated the crisis in education. However, as stated earlier, this decade of the educational reform movement virtually ignored the serious problems facing urban schools. In this part, the editors have chosen authors who they believe provide leadership and vision in identifying some of the major barriers to urban educational reform and in providing potential solutions to solving these problems and transforming urban schools. Recently, a number of alternative programs and theories have developed with the hope that the 1990s will bring some solutions to the problems identified in the previous sections. However, it is clear that transforming the nature and function of urban schools will be no easy task.

Many educators are now beginning to abandon the traditional structural-functionalist perspective that has dominated educational theory and practice since the mid-1920s. Right-wing and left-wing reformers are now speaking of restructuring schools; empowering teachers and students, including parents and community; and transforming the education system. Part III gives the reader some insight into the education revolution that the coming decade promises. Part III helps the reader to (1) understand the concept of empowerment and how it applies to the educational process, (2) identify several innovative ideas to transform the nature of urban education, (3) develop strategies for teaching urban children, and (4) identify areas of study for educators who teach in urban areas.

Social transformation is made possible, in part, through the ability of the young to grow and mature as critical thinkers in a democratic society. Thus, education is an active and constructive process of continual critical growth (Dewey, 1944). The knowledge, social relations, culture, and values presented and legitimated in schools are to be interrogated with reference to democratic social ideals. They are viewed as social constructs that can be analyzed and reconstructed. The strategic point for educators, however, is progressively realizing present possibilities for the growth and development of the young. It is important to stress that students must participate and provide the initiative in the directions in which their actions will proceed. Thus, education becomes the practice of freedom. That is, it becomes the means by which men and women deal critically and creatively with reality and discover how to participate in the transformation of their world (Freire, 1985).

REFERENCES

Anyon, J. (1980). "Social class and the hidden curriculum of work." *Journal of Education,* 162 (Winter).

Apple, M.W. (1982). *Education and Power.* Boston: Routledge and Kegan Paul.

Aronowitz, S. and Giroux, H.A. (1985). *Education Under Siege.* South Hadley, MA: Bergin and Garvey.

Barth, R.S. (1986). "On sheep and goats and school reform." *Phi Delta Kappan,* 68(4):293–296.

Berliner, D.C. (1992). *Educational Reform in an Era of Disinformation.* Paper presented at the meeting of the American Association of Colleges of Teacher Education, San Antonio, Texas, February 1992.

Carson, C.C., Huelskamp, R.M., and Woodall, T.D. (1991). *Perspectives on Education in America.* Annotated briefing (third draft). Albuquerque, NM: Sandia National Laboratories.

Coleman, J.S., Campbell, E.Q., Hobson, C.J., McPartland, J., Mood, A.M., Weinfeld, F.D., and York, R.L. (1966). *Equality of Educational Opportunity.* Washington, D.C: U.S. Government Printing Office.

Dewey, J. (1944). *Democracy and Education.* New York: The Free Press.

Duncan, V. (1980). *Oregon Early School Leavers Study.* Salem: Oregon Department of Education.

Ekstrom, R.B., Goertz, M.E., Pollack, J.M., and Rock, D.A. (1986). "Who drops out of high school and why? Findings from a national study." *Teachers College Record,* 87:356–373.

Fine, M. (1983). "Perspectives on inequality: Voices from urban schools." In L. Bickman, ed. *Applied Social Psychology Annual IV.* Beverly Hills: Sage.

Fine, M. (1991). *Framing Dropouts.* Albany: SUNY Press.

Fine, M., and Rosenburg, P. (1983). "Dropping out of high school: The ideology of school and work." *Journal of Education,* 165(3):257–272.

Freire, P. (1985). *The Politics of Education.* South Hadley, MA: Bergin and Garvey.

Giroux, H.A. (1983). *Theory and Resistance in Education: A Pedagogy for the Opposition.* South Hadley, MA: Bergin and Garvey.

Giroux, H.A. (1988). *Teachers as Intellectuals: Toward a Critical Pedagogy of Learning.* South Hadley, MA: Bergin and Garvey.

Giroux, H.A., and McLaren, P. (1986). "Teacher education and the politics of engagement: The case for democratic schooling." *Harvard Educational Review,* 56(3):1–19.

Keddie, N. (1971). "Classroom knowledge." In M.F.D. Young, ed. *Knowledge and Control* London: College Macmillan.

Kretovics, J. (1985). "Critical literacy: Challenging the assumptions of mainstream educational theory." *Journal of Education,* 167(2):50–62.

Kretovics, J. (1986). *Schooling and the Hidden Curriculum: Empowering Teachers with Strategies for the Development of a Transformative Pedagogy.* PhD. diss., Miami University, Oxford, Ohio.

Kretovics, J., Farber, K., and Armaline, W. (1991). "Reform from the bottom up: Empowering teachers to transform schools." *Phi Delta Kappan,* 73(4):295–299.

Levin, H.M. (1986). *Educational Reform for Disadvantaged Students: An Emerging Crisis.* West Haven, CT: NEA Professional Library.

Levin, H.M. (1987). *Accelerating Elementary Education for Disadvantaged Students.* Unpublished manuscript.

Lewis, A. (1985). "Washington report: Young and poor in America." *Phi Delta Kappan,* 67(4):251–252.

National Coalition of Advocates for Students (NCAS) (1985). *Barriers to Excellence: Our Children at Risk.* Boston: NCAS.

Raywid, M.A. (1987). "Making school reform work for the new majority." *The Journal of Negro Education,* 56(2):221–228.

Rumberger, R.W. (1983). "Dropping out of high school: The influence of race, sex, and family background." *American Educational Research Journal,* 20:199–220.

Sizer, T.R. (1984). *Horace's Compromise.* Boston: Houghton Mifflin.

Sizer, T.R. (1986). "Rebuilding: First steps by the coalition of essential schools." *Phi Delta Kappan,* 68(1):38–42.

Sleeter, C., and Grant, C. (1986). "Success for all students." *Phi Delta Kappan,* 68(4):297–299.

Spring J. (1972). *Educating the Worker Citizen: The Social, Economic, and Political Foundations of Education.* New York: Longman, Inc.

Spring J. (1980). *Education and the Rise of the Corporate State.* Boston: Beacon Press.

Stedman, L. (1987). "It's time we changed the effective school formula." *Phi Delta Kappan,* 69(3):215–224.

▶ Part I

The Changing
Urban Scene

Urban schools do not exist in a vacuum. They are part of a larger social milieu that influences what happens in the classroom. Our most basic concern is that all children, regardless of race, class, gender, ethnicity, or community, will receive at least a chance at equality of educational opportunity. This is only a basic concern in that we further believe that children should have the opportunity for equal educational outcomes in spite of the differences in prepararation that they bring to the classroom. However, the study of urban education can go no further until the concept of equality of educational opportunity is grasped and accepted as a basic right of all children.

Therefore, we begin Part I with an explication of the concept of equality of educational opportunity by James Coleman. Most notably, Coleman provides evidence that there has been a definitional shift in the concept of equality of educational opportunity that has changed the focus of responsibility. Gene I. Maeroff then offers evidence that situations in urban schools often frustrate efforts at good education and impede equality of educational opportunity. While decrying the conditions of urban schools, he offers hope that things can change. The purpose of this book is not despair but the hope for action and change.

The remaining articles in Part I describe in detail various aspects of the social scene external to the school. There is little doubt that the issues raised by these articles place urban education in the midst of controversy. Given descriptions of the problems of the urban poor and their families, educators are nevertheless expected to develop strategies that will provide successful experiences for all children. The recurring issue that haunts teachers is whether they have the resources and continued professional development opportunities to meet that challenge. Some of their resulting difficulties are described in Part II, with recommendations for improving education found in Part III.

Another social force impinging on educational practice, the changing demography of the city is the focus of Chapter 2. The exodus of many white and middle-class families from most of the largest cities in the United States has presented educators with new problems. Most urban educators are now faced with lower-class students from diverse racial and ethnic backgrounds. The needs and interests of these students differ greatly from those recently departed students for whom they had been prepared to teach. This change has disrupted what teachers were accustomed to doing and, for many teachers, the adjustment has been difficult if not impossible.

Efforts by the courts to disperse children of color and balance enrollments racially added to the demographic changes. The well-intentioned integrationists, in an effort to improve educational opportunity, perhaps caused additional disruptions and exacerbated the demographic shifts. Further, by ignoring in the educational process the very differences that they were attempting to accommodate in the organization of schools through desegregation, the struggle for equality of educational opportunity was set back. Race, class, and ethnic differences became deficiencies that needed to be acted on by the schools. Schools and communities need to work cooperatively to forge new partnerships and offer new hope for equality of educational opportunity. Thus, Chapter 3 examines the urban community and family.

In Chapter 4, this mosaic of conflicts and controversies focuses on the bureaucratic organization of school systems. Obviously, structure is necessary for the delivery of services in any social organization. However, is a structure designed for efficiency, control, and predictability the most effective approach for dealing with the heterogeneous nature of school populations? Can the present structure be flexible enough to meet the needs of the changing urban scene? Many critics argue that the present structure of urban schooling encourages conformity to a past system that can no longer exist. As such, the bureaucracy of schooling becomes the albatross that often obstructs constructive change. How do we begin to understand bureaucracy, school structure, and their effects on equality of educational opportunity so that we might advocate informed change?

It's clear that the study of urban education is interdisciplinary—social, political, economic, cultural, and historical. How the many external forces have affected education in urban areas is the thrust of Part I. We offer a limited number of selections from a large body of literature that we believe are both classic and representative of the larger debate. Because the study of urban education is interdisciplinary, searching for solutions to the problems of urban schools and the enhancement of educational opportunities for all students needs to come from many sources. We trust that the selections we have chosen will serve as a starting point for serious discussion about improving urban schools.

▶ 1

Equality of Educational Opportunity and Urban Schools

The statement "All men are created equal" is one that resounds throughout American history. The words are found in the Declaration of Independence and Lincoln's Gettysburg Address; they are also paraphrased and applied in numerous settings. Unfortunately, this statement has been used historically to exclude women, minorities, and the poor. For educators, it has meant that American schools are charged with offering every child equality of educational opportunity; however, the question of who gets excluded must still be asked.

Prior to the 1960s "the traditional notion of what constituted equality of educational opportunity was placidly assumed to be such school factors as teacher-pupil ratios, per pupil expenditures, laboratory facilities, number of volumes per student in the library, and several measures of quality of the curriculum" (Kent, 1968, p. 242). In even the most progressive of circumstances, equality of educational opportunity was often translated as sameness and rarely dealt with an examination of the underlying causes for unequal performance, consideration of equality of educational outcomes, or even a close look at the facilities provided. When even the most naive teacher heard the charge of inequities in educational opportunities, it was dismissed with a comment such as: "Of course, I believe in equality of educational opportunity. Every child in my class is treated equally—the same."

It's not that American educators were totally unfamiliar with the uneven performance of children. Problems relating to class and race were recorded as early as 1948 with Allison Davis's Inglis lecture. He criticized the narrow middle-class orientation of school personnel and noted language problems of children from lower socioeconomic groups because they didn't speak "standard English" (Davis, 1962). He also expressed grave reservations about homogeneous grouping that "really sets up different social and cultural groups within the school" (Davis, 1962, p. 95).

Despite the work of Davis and others, the issue of educational inequality did not become a national concern until the publication of James Coleman's *Equality of Educational Opportunity* in 1966. He clarified that facilities, staff, and services were distributed unequally. His data revealed that gaps in achievement between whites, blacks, and Puerto Ricans widened and favored whites the longer the students remained in school. The report was not without its critics; however, it was widely studied, evaluated, and argued, and was generally accepted as accurate. The data made apparent the evidence of inequalities between groups that could no longer be denied, dismissed, or ignored. This information, coupled with numerous federal court decisions beginning with Brown vs. Board of Education in 1954, brought the educational community to the realization that the American ideal of equality of educational opportunity was flawed.

Even if the ideal is accepted, how can it be actualized? Kerber and Smith (1964) remind us that "all men are physically, mentally, socially and idiosyncratically unequal. Yet we equally note, have equal privileges and immunities, and we most fervently demand our equal rights" (p. 126). Furthermore, even if the ideal were to somehow become a reality, how can we sustain and guarantee its continuance in the face of a rapidly changing, technological society? One only needs to review attempts at achieving racial balance in schools to see that some initial success was frustrated by demographic shifts. Therefore, how can the ideal become a reality?

The editors are comfortable with beginning this collection with Coleman's developmental essay on "The Concept of Equality of Educational Opportunity," which he originally presented on October 21, 1967. In this article, he reviews the historical roots of the concept. He also submits that the concept contains dilemmas when it is applied to the school setting. Conversely, he reminds us that the child is influenced by environments and groups external to the school. Nevertheless, if educational resources are developed with enough intensity all children should achieve at least a "degree of proximity to equality of opportunity" (Coleman, 1968, p. 22).

Turning to the current state of affairs, we ask: "How far has American education moved in the direction of equality of educational opportunity, particularly in urban centers?" Maeroff (1988) describes a depressing, "dismal panorama" of situations where success with students' education may be accidental rather than commonplace. The sense of isolation and lack of control earlier described by Coleman is reiterated by Maeroff. He reports that "many urban minority students have not the slightest clue of what it takes to attain academic goals" (Maeroff, 1988, p. 635). Teachers are beset with frustrations and dilemmas in addressing the causes of academic failure for poor and minority students without blaming the victims for the effects of an unequal system.

We raise these issues not for the sake of controversy but to ask the reader if American society, in general, and American education, in particular, still harbor a commitment to equality of educational opportunity. How far have we come? How far can we go? Is there a way out of the dilemmas? We hope to offer some meaningful alternatives.

REFERENCES

Coleman, J. (1968). "The concept of equality of educational opportunity." *Harvard Educational Review,* 38(1):7–22.

Davis, A. (1962). *Social Class Influences Upon Learning.* Cambridge, MA: Harvard University Press.

Kent, J.K. (1968). "The Coleman Report: Opening Pandora's Box." *Phi Delta Kappan,* 49:242–245.

Kerber, A., and Smith, W.R., eds., (1964). *Educational Issues in a Changing Society,* Rev. ed. Detroit: Wayne State University Press.

Maeroff, G.I. (1988). "Withered hopes, stillborn dreams: The dismal panorama of urban schools." *Phi Delta Kappan,* 69:632–638.

The Concept of Equality of Educational Opportunity*

JAMES COLEMAN

The concept of "equality of educational opportunity" as held by members of society has had a varied past. It has changed radically in recent years, and is likely to undergo further change in the future. This lack of stability in the concept leads to several questions. What has it meant in the past, what does it mean now, and what will it mean in the future? Whose obligation is it to provide such equality? Is the concept a fundamentally sound one, or does it have inherent contradictions or conflicts with social organization? But first of all, and above all, what is and has been meant in society by the idea of equality of educational opportunity?

To answer this question, it is necessary to consider how the child's position in society has been conceived in different historical periods. In pre-industrial Europe, the child's horizons were largely limited by his family. His station in life was likely to be the same as his father's. If his father was a serf, he would likely live his own life as a serf; if his father was a shoemaker, he would likely become a shoemaker. But even this immobility was not the crux of the matter; he was a part of the family production enterprise and would likely remain within this enterprise throughout his life. The extended family, as the basic unit of social organization, had complete authority over the child, and complete responsibility for him. This responsibility ordinarily did not end when the child became an adult because he remained a part of the same economic unit and carried on this tradition of responsibility into the next generation. Despite some mobility out of the family, the general pattern was family continuity through a patriarchal kinship system.

---

* This paper was delivered at the Conference on the *Equality of Educational Opportunity* Report sponsored by the Colloquium Board of the Harvard Graduate School of Education, October 21, 1967.

From Coleman, James S., "The Concept of Equality of Educational Opportunity," *Harvard Educational Review,* 38:1, pp. 7–22. Copyright © 1968 by the President and Fellows of Harvard College. All rights reserved.

There are two elements of critical importance here. First, the family carried responsibility for its members' welfare from cradle to grave. It was a "welfare society," with each extended family serving as a welfare organization for its own members. Thus it was to the family's interest to see that its members became productive. Conversely, a family took relatively small interest in whether someone in *another* family became productive or not—merely because the mobility of productive labor between family economic units was relatively low. If the son of a neighbor was allowed to become a ne'er-do-well, it had little real effect on families other than his own.

The second important element is that the family, as a unit of economic production, provided an appropriate context in which the child could learn the things he needed to know. The craftsman's shop or the farmer's fields were appropriate training grounds for sons, and the household was an appropriate training ground for daughters.

In this kind of society, the concept of equality of educational opportunity had no relevance at all. The child and adult were embedded within the extended family, and the child's education or training was merely whatever seemed necessary to maintain the family's productivity. The fixed stations in life which most families occupied precluded any idea of "opportunity" and, even less, equality of opportunity.

With the industrial revolution, changes occurred in both the family's function as a self-perpetuating economic unit and as a training ground. As economic organizations developed outside the household, children began to be occupationally mobile outside their families. As families lost their economic production activities, they also began to lose their welfare functions, and the poor or ill or incapacitated became more nearly a community responsibility. Thus the training which a child received came to be of interest to all in the community, either as his potential employers or as his potential economic supports if he became dependent. During this stage of development in eighteenth-century England, for instance, communities had laws preventing immigration from another community because of the potential economic burden of immigrants.

Further, as men came to employ their own labor outside the family in the new factories, their families became less useful as economic training grounds for their children. These changes paved the way for public education. Families needed a context within which their children could learn some general skills which would be useful for gaining work outside the family; and men of influence in the community began to be interested in the potential productivity of other men's children.

It was in the early nineteenth century that public education began to appear in Europe and America. Before that time, private education had grown with the expansion of the mercantile class. This class had both the need and resources to have its children educated outside the home, either for professional occupations or for occupations in the developing world of commerce. But the idea of general educational opportunity for all children arose only in the nineteenth century.

The emergence of public, tax-supported education was not solely a function of the stage of industrial development. It was also a function of the class structure in the society. In the United States, without a strong traditional class structure, universal education in publicly-supported free schools became widespread in the early nineteenth century; in England, the "voluntary schools," run and organized by churches with some instances of state support, were not supplemented by a state-supported system until the Education Act of 1870. Even more, the character of educational opportunity reflected the class structure. In the United States, the public schools quickly became the common school, attended by representatives of all classes; these schools provided a common educational experience for most American children—excluding only those upper-class children in private schools, those poor who went to no schools, and Indians and Southern Negroes who were without schools. In England, however, the class system directly manifested itself through the schools. The state-supported, or "board schools" as they were called, became the schools of the laboring lower classes with a sharply different curriculum from those voluntary schools which served the middle and upper classes. The division was so sharp that two government departments, the Education Department and the Science and Art Department, administered external examinations, the first for the products of the board schools, and the second for the products of the voluntary schools as they progressed into secondary education. It was only the latter curricula and examinations that provided admission to higher education.

What is most striking is the duration of influence of such a dual structure. Even today in England, a century later (and in different forms in most European countries), there exists a dual structure of public secondary education with only one of the branches providing the curriculum for college admission. In England, this branch includes the remaining voluntary schools which, though retaining their individual identities, have become part of the state-supported system.

This comparison of England and the United States shows clearly the impact of the class structure in society upon the concept of educational opportunity in that society. In nineteenth-century England, the idea of *equality* of educational opportunity was hardly considered; the system was designed to provide *differentiated* educational opportunity appropriate to one's station in life. In the United States as well, the absence of educational opportunity for Negroes in the South arose from the caste and feudal structure of the largely rural society. The idea of differentiated educational opportunity, implicit in the Education Act of 1870 in England, seems to derive from dual needs: the needs arising from industrialization for a basic education for the labor force, and the interests of parents in having one's own child receive a good education. The middle classes could meet both these needs by providing a free system for the children of laboring classes, and a tuition system (which soon came to be supplemented by state grants) for their own. The long survival of this differentiated system depended not only on the historical fact that the voluntary schools existed before a public system came into existence but on the fact that it allows both of these needs to be met: the community's collective need for a trained labor force, and the middle-class individual's interest in a better education for his own child. It served a third need as well: that of maintaining the existing social order—a system of stratification that was a step removed from a feudal system of fixed estates, but designed to prevent a wholesale challenge by the children of the working class to positions held for children of the middle classes.

The similarity of this system to that which existed in the South to provide differential opportunity to Negroes and whites is striking, just as is the similarity of class structures in the second half of nineteenth-century England to the white-Negro caste structure of the southern United States in the first half of the twentieth century.

In the United States, nearly from the beginning, the concept of educational opportunity had a special meaning which focused on equality. This meaning included the following elements:

(1) Providing a *free* education up to a given level which constituted the principal entry point to the labor force.

(2) Providing a *common curriculum* for all children, regardless of background.

(3) Partly by design and partly because of low population density, providing that children from diverse backgrounds attend the *same school.*

(4) Providing equality within a given *locality,* since local taxes provided the source of support for schools.

This conception of equality of opportunity is still held by many persons; but there are some assumptions in it which are not obvious. First, it implicitly assumes that the existence of free schools eliminates economic sources of inequality of opportunity. Free schools, however, do not mean that the costs of a child's education become reduced to zero for families at all economic levels. When free education was introduced, many families could not afford to allow the child to attend school beyond an early age. His labor was necessary to the family—whether in rural or urban areas. Even after the passage of child labor laws, this remained true on the farm. These economic sources of inequality of opportunity have become small indeed (up through secondary education); but at one time they were a major source of inequality. In some countries they remain so; and certainly for higher education they remain so.

Apart from the economic needs of the family, problems inherent in the social structure raised even more fundamental questions about equality of educational opportunity. Continued school attendance prevented a boy from being trained in his father's trade. Thus, in taking advantage of "equal educational opportunity," the son of a craftsman or small tradesman would lose the opportunity to enter those occupations he would most likely fill. The family inheritance of occupation at all social levels was still strong enough, and the age of entry into the labor force was still early enough, that secondary education interfered with opportunity for working-class children; while it opened up opportunities at higher social levels, it closed them at lower ones.

Since residue of this social structure remains in present American society, the dilemma cannot be totally ignored. The idea of a common educational experience implies that this experience has only the effect of widening the range of opportunity, never the effect of excluding opportunities. But clearly this is never precisely true so long as this experience prevents a child from pursuing certain occupational paths. This question still arises with the differentiated secondary curriculum: an academic program in high school has the effect not only of keeping open the opportunities which arise through continued education, but also of closing off opportunities which a vocational program keeps open.

A second assumption implied by this concept of equality of opportunity is that opportunity lies in *exposure* to a given curriculum. The amount of opportunity is then measured in terms of the level of curriculum to which the child is exposed. The higher the curriculum made available to a given set of children, the greater their opportunity.

The most interesting point about this assumption is the relatively passive role of the school and community, relative to the child's role. The school's obligation is to "provide an opportunity" by being available, within easy geographic access of the child, free of cost (beyond the value of the child's time), and with a curriculum that would not exclude him from higher education. The obligation to "use the opportunity" is on the child or the family, so that his role is defined as the active one: the responsibility for achievement rests with him. Despite the fact that the school's role was the relatively passive one and the child's or family's role the active one, the use of this social service soon came to be no longer a choice of the parent or child, but that of the state. Since compulsory attendance laws appeared in the nineteenth century, the age of required attendance has been periodically moved upward.

This concept of equality of educational opportunity is one that has been implicit in most educational practice throughout most of the period of public education in the nineteenth and twentieth centuries. However, there have been several challenges to it; serious questions have been raised by new conditions in public education. The first of these in the United States was a challenge to assumption two, the common curriculum. This challenge first occurred in the early years of the twentieth century with the expansion of secondary education. Until the report of the committee of the National Education Association, issued in 1918, the standard curriculum in secondary schools was primarily a classical one appropriate for college entrance. The greater influx of noncollege-bound adolescents into the high school made it necessary that this curriculum be changed into one more appropriate to the new majority. This is not to say that the curriculum changed immediately in the schools, nor that all schools changed equally, but rather that the seven "cardinal principles" of the N.E.A. report became a powerful influence in the movement toward a less academically rigid curriculum. The introduction of the new nonclassical curriculum was seldom if ever couched in terms of a conflict between those for whom high school was college preparation, and those for whom it was terminal education; nevertheless, that was the case. The "inequality" was seen as the use of a curriculum that served a minority and was not designed to fit the needs of the majority; and the shift of curriculum was intended to fit the curriculum to the needs of the new majority in the schools.

In many schools, this shift took the form of *diversifying* the curriculum, rather than supplanting one by another; the college-preparatory curriculum remained though watered down. Thus the kind of equality of opportunity that emerged from the newly-designed secondary school curriculum was radically different from the elementary-school concept that had emerged earlier. The idea inherent in the new secondary school curriculum appears to have been to take as given the diverse occupational paths into which adolescents will go after secondary school, and to say (implicitly): there is greater equality of educational opportunity for a boy who is not going to attend college if he has a specially-designed curriculum than if he must take a curriculum designed for college entrance.

There is only one difficulty with this definition: it takes as *given* what should be problematic—that a given boy is going into a given post-secondary occupational or educational path. It is one thing to take as given that approximately 70 per cent of an entering high school freshman class will not attend college; but to assign a *particular child* to a curriculum designed for that 70 per cent closes off for that child the opportunity to attend college. Yet to assign all children to a curriculum designed for the 30 per cent who will attend college creates inequality for those who, at the end of high school, fall among the 70 per cent who do not attend college. This is a true dilemma, and one which no educational system has fully solved. It is more general than the college/noncollege dichotomy, for there is a wide variety of different paths that adolescents take on the completion of secondary school. In England, for example, a student planning to attend a university must specialize in the arts or the sciences in the later years of secondary school. Similar specialization occurs in the German gymnasium; and this is wholly within the group planning to attend university. Even greater specialization can be found among noncollege curricula, especially in the vocational, technical, and commercial high schools.

The distinguishing characteristic of this concept of equality of educational opportunity is that it accepts as given the child's expected future. While the concept discussed earlier left the child's future wholly open, this concept of differentiated curricula uses the expected future to match child and curriculum. It should be noted that the first and simpler concept is easier to apply in elementary schools where fundamental tools of reading and arithmetic are being learned by all children; it is only in secondary school that the problem of diverse futures arises. It should also be noted that the dilemma is directly due to the social structure itself: if there were a virtual absence of social mobility with everyone occupying a fixed estate in life, then such curricula that take the future as given would provide equality of opportunity relative to that structure. It is only because of the high degree of occupational mobility between generations—that is, the greater degree of equality of *occupational* opportunity—that the dilemma arises.

The first stage in the evolution of the concept of equality of educational opportunity was the notion that all children must be exposed to the same curriculum in the same school. A second stage in the evolution of the concept assumed that different children would have different occupational futures and that equality of opportunity required providing different curricula for each type of student. The third and fourth stages in this evolution came as a result of challenges to the basic idea of equality of educational opportunity from opposing directions. The third stage can be seen at least as far back as 1896 when the Supreme Court upheld the southern states' notion of "separate but equal" facilities. This stage ended in 1954 when the Supreme Court ruled that legal separation by race inherently constitutes inequality of opportunity. By adopting the "separate but equal" doctrine, the southern states rejected assumption three of the original concept, the assumption that equality depended on the opportunity to attend the same school. This rejection was, however, consistent with the overall logic of the original concept since attendance at the same school was an inherent part of that logic. The underlying idea was that opportunity resided in exposure to a curriculum; the community's responsibility was to provide that exposure, the child's to take advantage of it.

It was the pervasiveness of this underlying idea which created the difficulty for the Supreme Court. For it was evident that even when identical facilities and identical teacher salaries existed for racially separate schools, "equality of educational opportunity" in some sense did not exist. This had also long been evident to Englishmen as well, in a different context, for with the simultaneous existence of the "common school" and the "voluntary school," no one was under the illusion that full equality of educational opportunity existed. But the source of this inequality remained an unarticulated feeling. In the decision of the Supreme Court, this unarticulated feeling began to take more precise form. The essence of it was that the *effects* of such separate schools were, or were likely to be, different. Thus a concept of equality of opportunity which focused on *effects* of schooling began to take form. The actual decision of the Court was in fact a confusion of two unrelated premises: this new concept, which looked at results of schooling, and the legal premise that the use of race as a basis for school assignment violates fundamental freedoms. But what is important for the evolution of the concept of equality of opportunity is that a new and different assumption was introduced, the assumption that equality of opportunity depends in some fashion upon effects of schooling. I believe the decision would have been more soundly based had it not depended on the effects of schooling, but only on the violation of freedom; but by introducing the question of effects of schooling, the Court brought into the open the implicit goals of equality of educational opportunity—that is, goals having to do with the *results* of school— to which the original concept was somewhat awkwardly directed.

That these goals were in fact behind the concept can be verified by a simple mental experiment. Suppose the early schools had operated for only one hour a week and had been attended by children of all social classes. This would have met the explicit assumptions of the early concept of equality of opportunity since the school is free, with a common curriculum, and attended by all children in the locality. But it obviously would not have been accepted, even at that time, as providing equality of opportunity, because its effects would have been so minimal. The additional educational resources provided by middle- and upper-class families, whether in the home, by tutoring, or in private supplementary schools, would have created severe inequalities in results.

Thus the dependence of the concept upon results or effects of schooling, which had remained hidden until 1954, came partially into the open with the Supreme Court decision. Yet this was not the end, for it created more problems than it solved. It might allow one to assess gross inequalities, such as that created by dual school systems in the South, or by a system like that in the mental experiment I just described. But it allows nothing beyond that. Even more confounding, because the decision did not use effects of schooling as a criterion of inequality but only as justification for a criterion of racial integration, integration itself emerged as the basis for still a new concept of equality of educational opportunity. Thus the idea of effects of schooling as an element in the concept was introduced but immediately overshadowed by another, the criterion of racial integration.

The next stage in the evolution of this concept was, in my judgment, the Office of Education Survey of Equality of Educational Opportunity. This survey was carried out under a mandate in the Civil Rights Act of 1964 to the Commissioner of Education to assess the "lack of equality of educational opportunity" among racial and other groups in the United States. The evolution of this concept, and the conceptual disarray which this evolution had created, made the very definition of the task exceedingly difficult. The original concept could be examined by determining the degree to which all children in a locality had access to the same schools and the same curriculum, free of charge. The existence of diverse secondary curricula appropriate to different futures could be assessed relatively easily. But the very assignment of a child to a specific curriculum implies acceptance of the concept of equality which takes futures as given. And the introduction of the new interpretations, equality as measured by results of schooling and equality defined by racial integration, confounded the issue even further.

As a consequence, in planning the survey it was obvious that no single concept of equality of educational opportunity existed and that the survey must give information relevant to a variety of concepts. The basis on which this was done can be seen by reproducing a portion of an internal memorandum that determined the design of the survey:

> *The point of second importance in design [second to the point of discovering the intent of Congress, which was taken to be that the survey was not for the purpose of locating willful discrimination, but to determine educational inequality without regard to intention of those in authority] follows from the first and concerns the definition of inequality. One type of inequality may be defined in terms of differences of the community's input to the*

school, such as per-pupil expenditure, school plants, libraries, quality of teachers, and other similar quantities.

A second type of inequality may be defined in terms of the racial composition of the school, following the Supreme Court's decision that segregated schooling is inherently unequal. By the former definition, the question of inequality through segregation is excluded, while by the latter, there is inequality of education within a school system so long as the schools within the system have different racial composition.

A third type of inequality would include various intangible characteristics of the school as well as the factors directly traceable to the community inputs to the school. These intangibles are such things as teacher morale, teachers' expectations of students, level of interest of the student body in learning, or others. Any of these factors may affect the impact of the school upon a given student within it. Yet such a definition gives no suggestion of where to stop, or just how relevant these factors might be for school quality.

Consequently, a fourth type of inequality may be defined in terms of consequences of the school for individuals with equal backgrounds and abilities. In this definition, equality of educational opportunity is equality of results, given the same individual input. With such a definition, inequality might come about from differences in the school inputs and/or racial composition and/or from more intangible things as described above.

Such a definition obviously would require that two steps be taken in the determination of inequality. First, it is necessary to determine the effect of these various factors upon educational results (conceiving of results quite broadly, including not only achievement but attitudes toward learning, self-image, and perhaps other variables). This provides various measures of the school's quality in terms of its effect upon its students. Second, it is necessary to take these measures of quality, once determined, and determine the differential exposure of Negroes (or other groups) and whites to schools of high and low quality.

A fifth type of inequality may be defined in terms of consequences of the school for individuals of unequal backgrounds and abilities. In this definition, equality of educational opportunity is equality of results given individual inputs. The most striking examples of inequality here would be children from households in which a language other than English, such as Spanish or Navaho, is spoken. Other examples would be low-achieving children from homes in which there is a poverty of verbal expression or an absence of experiences which lead to conceptual facility.

Such a definition taken in the extreme would imply that educational equality is reached only when the results of schooling (achievement and attitudes) are the same for racial and religious minorities as for the dominant group.

The basis for the design of the survey is indicated by another segment of this memorandum:

Thus, the study will focus its principal effort on the fourth definition, but will also provide information relevant to all five possible definitions. This insures the pluralism which is obviously necessary with respect to a definition of inequality. The major justification for this focus is that the results of this approach can best be translated into policy which will improve education's effects. The results of the first two approaches (tangible inputs to the school, and segregation) can certainly be translated into policy, but there is no good evidence that these policies will improve education's effects; and while policies to implement the fifth would certainly improve education's effects, it seems hardly possible that the study could provide information that would direct such policies.

Altogether, it has become evident that it is not our role to define what constitutes equality for policy-making purposes. Such a definition will be an outcome of the interplay of a variety of interests, and will certainly differ from time to time as these interests differ. It should be our role to cast light on the state of inequality defined in the variety of ways which appear reasonable at this time.

The survey, then, was conceived as a pluralistic instrument, given the variety of concepts of equality of opportunity in education. Yet I suggest that despite the avowed intention of not adjudicating between these different ideas, the survey has brought a new stage in the evolution of the concept. For the definitions of equality which the survey was designed to serve split sharply into two groups. The first three definitions concerned input resources: first, those brought to the school by the actions of the school administration (facilities, curriculum, teachers); second, those brought to the school by the other students, in the educational backgrounds which their presence contributed to the school; and third, the intangible characteristics such as "morale" that result from the interaction of all these factors. The fourth and fifth definitions were concerned with the effects of schooling. Thus the five definitions were divided into three concerned with inputs to school and two concerned with effects of schooling. When the Report emerged, it did not give five different measures of equality, one for each of these definitions; but it did focus sharply on this dichotomy, giving in Chapter Two information on inequalities of input relevant to definitions one and two, and in Chapter Three information on inequalities of results relevant to definitions four and five, and also in Chapter Three information on the relation of input to results again relevant to definitions four and five.

Although not central to our discussion here, it is interesting to note that this examination of the relation of school inputs to effects on achievement showed that those input characteristics of schools that are most alike for Negroes and whites have least effect on their achievement. The magnitudes of differences between schools attended by Negroes and those attended by whites were as follows: least, facilities and curriculum; next, teacher quality; and greatest, educational backgrounds of fellow students. The order of importance of these inputs on the achievement of Negro students is precisely the same: facilities and curriculum least, teacher quality next, and backgrounds of fellow students, most.

By making the dichotomy between inputs and results explicit, and by focusing attention not only on inputs but on results, the Report brought into the open what had been underlying all the concepts of equality of educational opportunity but had remained largely hidden: that the concept implied *effective* equality of opportunity, that is, equality in those elements that are effective for learning. The reason this had remained half-hidden, obscured by definitions that involve inputs is, I suspect, because educational research has been until recently unprepared to demonstrate what elements are effective. The controversy that has surrounded the Report indicates that measurement of effects is still subject to sharp disagreement; but the crucial point is that *effects* of inputs have come to constitute the basis for assessment of school quality (and thus equality of opportunity) in place of using certain inputs by definition as measures of quality (e.g., small classes are better than large, higher-paid teachers are better than lower-paid ones, by definition).

It would be fortunate indeed if the matter could be left to rest there—if merely by using effects of school rather than inputs as the basis for the concept, the problem were solved. But that is not the case at all. The conflict between definitions four and five given above shows this. The conflict can be illustrated by resorting again to the mental experiment discussed earlier—providing a standard education of one hour per week, under identical conditions, for all children. By definition four, controlling all background differences of the children, results for Negroes and whites would be equal, and thus by this definition equality of opportunity would exist. But because such minimal schooling would have minimal effect, those children from educationally strong families would enjoy educational opportunity far surpassing that of others. And because such educationally strong backgrounds are found more often among whites than Negroes, there would be very large overall Negro-white achievement differences—and thus inequality of opportunity by definition five.

It is clear from this hypothetical experiment that the problem of what constitutes equality of opportunity is not solved. The problem will become even clearer by showing graphs with some of the results of the Office of Education Survey. The highest line in Figure 1-1 shows the achievement in verbal skills by whites in the urban Northeast at grades 1, 3, 6, 9, and 12. The second line shows the achievement at each of these grades by whites in the rural Southeast. The third shows the achievement of Negroes in the urban Northeast. The fourth shows the achievement of Negroes in the rural Southeast.

When compared to the whites in the urban Northeast, each of the other three groups shows a different pattern. The comparison with whites in the rural South shows the two groups beginning near the same point in the first grade, and diverging over the years of school. The comparison with Negroes in the urban Northeast

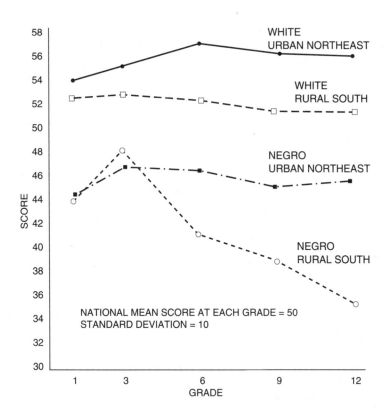

FIGURE 1-1 **Patterns of Achievement in Verbal Skills at Various Grade Levels by Race and Region**

shows the two groups beginning farther apart at the first grade and remaining about the same distance apart. The comparison with Negroes in the rural South shows the two groups beginning far apart and moving much farther apart over the years of school.

Which of these, if any, shows equality of educational opportunity between regional and racial groups? Which shows greatest inequality of opportunity? I think the second question is easier to answer than the first. The last comparison showing both initial difference and the greatest increase in difference over grades 1 through 12 appears to be the best candidate for the greatest inequality. The first comparison, with whites in the rural South, also seems to show inequality of opportunity, because of the increasing difference over the twelve years. But what about the second comparison, with an approximately constant difference between Negroes and whites in the urban Northeast? Is this equality of opportunity? I suggest not. It means, in effect, only that the period of school has left the average Negro at about the same level of achievement relative to whites as he began—in this case, achieving higher than about 15 per cent of the whites, lower than about 85 per cent of the whites. It may well be that in the absence of school those lines of achievement would have diverged due to differences in home environments; or perhaps they would have remained an equal distance apart, as they are in this graph (though at lower levels of achievement for both groups, in the absence of school). If it were the former, we could say that school, by keeping the lines parallel, has been a force toward the equalization of opportunity. But in the absence of such knowledge, we cannot say even that.

What would full equality of educational opportunity look like in such graphs? One might persuasively argue that it should show a convergence, so that even though two population groups begin school with different levels of skills on the average, the average of the group that begins lower moves up to coincide with that of the group that begins higher. Parenthetically, I should note that this does *not* imply that all students' achievement comes to be identical, but only that the *averages* for two population groups that begin at different levels come to be identical. The diversity of individual scores could be as great as, or greater than, the diversity at grade 1.

Yet there are serious questions about this definition of equality of opportunity. It implies that over the period of school there are no other influences, such as the family environment, which affect achievement over the twelve years of school, even though these influences may differ greatly for the two population groups. Concretely, it implies that white family environments, predominantly middle class, and Negro family environments, predominantly lower class, will produce no effects on achievement that would keep these averages apart. Such an assumption seems highly unrealistic, especially in view of the general importance of family background for achievement.

However, if such possibilities are acknowledged, then how far can they go before there is inequality of educational opportunity? Constant difference over school? Increasing differences? The unanswerability of such questions begins to give a sense of a new stage in the evolution of the concept of equality of educational opportunity. These questions concern the *relative intensity* of two sets of influences: those which are alike for the two groups, principally in school, and those which are different, principally in the home or neighborhood. If the school's influences are not only alike for the two groups, but very strong relative to the divergent influences, then the two groups will move together. If school influences are very weak, then the two groups will move apart. Or more generally, the relative intensity of the convergent school influences and the divergent out-of-school influences determines the effectiveness of the educational system in providing equality of educational opportunity. In this perspective, complete equality of opportunity can be reached only if all the divergent out-of-school influences vanish, a condition that would arise only in the advent of boarding schools; given the existing divergent influences, equality of opportunity can only be approached and never fully reached. The concept becomes one of degree of proximity to equality of opportunity. This proximity is determined, then, not merely by the *equality* of educational inputs, but by the *intensity* of the school's influences relative to the external divergent influences. That is, equality of output is not so much determined by equality of the resource inputs, but by the power of these resources in bringing about achievement.

Here, then, is where the concept of equality of educational opportunity presently stands. We have observed an evolution which might have been anticipated a century and a half ago when the first such concepts arose, yet one which is very different from the concept as it first developed. This difference is sharpened if we examine a further implication of the current concept as I have described it. In describing the original concept, I indicated that the role of the community and the educational institution was relatively passive; they were expected to provide a set of free public resources. The responsibility for profitable use of those resources lay with the child and his family. But the evolution of the concept has reversed these roles. The implication of the most recent concept, as I have described it, is that the responsibility to create achievement lies with the educational institution, not the child. The difference in achievement at grade 12 between the average Negro and the average white is, in effect, the degree of inequality of opportunity, and the reduction of that inequality is a responsibility of the school. This shift in responsibility follows logically from the change in the concept of equality of educational opportunity from school resource inputs to effects of schooling. When that change occurred, as it has in the past few years, the school's responsibility shifted from increasing and distributing equally *its* "quality" to increasing the quality of its *students'* achievements. This is a notable shift, and one which should have strong consequences for the practice of education in future years.

Withered Hopes, Stillborn Dreams: The Dismal Panorama Of Urban Schools

GENE I. MAEROFF

No white suburb in America would long tolerate the low academic achievement taken for granted in urban high schools attended largely by blacks and Hispanics. In big city after big city, minority students by the tens of thousands leave school each year—some as dropouts, some as graduates—utterly unprepared to participate in and contribute to a democratic society. They lack the skills that will allow them to obtain gainful employment, and they are devoid of the preparation that will lead to success in further education. They are what the Carnegie Council on Policy Studies warned almost a generation ago could become the nation's "lumpen proletariat."

A reform movement that was supposed to improve public education has been largely irrelevant to the needs of urban minority students. The reforms have either totally bypassed big-city school districts or have produced changes that lengthened the time for instruction or raised requirements for diplomas without addressing the underlying circumstances that lead to failure for these students.

My visits to urban high schools across the country showed them to be large, impersonal places in which students lack a sense of belonging and see no connection between what they are asked to do in the classroom and the world that awaits them outside the school. I found the atmosphere in such schools often unsupportive of education and the demands and expectations low. Students say that they are unmotivated and that they see no reason to attend school, except that there is little else to do with their time.

Attendance is atrocious, and statistics that show students marked present at the beginning of the day do not reflect the degree to which individual classes are cut. There is in urban high schools throughout the country what the Chicago Panel on

Reprinted from *Phi Delta Kappan*, 69:632–638, 1988, by permission of the author and the publisher.

Public School Policy and Finance described as "a widespread 'culture of cutting.' "[1] What passes as work in many courses is embarrassingly simple, and the level of discussion and the papers written by students (mostly in class, because few do any homework) are not truly on a high school level. Large-scale low achievement is accepted as the norm.

Readers can get a taste of the problem by looking in on a ninth-grade English class at a Chicago high school. During a composition lesson, the students were asked to write briefly about why they would choose a particular occupation. "We concentrate on the mechanics of writing so far as their second-, third-, and fourth-grade reading levels will allow," said the teacher. Indeed, the products of their labors, which lasted an entire period, very much resembled what might be produced in the lower grades of many suburban elementary schools. Wrote one student: "I would like to Be a judge and put Bad people in jail and judge make a lot of money to just like the foot ball player even More and I am glad that it is judges in the World to put the people in jail."

What is clearly needed is a fresh approach to urban education, involving smaller learning units and a different philosophy of instruction. The goal must be to create within each learning unit a sense of community and a desire on the part of students to belong to that community. Teachers must have fewer students and spend more time getting to know them. The curriculum must be narrower in scope—as it ought to be in all schools—so that students learn a few topics well, learning how to learn in the process, rather than trying to skim across a vast ocean of material. More classes must be organized around seminars, discussions, and cooperative learning, and students must be encouraged to take greater responsibility for their own education. Ideas and concepts, not facts and statistics, should form the core of this experience.

This reshaping of schools to better serve black students is a mission that America has historically been reluctant to accept. During the days of slavery, those in power acknowledged that laws prohibiting the education of blacks were intended to perpetuate "compulsory ignorance." Even five years after the Civil War, 90% of school-age blacks were not in school. As recently as 1940, public schools in the South operated on an average school year of 175 days for whites and 156 days for blacks, according to a report sponsored by the National Institute of Education.[2]

"The notion that this nation once had good schools for the masses of African-American students but has since let them deteriorate is inaccurate," the National Alliance of Black School Educators stated in a 1984 report. "The institutionalization of deprivation and disenfranchisement among schools has permitted race and socio-economic status to function as the chief determinants of access to quality treatment for children. The public schools often represent an integration of society's most crippling diseases—indifference, injustice, and inequity."[3]

Schools in big cities must do more to lure poor minority youngsters into the mainstream by countering the isolation of their lives. Urban black students, in particular, are surrounded by failure, both in and out of school. Normally they see but few examples of success, except possibly in sports, entertainment, and illicit activities. Their sense of the future is stunted, and, unlike more advantaged youngsters, it does not include academic achievement in any way.

Hopes wither; dreams are stillborn. The isolation suffered by these students is underscored from the moment they enter school. A visit to an urban elementary school, the place where it all starts, will quickly bring home the reality of this isolation. Such a place is the Beethoven Elementary School on Chicago's depressed South Side, a school dwarfed by the Robert Taylor Homes, the huge housing project it faces—26 buildings in which 20,000 people live, mostly women and children on welfare.

The inner city has long been populated by poor people, but what makes the situation different today—and exacerbates the isolation—is the flight of middle-class blacks and the virtual abandonment of entire black neighborhoods to the poorest of the poor. There has been a bifurcation, described by Nicholas Lemann in *The Atlantic,* that has drained the ghettos of many of those who might be constructive role models for the young. A new kind of society is emerging in these neighborhoods, one with its own values, one that is "utterly different from that of the American mainstream."[4] Education does not have a high priority in this setting.

Claude Brown and other commentators note the emergence of a black urban youth culture in which time in prison and unwed parenthood are the rituals of coming of age. *Time* called inner-city black males "America's newest lost generation,"[5] and the *Christian Science Monitor* called poor blacks the "exiles among us."[6] William Julius Wilson wrote of neighborhoods in which "the chances are overwhelming that children will seldom interact on a sustained basis with people who are employed or with families that have a steady breadwinner . . . [where] the relationship between schooling and postschool employment takes on a different meaning."[7]

The urban public schools, bequeathed to the impoverished, have an almost eerie aura about them, as though they were situated in one of the "homelands" to which blacks in South Africa have been confined. Despair reigns supreme among the young. "I don't have any goals," said a young male student in a Houston high school. "I live with my grandmother, and she tells me to do my schoolwork, but she can't read, so she can't help me. Nobody can help me."

Isolation of this sort strengthens the hold of the subculture, giving free play to values that neither reinforce schooling nor encourage the development of the habits of mind needed for academic success. Little happens in many schools or in many homes to build confidence in educational abilities. "They have been filled with so many stereotypes of low achievement that they tend to accept them," said the assistant principal of a high school in New Orleans. "Our goal must be to get students without a history of achievement to believe they can be successful."

Many students whose existence is rooted in urban poverty simply do not have the everyday experiences that might nurture their intellectual development and complement the mission of the school. "Some kids in this school just don't have anyone at home to say, 'I'm proud of you—keep up the good work,' " noted a student at a high school in Houston.

A sad result of their isolation is that many minority students, lagging hopelessly behind in academic achievement for their age, cannot appraise clearly the work they are doing and do not realize that it is not on the high school level. Frequently they do not possess a realistic understanding of just how badly they are lagging. They have no basis for drawing such academic comparisons, because they hardly ever come in contact with anyone other than similarly low-achieving students.

"I don't think I'm having too much trouble with reading," said a young woman at a high school in New Orleans. She was in the 10th grade and had a reading test score that placed her on the third-grade level. An 11th-grader at a high school in Los Angeles, who had not taken algebra or geometry and was currently enrolled in a course called "High School Mathematics," in which the class was learning to add mixed numbers, said: "I'll need this more than I'll need geometry and algebra in the world, and it'll help me more in life. I want to be an architect." He had little comprehension of the field to which he said he aspired, and even less knowledge of what is required to get there.

Many urban minority students have not the slightest clue of what it takes to attain academic goals. The climate in the schools they attend often bodes ill for achievement. Students routinely arrive after the bell has rung—perhaps a quarter of the class comes late—slamming the door behind them, one after the other; walking in front of the teacher; and repeatedly disrupting the lesson as if the teacher were doing nothing of consequence.

During lessons, teachers are frequently forced to compete for attention with unruly and disrespectful students. A world history teacher in a Chicago high school had apparently come to terms with such disruptions by pretending they were not occurring. Students kept talking among themselves and blurting out sarcastic comments as he lectured on Italy. "Put your feet on the floor and your elbows on the desk" he finally said to a rambunctious student, almost without breaking verbal stride. "Do you have your book open to the page?" he asked another student, when he was trying to get the class to look at a map of Italy in the textbook. Before many minutes had passed, four students, their eyes closed, had put their heads down on their desks and were oblivious to the teacher, who was now talking about the Pope's reaction to the Reformation. And so it went.

Caught in a milieu in which classmates often disparage conscientiousness about school, many minority students have no countervailing force at home to reinforce the values that the school wishes to instill. Schools in the heart of the city tend to have a sour atmosphere that strips them of the spirit and vitality that might motivate the young. Students, often consumed by poverty, simply do not participate in the kinds of activities that would enrich the school community.

In one urban high school, where the dimly lit corridors and the shabbiness of the building belied its relative newness, there was no cheerleading squad, the band was shrinking from a shortage of members, and the student newspaper had stopped publishing for lack of money. "There is virtually no enthusiasm among the students," said one young woman, an honors student who had found that being chosen editor of the school newspaper was an empty honor. "The kids need incentives to keep them from being down on themselves."

At school and after school, the peer pressure against academic achievement is strong, especially on black males. "The fact that I like to read makes me exceptional at this school," said a young man who was a sophomore at a high school in New Orleans. "Other kids don't want to read, and their parents don't make them study. Some of them seem jealous of me because I go into the school library a lot."

The existence of this negative peer pressure has been documented by such researchers as Signithia Fordham and John Ogbu, who studied a high school in Washington, D.C. They found that fear of being accused of "acting white" created social and psychological pressures against exerting academic effort. "Peer group pressures against academic striving take many forms, including labeling, exclusion from peer activities or ostracism, and physical assault," the researchers said.[8]

Accumulated academic neglect is abundantly evident. In subject after subject, in classroom after classroom, a large portion of the students never encounter subject matter of the sort presented to students of their age in other kinds of schools.

As a result, most graduates of urban high schools serving primarily impoverished minority students have not read and explored the same literature as their counterparts in suburbs and small towns, have not gotten as thorough a grounding in science and mathematics, have not moved into the more sophisticated areas of social studies, have not gained as much proficiency in foreign languages, and have not had as wide an exposure to art and music. The cruel joke is that most of the dropout prevention programs intended to keep them in school set them up to obtain nothing but a meaningless diploma.

The question is, What are urban minority students giving up when they drop out? Michael Sherraden, writing in the *Educational Forum,* said:

> *In many respects it is inaccurate to view these young people as "dropouts." They never really dropped in. They have attended school, often erratically because school is compulsory and because there are tremendous social pressures to attend. But they had been marginal for many years. They have gone through the motions but they have not been engaged in the educational process. Dropping out is only a visible sign of this underlying pattern of disengagement.*[9]

In Cleveland, 11th- and 12th-graders at one high school were taking a course called "Consumer Mathematics" at a point in their education when many of their counterparts in the suburbs were studying calculus. The teacher was leading them through a lesson on the metric system, explaining that it is based on units of 10 and asking them to make calculations of the sort typically assigned in elementary school. They reviewed the problems the teacher had assigned for homework: "8/10 of a kilometer equals how many meters? 3.5 meters equals how many millimeters?"

In a biology class in a New York City high school, students looking at samples of pond water under microscopes were drawing pictures of the rotifers, oligio-chaetes, and nematodes they saw. The pictures, however, were as far as they would go, according to the teacher, who said it was his experience that they would not take the next step and learn the distinctions among the organisms.

The possibility of pursuing careers in mathematics and science is foreclosed for most urban minority students long before they finish high school. The result is that, in the entire United States in 1986, of the 3,003 doctorates in the physical sciences awarded to American citizens, only 25 were awarded to blacks and 53 to Hispanics. Of the 1,379 doctorates in engineering awarded to Americans, only 14 were awarded to blacks and 25 to Hispanics.[10]

At a point in the term by which she should have covered 10 chapters in the textbook, a chemistry teacher at a high school in New Orleans had completed just five. "They don't read enough, and only half of them will do the homework assignments," she said. "They tell me my expectations for them are too high, but at this rate they will go off to college at a disadvantage."

This is a high school that sends fewer than 20% of its graduates to college. Those who try to make the leap into higher education are generally at a severe disadvantage because the school offers no physics course, has barely enough students for one calculus class, and offers a maximum of two years of foreign language instruction by a single overworked teacher who must teach every foreign language class in the school. As it is, she said, the students struggle every step of the way in French and Spanish—the only two languages offered—and what they learn in two years is the equivalent of what better-prepared students in suburban high schools learn in one year. "They don't recognize words that are cognates to those in English, because their English vocabulary is so weak," she said.

Data from the American College Testing Program show that, although a large number of minority students say that they plan to enter rigorous programs in higher education, they have generally taken fewer years of college-preparatory courses in English, mathematics, social studies, and natural sciences than non-Hispanic white students.[11]

Some minority students in big cities purposely gravitate toward the lower end of the academic offerings, seeking neither challenge nor substance. "My idea is that it doesn't matter what you're taking just so you can pass it without a problem," said a student at a high school in Houston who was enrolled in a bottom-level mathematics course. "If you move to a higher level and fail, you may as well stay where you were rather than try something you can't accomplish."

Teachers in urban schools are confronted by a dilemma, especially in the upper grades, where the lack of earlier preparation leaves a mark of destruction on young people who are academically ill-prepared. A teacher who asks too much of students who have not been equipped to meet the demands may not only be unrealistic, but may also be setting students up for frustration and failure. On the other hand, not having high expectations for students implies that minority students are incapable of doing the work and dooms them to the ranks of the underclass.

Some students recognize the dilemma. "We should have had a lot more reading and math before we got here," said a 14-year-old in the ninth grade at a Chicago high school, where only 10% of the entering students are able to read at grade level. "The teachers should have been harder on us. We should have been given homework. But I know that if they gave the work, some of the kids wouldn't have done it anyhow."

Homework, in fact has gone the way of inkwells in the high schools that minority students attend in big cities. Many teachers have simply stopped assigning homework; those who do so have little hope that it will be completed. In a Los Angeles high school located on the edge of Watts, a social studies teacher had set aside part of the class period to let the students start their homework because that was the only homework that most would do. She had put five questions on the board for them to address:

1. Why are natural resources important to a country?
2. What did Thomas Hobbes believe?
3. List some of the reasons for the rise of nations?
4. Explain how England became a nation.
5. What were the causes of the Hundred Years' War?

Twelve of the 26 students listed on the roll were in class. One of the 12 was doing nothing, explaining that he had lost his book. The teacher said that one advantage of letting students do their homework in class was that she could help them. "They can read the words, but sometimes they have comprehension problems," she said. "It is difficult for them to understand concepts. They come to me without a lot of prior knowledge on which to build. I'm lucky if they can identify England as a country."

Given a pool of students in which so many are performing so abysmally, what passes as an honors course at most big-city high schools that serve minority clienteles is a course that draws on the small number of students achieving at or near grade-level. These so-called honors courses usually do not remotely resemble honors courses at good suburban high schools.

In a Cleveland high school that has not offered a College Board Advanced Placement course since 1975, the teacher of an honors English course for seniors said that the best student, the only one who had scored in the top stanine on a standardized reading test, had spent most of the school year in prison. The course was titled Advanced Placement English because it was thought that the designation "might help the students psychologically," even though this was not actually a course that would prepare students for an Advanced Placement exam. Twenty-four students were in the class at the start of the term, but 12 who seldom showed up were dropped. On this day, eight of the remaining 12 were absent.

"I've taught at this school since 1959, when what we called Advanced Placement *was* Advanced Placement," the teacher said. "Now, even in this class, I have to go back and teach about usage and about complex sentences."

She sat quietly for a moment and then spoke of larger problems. "Our students are having children," she said. "Their own mothers are 32 years old, and the house is full of kids. These students can't get the values at home that they need for school. The problems are tremendous, and we don't know how to handle them. These children have given up. I grew up poor and black in the South, but we didn't give up. It's a really sad situation."

Because urban problems have grown so much worse, students in big cities suffer in ways that seem much more resistant to improvement than the educational woes of students elsewhere. Many of the difficulties are not of the school's making and are not within the school's ability to solve, leaving urban education captive to forces beyond its control. Thus impoverished minority students in big cities, who suffer the worst educationally, are doubly afflicted by the ills peculiar to urban life, as well as possible racism.

The network of support systems that surrounds the urban poor is an Ottoman Empire of services, old and creaky, inefficient, and out of touch with changing needs. Life on welfare has become a devastating cycle of indigence, neither adequate to meet a family's needs or designed to breed self-sufficiency. Structural unemployment has embedded itself in a way that makes a mockery of job training and robs the underclass of the dignity of productive work. Housing for the poor is an embarrassment of paltry contrivances in a land of manicured suburbs and sumptuous condominiums.

Health delivery is inadequate and fragmented, haunting the poor from the moment of conception to the moment of death. The justice system is an oxymoron, since it provides scant justice and is too disjointed to be a true system. It has been stripped of all pretense of rehabilitation and does little more than put souls on ice, as Eldridge Cleaver once said.

In recent years reports have circulated of reading scores in big-city districts that surpass national norms on standardized tests. But one who visits urban high schools quickly discovers a gap between the reality of the work of most students and the overall scores. The questions raised by Friends of Education about the misleading nature of the above-average scores cut to the heart of the issue.[12] If minority students in urban elementary schools are in fact reaching national norms, then these levels of achievement do not seem to be sustained in the high schools. If minority students are bringing higher scores with them to high school, those higher achievement levels do not appear to be used as a base for serious academic work appropriate to high school.

Part of the difficulty lies in the teaching. For every student inspired by a teacher, too often there is another turned off by a teacher unequipped to deal with the needs of disadvantaged children. The differences among teachers could not have been more vivid than in a Chicago junior high school in which the same group of eighth-graders was taught one period by a teacher for whom the students were well-behaved and responsive and the next period by a teacher whose rapport with them was so poor that they were disruptive and uninvolved.

In New Orleans a teacher in an American history course was presenting a unit on black Americans in connection with Black History Week. One by one he recited the names: Gwendolyn Brooks, Ralph Bunche, George Washington Carver, Frederick Douglass, rattling off a long list of dates and facts about each. No questions, no discussion, no interpretation. The students spent the entire period with their heads down, copying facts as the teacher dictated them—information that might better have been presented in a handout or assigned to the students to look up on their own.

Yet another teacher, this one at an elementary school in Houston, was confusing fourth-graders one day with an elaborate reading lesson on "eye syllables that we see" and "ear syllables that we hear." The students were identifying the two kinds of syllables as they went through a story instead of reading for enjoyment and comprehension.

Urban schools have no monopoly on uninspired teaching, but it takes a terrible toll on students who are already unmotivated. Students from advantaged back-grounds will often persevere despite poor teaching because of the rewards they expect by staying the course and earning their credentials. Delayed gratification seldom is enough to hold those who have no experience of reaping rewards that have been held in abeyance. The lack of success of minority students in urban schools is so prevalent that the expectation of failure is as much a part of many classrooms as the textbooks that the children struggle to read. Remediation is a permanent state of being rather than a temporary intervention.

So widespread are low expectations that, when a student in Los Angeles wanted to take algebra, she was dissuaded by a teacher who warned that it was too difficult for her and steered her into an easier course. Last spring, three years later, that same student, still steadfast in the face of discouragement, had shaken free of the ill-founded advice and was taking Advanced Placement calculus.

High schools in the inner city must become more like elementary schools, proffering supportive environments that bolster the confidence of students. Experts repeatedly reaffirm the merits of smallness, and yet urban high schools remain Goliaths, as though there were virtue in bigness. Urban high schools must insinuate themselves into the lives of students in ways that make the schools places where students want to be. The schools should present themselves to students not as places where they can work toward a better "tomorrow," but as places where they can create a better "today."

Building a sense of community among students can put the school in a position to foster the values essential for academic success. Students should help set the rules of the community and participate in its upkeep, as they do in Japanese schools and in some American boarding schools. There should be activities involving groups of students and teachers, so that bonding is enhanced and students feel that they belong to the school and the school belongs to them.

A high school of 200 to 300 students with a faculty of its own that is shared with no other school—even though schools may coexist on separate floors in the same building—can be an intimate institution in which students see the same small cadre of teachers over and over again. Time must be built into the schedule for teachers to meet regularly for several hours a week with small groups of students to talk about life and its problems. More effort must be made to inform the adults at home about what students are studying, so that the adults will take more interest in what is occurring in the classroom.

Borrowing from Theodore Sizer's Coalition of Essential Schools, urban high schools must embrace the philosophy that "less is more." The scope of the curriculum should be reduced and focused on a more limited body of material that can be taught in depth—adapted to individual needs along the way—so that it is better understood and serves as a possible base for widening interests.

Improving the big-city high schools that are attended largely by black and Hispanic students is possible. A pitifully few scattered instances have demonstrated that with fundamental restructuring it can be done. But there is a tendency to revel in delusions of improvement. Order may be restored, but oppression reigns. Test scores may rise, but concepts remain ungrasped. Facts may be memorized, but students cannot apply them in solving problems. Dropouts may be kept in school, but the diplomas they receive are not backed by skills and knowledge.

Nonetheless, some students persist, hoping that school can lead to a life better than the one they have known. A student in Houston, who said that his parents showed little interest in his education, found his reinforcement in a letter written by his older sister. He pulled it from his back pocket, where he said he always carried it, and unfolded the creased, dog-eared stationery. His sister had set out a philosophy that she summed up in just a few words: "Love, Goals, Education, Drive, Resourcefulness, Perseverance, God."

ENDNOTES

1. *'Where's Room 185?': How Schools Can Reduce the Dropout Problem, Part I* (Chicago: Chicago Panel on Public School Policy and Finance, 1986), pp. iii, vii.

2. Meyer Weinberg, *Minority Students: A Research Appraisal* (Washington, D.C.: National Institute of Education, 1977), pp. 1, 3, 5.

3. *Saving the African American Child* (Washington, D.C.: National Alliance of Black Educators, 1984), p. 37.

4. Nicholas Lemann, "The Origins of the Underclass," *The Atlantic,* June 1986, pp. 31–68.

5. "Today's Native Sons: Inner-City Black Males Are America's Newest Lost Generation," *Time,* 1 December 1986.

6. Kristin Helmore and Karen Laing, "Exiles Among Us: Poor and Black in America," *Christian Science Monitor,* 13 November 1986, p. 1.

7. William Julius Wilson, *The Truly Disadvantaged: The Inner City, the Underclass, and Public Policy* (Chicago: University of Chicago Press, 1987).

8. Signithia Fordham and John U. Ogbu, "Black Students' School Success: Coping with the 'Burden of "Acting White," ' *Urban Review,* vol. 18, 1986, p. 183.

9. Michael W. Sherraden, "School Dropouts in Perspective," *Educational Forum,* Fall 1986, p. 23.

10. Michael W. Hirschorn, "Doctorates Earned by Blacks Decline 26.5 Pct. in Decade," *Chronicle of Higher Education,* 3 February 1988, p. A-1.

11. "Minority Students Will Benefit from Early Planning, Improved Academic Preparation," *Activity,* October 1986, p. 5. (This is a publication of the American College Testing Program, Iowa City, IA.)

12. John Jacob Cannell, *Nationally Normed Elementary Achievement Testing in America's Public Schools: How All Fifty States Are Above the National Average* (Daniels, W. Va.: Friends of Education, 1987).

▶ 2

Demographic Change and the Schools

Dramatic shifts in population since about 1950 have caused important changes in urban schools. Veterans of World War II and the Korean War were able to use their G.I. loans to move to outlying sections of the city or to the new suburban tracts springing up in areas immediately beyond the core city. Left behind in the city were the poor, the elderly, the new migrants (Asian and Hispanic), and a large proportion of blacks. Although the majority of economically depressed families in the United States are Caucasian, the concentration of one parent, minority families found in the cities has changed the challenges presented to urban schools.

Wegmann (1977) describes some of the difficulties encountered in urban schools because of these changes. He explains that the term "white flight" may be a misnomer. He argues that, in reality, the population shift has been and continues to be middle class. By the 1980s it also included blacks, as restrictive housing covenants became more difficult to implement. The effort to desegregate the public schools was also a contributing factor, but some cities changed racially and socio-economically without court-ordered action.

The trends depicted by Wegmann have continued unabated into the 1990s. Whether the development of the suburbs is a class or race phenomenon may be moot. Wegmann's (1977) data on Atlanta indicate that the city was 38% minority in 1960 and by 1970 had become 52%. We can now add that by 1980 the figure had become 67%; by 1990, 71%. At the same time, we are aware that from 1950 to 1966 blacks in the suburbs ranged from 4% to 5%; by 1990 it was 25%. Most of the latter figure, as will be pointed out later, are middle class.

According to *USA Today,* minorities represent a majority in 51 American cities. Further, the article reports: "This urban equation is equal to the sum of three parts: The largest wave of immigrants since the early 1990's—most Asian or Hispanic; Continuing white flight; The slow suburbanization of blacks" (Usdansky, 1991, p. A-1).

Wegmann's point that the black school population is *well ahead* of the overall city percentage is quite correct. For example, the minority population of Washington, DC is 73%; 66% of which are black. Detroit has 79% minorities; 76% of which are black. In these cities, there are virtually no white children attending public schools. Those that remain are usually from economically depressed families. Complaints about the Clintons sending their daughter to a private school only highlighted what Caucasian public officials have done consistently in Washington—including the previous education secretary, Lamar Alexander.

Hispanic concentrations are noteworthy in other cities. In New York City, the total minority population is 56.8%; 29% black and the remainder mostly Hispanic. In San Antonio, the minority population is 64% of which 56% is Hispanic. In El Paso, the minority population is 74% of which 69% is Hispanic. Los Angeles and Miami also have large Hispanic populations.

These urban concentrations are predominantly economically depressed families. In 1990, 32% of blacks and 28% of Hispanic families lived below the poverty line, while the same was true of only 12% of Asians and 11% of Caucasian families (U.S. Department of Commerce, 1990).

Obviously, most large cities have become the center of large concentrations of poor people of color. Early in 1993, Jimmy Carter stated: "Now, I think, our society is as segregated as it was 30 years ago. But it is not on the basis of race anymore. Segregation today is between the rich and those who are poverty stricken" (*Toledo Blade,* 1993, p. P-1).

Wegmann concludes that the changes related to desegregation and resegregation of schools have created a "complicated phenomenon." It appears that what is true in one community may not be true in another.

The consequence for urban educators is that this poverty stricken segment of the population have the children who attend public schools. These are the people that Singh refers to as an *underclass.* To some, such a term carries a pejorative label not unlike the progression of labels such as *culturally deprived* or *disadvantaged* that were popularized during the 1960s and 1970s. The latter term became the most acceptable, although some would argue that such language tends to blame the victim. In a major work, Riessman developed what he meant by culturally deprived and was an important, early contributor in attempting change in the inner-city schools (Riessman, 1962). However, problems arose with this usage because in a practical sense no human being can be deprived of a culture. Therefore, *disadvantaged* became a popular substitution because these children, for a variety of reasons, were placed at a disadvantage relative to middle-class children (Fantini and Weinstein, 1968).

The term *underclass* has more recent origins. Wilson (1987) used it extensively but explained that there were some problems (often political) with its usage. In the end we are comfortable with Wilson (1987) who wrote: "Regardless of which term is used, one cannot deny that there is a heterogeneous grouping of inner-city families and individuals whose behavior contrasts sharply with that of mainstream America" (p. 7). In our view this contrast should not be viewed as pejorative, but most often it is. In an article from *The New York Times* that appeared in a Miami paper, the point was made that the development of an underclass is in part due to the expansion of a black middle-class. This meant that "the old ghetto neighborhood became ever more impoverished, bereft of professionals, businessmen and artists who had provided it with vitality and hope. Now, black flight from the inner city has left an underclass equally alienated from mainstream white society and mainstream black society alike" ("Underclass alienated," 1988, p. 4A).

This view offers useful parallels to Singh (1991). He emphasizes how the changing employment market took jobs out of the cities and moved them to the suburbs. Upwardly mobile blacks and whites moved to the suburbs and left the inner city with a homogeneous population of the poor underclass. The attendant problems of community and family breakdown followed. What was left of the job market became even more complicated by discrimination in hiring practices.

It appears that most of the problems discussed in these articles have been induced by forces outside the control of educators. Nevertheless, educators are expected to adjust and offer programs that ensure equality of educational opportunity. The evidence suggests that they haven't done so. Yet, the question persists that in the face of such dynamic change, do the public schools, as currently structured, have the wherewithal to meet the complex needs of urban children? We hope to offer some answers later in the text.

REFERENCES

Fantini, M.D., and Weinstein, G. (1968). *The Disadvantaged Challenge to Education.* New York: Harper & Row. (See Chapter 1 for a complete discussion on the disadvantaged.)

Riessman, F. (1962). *The Culturally Deprived Child.* New York: Harper & Row.

Singh, V.P. (1991, Fall). "The underclass in the United States: Some correlates of economic change." *Sociological Inquiry,* 61(4):505–521.

Toledo Blade. (1993, January 12). Quoted from a speech at the Boston Public Library, January 10, 1993, p. P-1.

"Underclass alienated from whites, other blacks." (1988, March 6). *News/Sun Sentinel,* p. 4A.

Usdansky, M.L. (1991, September 17). "Minorities a majority in 51 cities." *USA Today,* p. A-1.

U.S. Department of Commerce, Bureau of the Census. (1990). Washington, DC: U.S. Government Printing Office.

Wegmann, R.G. (1977). "White flight and school resegregation: Some hypotheses." *Phi Delta Kappan,* 58:389–393.

Wilson, W.J. (1987). *The Truly Disadvantaged.* Chicago: The University of Chicago Press.

White Flight and School Resegregation: Some Hypotheses

ROBERT G. WEGMANN

As the recent debate between James Coleman and his critics has made clear,* desegregated schools exist within a multitude of contexts, and each of these contexts influences what does or does not happen in the school. There is an ongoing process of suburbanization which surely would have occurred if there were no racial minorities, but which in fact disproportionately involves the white middle class. There has been a major downturn in white birthrates which is now causing, in most school districts, a loss of white enrollment quite unconnected with desegregation. Longitudinal studies of school desegregation are complicated by the fact that school attendance areas and school district boundaries change over time. Comparisons with city census data can be difficult because many school systems have boundaries not conterminous with city boundaries. Further, there are minority groups other than blacks in most school systems. Some authors add these other minority students to the white population when analyzing white flight, others do not. Despite these problems, the available research on white withdrawal from desegregated schools does reveal some reasonably clear patterns.

Two Initial Distinctions

Before examining these patterns, however, it is particularly important to note the degree to which issues of race and class are consistently confounded when studying school resegregation. Blacks and most other minority groups are, of course, disproportionately poor. The poor do not do well in school, and schools where the poor

Reprinted from *Phi Delta Kappan,* 58:389–393, 1977, by permission of the author's family and the publisher.

* James Coleman, "Racial Segregation in the Schools: New Research with New Policy Implications," *Phi Delta Kappan,* October 1975, pp. 75–78; Robert Green and Thomas Pettigrew, "Urban Desegregation and White Flight: A Response to Coleman," *Phi Delta Kappan,* February, 1976, pp. 399–402.

are concentrated are no more attractive to minority-group parents (especially middle-class minority parents) than they are to white parents. The schools in communities such as Richmond, Virginia, are reported to be experiencing "black flight" as they become increasingly black and poor; they are just as unattractive to the black middle class as to the white middle class. Similarly, some 10,000 black students in Washington, D.C., are in private schools. What is often called "white flight" is, in fact, a class phenomenon as well as a racial phenomenon.

Further, it is useful to make a distinction between withdrawal and nonentrance. The phrase "white flight" tends to suggest that white students were attending a school, the school was integrated, and then white students found this undesirable and left. In fact, reported drops in white attendance in the first year of school desegregation really refer to students who never showed up at all. It wasn't that they experienced desegregation and found it undesirable; rather, they declined to try the experience in the first place. Some of this decline in white enrollment may consist of students who formerly attended a given school; but part may also consist of students who, in the absence of school integration, would have moved into a neighborhood but now have not done so.

In addition to nonentrance into the neighborhood served by a particular set of schools (elementary and secondary), there is also the issue of nonentrance into a particular school. Schools are particularly susceptible to nonentrance, not only because there are private and parochial alternatives but because the transition from elementary school to junior high, and from junior high to senior high (each school often serving a wider attendance area and having a different reputation and racial composition), repeatedly presents parents and students with the decision to enter or not enter.

Issues of Quality, Safety, and Status

Surprisingly, little research seems to be available on the motives that lead parents to avoid desegregated schools. Such discussions as are found center on three areas: parental perceptions of school quality, parental perceptions of student safety in the desegregated school, and parental concerns about social status. In view of the very limited data, however, any conclusions about the relative importance of these concerns (or their actual impact on the decision to withdraw from a desegregated school) must remain very tentative.

Neil Sullivan, the superintendent of schools who presided over the desegregation of the Berkeley (California) public schools, describes the main fears of white parents when school desegregation is proposed as fear for their children's safety and fear that educational quality will be lost. Concerns about educational quality do seem widespread; national polls show that a fourth of the public believes that the test scores of white students decline sharply in desegregated schools. Although such declines do *not* generally occur, the quality of research in this area leaves much to be desired.

Parental perceptions of student safety may also be involved in decisions to reject desegregated schooling. Black and white students bring differing perceptions of each other to the desegregated school. They may exhibit different behavior patterns and ways of handling conflict and hostility. Rumors can fly as latent parental fears are triggered by incidents which would otherwise be ignored. In some cases, of course, inner-city schools in our major cities are *not* safe, and physical attacks, shakedowns, and threats are real occurrences. What seems to be involved in some of these situations is the fact that, though desegregated, these schools are not truly integrated. Though black and white students are physically present in the same school, the degree of friendship, understanding, and community can be very low.

Finally, just as some individuals do not wish to live in a neighborhood with members of a group whose social status they view as below their own, some parents who do not have specific concerns about educational quality or safety as such may still object to having their children attend school with students from a lower social class. Desegregation generally brings not only an influx of black children into the white child's environment, but also in influx of lower-class children into a middle-class environment.

Although parental concerns about educational quality, safety, and status may be present no matter how the desegregated situation comes about, the available evidence suggests considerable differences in the likelihood of a school's resegregating and the process by which this may occur, depending on whether the racial mix in the school is a reflection of the neighborhood served by the school or whether some level of government has intervened to bring about school desegregation quite apart from the situation in the surrounding neighborhood. The resulting racial and class conflicts as well as patterns of flight and nonentrance (should these occur) can work themselves out in markedly different ways.

I. NEIGHBORHOODS AND SCHOOLS IN RACIAL TRANSITION

Atlanta has been judicially cited as having a great deal of white flight from its school system, so much as to render further attempts at integration futile. The system, once majority white, was 69% minority by 1970. The minority population of the city as a whole, however, also went from 38% minority in 1960 to 52% in 1970. (It is routinely the case that the proportion black in a city's school system is well ahead of the proportion black in the general population.) Hence the change in the racial make-up of Atlanta's public schools took place within the context of a general change in the racial make-up of the entire city (witness the fact, for example, that Atlanta now has a black mayor). Indeed, all of Coleman's findings as he *initially* presented them must be considered to have happened within the context of the changing neighborhoods of large central cities, since a check by the *New York Times* revealed that there was no court-ordered busing, redistricting, or other "forced" integration in any of the 19 cities initially studied.

These changes in central-city racial balance are of considerable magnitude. According to the U.S. Commission on Civil Rights, enrollment in the 100 largest school districts (which have half of the nation's black pupils) dropped by 280,000 students between 1970 and 1972. Since there was a gain of 146,000 black students during this same period, the data suggest a very considerable loss of white students. Some of this loss, of course, can be attributed to a drop in the white birthrate and to other factors. Nonetheless, it is clear that whites with children are disproportionately likely to live in suburban areas. According to the U.S. Census Bureau, 60.1% of the white population (age 18 and over) of metropolitan areas lived in the suburbs in 1974; but 66.6% of the school-age whites (ages 5 to 17) were to be found in suburbs. Note that this is the opposite of what one might expect, since the poor are more likely to live in the city, and are also more likely to have large families. Of course, this situation need not be totally attributed to problems with schools; suburbanization would no doubt be going on if there were no racial minorities in the U.S., and suburbs hold special attractions for families with school-age children for other reasons. The data suggest, however, that schools do play a part.

The most obvious fact about the neighborhood context of school racial proportions is the very high degree of residential segregation that characterizes every U.S. city; there are only a few stable interracial neighborhoods in American cities. Some of this segregation is due, of course, to differences in income level, but rather convincing data show that economic factors account for only a small part of the concentration of blacks in the central city. According to the Census Bureau, blacks constituted only 5% of suburban populations in both 1970 and 1974, despite the fact that a majority of metropolitan residents now live in the suburbs rather than the central city.

Thus while it is important to understand how the process of school and neighborhood resegregation proceeds, it is initially necessary to point out that one fundamental fact cannot be ignored: Given constant density, a growing minority population staying within the central city will inevitably produce an increasing number of segregated neighborhoods and segregated schools.

Interracial neighborhoods are commonly found on the fringes of the black ghetto. What is striking as one reviews studies of the process of racial transition in these areas is the degree to which white *nonentrance* is much more involved than white flight as such. This is not to deny that some individuals move from racially changing neighborhoods specifically to avoid an interracial setting. The fundamental pattern, however, seems to be one of blacks moving short distances into racially mixed neighborhoods, while whites fail to compete with them for the available housing. One study in Milwaukee found that only 4% of a sample of black movers selected housing more than 10 blocks beyond the original ghetto neighborhood. At the same time, beyond 30% black occupancy, the number of new white housing purchases fell off sharply. Other data indicate that this is a common pattern; neighborhood racial change apparently is less a matter of invasion than of retreat. So long as blacks seek to occupy housing on the fringes of the ghetto while whites avoid it, racial change is inevitable. Such neighborhoods then go through a transition from a white to a black housing market.

The School and Neighborhood Change

The research on the school's role in the process of neighborhood change is sketchy, but suggests much. A study in Milwaukee found that in interracial neighborhoods the proportion of blacks within the school is consistently higher than the proportion of blacks within the school attendance area. And schools, like double beds, enforce a certain intimacy. One can ignore a neighbor down the street; it is harder to ignore someone sitting beside you in the classroom. The school, moreover, is a social institution which serves as the focal point for much community interaction.

Parents, students, and schools may or may not be ready for racial integration. To the extent that they are unprepared and fearful of racial change, the schools can become a focus of discontent. And the schools are, indeed, often unprepared and fearful of racial change. A study of riots and disruptions in public schools indicates that such disruptions are most likely to occur in schools with 6–25% minority population and lacking an integrated faculty—precisely the situation found in most urban schools as the neighborhoods they serve begin the process of racial transition.

The available research suggests that school and neighborhood have a reciprocal relationship, with the school seemingly more sensitive to racial transition. To consider what is happening to the racial make-up of the urban school outside the context of the racial make-up of its school attendance area and the changing racial proportions of the entire school district is to risk serious misunderstanding.

Any consideration of the "tipping point" controversy might most profitably occur within this framework. Various authors, including myself, have referred to a point where white departures accelerate or at least become irreversible, leading shortly to a neighborhood or school's becoming all black. References to this concept can be found in several school desegregation suits. A careful examination of racial change in Milwaukee's schools over the eight years for which data exist convinces me that, though there are occasional "surges" of white departures in individual schools in changing neighborhoods, the more common phenomenon seems to be a relatively steady pattern of black entrance combined with white departure and/or nonentrance. Schools do not "tip" by themselves. They resegregate because there is a growing black population which has to go *somewhere,* and which is being steered by a dual housing market to transitional neighborhoods; simultaneously, white buyers avoid these same neighborhoods, anticipating that they and the schools which serve them will shortly be resegregating. Thus it now seems to me that tipping is not a particularly useful concept to describe the changing racial proportions of schools, because it ignores the contexts within which resegregation takes place and tends to imply that there is no such thing as stable integration—which is not true.

Class Levels and Neighborhood Change

One additional variable which may be closely related to school resegregation is the social-class level of the white population in the changing neighborhood. One study in Detroit found that the moving-order of white households is markedly affected by family income, with the more prosperous families moving first; racial attitudes were irrelevant. Indeed, the disorders which have sometimes accompanied court-ordered busing seem to be concentrated in working- and lower-class areas, perhaps because these groups are more prone to physical expressions of their frustrations, and perhaps because, unlike the middle class, they cannot easily afford to move quietly away.

Taken as a whole, the research evidence indicates rather strongly that, so long as in-migration and natural increase provide a growing minority population, it is most unlikely that the process of school "desegregation" in these changing neighborhoods around the fringes of the inner city will be anything but a temporary situation. Without government intervention to provide a stable level of integration in these schools, and simultaneously to provide adequate, safe, and desirable living opportunities for minority citizens in areas other than those immediately surrounding the inner city, the process of resegregation cannot but continue. In some cases (such as Inglewood, California), this process has passed the boundary of the central city and is continuing on into the suburbs.

II. SCHOOL DESEGREGATION BY GOVERNMENTAL ACTION

The second broad type of school desegregation develops when the local school board, the executive branch of either federal or state government, or the courts intervene to bring about the desegregation of previously segregated schools. In the South this has occasionally meant changing from a dual to a unitary—but still neighborhood—school system, particularly in small towns. In many Southern towns of any size, however, as in many Northern areas, segregated neighborhoods are large enough so that students must be transported if school desegregation is to be accomplished.

School resegregation may or may not occur in such situations. White Plains, New York, which began busing students to desegregate its schools in 1964, did a follow-up study in 1970. White students were doing as well or better academically than before integration, black students were doing better, and there had been no white flight. Pasadena, California, on the other hand, recently completed a four-year follow-up study of its experience with school desegregation. Achievement levels of students throughout the district have dropped significantly. Simultaneously, white enrollment has declined precipitously, from 18,000 in 1969 to 11,000 in 1973. Although much of this wide variation in the consequences of school desegregation may be attributable to the particular characteristics of individual cities and school districts, there do seem to be some general patterns.

Racial Proportion and Class Effects

Studies dating back to the period immediately after the 1954 *Brown* decision indicate that resistance to desegregation is closely related to the proportion of black students in the schools. Just as resistance to school desegregation seems to mount as the proportion of black students increases, so apparently does the likelihood of some white withdrawal. There was less than a 1% additional decline in white enrollment after busing began in the 18%-black Kalamazoo (Michigan) school system, but an additional 4.7% decline in white enrollment in the 38%-black Pontiac school system. A similar relationship between the proportion of blacks and white flight in Mississippi has been reported, with particularly heavy withdrawal from majority-black schools. In Nashville the number of whites in one school declined from 560 to 268 when busing to a 40%-black inner-city school began; the white decline in a similar school was only 15% when students were to be bused to a school which was 20% black. (There was an additional factor, however; the former students were to be bused through high school, while the latter were to be bused only for one year.) In a major research project in Florida, the proportion of whites withdrawing to private schools was found to have a 30% black "threshold" beyond which white withdrawal increased, as well as a close connection to white family income.

The impact of the proportion of blacks on white withdrawal may not only be a matter of the proportion itself, but also of the difference in social-class level between black and white students. Memphis, Tennessee, and Jackson, Mississippi, for instance, are often cited as particularly striking examples of white withdrawal from desegregated schooling. Shortly after the Memphis busing order, white enrollment in public schools fell by 20,000, while the number in private schools rose by 14,000. Memphis lost 46% of its white public school students between 1970 and 1973. What is striking about white withdrawal from public schools in Memphis is that it occurred in a situation where the black school population was both large (54% even in 1968) and unusually poor. According to 1970 census data, 35.7% of black families in Memphis were below the poverty line, compared with only 5.7% of the nonblack families. By one estimate, Memphis is second among the major cities of the nation in poverty, with 80% of it found in the black ghetto.

A similar example can be found in the case of Jackson, Mississippi. The Jackson school system, 55% white before mid-year desegregation, lost 9,000 whites and dropped to 40% upon desegregation; 1,500 additional whites left in the following year, dropping the proportion of whites to 36%. Half of all the white pupils in

Jackson now attend private schools. Here again is a combination of high proportion black and extreme poverty. According to recent census data, 27.3% of the black population in Jackson are high school graduates, compared to 77.5% of the non-black population; and 40.3% of the black families are below the poverty line, compared to only 6.3% of the nonblack families.

Just as the social-class level of minority students involved in school integration may be important in determining the presence and extent of racial instability, so may the social-class level of the white students. One study of white withdrawal to private schooling in the Charlotte-Mecklenburg (North Carolina) school district found that income alone explained 54% of white abandonment of the public schools after integration. Thirteen new private schools have opened in Charlotte-Mecklenburg since the 1969 desegregation order. The Florida study already mentioned found that rejection rates for white-students assigned to schools more than 30% black were 4% for low-income students, 7% for middle income, and 17% for high income. It is important to note that though such losses did not represent a very high percentage of the public school population (only 3.6% overall), they can deprive the public schools of a disproportionate number of students from the most affluent part of the community.

The available data suggest, then, that the proportion and social-class level of minority students, the social-class level of the white students, and the cost and availability of schooling alternatives are among the variables which may have a significant relationship to whether or how much white withdrawal may be expected to occur if there is government intervention to desegregate formerly segregated public schools.

III. CONCLUDING COMMENTS

The relationship of one aspect of desegregated schooling to white withdrawal has not, so far as I know, been formally investigated, yet it seems to me to be at the heart of the whole issue: To what extent is the racially mixed school truly integrated? Are the students merely physically co-present, or are they relating to one another in an environment of mutual understanding and respect?

Anyone who has spent any time in racially mixed schools, especially high schools, knows that students in these schools can be as distant from each other as if they were on separate planets. Blacks sit in one part of the cafeteria, whites in another; ditto in classrooms, assemblies, athletic events. Some social events may even be held separately. Indeed, there is evidence that school desegregation may actually *increase* feelings of racial identity. And yet, although a number of studies have investigated interracial attitudes in desegregated schools, the literature contains few reports of programs which foster interracial cooperation and understanding. Yet it should be obvious that schools were never organized to help people understand each other, and there is no evidence that bringing students from different racial, class, and neighborhood backgrounds into them will automatically lead to understanding, appreciation, and friendship. Though some good studies have been done on the relationships among interracial friendship, self-esteem, and academic accomplishment, almost nothing is available that could serve as a blueprint for the school administrator trying to decide what to do tomorrow in order to overcome the racial, class, and cultural gulfs that are so frequently a part of racially mixed education. The answer to this dilemma may contain the key not only to the control of white flight but to the survival of our national commitment to school integration.

Summary and Conclusions

The issue of white withdrawal from desegregated schools is an unusually complex one, and the research done to date has not been equal to the task of explaining all that is involved. Trying to understand this complicated phenomenon is much like trying to put together a giant, confusing jigsaw puzzle with many of the pieces missing. For almost every pattern there seems to be a contrary instance. The available research is characterized by many data gaps, unanswered questions, and unverified assumptions. Nonetheless, the following tentative conclusions seem justified:

1. Whites do not necessarily withdraw from desegregated schools. Some schools maintain a high level of integration for years, some change slowly, and some resegregate very rapidly. Others may experience some white withdrawal followed by stability, or even by white reentrance.

2. Racially mixed schools located in areas bordering the inner city present some markedly different patterns of resegregation from schools located in school districts which have experienced districtwide desegregation. It is important not to extrapolate from the one situation to the other.

3. In situations where there has been no governmental action to bring about desegregation, white withdrawal seems to be linked more than anything else to the underlying demographic consequences of increased minority population growth. This growth takes place primarily in neighborhoods located on the edge of the inner city, as area after area "turns" from black to white. The schools "turn" more quickly than the area generally, and play a significant role in making this process relatively rapid and apparently irreversible. Stable school integration seems to be a necessary if not sufficient precondition for stable neighborhood integration.

4. Decisions on where to purchase a home or where to send one's children to school are made not only on the basis of the present situation but on estimates of what is likely to happen in the future. The belief that presently integrated schools and neighborhoods will shortly resegregate is a major barrier to attracting whites to integrated settings.

5. Little formal research has been done on the motivations behind white withdrawal from desegregated schooling. Worries about the quality of education, student safety, and social-status differences may be among the chief causes. To the extent

that this is true, it could be expected that, other things being equal, school integration would more likely be stable and successful when combined with programs of educational improvement, in settings where concerns about safety are adequately met, and when programs of which parents can be proud are featured.

6. School desegregation ordinarily creates situations which have the potential for both racial and class conflict. The degree of white withdrawal to be expected when there is governmental intervention to desegregate schools may vary, depending on the proportion of minority students who are being assigned to a given school and on the social-class gap between the minority and white students.

7. White withdrawal from desegregated schooling has widely varying costs in different settings. Moving to a nearby segregated suburb, moving outside a county school district, attending a parochial school, attending a private school, transferring to a segregated public school within the same system, or leaving the state are examples of options which may or may not be present in a given situation. Each of these options, if available, will have different costs for different families, just as families will have varying abilities to meet these costs. So long as school desegregation is feared (or experienced) as painful, threatening, or undesirable, it can be expected that the number of families fleeing the desegregated school will be proportionate to these costs and to their ability to pay these costs.

8. Although there is a certain degree of racial mixing in many public schools, there may also be a notable lack of cross-racial friendship, understanding, and acceptance. Superintendents in desegregated districts tend to describe racial relations as "calm" or characterized by few "incidents." Few claim that they have attained anything like genuine community, nor is there much indication that extensive efforts are being made toward this end.

Some Policy Implications

Given the incomplete nature of research on white withdrawal from desegregated schools, policy implications are perhaps better stated as personal opinion rather than as "proven" by the available research. The suggestions given below are so offered.

1. A thorough, national study of school resegregation is needed. Scattered case studies and sketchy national data are not enough. Unless the public schools of this country are going to continue to contribute heavily to the development of two societies, one white and one black, neither understanding nor trusting the other, white withdrawal from desegregated schools needs to be better understood—and avoided. It is significant that the available research is found in journals of law, political science, economics, education, geography, sociology, psychology, and urban affairs. Any such study would have to be a significantly interdisciplinary effort.

2. Although it may be true that government intervention to desegregate schools has in some instances precipitated white withdrawal, it is equally true that the lack of any positive government intervention in the so-called "changing neighborhoods"

surrounding the inner city has been responsible for continuous and ongoing resegregation. In discussing problems of school desegregation in major metropolitan areas, it is desirable to separate the discussion of what to do about inner-city schools from the special problems of resegregating schools on the fringes of the ghetto. If the steady growth of the ghetto is to be arrested, it must be done in these areas. A comprehensive approach to fostering racially stable and integrated neighborhoods and schools would go a long way toward removing the present connection in the minds of many Americans between school desegregation and eventual resegregation.

3. Finally, there is a great need to emphasize the *quality* of school integration and to develop and communicate practical approaches to overcome the cultural and class barriers between the races. The available evidence does not suggest that, if one can just get black and white students into the same building, the rest will take care of itself. It will not. School integration worthy of the name will only come about as the result of conscious, deliberate effort.

The Underclass in the United States: Some Correlates of Economic Change

VIJAI P. SINGH

INTRODUCTION

Much scholarly research and policy analysis has been devoted to the study of poverty, yet it is only recently that serious attention has been given to the underclass phenomenon in the United States. A variety of scholarly conceptualizations, definitions and estimates of underclass size have begun to provide a foundation for distinguishing this phenomenon from that of simply being poor (Glasgow 1980, pp. 3–15; Auletta 1982, pp. 1125–1130; Wilson 1987, pp. 8–9; Ricketts and Sawhill 1988, pp. 317–321; Sawhill 1988, pp. 215–230; Haitsma 1989, pp. 27–31; Ellwood 1989, pp. 6–13). The causes and consequences of the existence and growth of the underclass are analyzed by some scholars from the standpoint of failure of the society (Wilson 1985, pp. 551–557; Cook and Curtin 1987, pp. 217–264; Gans 1990, pp. 276–277; Massey 1990, pp. 329–357), while others find that it is the individual who, for a variety of reasons, has rejected such main-stream values as self-improvement, individual initiative and independence (Murray 1984, pp. 154–177; Berlin and Sum 1988, pp. 26–38; Mead 1989, pp. 156–164). The understanding of the multi-faceted nature of the underclass has involved interdisciplinary perspectives, relevant levels of analysis, quantitative and qualitative data collection, and community studies.

Though the focus is mainly on the black underclass, it is recognized that this is a multi-racial-ethnic phenomenon. The poor in the United States, i.e., those below poverty level, have been changing in composition, but what has baffled scholars and

Reprinted from "The Underclass in the United States: Some Correlates of Economic Change," by V.P. Singh, *Sociological Inquiry*, Vol. 61:4, Fall 1991 by permission of the author and the University of Texas Press.

policy makers is the magnitude and persistence of poverty in certain groups. A significant proportion of persons in low-income groups experiences poverty sometime in their lifetime as a result of loss of employment, marital breakup, catastrophic illness, and other factors (Duncan 1984). The benefits of unemployment compensation, welfare and other types of transfer payments were originally designed to provide a means of sustenance during the interim when people are struggling to overcome temporary setbacks or misfortunes (Duncan 1984, pp. 33–69; Murray 1984, pp. 13–68). While the major economic and population shifts in this country in recent decades have increased the public's awareness of the problem of poverty, most Americans still believe that those who are ambitious, hardworking and self-reliant can take advantage of opportunities and eventually overcome their economic and social disadvantages.

The income gap between the top one-fifth and bottom one-fifth of the population has grown during much of the last decade; worse yet is that, unlike in the past, it is the younger persons who disproportionately constitute the poverty population. The popular perception of the causes of poverty include a low level of education, laziness, low self-esteem and lack of individual aspirations. However, the poor also aspire to a good job, a home, family and self-respect, and many of them succeed in obtaining some or all of these at some point in their lifetime (Lemann 1986, pp. 37–38; Cook and Curtin 1987, pp. 231–234). But a small proportion of this group known as the underclass poses a real challenge to society by disengaging itself from the larger social and economic fabric of the American mainstream.

Conceptualization of Underclass

The concept of underclass has readily observable spatial, economic and demographic components as well as behavioral dimensions. For Wilson (1987, p. 8), the underclass includes ". . . individuals who lack training and skills and either experience long-term unemployment or are not members of the labor force, individuals who are engaged in street crime and other forms of aberrant behavior, and families that experience long-term spells of poverty and/or welfare dependency." This is a group of people concentrated in certain neighborhoods in the inner city who suffer not only from low income, but also have low education, unstable family relationships, limited work opportunities and a slim chance for mobility (Auletta 1982, p. 27; Magnet 1987, p. 130; Gephart and Pearson 1988, p. 1; Ricketts and Sawhill 1988, pp. 317–321; Jencks 1989, pp. 14–26).

The size of the underclass depends on the particular definition used. A definition which is broader will produce a larger size than will a highly specific one. There are many different estimates, but experts who consider this underclass group to be economically and socially isolated from the mainstream society place the number at approximately one percent of the U.S. population (Auletta 1982, pp. 27–29; Ricketts and Sawhill 1988; Sawhill 1988, pp. 229–230). The underclass family is predominantly non-white, female and has children under the age of 18. This group has grown in size during the 1980s and is primarily concentrated in the inner cities of the major urban metropolitan areas (Auletta 1982, pp. 27–80; Wilson 1987, pp. 8–10; Ricketts and Sawhill 1988, pp. 318–320). It is also argued that the number of people affected by poverty during the 1980s was higher than in the 1960s and 1970s. The close conceptual linkage between poverty and underclass may have produced a larger underclass size (Jencks 1989, pp. 14–17). It is not the size by itself that is of great significance but who these people are, how they feel about their connection with the larger society, especially its fundamental values, and the economy (Wilson 1985, pp. 541–543; Nathan 1987, pp. 59–62; Wilson 1989, pp. 189–192; Haitsma 1989, pp. 28–31).

In spite of shared aspirations, the values, life styles and behaviors of the underclass differ markedly from the rest of society (Wilson 1987, pp. 6–7; Hughs 1989, pp. 274–276). The behavioral dimensions which are important and difficult to measure are usually reflected in acts of crime, vandalism and other anti-social or illegal activities (Nathan 1987, p. 58). The social and physical isolation of these groups affords little opportunity for the young to experience the value systems that emphasize hope and opportunity and recognize at the same time the barriers that need to be overcome. Most children growing up in such an environment of poverty rarely encounter appropriate role models who could demonstrate the value of education, of holding a job, of raising children in a two-parent family, or of being a law-abiding citizen. For many in this underclass group, aspirations and dreams cannot be realized by pursuing legitimate means in light of the perceived hostility from representatives of the major societal institutions in the form of racism and stereotyping (Glasgow 1980, pp. 10–15; Auletta 1982, pp. 31–32; Wilson 1985, pp. 551–555; Newport 1989, 165–168). These people often see only formidable barriers to taking initiatives and seeking self-sufficiency beyond the boundaries of the ghetto, a ghetto that does not have much to offer.

The Black Underclass

A variety of social, economic, and demographic factors are associated with the causes and growth of the underclass (Auletta 1982, pp. 25–33; Murray 1984, pp. 154–191; Wilson 1985, pp. 544–556; Wilson 1987; Ricketts and Sawhill 1988; Kasarda 1989; McLanahan and Garfinkel 1989, pp. 93–100; Haitsma 1989, pp. 30–31; Jencks 1989; Massey and Eggers 1990). There is a high degree of association between these characteristics, but no causal relationships are suggested. The underclass is not entirely homogeneous, however, it is disproportionately black and urban. The recency of this phenomenon is readily established by examining changes in the social and economic structures of many inner-city neighborhoods. Prior to the 1960s, the ghettos were different from what they are today; there were leaders, community organizations, and other institutions that enforced community norms in which aberrant behavior was not condoned (Glasgow 1980, pp. 8–10; Wilson 1985; Lemann 1986, pp. 35–39; Wilson 1987, pp. 6–12; Wacquant and Wilson 1989, pp. 14–16). A substantial number of persons living in the inner city ghettos held jobs, encouraged their children to go to school, and participated in local organizations; and some of these people fought those institutional barriers that limited their economic and social opportunities. But progress occurred, leading to affirmative action and desegregation in housing, thus making it possible for those with jobs and skills to move out of the ghetto to other, more desirable areas with better schools and opportunities for mobility. The decision to do so and the actions were in complete conformity with the mainstream social values and expectations.

The departure of socially mobile middle- and working-class blacks made the ghetto even more homogeneous with respect to joblessness, unwed parenting and low aspirations. The poor and underclass who were left behind became still more socially and economically isolated, in part because the effectiveness of many of the mediating institutions waned as community leaders left the ghetto neighborhood (Woodson 1981, pp. 35–42). In spite of such other factors that have contributed to the growth of the underclass, race remains significant. Auletta (1982, p. 31) puts it succinctly, "Inevitably, racism conditioned many blacks to turn their hatred inward, sometimes resulting in negative self-images, and crippling inferiority complexes, in physical and sexual violence, or escape into alcohol and drugs."

The way of life that evolved in the ghetto since the departure of working- and middle-class blacks continues to isolate those left behind from the rest of society. The social fabric broke down as the sense of community and neighborhood diminished and the role of the extended family became less relevant to many young people. Weak social ties pave the way for anti-social behavior and allow illicit activities to flourish (Wilson 1985, pp. 541–542; Wilson 1987, pp. 143–144; Wacquant and Wilson 1989, pp. 15–23). In spite of this growing homogeneity, the ghetto does not foster a "culture of poverty" in which the norms of dependency are passed on from one generation to the next. Recent changes in the American economy have contributed significantly to the growth of the black underclass in older urban-industrial regions.

Causes of Underclass: Some Competing Explanations

There are two competing explanations for the persistence of poverty and the emergence of the underclass in the United States. The first position is that recent changes in the American economy have substantially contributed to the growth of the underclass population (Wilson 1987, pp. 93–106; Kasarda 1989; Wacquant and Wilson 1989, pp. 11–16). The massive elimination of blue-collar, entry-level jobs and the emergence of knowledge-based jobs have not favored many blacks who did not possess sufficient levels of education, skill or work experience. Unemployment and growing isolation from the mainstream economy have led to unwed parenting, dependency, lawlessness, joblessness, and school failure among some blacks. But Mead (1989, p. 159) asserts that proponents of this theory have "not demonstrated a concrete connection between the workers victimized by deindustrialization and jobless poor people in the inner city." Mead challenges the notion of unemployment as the cause of growth of the underclass. He joins Murray (1984) by empirically demonstrating that the poor would rather be on welfare than accept low-paying jobs (Mead 1989, pp. 156–157). Mead further elaborates by implying the culture of poverty argument in which

> *work is something they would like to do, but not something they feel they must do at any cost. It is an aspiration but not an obligation (1989, p. 162).*

The conservative explanation of the underclass phenomenon is that the value system of this group has been fostered and, indeed, reinforced by programs originally conceived to help abate existing racial and class disparities (Murray 1984; Mead 1989). Conservatives insist that the black underclass is a product of unique cultural attributes which generally encourage dependency, and that generous, liberal-inspired welfare programs have contributed to the persistence of this dependency (Lemann 1986, pp. 32–33). Lemann perhaps echoes the most conservative position when he asserts that "in the ghettos, though, it appears that the distinctive culture is now the greatest barrier to progress by the black underclass, rather than either unemployment or welfare" (1986, p. 35). The distinctiveness of culture is reflected in the black underclass not valuing mobility, education, work, marriage or economic progress. All these have been accentuated by the departure of the black middle-class and working-class from the ghetto.

Lemann attributes the cultural distinctiveness of poor blacks to the high propensity for crime, poverty, poor education and out-of-wedlock births. This cultural thesis has been based on the assumption that potential underclass members are not fully socialized into the mainstream norms and values of society. However, Glasgow (1980) found that inner city young men had ". . . many of the same attitudes regarding consumerism, status symbols and goals for attainment" (p. 155). Yet, when these youth begin to encounter institutional barriers, they cope by lowering their level of expectation for themselves rather than continuing to try to get ahead. As a consequence, the behavior of the underclass is different from the mainstream society in relation to schooling, job and family relationships (Cook and Curtin 1987, pp. 217–264). However, there is no evidence that underclass people have developed elaborate institutions and customs to pass on these pathologies as cultural goals to their children.

Ellwood (1989) has elaborated that people do make choices based on utility or satisfaction. Therefore, even single women with mainstream values may choose welfare because of their limited earning potential. However, according to Ellwood (1989, p. 12) it is not clear "whether the problem is that choices are much more limited there because quality education and well-paying jobs are lacking, or whether the problem is more the result of isolation and distorted values. . . ." Thus, it is not just a question of one's position in the labor market or distorted values, but how each of these factors contributes by itself and in concert with other factors to produce and perpetuate the underclass phenomenon. The detachment from the world of work or society in general is to avoid repeated humiliation, frustrations, disappointments and stereotyping.

Murray (1984) implies that society allowed a vicious synergism between various factors for many growing up in ghettos in the 1970s to become members of the underclass.

> *It was easier to get along without a job. It was easier for a man to have a baby without being responsible for it, for a woman to have a baby without having a husband. It was easier to get away with crime. Because it was easier for others to get away with crime, it was easier to obtain drugs. Because it was easier to get away with crime, it was easier to support a drug habit. Because it was easier to get along without a job, it was easier to ignore education. (1984, p. 175)*

But such arguments ignore the reality of the economic market place for blacks living in the ghetto, poor institutional support structure and the presence of racial discrimination in hiring. The desegregation and affirmative action programs born of a liberal perspective may have indirectly contributed to the spatial concentration of the black underclass when many in the middle- and working-classes left their neighborhoods, but, without these programs, the level of persistent poverty and the size of the underclass would have been far higher than the levels in recent years. Migration of blacks out of the ghetto was consistent with the historical trends of residential mobility of ethnic whites to more desirable neighborhoods as their economic situation improved.

There is a significant association between the unemployment status of men and out-of-wedlock birth (Lemann 1986, p. 50). Various estimates exist of the proportions of single mothers who become part of the underclass, but the duration and effect this has on their children should be carefully studied before sweeping generalizations are made. The reliance on welfare on the part of single mothers insulates many of them from the mainstream economy (McLanahan and Garfinkel 1989, pp. 99–104). Clearly some of their children are likely to become part of the underclass and engage in antisocial and illegal activities, but it still should not be interpreted as intergenerational transmission of values and life style that promote dependency and deliberate rejection of legitimate economic opportunities. Many underclass youth, as Woodson (1981) notes, do not have an adequate support system composed of schools, community organizations, churches, vibrant neighborhoods that can assist them to seek education and legitimate economic opportunities. Welfare dependency and illicit economic activities that are highly lucrative become part of an adaptation to what many youth consider to be a hostile environment.

People with liberal perspectives generally ignore the economic position of blacks, especially the disadvantaged, in the changing economy while lending credence to discrimination and prejudice as primary causes in the growth of the underclass (Wilson 1987, pp. 10–12). Newport (1989) points out that any solution to the black underclass problem must pay special attention to the economic plight of black men. Citing a Ford Foundation study Newport states that

> *As late as 1974 nearly half of all employed young black men worked at relatively high paying blue collar jobs in the manufacturing sector. Ten years later, after companies cut the number of these jobs or moved them off shore, the portion of young black men laboring at them had fallen to 26 percent . . . (Newport 1989, p. 166).*

The evidence contradicts the arguments that removal of the welfare system and other support programs or elimination of racial prejudice and discrimination should eventually eliminate the underclass phenomenon. Participation in the mainstream economy may represent the key to addressing the problem of the underclass.

Irrespective of their positions, both liberals and conservatives are troubled by the staying power of this underclass phenomenon in a society that legitimately takes pride in its compassion and equality of opportunity. The conservative position has shifted from blaming the welfare system for joblessness and other underclass pathologies to enhancing the work ethic and family values as possible solutions (Jencks 1989, p. 18). Recent research efforts and public debate on this subject are promising as the causes and correlates of this phenomenon have become clearer.

Economic Change and the Underclass

The foregoing discussion has established that, irrespective of liberal or conservative positions, economic factors are of paramount importance in understanding the underclass phenomenon. It is within this context that the effect of industrial restructuring on employment in selected metropolitan regions of the United States is examined. This analysis is intended to show the magnitude of economic plight which has made a greater impact on blacks than on any other group. It also indicates that the economy of the inner city and nearby industrial towns located in metropolitan regions are inextricably tied to larger economic forces and therefore, ameliorative policies for the underclass must be sensitive to these facts.

Global competition, technological changes and product substitutions have forced accelerated economic restructuring in several mature industrial regions in the Unites States. Some economic sectors, especially those that were recession-prone and less competitive in the global market place, suffered dramatic declines producing massive employment losses during the early 1980s. Many plants and factories closed permanently, creating despair and helplessness among those who could not find work. Communities that depended on such enterprises lost population and tax base and faced deteriorating infrastructure and inadequate public services.

The older industrial regions, a sampling of which is presented in Table 2-1, show the magnitude of decline in the manufacturing industry. The major manufacturing sectors such as steel, rubber, automobile, chemical and textile contributed to much of the decline. According to Table 2-1, between 1968 and 1988 New York and Pittsburgh lost more than one-half of their manufacturing jobs; Cleveland, Baltimore and Chicago lost about one-third; Detroit and St. Louis lost more than one-fourth. It is also noteworthy that much of the recovery of the manufacturing industry in the form of employment gains after the recession of the early 1980s is reflected in these numbers. Other regions such as Philadelphia, Cincinnati and Boston, which had fewer recession-prone industries, still lost manufacturing jobs during the 1968–88 period. However, areas such as Atlanta and Columbus, which were not as burdened with outmoded plants and equipment or poor labor-management relations gained new investments and experienced substantial growth in manufacturing jobs. Many older industrial regions in the northeast and midwest that once were the centers for economic growth and employment opportunity found a substantial proportion of their manufacturing labor force out of work.

When examining the consequences of restructuring in Pittsburgh, for example, the durable goods industry lost 87,000 jobs between 1979 and 1986, much of this loss being attributed to the steel industry. In spite of some gains achieved in the manufacturing sector, after the recession of the early 1980s there were 90,500 fewer jobs in 1986 than in 1975. In the case of Pittsburgh, job losses were concentrated in steel towns which are still struggling for economic survival. The growth in the non-manufacturing industries, especially the services, has compensated for job losses in manufacturing, but it has not served as a major avenue for long-term employment for those who lost jobs due to plant closings (Singh 1987; Giarratani and Houston 1988, pp. 68–74; Singh and Borzutzky 1988; Glennan 1989, pp. 4–5). Some improvements in the manufacturing industries have begun in the recent past, but such improvement is small compared to the magnitude of the loss in manufacturing jobs in the past two decades.

In this paper the relationship between the recent economic changes in the major industrial regions and the growth of the underclass is reviewed. One important inference that has been developed is that restructuring of the basic industries has contributed to the growth of the underclass, however, its level of impact in different contexts has not been fully established. The most commonly used methods have been surveys and community studies in linking economic change and the underclass, but the approach suggested by Ricketts and Sawhill (1988), which uses census data, allows us to link spatial concentration of the underclass with the changes in the economy of the area. Since the debate on the relationship between the recent economic changes and the underclass is not yet settled, it is important to continue to bring new approaches in the analysis to further our understanding of this relationship. This relationship between economic change and the underclass phenomenon in the Pittsburgh region will be analyzed using the method suggested by Ricketts and Sawhill.

TABLE 2-1 **Manufacturing Employment in Selected Metropolitan Regions (1968, 1978, 1988)**

	1968	1978	1988	Percent Change (1968–1988)
Pittsburgh	260,255	216,881	125,788	−51.67
Philadelphia	308,762	308,515	281,165	−8.94
Cincinnati	163,771	165,255	153,309	−6.39
Cleveland	316,255	276,535	200,529	−36.59
Baltimore*	212,108	163,330	147,163	−30.62
Boston*	613,160	555,713	520,216	−15.16
Detroit	621,137	604,939	454,163	−26.88
Chicago	890,330	794,824	604,707	−32.08
New York	1,004,738	681,655	487,216	−51.51
St. Louis*	301,015	264,798	225,077	−25.23

Sources: U.S. Department of Commerce, Bureau of the Census. *County Business Patterns.* Please see sources in the references.
* Baltimore MSA, Boston CMSA and St. Louis MSA.

Ricketts and Sawhill (1988) chose four variables, namely high school dropouts, males who are 16 years of age and older and not regularly attached to the labor force, welfare recipients and female heads of household to identify underclass areas based on the presence of high proportions of these variables. For a census tract to be designated an underclass area, it must score one standard deviation above the mean for the United States for each of the four variables (1988, p. 321).

The Ricketts and Sawhill approach allows us to evaluate the tendency of the underclass to be concentrated in certain neighborhoods where its behavioral characteristics can be observed. Using their definition, only four of the 680 tracts in the four-county metropolitan region of Pittsburgh can be identified as underclass areas. Since significant impacts of the restructuring in the region have been felt beginning in the mid-1970s and most of the job losses were recorded during the latter part of the decade, either the underclass is thinly dispersed throughout the region or the hypothesis that restructuring produces the underclass phenomenon is open to question. Before investigating these two issues, the efficacy of the above method itself is evaluated in the context of the Pittsburgh metropolitan area.

According to Table 2-2, the census tracts in the Pittsburgh region that have a large number of female-headed households are also likely to have people dependent on public assistance, because many of them are persistently poor and unemployed. The strong association between these variables confirms the spatial concentration of the underclass. However, the level of association between these indicators may vary due to other demographic differences between the geographic areas.

Excluding the four tracts meeting all criteria, 48 tracts in the Pittsburgh region meet the three criteria other than the high proportion of high school dropouts, while

TABLE 2-2   **Correlations Between Indicators of Underclass for the 1980 Census Tracts* in Pittsburgh**

	WHEAD	DROPOUT	ASSIST	MNLFU	PPOV
WHEAD	1.00	.27	.82	.62	.78
DROPOUT	.27	1.00	.31	.36	.25
ASSIST	.82	.31	1.00	.72	.86
MNLFU	.62	.36	.72	1.00	.78
PPOV	.78	.25	.86	.78	1.00

* Total number of tracts 680.
WHEAD—Households headed by women with children.
DROPOUT—16–19-year-olds who are not enrolled in school and are not high school graduates.
ASSIST—Households receiving public assistance income.
MNLFU—Males, 16-years-old and over who are not working regularly.
PPOV—Percent of persons below poverty level.

only fifteen totally different tracts meet the high school dropout criterion and these, in general, meet few of the other criteria such as households headed by women with children, male unemployment, welfare dependency and poverty.

Clearly the dropout rate is a limiting variable and has the weakest relationship to the others while the remaining variables are much more strongly intercorrelated with each other.

In Table 2-2, the correlations of the three other variables with the dropout rate range between .25 and .36, while intercorrelations of these variables among themselves range from .62 to .86. Many of the 48 tracts meeting the three criteria are heavily black and are located within the city of Pittsburgh. Many tracts are also characterized by high levels of poverty and persistent unemployment and are, thus, the prime target for underclass status. According to Hughs (1989), this high level of persistent poverty, when spatially concentrated, produces some of the same behavioral and economic consequences that are associated with the underclass phenomenon. Some confirmation for this statement is found in the Pittsburgh data. However, Hughs (1989) finds this methodology defective, because the measures are linked to the national average even though there is tremendous diversity between different metropolitan regions.

In a study of Pittsburgh it was found that the national means for female-headed households with children and high school dropouts were higher than the regional means. However, the national means for men not participating in the labor force and households receiving public assistance were lower than the regional means. When regional means were used, thirteen census tracts met all four criteria for the underclass area as compared to only four tracts when using the national means. Four census tracts met all four criteria and also the criterion of 40 percent or more of the population below poverty level when regional means were used, but none of the census tracts met these requirements using national means. Our analysis of the

Pittsburgh data shows that results of using national or regional means are mixed; however, when the most stringent requirements are used, more census tracts qualify as underclass areas using regional means than when using the national means.

Ricketts and Sawhill (1988) have acknowledged the limitations of their measures (i.e., that some important dimensions of the underclass such as drug abuse and teenage child bearing cannot be compared), but they still insist that an absolute measure is easier to interpret than a relative one (Sawhill 1989, pp. 282–283).

A single indicator, no matter how valid or reliable, cannot fully capture all the significant manifestations of the underclass, but an area that has at least forty percent of its population below the poverty level can be expected to contain many of the behavioral manifestations of the underclass, including welfare dependency, female-headed households, and disengagement from the labor force. There are nineteen census tracts in Pittsburgh that meet the poverty criterion of the underclass. Fourteen of these tracts also meet the three criteria of unemployment, welfare dependency and female-headed households with children. Many people in these areas were dependent directly or indirectly on the manufacturing and mining activities around the city.

The plant closings in the early 1980s worsened the economic prospects for people who were already marginal in the labor market. Several studies conducted in the Pittsburgh region have confirmed that the economic recovery that has been underway since 1983 has provided employment opportunities to persons who have some skills and are able to move, if necessary, to find work. Even though there are underclass tracts in Pittsburgh which exhibit some of the same characteristics as underclass areas elsewhere, the spatial concentration is much less pronounced because of relatively lower proportions of minority population in the region and dispersed manufacturing facilities. A Rand Corporation study of Pittsburgh found that even though the employment opportunities have improved, "Many of the good jobs for which the minority workers are qualified don't seem to be located close to the neighborhoods where they live" (Glennan 1989, p. 17). The most severe effect of restructuring has been felt by those who are least able to cope with it (Bluestone and Harrison 1982, pp. 25–48; Pearson 1989). The expectation that new jobs will help the unemployed in the manufacturing industries has been disappointing.

DISCUSSION AND CONCLUSION

Economic restructuring and the ensuing polarization of the labor force into high- and low-wage occupations has not enhanced job opportunities for inner-city youth and other black workers (Duster 1987; 1988; Wilson 1987, pp. 121–123; Berlin and Sum 1988). Although the economic recovery of the 1980s created millions of new jobs and reduced overall unemployment, it primarily benefitted educated and skilled workers and those with job experience. As Duster (1988) noted, the reason more than one-half of the black youth are unemployed is because entry-level jobs in the manufacturing industries have been largely eliminated. Other jobs that are available are low paying, often temporary, and are concentrated in marginal industries. For many black youth, such jobs do not provide a stable means of sustenance or dignity and, therefore, are rejected (Duster 1988, pp. 2–7).

Some analysts attribute the growth of low-paying jobs to the demand side and others to the supply side of the labor market (Mead 1988, pp. 45–48; Pearson 1989, pp. 17–18). But sufficient evidence exists to suggest that new jobs consist of professional and managerial jobs as well as low-paying, deadend jobs (Loveman and Tilly 1988; Mead 1988). As the economy changed and newly created jobs that required substantial levels of education and skills grew, the education of blacks did not keep pace (Kasarda 1989, pp. 30–35). High school dropout rates increased and generally deficient schooling of blacks created a mismatch between available jobs and skill levels. Those who do not finish high school or remain unemployed for a prolonged period of time become prime candidates for the underclass (Auletta 1982, pp. 33–35; Mead 1988, pp. 158–159).

There is no evidence that the economic recovery of the 1980s has significantly benefitted those who live in the inner city or old industrial towns. Many underclass blacks lacking in technical and interpersonal skills could work in the fast food industry and personal care services, except that these, too, are outside the inner city. The erosion of the economic base of the inner city and the lack of opportunities in the emerging economy contributed to the growth of the underclass which has become quite homogeneous with respect to joblessness, welfare dependency, single-parent households, and the prevalance of drugs and crime (Gephart and Pearson 1988, pp. 2–7).

Massey and Eggers (1990, pp. 1153–1188) recently reported that there are regional differences in the concentration of the poor and the underclass, and these can be substantially explained through the differences among regions in their patterns of racial segregation. A similar conclusion can be drawn for the Pittsburgh region where a high degree of concentration is observed in the city but less so in the old industrial towns. These conclusions reaffirm the fact that rapid changes in the industrial economy have contributed to the growth of the underclass and, because such changes cannot be stopped, it is imperative that effective policies be developed to address this problem.

Affirmative action programs conceivably will demonstrate their effect when members of the underclass acquire skills that enable them to participate in the emerging economy. Social policies must be sensitive to the multiple causes of the underclass phenomenon even though emphasis should be placed on the economic integration of this group. The role models, if they are important, must be identified within the underclass neighborhood. In this context, assisting people to become self-sufficient and economically independent is important. Since most jobs are created by the private sector, however, its involvement in determining a broad national policy related to the underclass is critical.

Economic revitalization and job creation strategies should include special programs for inner-city neighborhood development where most unemployed and low-income people are concentrated. Cooperation between the private and the public sector is essential, in this regard, and the public sector must become an active partner in protecting and diversifying the economic base of industrial communities while also developing plans for transforming inner-city areas into viable, profitable business sites. The private sector should identify types of jobs for which the underclass persons can be trained. It must also make a commitment to hire some of these persons, at least initially, so that the promise of integrating them in the mainstream economy is reaffirmed.

Philanthropic organizations, especially the corporate and community foundations, can share this responsibility, at least temporarily, in helping revitalize neighborhoods and communities where the underclass are concentrated. It is equally important that public transportation facilities be provided to locations where employment opportunities exist. Public debate, legislation or sanctions will not change the condition of people who are outside of the economic mainstream. Pragmatic and effective programs for economic participation along with provisions for continuous monitoring and evaluation would be appropriate. As programs for economic integration of the underclass are implemented, it is important that the federal government continuously monitor the effects of major changes in the domestic economy on regions, communities and subpopulations.

ENDNOTE

* The author acknowledges the contribution of Don Musa who provided the analysis of the Pittsburgh data and made substantive comments on the earlier version of this paper. The editorial comments of Laurie Fowler and Jo Ann Kurutz were also helpful.

REFERENCES

Auletta, Ken. 1982. *The Underclass.* New York: Random House.

Berlin, Gordon, and Andrew Sum. 1988. *Toward a More Perfect Union: Basic Skills, Poor Families and Our Economic Future.* New York: Ford Foundation.

Bluestone, Barry, and Bennett Harrison. 1982. *The Deindustrialization of America.* New York: Basic Books.

Cook, Thomas D., and Thomas R. Curtin. 1987. "The Mainstream and the Underclass: Why are Differences so Salient and the Similarities so Unobtrusive?" Pp. 217–264 in *Social Comparison, Social Justice and Reactive Deprivation: Theoretical Empirical and Policy Perspectives,* edited by J.C. Masters and W.P. Smith. Hillsdale, NJ: Lawrence E. Associates, Publishers.

Duncan, Greg J. 1984. *Years of Poverty, Years of Plenty.* Ann Arbor: Institute for Social Research.

Duster, Troy. 1987. "Crime, Youth Unemployment, and the Black Underclass." *Crime and Delinquency* 33:300–316.

———. 1988. "Social Implications of the 'New' Black Urban Underclass." *The Black Scholar* 19:2–9.

Ellwood, David T. 1989. "The Origins of 'Dependency': Choices, Confidence and Culture." *Focus* 12:6–13.

Gans, Herbert. 1990. "Deconstructing the Underclass: The Term's Dangers as a Planning Concept." *APA Journal* 56:271–277.

Gephart, M.A., and Robert W. Pearson. 1988. "Contemporary Research on the Underclass." *Items* 42: 1–10.

Glasgow, Douglas G. 1980. *The Black Underclass: Poverty, Unemployment and Entrapment of Ghetto Youth.* New York: Vintage Books.

Glennan, Thomas K. 1989. *Education, Employment and Economy: An Examination of Work-related Education in Greater Pittsburgh.* Santa Monica: The Rand Corporation.

Giarratani, Frank, and David B. Houston. 1988. "Economic Change in Pittsburgh." Pp. 49–87 in *Regional Structural Change in International Perspective: United States, Great Britain, France, Federal Republic of Germany.* Baden-Baden: Nomos Verlagsgesellschaft.

Haitsma, Martha Van. 1989. "A Contextual Definition of Underclass." *Focus* 12:27–31.

Hughs, Mark Alan. 1989. "Concentrated Deviance and the 'Underclass' Hypothesis." *Journal of Policy Analysis and Management* 8:274–281.

Jencks, Christopher. 1989. "What is Underclass—and Is It Growing?" *Focus* 12:14–26.

Kasarda, John D. 1989. "Urban Industrial Transition and The Underclass." *Annals of the American Academy of Political and Social Science* 501:26–47.

Lemann, Nicholas. 1986. "The Origins of Underclass." *The Atlantic Monthly,* June:31–55.

Loveman, Gary W., and Chris Tilly. 1988. "Good Jobs or Bad Jobs: What does the Evidence Say?" *New England Economic Review: Federal Reserve Bank of Boston* (January—February): 46–65.

Magnet, Myron. 1987. "America's Underclass: What To Do?" *Fortune* (May): 130–133.

Massey, Douglas S. 1990. "American Apartheid: Segregation and the Making of the Underclass." *American Journal of Sociology* 96:329–357.

Massey, Douglas S., and Mitchell L. Eggers. 1990. "The Ecology of Inequality: Minorities and the Concentration of Poverty, 1970–1980." *American Journal of Sociology* 95:1153–1188.

McLanahan, Sara, and Irwin Garfinkel. 1989. "Single Mothers, the Underclass and Social Policy." *Annals of the American Academy of Political and Social Science* 501:93–106.

Mead, Lawrence M. 1988. "The Hidden Job Debate." *The Public Interest* 91:40–58.

———. 1989. "The Logic of Workforce: The Underclass and Work Policy." *Annals of the American Academy of Political and Social Science* 501: 157–169.

Murray, Charles. 1984. *Losing Ground: American Social Policy 1950–1980.* New York: Basic Books.

Nathan, Richard P. 1987. "Will the Underclass Always Be With Us?" *Society* 24:57–62.

Newport, John Paul. 1989. "Steps to Help the Urban Black Man." *Fortune* (December): 164–172.

Pearson, Robert W. 1989. "The Growing Underclass." *Evaluation Forum* 5–6:14–18.

Ricketts, E.R., and Isabel V. Sawhill. 1988. *Journal of Policy Analysis and Management* 7:316–325.

Sawhill, Isabel V. 1988. "Poverty and the Underclass." Pp. 215–252 in *Challenge to Leadership: Economic and Social Issues for the Next Decade,* edited by Isabel V. Sawhill. Washington, D.C.: The Urban Institute Press.

————. 1989. "Comment on Concentrated Deviance and the Underclass Hypothesis." *Journal of Policy Analysis and Management* 8:282–283.

Singh, Vijai P. 1987. *Regional Structural Change in International Perspective: The Case of Public-Private-University Partnership in Regional Revitalization* (in German). Bonn: Friedrich Ebert Stiftung.

Singh, Vijai P., and Silvia Borzutzky. 1988. "The State of the Mature Industrial Regions in Western Europe and North America." *Urban Studies* 25:212–227.

U.S. Department of Commerce, Bureau of the Census. 1970. *County Business Patterns, Illinois: 1968.* Washington, DC: U.S. Government Printing Office.

————. 1980. *County Business Patterns, Illinois: 1978.* Washington, DC: U.S. Government Printing Office.

————. 1990. *County Business Patterns, Illinois: 1988.* Washington, DC: U.S. Government Printing Office.

————. 1970. *County Business Patterns, Kentucky: 1968.* Washington, DC: U.S. Government Printing Office.

————. 1980. *County Business Patterns, Kentucky: 1978.* Washington, DC: U.S. Government Printing Office.

————. 1990. *County Business Patterns, Kentucky: 1988.* Washington, DC: U.S. Government Printing Office.

————. 1970. *County Business Patterns, Maryland:1968.* Washington, DC: U.S. Government Printing Office.

————. 1980. *County Business Patterns, Maryland: 1978.* Washington, DC: U.S. Government Printing Office.

————. 1990. *County Business Patterns, Maryland: 1988.* Washington, DC: U.S. Government Printing Office.

————. 1970. *County Business Patterns, Massachusetts: 1968.* Washington, DC: U.S. Government Printing Office.

————. 1980. *County Business Patterns, Massachusetts: 1978.* Washington, DC: U.S. Government Printing Office.

————. 1990. *County Business Patterns, Massachusetts: 1988.* Washington, DC: U.S. Government Printing Office.

————. 1970. *County Business Patterns, Michigan: 1968.* Washington, DC: U.S. Government Printing Office.

————. 1980. *County Business Patterns, Michigan: 1978.* Washington, DC: U.S. Government Printing Office.

————. 1990. *County Business Patterns, Michigan: 1988.* Washington, DC: U.S. Government Printing Office.

————. 1970. *County Business Patterns, Missouri: 1968.* Washington, DC: U.S. Government Printing Office.

————. 1980. *County Business Patterns, Missouri: 1978.* Washington, DC: U. S, Government Printing Office.

————. 1990. *County Business Patterns, Missouri: 1988.* Washington, DC: U.S. Government Printing Office.

————. 1970. *County Business Patterns, New Jersey: 1968.* Washington, DC: U.S. Government Printing Office.

————. 1980. *County Business Patterns, New Jersey: 1978.* Washington, DC: U.S. Government Printing Office.

————. 1990. *County Business Patterns, New Jersey: 1988.* Washington, DC: U.S. Government Printing Office.

————. 1970. *County Business Patterns, New York: 1968.* Washington, DC: U.S. Government Printing Office.

————. 1980. *County Business Patterns, New York: 1978.* Washington, DC: U.S. Government Printing Office.

————. 1990. *County Business Patterns, New York: 1988.* Washington, DC: U.S. Government Printing Office.

————. 1970. *County Business Patterns, Ohio: 1968.* Washington, DC: U.S. Government Printing Office.

————. 1980. *County Business Patterns, Ohio: 1978.* Washington, DC: U.S. Government Printing Office.

————. 1990. *County Business Patterns, Ohio: 1988.* Washington, DC: U.S. Government Printing Office.

————. 1970. *County Business Patterns, Pennsylvania: 1968.* Washington, DC: U.S. Government Printing Office.

————. 1980. *County Business Patterns, Pennsylvania: 1978.* Washington, DC: U.S. Government Printing Office.

————. 1990. *County Business Patterns, Pennsylvania: 1988.* Washington, DC: U.S. Government Printing Office.

Wacquant, Loic J.D., and William Julius Wilson. 1989. "The Cost of Racial and Class Exclusion in the Inner City." *Annals of the American Academy of Political and Social Science* 501:8–25.

Wilson, William Julius. 1985. "Cycles of Deprivation and Underclass Debate." *Social Service Review* 54:541–559.

————. 1987. *The Truly Disadvantaged: The Inner City, The Underclass and Public Policy.* Chicago: The University of Chicago Press.

————. 1989. "The Underclass: Issues, Perspectives and Public Policy." *Annals of the American Academy of Political and Social Science* 501:182–192.

Woodson, Robert L. 1981. *A Summons to Life: Mediating Structures and the Prevention of Youth Crime.* Cambridge: Ballinger Publishing Company.

▶ 3

Poverty and The Urban Family

It is clear that in the last two decades of the twentieth century, the urban family in the United States has undergone profound changes. Poverty, homelessness, drugs, and teen pregnancy are among the many social and economic problems that have been highlighted in the media to underscore the decline of urban America. These problems have been prompted in large measures by the departure of the older industries that depended on skilled and semiskilled immigrant labor. As industries abandoned the urban centers and the economic base of the cities eroded, those who had the education or training that allowed them to be mobile left. Poor and minority families were left to struggle for increasingly limited resources found in the inner-city streets. The struggle over these scarce resources has had an enormous impact on the ability of poor and minority families to negotiate everyday life. Single-parent families of low socioeconomic means have become the norm.

The question of the quality of the early socialization of the children from these families is a perplexing one. Surely, the preschool years are crucial in setting the tone for future academic and social growth. Kozol (1990) describes the situation as grim as he portrays the children of the poor as social outcasts. He warns us of the gulf that is being perpetuated between the *haves* and *have nots* and wonders what kind of adults the latter will become. He cites differences in school expenditure, infant mortality rates, homelessness, and school standards, all of which compound the problems of the poor.

Slaughter and Epps (1987), in an extensive research review, validate the results of Kozol's description. They demonstrate the importance of communication between parent and child in affective bonding. However, communication between low-income black children and teachers is not as satisfactory. What might that indicate about the relationships of socioeconomic status and race to family influence and school achievement? There do appear to be some negative perceptions about education held by lower-class black children. Where do they come from and how are they sustained?

Slaughter and Epps emphasize the variety of family roles, which include teacher, mediator, supporter, and decision maker. They conclude by suggesting various ways that school personnel can work more cooperatively with parents of low socioeconomic status. These strategies will be developed later in this text.

REFERENCES

Kozol, J. (1990). "The new untouchables." *Newsweek,* (Winter/Spring):48–53.
Slaughter, D.T., and Epps, E.G. (1987). "The home environment and academic achievement of black American children and youth: An overview." *The Journal of Negro Education,* 56:3–20.

The New Untouchables

JONATHAN KOZOL

On an average morning in Chicago, about 5,700 children in 190 classrooms come to school only to find they have no teacher. Victimized by endemic funding shortages, the system can't afford sufficient substitutes to take the place of missing teachers. "We've been in this typing class a whole semester," says a 15-year-old at Du Sable High, "and they still can't find us a teacher."

In a class of 39 children at Chicago's Goudy Elementary School, an adult is screaming at a child: "Keisha, look at me . . . Look me in the eye!" Keisha is fighting with a classmate. Over what? It turns out: over a crayon, said *The Chicago Tribune* in 1988. Last January the underfunded school began rationing supplies.

The odds these black kids in Chicago face are only slightly worse than those faced by low-income children all over America. Children like these will be the parents of the year 2000. Many of them will be unable to earn a living and fulfill the obligations of adults; they will see their families disintegrate, their children lost to drugs and destitution. When we later condemn them for "parental failings," as we inevitably will do, we may be forced to stop and remember how we also failed them in the first years of their lives.

It is a commonplace that a society reveals its reverence or contempt for history by the respect or disregard that it displays for older people. The way we treat our children tells us something of the future we envision. The willingness of the nation to relegate so many of these poorly housed and poorly fed and poorly educated children to the role of outcasts in a rich society is going to come back to haunt us.

With nearly 30 percent of high-school students dropping out before they graduate—60 percent in segregated high schools—it is not surprising that illiteracy figures have continued to grow worse. The much publicized volunteer literacy movement promoted for the last six years by Barbara Bush serves only 200,000 of the nation's estimated 30 million functional illiterates. Meanwhile, the gulf in income between rich and poor American families is wider than at any time since figures were recorded, starting in the 1940s. The richest 20 percent received 44 percent of national family income; the poorest 20 percent got only 4.6 percent. More than 5 million of the poorest group are children.

Reprinted from *Newsweek*, Winter/Spring:48–53, 1990, by permission of the author.

Disparities in wealth play out in financing of schools. Low-income children, who receive the least at home, receive the least from public education. New Trier High School, for example, serving children from such affluent suburbs as Winnetka, Ill., pays its better teachers 50 percent above the highest paid teachers at Du Sable, by no means the worst school in Chicago. The public schools in affluent Great Neck and White Plains, N.Y., spend twice as much per pupil as the schools that serve the children of the Bronx.

Infant-mortality figures, classic indices of health in most societies, have also worsened for poor children and especially for nonwhite children. The gap between white and black mortality in children continues to widen, reaching a 47-year high in 1987 (the most recent year for which data are available). Black children are more than twice as likely to die in infancy as whites—nine times as likely to be neurologically impaired. One possible consequence: black children are three times as likely as whites to be identified as mentally retarded by their public schools.

Federal programs initiated in the 1960s to assist low-income children, though far from universally successful, made solid gains in preschool education (Head Start), compensatory reading (Chapter I) and precollege preparation (Upward Bound), while sharply cutting the rates of infant death and child malnutrition. Limited funding, however, narrowed the scope of all these efforts. Head Start, for example, never has reached more than one of five low-income children between its start-up in the '60s and today.

Rather than expand these programs, President Reagan kept them frozen or else cut them to the bone. Living stipends paid to welfare families with children dropped to 35 percent (adjusted for inflation) below the 1970 level. Nearly half a million families lost all welfare payments. A million people were cut from food stamps. Two million kids were dropped from school-lunch programs. The WIC program (Women, Infants, Children), which provides emergency nutrition supplements to low-income infants, young children and pregnant women, was another target of Reagan administration cuts, but Congress successfully fought them off. Despite their efforts, the WIC budget is woefully inadequate, and has never been able to provide services to even half of the children and women who meet the eligibility requirements.

Federal housing funds were also slashed during these years. As these cutbacks took their tolls, homeless children were seen begging in the streets of major cities for the first time since the Great Depression. A fivefold increase in homeless children was seen in Washington, D.C., in 1986 alone. By 1987 nearly half the occupants of homeless shelters in New York City were children. The average homeless child was only 6 years old.

The lives of homeless children tell us much of the disregard that society has shown for vulnerable people. Many of these kids grow up surrounded by infectious illnesses no longer seen in most developed nations. Whooping cough and tuberculosis, once regarded as archaic illnesses, are now familiar in the shelters. Shocking numbers of these children have not been inoculated and for this reason cannot go to school. Those who do are likely to be two years behind grade level.

Many get to class so tired and hungry that they cannot concentrate. Others are ashamed to go to school because of shunning by their peers. Classmates label them "the hotel children" and don't want to sit beside them. Even their teachers sometimes keep their distance. The children look diseased and dirty. Many times they are. Often unable to bathe, they bring the smell of destitution with them into school. There *is* a smell of destitution, I may add. It is the smell of sweat and filth and urine. Like many journalists, I often find myself ashamed to be resisting the affection of a tiny child whose entire being seems to emanate pathology.

So, in a terrifying sense, these children have become American untouchables. Far from demonstrating more compassion, administration leaders have resorted to a stylized severity in speaking of poor children. Children denied the opportunity for Head Start, sometimes health care, housing, even certified schoolteachers, have nonetheless been told by William J. Bennett, preaching from his bully pulpit as U.S. Secretary of Education under Reagan, that they would be held henceforth to "higher standards." Their parents—themselves too frequently the products of dysfunctional and underfunded urban schools—have nonetheless been lectured on their "lack of values." Efforts begun more than 10 years ago to equalize school funding between districts have been put on the back burner and are now replaced by strident exhortations to the poor to summon "higher motivation" and, no matter how debilitated by disease or hunger, to "stand tall." Celebrities are hired to sell children on the wisdom of not dropping out of school. The White House tells them they should "just say no" to the temptations of the streets. But hope cannot be marketed as easily as blue jeans. Certain realities—race and class and caste—are there and they remain.

What is the consequence of tougher rhetoric and more severe demands? Higher standards, in the absence of authentic educative opportunities in early years, function as a punitive attack on those who have been cheated since their infancy. Effectively, we now ask more of those to whom we now give less. Earlier testing for schoolchildren is prescribed. Those who fail are penalized by being held back from promotion and by being slotted into lower tracks where they cannot impede the progress of more privileged children. Those who disrupt classroom discipline are not placed in smaller classes with more patient teachers; instead, at a certain point, they are expelled—even if this means expulsion of a quarter of all pupils in the school. The pedagogic hero of the Reagan White House was Joe Clark—a principal who roamed the hallways of his segregated high school in New Jersey with a bullhorn and a bat and managed to raise reading scores by throwing out his low-achieving pupils.

In order to justify its abdication, the federal government has called for private business to assist the underfunded urban schools. While business leaders have responded with some money, they have also brought a very special set of values and priorities. The primary concern of business is the future productivity of citizens. Education is regarded as capital investment. The child is seen as raw material that needs a certain processing before it is of value. The question posed, therefore, is how much money it is worth investing in a certain child to obtain a certain economic gain. Educators, eager to win corporate support, tell business leaders what they want to hear. "We must start thinking of students as workers," says the head of the American Federation of Teachers, Albert Shanker.

The notion of kids as workers raises an unprecedented question. Is future productivity the only rationale for their existence? A lot of the things that make existence wonderful are locked out of the lives of children seen primarily as future clerical assistants or as possible recruits to office pools at IBM. The other consequence of "productivity" thinking is an increased willingness to make predictions about children, based almost entirely on their social status. Those whose present station seems to promise most are given most. Those whose origins are least auspicious are provided with stripped-down education. IQ testing of low-income babies has been recently proposed in order to identify those who are particularly intelligent and to accord them greater educational advantages, although this means that other babies will be stigmatized by their exclusion.

A heightened discrimination in the use of language points to a dual vision: we speak of the need to "train" the poor, but "educate" the children of the middle class and rich. References to "different learning styles" and the need to "target" different children with "appropriate" curricula are now becoming fashionable ways of justifying stratified approaches. Early tracking is one grim result. A virtual retreat from any efforts at desegregation is another: if children of different social classes need "appropriate" and "different" offerings, it is more efficient and sensible to teach them separately.

A century ago, Lord Acton spoke thus of the United States: "In a country where there is no distinction of class a child is not born to the station of its parents, but with an indefinite claim to all the prizes that can be won by thought and labor. It is in conformity with the theory of equality . . . to give as near as possible to every youth an equal start in life." Americans, he said, "are unwilling that any should be deprived in childhood of the means of competition."

That this tradition has been utterly betrayed in recent years is now self-evident. The sense of fairness, however, runs deep in the thinking of Americans. Though frequently eclipsed, it is a theme that stubbornly recurs. A quarter century ago, it took disruptions in the streets to force Americans to question the unfairness of de jure segregation. Today it is not law but economics that condemns the children of the very poor to the implacable inheritance of a diminished destiny. "No matter what they do," says the superintendent of Chicago's public schools, "their lot has been determined."

Between the dream and the reality there falls the shadow of the ghetto school, the ghetto hospital, the homeless shelter. Appeals to the pocketbook have done no good. Black leaders have begun to contemplate the need for massive protest by poor people. Middle-class students, viscerally shocked by the hard edge of poverty they see in city streets, may be disposed to join them. The price may be another decade of societal disruption. The reward may be the possibility that we can enter the next century not as two nations, vividly unequal, but as the truly democratic nation we profess to be and have the power to become. Whether enough people think this outcome worth the price, however, is by no means clear.

The Home Environment and Academic Achievement of Black American Children and Youth: An Overview

DIANA T. SLAUGHTER   EDGAR G. EPPS

INTRODUCTION

What roles do Black parents have in their children's schooling? One way to address this important question is to explore the contributions that parents make to student achievement. The question is important for at least three reasons. First, American family structure and organization are presently undergoing rapid social change. Second, the current and projected costs of higher education exacerbate the importance of a solid academic foundation in the elementary and secondary school years. Third, there is increased evidence that American schools, as presently operated, are biased learning environments for many Black children.

In the research literature, four approaches to parental impact upon the achievements of children and youth can be identified: parent as decision maker, parent as supporter, parent as mediator, and parent as teacher. Each approach will be illustrated in this selective review of the contributions of families to Black children's elementary and secondary schooling achievements.

A number of reviews on this topic are available for children in general.[1] The purpose of the present review is not to duplicate those statements, but to discuss briefly what is known today of how social class and race affect childhood and adolescent socialization for academic achievement. For brevity, with regard to dependent variables, this review is confined to direct measures of academic achievement, their proxies (e.g., I.Q. scores, grades, and so forth), or to educational attainment. We acknowledge, however, that student academic achievement motiva-

Reprinted from *The Journal of Negro Education,* 56(1):3–20, 1987, by permission of the authors and the publisher.

tion and educational aspirations and expectations are important intervening variables that affect these behavioral outcomes.

PARENTS, TEACHERS, AND STUDENT ACHIEVEMENT: THE HISTORICAL CONTEXT

Fantini[2] noted that shifts in the nature of economic life in England and America, particularly during colonial times, caused a shift in the social institutions deemed primarily responsible for children's education for citizenship. As the economy became increasingly industrial, the family had less of the collective wisdom needed by each new generation to participate competently in society. Schools gradually replaced families as the primary source of this wisdom. Black Americans' early and determined struggle for formal education, including the perception that this was a key, if not *the* key, to attaining full citizenship in America, has been well documented.[3] Immediately following the Civil War, for example, Blacks worked diligently with the help of the Freedmen's Bureau to establish schools and colleges for themselves.

Another impetus for the shift from familial to school control of children's education included the high rates of immigration and migration after the Civil War, particularly to urban industrial areas, and the corresponding need for political unity within a socially diverse nation. The role conceived for public education during these times was to establish a literate electorate. Black American families supported schools because they had considerable faith in the power of the American educational system to produce literacy, which in turn would assure freedom and prosperity to Black children and youth. Increasingly, the school as an institution has, of necessity, assumed other educative functions that once were the domain of the family.[4]

By the mid 1960s, when compensatory educational programs for prospective low-income school children had gained maximal societal support, Clark[5] published *Dark Ghetto*. He reported the findings of New York's *HARYOU* project, and placed blame for the children's academic achievements squarely on school teachers' expectations. Teachers, rather than parents, were to blame for student underachievement. The prevailing view[6] was that parents were primarily responsible for these children's early learning and, therefore, subsequent educability. Preschool programs such as Project Head Start were partly designed to compensate for the earlier absence of appropriate parental input.[7] The debate over what educators such as Riessman[8] labelled the "culturally deprived" or "culturally disadvantaged" child is well known. However, the mid 1960s debate was merely part of a history in which families and schools had become increasingly perceived as oppositional rather than mutually interdependent institutions that educate children.

Coleman's 1966 research[9] indicates that family background and associated parental influences may be the primary forces affecting student achievement over time. Bloom has argued that parents may be more important simply because they are the most consistent figures in the child's life.[10] However, it is also clear that schools, and particularly quality of teaching in schools, do make a difference. Because of the changing nature of the society, its families, and its schools, and because we do not yet know precisely how family environments interact with the schooling process for different age and sociocultural populations, the study of home environment and student achievement continues to be important.

PARENTAL INFLUENCES ON EARLY LEARNING AND ACHIEVEMENT: DEFINING "HOME ENVIRONMENT"

Specific parental influences on children's intellectual development have been found in children as young as three months. When a mother responds to her baby's specific vocalizations as if a conversation were occurring, the baby's language development is affected in a positive way. By age one, the mother's crucial teaching role is even more apparent. Clarke-Stewart, Blumenthal, and Caldwell and colleagues have shown in their studies[11] that between 9 and 36 months of age the Black child's advances in language development are stimulated by maternal verbal behaviors that are contingently responsive to the child's speech behaviors, and by verbal and nonverbal behaviors indicative of active participation in the child's ongoing play. Schachter believes that the value of verbal responsivity, from the child's perspective, is not primarily intellectual, but social and emotional.[12] The verbal behaviors of the mother increase the child's sense of self-worth and security. Clarke-Stewart also believes that the child thus develops expectancies of affecting and controlling its home environment.

Even before nursery school, the family shapes the child through stimulation of his verbal, conversational skills and creation of affective bonds that may often be transformed into a press for evidence of independence and achievement as the child matures. Parents are, in effect, the child's earliest teachers, not simply because they have the "right" to be, but because they do, in their priorities, expectancies, and behaviors, influence the course of the child's achievement development. Recent research suggests that when Black primary caregivers feel supported by extended family members, they are better informal "educators" to children.[13]

Slaughter[14] found that low-income Black preschool children who are successful school achievers through the first kindergarten year have mothers who set clear, firm, consistent standards for behavior, but who also are warm, accepting, and flexible enough to consider the child's viewpoint and to communicate this understanding. In addition, these mothers experience less social isolation in their communities. In the American society, the least effective parenting style for the early development of social and academic competence is one which expects the child merely to respond to the parent's authority.

The family exists within the community, and the community within society. The home environment's role as educator to the child is interdependent with many other, continuing, changing, and frequently competing roles that it fulfills. While we have some idea of what would be beneficial to children's early reading, we have little idea of how these processes manifest themselves in the roles enacted by culturally and socially different families in their natural settings. More accurate characterization of these environments, especially during the primary school years, will enable educators to work with parents to design and implement more useful reading intervention programs in which homes and schools work as partners, specifically parents and primary-grade teachers.

Three studies of the home language environments of Black children, for example, have produced some important findings. Ward studied the home language environment of young lower-income Black children in an all-Black southern community, using an ethnographic approach and some of Bernstein's theoretical formulations.[15] She found that beliefs about children, such as "Children should be seen and not heard," rather than books or articles about childrearing or various developmental time-tables governed the adult community's interactions with them. Preschool children were not expected to enter into adult conversations, and adults rarely made "polite" conversation with them. There were few educational toys, little direct language instruction was observed, and family members did not correct children's speech. While younger children, ages 0–3 years, received much affective attention from adults, children between ages 3 and 5 were relatively ignored. Conversations between children and adults increased after first grade, but even then emphasis tended to be on the business of the day rather than on personal, affective perspectives.

Ward emphasized that the extended family and community, including peers, siblings, and other related adults, constitute the child's real human language environment. Children freely and openly explore their total community. If one is to understand their early language development, these communities and extended families must be studied.

Teale[16] reported some of the major preliminary findings of an ongoing exploratory study of the home language environments of lower-income preschool-age Black, Anglo, and Mexican American children in a mid-sized Californian city. The study focused on the occurrence of literacy events in each home, with literacy defined simply as events directly related to the reading process, where adults or children (including the focal child) produced or attempted to produce written language.

Teale found wide variation in the incidence, timing, types, and functions of literacy events among the homes. He also found that the context and materials of these events are closely linked to other, extrafamilial institutions and to family activities in which adults and children participated. An understanding of family activities and life styles is crucial to any effective home-based intervention program. For example, church-going adults might read the Bible to the children, or use the Bible to model the reading process for them.

Brice-Heath[17] also conducted an extensive ethnography of language socialization in a lower-income Black community of a midsized southeastern city whose school system had recently been desegregated. Both teachers and parents had complained that communication between the Black children and their teachers was poor. A major focus of the study was upon the discontinuities between how questions or interrogatives were used in the community and how they were used by the teachers in the children's classrooms.

The results of Brice-Heath's five-year field study emphasize that questions are used by adults in the community to stimulate understanding by analogy. Nonspecific, unexplained comparisons are thus perfectly acceptable child responses. Conversely, with their own preschool children, as well as with their primary-grade students, teachers used questions to stimulate conversational interactions between themselves and the children, often around highly specific information that had been given previously. Community adults frequently addressed comments about children to third parties, whereas in similar situations teachers would direct specific questions to children. Community adults almost never asked children to label and discuss obvious object attributes for which the child knew the adult already had the answer, nor were children socialized to feel compelled to answer questions. Rather, children were asked about obviously unknown (to the inquirer) facts or stories, or for commentary or related experiences, activities, and so forth. Questions were used by community adults as accusatory devices, relative to past infractions. Questions were not used to indirectly signal that certain ongoing behaviors should cease. Finally, Brice-Heath found that teachers often asked questions for which the "obvious" answers were outside the actual life experiences of the Black children.

Like Hall and Tirre,[18] Brice-Heath emphasizes that lower-income Black children are quite "verbal," but that the norms governing when and how they should speak are different from middle-class norms. To be effective educators, teachers need to know some of these norms, to adapt them to their own classroom behaviors, and, conversely, to point out the differences between in-school and out-of-school speech to the students.

Each of the preceding ethnographic case studies focused upon factors associated with preschool and primary-grade Black children's school achievement, including home/school relations, in smalltown and/or rural southern communities. Similar research is needed in urban settings, where the majority of Black children attend school. Gouldner has published one such study, and Massey is conducting a longitudinal follow-up of primary-grade Black children initially studied in infancy.[19]

Researchers have only occasionally emphasized the varieties of strengths to be found in careful examination of social differences in studies of parenting and student achievement. Many have thought the more important task to be one of determining which parental behaviors account for student achievement regardless of familial social status. Researchers have sought to achieve equity or parity in education by focusing on commonalities relative to beneficial parental influences on student achievement rather than on intersocietal and intrasocietal diversity in parenting styles which could result in similar desired outcomes. However, by neglecting the role of such social stratification variables as class, race, and ethnicity in the everyday lives of school children, we have narrowed the focus to only a few. The younger the child, the easier it is to neglect such variables, but even in studies of infants and preschoolers they emerge as important.

SOCIOECONOMIC STATUS AND ACHIEVEMENT: THE FAMILY AS MEDIATOR?

Social status in America, for purposes of educational research, is usually defined by measures of social class position: occupation of household heads, education, and income. Hess[20] reports that the higher a person's social status position is ranked, the more likely he or she is to have a higher level of performance on achievement tests. White[21] reports, on the basis on meta-analysis of two hundred studies, that socioeconomic status (SES) correlates about .22 with individual student achievement. Many family characteristics have been found to be associated with individual student achievement—characteristics believed by some educational researchers to be linked to SES and family life style. Measures of these characteristics correlate about .55 with individual student achievement. White does not report the typical correlation between SES and family characteristics, but he does indicate that when the dependent variable is aggregated (e.g., schools), the correlation between SES and mean achievement level is typically as high as .79. White also notes that SES may be an indirect measure of home atmosphere and that student achievement differences may be influenced more by childrearing practices (e.g., reading to the children, taking them to the library, encouraging them in school, and the like) than by the occupation, income, or education of the parents.

Policy positions that emphasize child resocialization in school were criticized[22] because they seemed to hold families living in poverty solely responsible for their children's school failures. Despite theories that stress links between social structures to parenting processes and educational outcomes, recommendations often stress only changes in lower-status Black families and children. Therefore, educators can declare children uneducable because of their social backgrounds; and thus, "family" replaces "IQ" in determining the children's learning potentials. Finally, many reject the basic assumption that families, particularly Black families, simply mediate and reflect societal influences without also actively filtering and thus protecting their children from perceived threats to the children's images of themselves as learners and as persons.[23]

However, families are much more vulnerable to the influences of social structure than is commonly believed. Middle- and upper-income Black families have problems with schools because they must also accommodate to the peculiar pressures the institutions generate for their children. Slaughter and Schneider[24] found that Black parents who could afford to send their children to private schools often reported experiencing some marginality within these school environments, and most were concerned that their children receive the necessary social skills to sustain the family's social standing in the next generation. A few expressed concern that the children retain a strong sense of identification with the Black American community. Black families of all social status groups have been remarkably effective and resilient at helping their children cope with the schooling process. Each group can teach the other about relationships within society as a whole, its own family life, and the consequent meaning of education to its members.

ACADEMIC ACHIEVEMENT: WHAT IS THE ROLE OF ETHNICITY AND FAMILY?

Ogbu[25] has argued that whenever a subcultural minority has historically experienced caste-like restrictions in its access to legitimate power and status within a dominant culture, the adult members of the subculture develop different, largely negative, cultural attitudes toward such settings—attitudes that are transmitted to its children. According to Ogbu, many Black American children and youth may learn that education is not a vehicle to social mobility and opportunity, and thus develop negative attitudes toward schooling. The result is widespread school failure within the Black community. This theory suggests that we need to understand more of how the Black child's family interfaces with the educational process to affect school achievement.

We are in need of mini-theories and innovative research strategies to examine this important question. For example, Holliday[26] has argued that in the Black subculture children are socialized to assume a posture of persistence and assertiveness in relation to problem-solving. When displayed by Black children in the classroom, however, these traits are rejected by teachers as being inappropriate for Blacks in America. By the middle-school years, according to Holliday, the cumulative impact of these rejections is to "transform young Black children's achievement efforts into learned helplessness." Hare and Castenell,[27] in considering the fates of Black male school children, argue that by the middle-school years the peer culture easily competes with the school culture because, unlike the latter, the former provides opportunities for the boys to demonstrate competence and, therefore, maintain a sense of self-respect. Hare and Castenell view meeting esteem needs as a primary element of human motivation.

Slaughter[28] conducted a follow-up study of 56 lower-income Black children who had been studied while in a 1965 summer preschool program. The children were in grade six at the time of the follow-up. Twenty-seven of these children were surveyed again in 1978, the point of expected high-school graduation.[29] The status and power of the children's lower-income families were decidedly not equivalent to the status and power held by the middle-class school system. Slaughter predicted and found that in such a situation, teacher evaluations (cumulative report card grades) would affect both the children's and the mothers' perceptions of the children's academic ability.

However, despite teacher feedback which differentiated maternal and child perceptions of the child's achievement effort and performance in grades kindergarten through five, the schools' criteria of academic success (standardized tests) indicated no differences among the children: by grade six, academic performances were almost uniformly substandard for all. Although the early home environment did relate positively to the children's academic readiness for school, teachers' feedback either did not convey the schools' high standards to these children and their mothers or, if the standards were conveyed, the means for realizing them were not. Further, because children and mothers were being led to believe that the children were learning more in school than they actually were, their images of themselves were being manipulated. There were long-term consequences to these earlier distortions: increasingly poor achievement performance and reduced actual expectations for future educational attainment at the point of high-school graduation. Parents in the Slaughter study did not know from prior experiences what the achievement standards of the schools were. Therefore, their best earlier efforts with their children were not sufficient to sustain achievement in school. The nature of the teacher feedback exacerbated the social discontinuities between these lower-income Black families and the middle-income, predominantly white, school system.

Some studies have used innovative research designs to examine the problems of Black academic achievement during the middle-school years. Moore[30] shows how community-based norms enter the individual achievement testing situation. She recorded the verbal and nonverbal behaviors of forty-six urban black adopted children (average age, 8.0 years) during IQ testing. Twenty-three of the children lived in middle-class Black homes and twenty-three in middle-class white homes from at least fifteen months of age. Moore attributed the 13.5 difference in average IQ score favoring white homes over Black homes to the work styles used by the two groups of children during testing, work styles she found reinforced by observed differences in interactive maternal behaviors. Black adopted children from white homes more often justified what they did not know aloud. They seemed to pursue the testing situation as if it were a competitive game between themselves and the tester. Their verbal behaviors seemed directed at reassuring and buttressing their own positive images of themselves in the event that they had given the "wrong" answer. In contrast, children in Black homes were far less likely to engage in such behavior; they assumed a more passive posture, often nonverbally shaking their heads when they did not know an answer. They behaved as if they perceived the situation as a test, not as a game.

Moore observed that Black middle-class adopters were typically of first-generation middle-class status. The study points to possible differences in the cultural problem-solving styles associated with maternal achievement training. It suggests that parents' social class of origin may be more crucial to immediate parental behaviors associated with early achievement development than to their attained social status. Blau[31] holds a similar view. She reports that the achievement performance of fifth graders is more consistently predicted by maternal socialization variables for whites than for Blacks. Variability in the achievements of Black children is more consistently predicted by measures of mothers' structural involvements: SES, marital status, organizational memberships, and nondenominational religious affiliation.

The studies reviewed above emphasized families' roles as teacher, mediator, or supporter. At least one other role should be noted: parents as decision makers. For example, there are documented instances in which Black parents experience a genuine sense of potency and significance within their children's school communities. Black parents who can afford to send their children to private schools, or who actively participate in special decentralized public school demonstration projects, appear to have children who, using the criteria outlined for this review, are more often successful school achievers.[32] It is possible that the children's real and tangible academic successes induce this "sense of potency," but it is equally likely that the feeling that these Black family members have that their children's school is serving them contributes directly to the children's confidence in their own ability to "make something of themselves."

FAMILY INFLUENCES ON SECONDARY SCHOOL ACHIEVEMENT

By the time students reach high school, much of their socialization for academic achievement has already been completed. Parents, peers, and school personnel have helped to create the kind of person, and the kind of student, the adolescent has become. In traditionally organized classrooms, achievement is remarkably stable across the school years. Maruyama, Rubin, and Kingsbury[33] reported correlations of .67 to .72 for verbal achievement between ages 9 and 12, and of .75 to .79 for verbal achievement between ages 12 and 15. Similarly, in summarizing results of longitudinal studies, Bloom[34] reported that measures of achievement after grade three yielded a median correlation with achievement at grade 12 of .70. In addition, White[35] found that the relation between SES and achievement drops off as students become older. The correlation between SES and achievement is about .21 in elementary school and about .17 in high school. These studies suggest that direct family influences on secondary-school achievement are probably somewhat weaker than on preschool and elementary-school achievement. However, experiences in lower grades, including the family's influences, are reflected in secondary-school students' attitudes toward school, their behaviors, and their academic achievement.

Studies that have investigated the influences of SES on the educational achievement and attainment of Black adolescents have usually found that socioeconomic background of students' families explains relatively little of the variation in achievement. Studies that use high-school grades or rank in class as indicators of achievement have generally found that SES is unrelated to Black students' academic performance.[36] The relationship of SES to ability and achievement test performance is usually weak but positive and statistically significant.[37]

Epps and Jackson[38] examined the relationship of SES, ability, and selected school variables to achievement test scores and grades of Black high-school seniors in two nationally representative samples: the National Longitudinal Study of 1972 sample, and the 1980 High School and Beyond sample. Their findings suggest that much of the family influence on grades and achievement of high-school students is indirect. The high achievers have high educational aspirations, and these aspirations are directly influenced by SES. Families also influence secondary school achievement by their choice of private versus public schools, by encouraging students to enroll in academic rather than vocational or general courses, and by encouraging them to do homework and to attend school regularly.

Bowman and Howard, in a national survey of 317 Black youths between the ages of 14 and 24, investigated the relationship of racial socialization by parents to the self-reported grades of respondents. Results indicated that grades were lowest for the one-third of the youths who reported that parents had told them nothing about race relations in the United States. Youths socialized to be aware of racial barriers reported significantly higher grades. The authors concluded that " . . . it is through an emphasis on ethnic pride, self-development, racial barriers, and egalitarianism that Black parents attempt to filter to the developing child the meaning of [his/her] racial status."[39]

Family characteristics may affect Black students' educational achievements and attainments differently across national regions. Bachman[40] found that Black students in northern segregated schools differed considerably from those in southern segregated schools in terms of test scores and socioeconomic levels, and Blacks in integrated schools differed from both segregated subgroups. There is also some evidence of regional variations in the way different SES measures relate to achievement.[41] However, there are some inconsistencies among the research results.[42]

Studies that have looked at educational attainment have usually found socioeconomic level of family of origin to have an important influence on the amount of education attained.[43] Porter[44] found small significant positive correlations between head of family's occupation and students' educational and occupational attainment, but no direct effect of parents' occupation when other variables were included in a multiple regression analysis. Wilson[45] reported that socioeconomic level of students' families was more strongly related to Black students' educational attainment in integrated schools than in segregated schools and was more important for "upper-class" Blacks than for lower-class Blacks. One indication of the way social status affects attainment comes from the study by Gurin and Epps.[46] This study of Black students attending traditionally Black colleges in the South found little effect of social status on academic performance or motivation. However, when students who aspired to post-graduate education were asked how certain they were that they would actually be able to attend graduate or professional school, those from poverty-level backgrounds were much less certain about their ability to attend in the near future.

What survey studies of the relation of family background to achievement fail to explain is why some economically poor families are able to translate their aspirations for their children into reality through their children's school successes while others are unable to obtain the desired outcomes. R. Clark[47] used a case study approach in his investigation of Black family influences on school achievement. The case studies of families of successful high-school achievers include retrospective descriptions of explicit literacy-enhancing activities during childhood such as reading, writing, word games, and hobbies. The families of successful achievers provided a home atmosphere that was strongly supportive of academic achievement. There was firm discipline, but it was not rigid or harsh. Parents were willing to explain decisions and involve students in the decision-making process. Clark also found that parents of high achievers were assertive in their efforts to keep themselves informed about their children's progress in school. The parents of low achievers, however, tended to avoid contact with school personnel as much as possible. Parents of successful students also appear to be more optimistic than parents of low achievers and tend to perceive themselves as persons who can successfully cope with life's problems. Parents of low achievers tend to see the world around them as unmanageable and devoid of opportunities for self-improvement.

The pessimism of the parents of low achievers reported in Clark's research is consistent with Ogbu's conclusion[48] that perceptions of a "job ceiling" among caste-like minorities lower their motivation to strive for academic success. The argument that perception of limited opportunities causes many low SES minority students to believe that academic excellence is unrelated to future occupational or economic success is more plausible for secondary- than for elementary-school pupils. The latter are less likely to have highly structured ideas about societal barriers to social mobility. However, what parents tell young children about opportunities, and how educational achievement affects success, may influence the way children respond to the negative pressures they encounter as adolescents.

CONCLUSIONS AND IMPLICATIONS

Prior to the secondary-school level, quality survey research and ethnographic case studies that are developmentally oriented are in short supply. Even fewer of the existing studies assume a macrosocial structural perspective (class, race, or ethnicity) in design or interpretation of obtained data. Studies of the natural variation in the patterns of parental involvement among Black and other minority families are only just emerging. In contrast, at the secondary level and beyond, few case studies exist that permit an in-depth understanding of the life course experienced by higher and lower achieving Black youth, including the social networks and institutions that condition these experiences. Many studies at both grade levels fail to examine sex differences in achievement performance within the Black community.

From a policy perspective, parents influence their children's academic achievement directly by the kind of educational environment they provide in the home, and indirectly by their impact on the schools their children attend. Low-SES and Black families often lack the human and material resources needed for a positive academic environment in the house. However, as research has shown, positive learning environments do exist in some low-SES Black homes. It is generally accepted that parental involvement in their children's educational experiences enhances students' achievement.

It is good that the prematurely closed question of the role of the child's cultural background in its achievements has been reopened for educational research. Recent studies suggest strategies and methods that can be used to approach these problems. We may just find that there are differing socialization routes to the same end for differing populations within this nation's highly diverse Black American communities.

School administrators typically give limited support to parental involvement in school affairs beyond participation in parent-teacher organizations. Attempts by parents to gain a voice in the decision-making process are usually frustrated. While more affluent parents are able to exercise choice in selecting their children's schools, either by choosing private schools or choosing housing near a desirable public school, most low-income parents do not have the resources to exercise such options. Magnet schools that do not restrict admittance to specific geographic attendance zones offer some choices to parents who have the assertiveness to obtain information needed to make informed choices, and who arrange transportation. However, most low-income families must resign themselves to the neighborhood school, which typically is poorly financed.

Schools should help parents provide better educational environments at home for their children. For example, schools should arrange regular home visits by specialists in early childhood education who would provide educational materials where needed as well as help parents improve their abilities to work effectively with their own children. Parent groups should be organized for regular meetings with educators to discuss what parents can do in conjunction with teachers to facilitate children's learning. Such discussions could help parents understand the curriculum of the school, what standards of achievement are expected, and what parents can do at home to improve their children's achievement and the quality of life of the school.

Parents should mobilize their extended families and communities to support the schools. McAdoo[49] and others have documented how extended family members, under certain conditions, can be sources of support to both two- and single-parent Black families in caring for school-age children. Community leaders and community organizations should work cooperatively with schools to rebuild bridges between Black communities and the schools.

If public schools are to survive as a primary source of collective, national unity, educators will have to make some accommodations to Black and poor families. The perpetuation of a "no-difference" ideology does not necessarily lead to equitable treatment; it may lead to an imbalanced focus on "negative" differences between children of different classes and races. Teacher-preparation programs should require completion of at least one course on the contribution of the home environment to the achievement development of children and youth. Courses on parent education which highlight (a) social diversity in parenting styles and (b) Black family life would also be desirable.

For many Black families, the daily struggle for survival takes precedence over all other concerns. A society that is committed to equal opportunity for all its citizens must give serious attention to the many problems faced by a sizable proportion of its families. Blacks will again perceive a strong, viable connection between educational attainment and work when they can see employment opportunities for themselves and their children as a reality in the society.

ENDNOTES

1. Allison Clarke-Stewart, "Evaluating Parental Effects on Child Development," in *Review of Research in Education,* ed. Lee Shulman (Itasca, Ill.: Peacock, 1978), pp. 47–119; Edgar Epps and Sylvia Smith, "School and Children: The Middle Childhood Years," in *Development During Middle Childhood: The Years from Six to Twelve,* ed. Andrew Collins (Washington, D.C.: National Academy Press, 1984), pp.283–334; Robert Hess and Susan Holloway, "Family and School as Educational Institutions," in *Review of Child Development Research,* ed. Ross Parke (Chicago: University of Chicago Press, 1985), vol.7, pp. 179–122; Hazel Leler, "Parent Education and Involvement in Relation to the Schools and to Parents of School-aged Children," in *Parent Education and Public Policy,* ed. Ronald Haskins and Diane Adams (Norwood, N.J.: Ablex, 1983), pp. 141–161; Kevin Marjoribanks, "Family Environments," in *Educational Environments and Effects,* ed. Herbert Walberg (Berkeley: McCutchan, 1979), pp. 15–37; Patricia Olmsted and Roberta Rubin, "Parent Involvement: Perspectives from the Follow-through Experience," in *Parent Education and Public Policy,* ed. Haskins and Adams, pp. 112–140; Diane Scott-Jones, "Family Influences on Cognitive Development and School Achievement," in *Review of Research in Education,* ed. Edmund Gordon (Itasca, Ill.: Peacock, 1984), vol. 11, pp. 259–304; Rachel Seginer, "Parents' Educational Expectations and Children's Academic Achievements: A Literature Review," *Merrill-Palmer Quarterly,* 29 (1983), 1–23.

2. Mario Fantini, "The Parent as Educator: A Home-School Model of Socialization," in *Parenting in a Multicultural Society,* ed. Mario and Roberto Cardenas (New York: Longman, 1981), pp. 207–222; and Mario Fantini, *What's Best for the Children? Resolving the Power Struggle Between Parents and Teachers* (Garden City, N.Y.: Anchor Press, 1974).

3. See Henry Bullock, *A History of Negro Education in the South* (Cambridge: Harvard University Press, 1967); and Vincent Franklin, *Black Self-Determination* (Westport, Conn.: Lawrence Hall & Co., 1984).

4. Paul Woodring, "The Development of Teacher Education," in *Teacher Education; The Seventy-Fourth Yearbook of the National Society for the Study of Education,* ed. Kevin Ryan (Chicago: University of Chicago Press, 1975), pp. 1–23.

5. Kenneth Clark, *Dark Ghetto* (New York: Harper, 1965).

6. Illustrated in the writings of Allison Davis, *Social Class Influences Upon Learning* (Cambridge: Harvard University Press, 1948); Benjamin Bloom, *Stability and Change in Human Characteristics* (New York: Wiley, 1965); and Robert Hess, "Educability and Rehabilitation: The Future of the Welfare Class," *Journal of Marriage and Family,* 26 (1964), 422–429.

7. See, for example, Edward Zigler and Jeanette Valentine, eds., *Project Head Start: A Legacy of the War on Poverty* (New York: Free Press, 1979); and Diane Slaughter, "What is the Future of Head Start?" *Young Children,* 37 (1982), 3–9.

8. Frank Riessman, *The Culturally Deprived Child* (New York: Harper, 1962).

9. James Coleman et al., *Equality of Educational Opportunity* (Washington, D.C.: U.S. Government Printing Office, 1966).

10. Benjamin Bloom, "Early Learning in the Home," in *All Our Children Learning,* ed. Benjamin Bloom (New York: McGraw-Hill, 1980), pp. 67–88.

11. Allison Clarke-Stewart, "Interactions Between Mothers and Their Young Children: Characteristics and Consequences," *Monographs of the Society for Research in Child Development,* 38 (1973), 6–7, Serial No. 153; Janet Blumenthal, "Mother-Child Interaction and Child Cognitive Development in Low-income Black Children" (Paper presented at the biennial meeting of the Society for Research in Child Development, Toronto, Canada, April, 1985); Richard Elardo, Robert Bradley, and Bettye Caldwell, "The Relation of Infants' Home Environments to Mental Test Performance from Six to Thirty-six Months: A Longitudinal Analysis," *Child Development,* 46 (1975), 71–76; and Robert Bradley and Bettye Caldwell, "Home Environment, Social Status, and Mental Test Performance," *Journal of Educational Psychology,* 69 (1977), 697–701.

12. Frances Schachter, *Everyday Mother Talk to Toddlers* (New York: Academic Press, 1979).

13. Joseph Stevens, "Parenting Skill: Does Social Support Matter?" (Paper presented at the biennial meeting of the Society for Research in Child Development, Toronto, Canada, April, 1985).

14. Diana Slaughter, "Maternal Antecedents of the Academic Achievement Behaviors of Afro-American Head Start Children," *Educational Horizons,* (1969), 24–28.

15. Martha Ward, *Them Children: A Study in Language Learning* (New York: Holt, Rinehart & Winston, 1971); and Basil Bernstein, "A Sociolinguistic Approach to Socialization: With Some Reference to Educability," in *Language and Poverty,* ed. Fred Williams (Chicago: Markham, 1970), pp. 25–61.

16. William Teale, in a lecture delivered at the School of Education and Social Policy, Northwestern University, April 29, 1982.

17. Shirley Brice-Heath, "Questioning at Home and at School: A Comparative Study," in *Doing Ethnography: Educational Anthropology in Action,* ed. George Spindler (New York: Holt, Rinehart & Winston, 1982), pp. 96–101.

18. William Hall and William Tirre, *The Communicative Environment of Young Children: Social Class, Ethnic, and Situational Differences* (Champaign: University of Illinois at Urbana-Champaign, Center for the Study of Reading, Tech. Rep. No. 125, May, 1979).

19. Helen Gouldner, *Teachers' Pets, Troublemakers, and Nobodies* (Westport, Conn.: Greenwood Press, 1978); and Grace Massey, Personal Communication, July 1986. Dr. Massey currently has a Rockefeller Foundation Fellowship grant to conduct this study.

20. Robert Hess, "Social Class and Ethnic Influences on Socialization," in *Carmichael's Manual of Child Psychology,* ed. Paul Mussen (New York: Wiley, 1970), vol. 2, pp. 457–558.

21. Karl White, "The Relations Between Socioeconomic Status and Academic Achievement," *Psychological Bulletin,* 91 (1982), 461–481.

22. See, for example, Steven Baratz and Joan Baratz, "Early Childhood Intervention: The Social Science Base of Institutional Racism," *Harvard Educational Review,* 40 (1970), 29–50; Steven Tulkin, "An Analysis of the Concept of Cultural Deprivation," *Developmental Psychology,* 6 (1972), 326–339; John Ogbu, "Origins of Human Competence: A Cultural-Ecological Perspective," *Child Development,* 52 (1981), 413–429.

23. See, for example: Andrew Billingsley, *Black Families in White America* (Englewood Cliffs, N.J.: Prentice-Hall, 1968); Robert Hill, *The Strengths of Black Families* (New York: Emerson-Hall, 1972); Edward Barnes, "The Black Community as the Source of Positive Self-concept for Black Children: A Theoretical Perspective," in *Black Psychology,* ed. Reginald Jones (New York: Harper, 1972). pp. 166–192.

24. Diane Slaughter and Barbara Schneider, *Newcomers: Blacks in Private Schools* (Washington, D.C.: National Institute of Education, Final Report on Contract No. NIE-G-82-0040, Project No. 2-0450, April 1986). See idem, "Parental Goals and Black Student Achievement in Urban Private Elementary Schools," *Journal of Intergroup Relations,* 13 (1985), 24–33, for a synopsis of the findings of this project.

25. See John Ogbu, *Minority Education and Caste* (New York: Academic Press, 1978); idem, *The Next Generation: An Ethnography of Education in an Urban Neighborhood* (New York: Academic Press, 1974).

26. Bertha Holliday, "Towards a Model of Teacher-Child Transactional Process Affecting Black Children's Academic Achievement," in *Beginnings: The Social and Affective Development of Black Children,* ed. Margaret Spencer, Geraldine Brookins, and Walter Allen (Hillsdale, N.J.: Lawrence Erlbaum, 1985), pp. 117–130.

27. Bruce Hare and Louis Castenell, "No Place to Run, No Place to Hide: Comparative Status and Future Prospects of Black Boys," in *Beginnings,* ed. Spencer, Brookins, and Allen, pp. 201–214.

28. Diana Slaughter, "Relation of Early Parent-Teacher Socialization Influences to Achievement Orientation and Self-esteem in Middle Childhood Among Low-income Black Children," in *The Social Context of Learning and Development,* ed. John Glidewell (New York: Gardner, 1977), pp. 101–131.

29. Henry Rubin, "Longitudinal Investigation of Factors Influencing the Development of Educational Aspirations among Low-income Black Students" (Ph.D. diss., Northwestern University, 1980).

30. Elsie Moore, "Language Behavior in the Testing Situation and the Intelligence Test Achievement of Transracially- and Traditionally-Adopted Black Children," in *The Language of Children Reared in Poverty,* ed. Lynne Feagans and Dale Farran (New York: Academic Press, 1982), pp. 141–162.

31. Zena Blau, *Black Children/White Children: Competence, Socialization and Social Structure* (New York: Free Press, 1981).

32. See James Comer, *School Power* (New York: Free Press, 1980); and Slaughter and Schneider, *Newcomers.*

33. Geoffrey Maruyama, Rosalyn Rubin and G. Gage Kingsbury, "Self-esteem and Educational Achievement: Independent Constructs with Common Cause," *Journal of Personality and Social Psychology,* 40 (1981), 962–975.

34. Benjamin Bloom, *Human Characteristics and School Learning* (New York: McGraw-Hill, 1976).

35. White, "The Relations Between Socioeconomic Status and Academic Achievement."

36. See, for example, Larry DeBord, Larry Griffin, and Melissa Clark, "Race and Sex Influences in the Schooling Process of Rural and Small Town Youth," *Sociology of Education,* 50 (1977), 85–102; Edgar Epps, "Correlates of Academic Achievement among Northern and Southern Urban Negro Students," *Journal of Social Issues,* 25 (1969), 55–70; Frank Howell and Wolfgang Freese, "Race, Sex and Aspirations: Evidence for the 'Race Convergence' Hypothesis," *Sociology of Education,* 52 (1970), 34–46; Alan Kerckhoff and Richard Campbell, "Black-White Differences in Educational Attainment," ibid., 50 (1977), 15–27; James Porter, "Race, Socialization, and Mobility in Early Occupational Attainment," *American Sociological Review,* 39 (1974), 303–316: Alejandro Portes and Kenneth Wilson, "Black-White Differences in Educational Attainment," ibid., 41 (1976), 414–431; and Gail Thomas, "Influence of Aspirations, Achievement, and Educational Expectations on Black-White Postsecondary Enrollment," *Sociological Quarterly,* 20 (1979), 202–222.

37. Epps, "Correlates of Academic Achievement"; and Howell and Freese, "Race, Sex, and Aspirations."

38. Edgar Epps and Kenneth Jackson, *Educational and Occupational Aspirations and Early Attainment of Black Males and Females* (Atlanta, Ga.: Final Report to the Southern Education Foundation, April 1985).

39. Philip Bowman and Cleopatra Howard, "Race-related Socialization, Motivation, and Academic Achievement: A Study of Black Youth in Three Generation Families," *Journal of the American Academy of Child Psychiatry,* 24 (1985), 134–141.

40. Jerold Bachman, *Youth in Transition: The Impact of Family Background and Achievement on Tenth-Grade Boys* (Ann Arbor: Survey Research Center, Institute for Social Research, 1970).

41. See Epps, "Correlates of Academic Achievement"; and Debord, Griffin and Clark, "Race and Sex Influences."

42. See Howell and Freese, "Race, Sex, and Aspirations"; Kerckhoff and Campbell, "Black-White Differences"; Alan Kerckhoff, "Race and Social Status Differences in the Explanation of Educational Ambition," *Social Forces,* 55 (1977), 701–714; and Walter Allen, "Moms, Dads, and Boys: Race and Sex Differences in the Socialization of Male Children," in *Black Men,* ed. Lawrence Gary (Beverly Hills, Calif.: Sage, 1981), pp. 99–114.

43. Kerckhoff and Campbell, "Black-White Differences"; Portes and Wilson, "Black-White Differences in Educational Attainment"; and Gail Thomas, "Race and Sex Differences and Similarities in the Process of College Entry," *International Journal of Higher Education,* 9 (1980), 179–202.

44. Porter, "Race, Socialization, and Mobility."

45. Kenneth Wilson, "Effects of Integration and Class on Black Attainment," *Sociology of Education,* 52 (1979), 84–98.

46. Patricia Gurin and Edgar Epps, *Black Consciousness, Identity and Achievement* (New York: Wiley, 1975).

47. Reginald Clark, *Family Life and School Achievement: Why Poor Black Children Succeed or Fail* (Chicago: University of Chicago Press, 1983).

48. Ogbu, *Minority Education and Caste.*

49. See, for example, Harriette McAdoo, "Stress Absorbing Systems in Black Families," *Family Relations,* 31 (1982), 479–488; Marie Peters and Harriette McAdoo, "The Present and Future of Alternative Life Styles in Ethnic American Cultures," in *Contemporary Families and Alternative Life Styles,* ed. Eleanor Macklin and Roger Rubin (Beverly Hills, Calif.: Sage, 1983), pp. 288–307.

► 4

Bureaucracy and Urban School Reform

American education is organized in a bureaucratic form. At any level—national, state, or local—the traditional pyramidal, hierarchical arrangement is in effect. At the district level, a superintendent is at the apex of a clearly delineated "line and staff" organization; thus, to effect change in urban schools the bureaucratic structure must be addressed. Proposals for reform of urban schools must consider how the bureaucratic functionaries might respond. Since a bureaucracy is "an institutionalized method of organizing social conduct in the interest of administrative efficiency," the issue of response is a genuine concern (Blau, 1956, p. 60). For example, site-based management, it is proposed, will permit individual school faculties to engage in efficient decision making without consulting with the central administration. From a bureaucratic standpoint, will such actions be more efficient or will irregularities arise that will force the central administration to revoke the newfound autonomy? Over which dimensions of school life will faculties develop control and in which areas will control be maintained by the central administrations? It is our contention that reform is easier to talk about than to implement because not enough time is spent considering organizational constraints.

Levine (1971) explains how four basic problems impede reform in urban schools:

1. institutional complexity and overload
2. goal displacement

3. deficiencies in communications and decision-making processes
4. social and psychological distance between client and institution

He believes that urban schools can make the necessary changes in their current condition but will need to involve new bureaucratic perspectives in order to succeed. Levine argues that educational leaders might need to emphasize development over efficiency for real change to transpire; thus, good intentions alone will not suffice. He concludes his article with seven specific recommendations, many of which are designed to improve communications within the organization or with the community it serves. These recommendations continue to be useful guidelines irrespective of the time period.

The extent of the challenge described by Levine is further developed by Sjoberg, Brymer, and Farris (1966). The typical bureaucrat who works with the urban poor is generally middle class and has to work within the formalized role imposed by his or her organization. When special problems arise, the bureaucrat is hard-pressed to react to those situations with creative solutions. Role constrictions or the lack of understanding or empathy with lower-class problems often inhibit creative problem solving within a bureaucracy. Furthermore, the lower-class person often does not understand how the bureaucracy functions or has developed an overly deterministic view of how the bureaucracy functions to maintain hierarchical relationships of power. Failure to resolve a problem may result in feelings of frustration, alienation, and powerlessness.

The lower-class community regularly interacts with a variety of bureaucratic organizations: welfare, housing authority, social work, police, and education. These organizations function to maintain the status quo by presenting a view of the world in which social structures are taken for granted, and the only questions that are permitted deal with how to function within that hierarchical structure. For example, Connell, Ashenden, Kessler, and Dowsett (1982) demonstrate how parents from different social classes come to view schools, teachers, and the ability to facilitate change differently. They argue that middle-class parents view teachers as workers who can be hired and fired while working-class parents view teachers as experts. This worldview often structures limitations on the ability of poor and minority groups to struggle for equality of educational opportunity and develop creative solutions to their problems. The problems presented by the editors suggest that we haven't made much progress in reducing lower-class stress in dealing with bureaucracies since the article was written in 1966. Unless such problems are rectified, change will not occur, nor will chances for equality of educational opportunity.

REFERENCES

Blau, P. (1956). *Bureaucracy in Modern Society.* New York: Random House.

Connell, R.W., Ashenden, D.J., Kessler, S., and Dowsett, G.W. (1982). *Making the Difference*. Sydney, Australia: George Allen & Unwin.

Levine, D.U. (1971). "Concepts of bureaucracy in urban school reform." *Phi Delta Kappan*, 52:329–333.

Sjoberg, G., Brymer, R.A., and Farris, B. (1966). "Bureaucracy and the lower class." *Sociology and Social Research*, 50:325–337.

Concepts of Bureaucracy In Urban School Reform

DANIEL U. LEVINE

The public school is a social system established to deliver good education to the students who attend it. Without quibbling about the definition of "good" education, let us assume that one major component is a minimal level of academic skills needed to compete successfully for rewarding employment. By this measure, many urban schools are unequivocally failing.

At another level of generality, most people would agree that a major goal of the public school is to teach students skills and attitudes needed for learning outside the school and for living satisfying lives as adults. Without implying that the schools in and of themselves can be held solely responsible for solving all the critical problems of urban society, it would be ludicrous to argue that most urban schools are succeeding in preparing students to live wisely and well in the bright new world (or, if you prefer, the new dark ages) of metropolitan complexity; to wit: dropouts, copouts, throwouts, flunkouts, tuneouts, and freakouts littered all over the metropolitan landscape.

Thus, whatever else one may say about them, urban schools today generally are not functioning as outstandingly effective delivery systems in terms of some of their major purposes.

ROOTS OF THE PROBLEMS

To understand why urban schools frequently are not delivering adequate education, it is best to begin by recognizing that they are bureaucratic institutions in the classic meaning of the term as defined by Max Weber and other nineteenth century sociologists. That is, both within the school and within the larger educational system of which it is a part, roles are defined impersonally, numerous rules and expectations

Reprinted from *Phi Delta Kappan*, 52:329–333, 1971, by permission of the author and the publisher.

are codified to fit each role within a hierarchy of other roles, and fitness to fill a role is defined with reference to technical training and previous experience thought to be necessary to carry it out properly.

So far so good: The urban school is conceived in an effort to use rational planning and technical competence in the task of educating masses of citizens in an urban society. Where did it all go wrong?

Basically, the urban school as it is now organized and operated is a victim of the same forces and problems which are generating failure in other rational bureaucracies such as hospitals, social welfare agencies, industrial corporations, the military, and municipal service departments; it is not just in education that reformers are concerned with improving the structure and performance of urban delivery systems. Among the most important of these problems are *institutional complexity and overload, goal displacement, deficiencies in communications and decision-making processes,* and *social and psychological distance between client and institution.*

This listing is not offered as an exhaustive catalogue of all the logically exclusive dysfunctions which rational bureaucracy is heir to, but it does call attention to some of the critical issues which reformers must specifically take into account in endeavoring to rebuild and revitalize urban schools.

Institutional complexity and overload refers to the tendency for institutions to be ineffective when their internal structures are too complicated to allow for adequate communications, or when the external frameworks in which they function are rendered inoperable by having too large a burden placed on them. In other words, the growing complexity of industrial society tends to make existing organizational structures and networks obsolete. Part of the problem is that a message retranslated 10 times is likely to be considerably more garbled than one transmitted directly to its recipient. Or, as was illustrated in the recent telephone crisis in New York City, the volume of messages may simply overwhelm available communications channels, making it necessary to tear out much of the existing system and replace it with new subsystems more adequate for the load.

Similar difficulties arise because multiplying the layers of complexity which exist in an organization tends to increase the number of points at which vested interests can counter organizational goals. In part, a complex institution becomes more vulnerable to dysfunctions merely because there are more places where things can go wrong—just as one comma out of place in a complicated computer program was responsible for the failure of a multimillion-dollar space probe.

In addition, adding layer upon layer to the organizational structure of modern society leads the individual to perceive the structure and his experience in it as artificial and unreal. Whether exemplified in the curriculum of the school, which becomes further and further removed from daily life, or in the impersonal humming of the Corporate State's computers, the byproducts of complexity become too abstract to be believed. The result, as Ortega y Gasset prophetically foresaw in *Man and Crisis,* is an exploding rejection of institutions and the philosophic presupposi-

by both distant and supporting primary groups" and hence in need "of a range of coordinating mechanisms."[10] The inner-city elementary school with a particularly alienated constituency probably comes closest in education to fitting the first situation; the comprehensive urban high school is a good example of the second.

In the first situation, Litwak and Meyer conclude, emphasis should be placed on 1) working with local opinion leaders in the client community; 2) delegating functions as much as possible to associated groups with presumably better access to primary units among clients; 3) a "settlement-house" approach which locates physical facilities and services in the client community and makes change agents available to work there; and 4) a "detached-expert" approach which gives professionals in the organization "relative autonomy" to participate directly in the affairs of external primary groups.[11]

In the second situation, emphasis should be placed on selecting a situationally appropriate mixture of the coordinating mechanisms described above plus traditional rational-bureaucratic coordinating mechanisms such as 1) sponsorship of voluntary associations bringing organization personnel and clients together in a formal setting (e.g., PTA's); 2) utilization as a "common messenger" of an individual who is regularly a member of both the organization and the primary group (e.g., the child); 3) utilization of formal authority as a "basis for communicating with external primary groups"; and 4) employment of mass communications media as a means to influence primary groups.[12]

The final point in Litwak and Meyer's paper is one it would pay us well to particularly keep in mind in education. After noting that some organizations have a better base than others for linking to the community, the authors point out that *"if an organization is not self-conscious about its coordinating mechanisms"* (italics added), then it will tend to communicate with primary groups using the common messenger and the opinion leader mechanisms, because these mechanisms develop informally and require little or no initiative from the organization.[13] This is precisely, of course, what has happened in education: Most public schools have relied on the child and on a few visible, presumably influential persons in the community for communications with constituent primary groups. That abdicating responsibility in this way has led to the bankruptcy of many urban schools is hardly open to question.

COMMENTS AND CONCLUSIONS

The material in the first section of this paper suggests that efforts to reform urban schools should: 1) aim to rebuild them as less complex institutions and/or equip clients and staff with better ways to handle institutional complexity; 2) reduce social and psychological distance between clients and the institution, particularly by increasing student and parent participation in decision making; and 3) provide specifically for additional information feedback in every aspect of the operation of the school.

The material on concepts of bureaucracy suggests that 1) urban schools should place major emphasis on gaining the cooperation of their clients rather than first using traditional efficiency criteria to allocate institutional roles and assess institutional processes; 2) this type of client-centered, service orientation is most likely to be achieved and maintained when authority is allocated laterally rather than hierarchically and organizational structures are experimental and fluid rather than fixed and permanent; and 3) urban educators should self-consciously select a situation-specific mixture of outreach-type as well as traditional communications mechanisms to coordinate the work of the school and the external primary groups whose cooperation is required to achieve the goals of education.

Some related points which should be made concerning the rebuilding of urban schools in general and inner-city schools in particular are that:

1. Making authority relations in a school or school district less "vertical" in order to place certain necessary decision-making powers and responsibilities in the hands of staff members who work directly with clients has little to do explicitly with "democratic" administration (whatever that is). As Fiedler has shown in an important but frequently ignored study on leadership, situations which are highly problematic for an organization create a need for administrators who supply relatively "structured" leadership.[14] To put it mildly, urban schools today are highly problematic institutions.

2. For this reason, outstanding administrative leadership is by far the most important variable necessary for successful reform in urban schools. Successful inner-city schools invariably have particularly outstanding building administrators who absolutely refuse to engage in bureaucratic games of any sort.[15]

3. The critical importance of the building principal is closely linked to the cherished dream of individualization of instruction. On the one hand it is an obvious truth that instruction for disadvantaged students cannot possibly be successful without individualized diagnosis and prescription of students' strengths and weaknesses. On the other hand it is also a truism that individualized instruction has seldom been achieved in schools anywhere in the United States. One thing that outstanding inner-city administrators have in common is that they organize their schools so that methods and materials actually are utilized to individualize instruction and then insist that nothing—but *nothing*—will be allowed to prevent achievement of this goal. Visitors to their schools can expect to hear of such incidents as the following two reports from unusually successful schools:

"My teachers were supposed to be attending a district-wide workshop that summer, but we found they could not achieve anything in these large groups so I pulled them out and brought them back to the school to work in small groups on planning for the next year."

"Our excellent new programmed reading materials were not working very well, mainly because teachers and aides had no space to work together on planning or to meet with students individually or in small groups.

*So the principal increased class size—the central office never found out—
in order to free space for this purpose."*

4. Much of the principal's leadership in establishing lateral authority relations
can be discussed in terms of what he does to provide each party (i.e., teachers,
students, parents) with a firm power base in school decision making. Once each
group is in a position to stand up and say, "I know from direct experience that the
way we are doing things is not working and I insist it be changed," the orientation
in the school becomes one of solving problems rather than keeping the lid on or
sweeping them under the rug. In a successful inner-city school, in other words, "End
the nonsense" is the operating theme not just of the principal but of every interest
group.

5. Urban schools should be built up of (or broken down into) small, relatively
autonomous operating units. It is not important whether functional units are referred
to as "houses," "grade levels," "families," "minibranches," or some other term, as
long as authority and responsibility are located primarily at the unit level and units
are supplied with the resources and supporting services necessary to carry out their
tasks.

6. The crucial factor in making use of promising practices from another school
is to make sure that the organizational structure of the receiving institution is
designed to implement the innovation effectively. For example, the receiving structure must be modified to ensure continuous feedback across hierarchical levels, to
minimize psychological distance between staff and clients, and to maintain a client-
centered service orientation, or promising practices borrowed either eclectically or
as a total package from outside sources are not going to make very much difference.

7. Urban schools are not going to be rebuilt as effective institutions unless we
first sweep the deck of existing organizational structures and practices which constitute fundamental obstacles to the attainment of educational goals. As Morris
Janowitz points out, specialists and technologists have a vital and indispensable part
to play in reforming urban education, but piling more specialists and new technologies on top of an already overloaded institutional structure will compound rather
than alleviate our problems. What all this boils down to is the old rule of first things
first—and the first priority in urban education is to introduce new concepts of
organization and bureaucracy that emphasize the creation of authentic institutional
communities, so that specialization and technique are not plugged into essentially
dysfunctional vessels.

Emphasis in most of the following papers is placed on the difficult practical
problems encountered in building or rebuilding an institution and on the crucial
decisions made in solving them. In describing specific problems involved in implementing effective programs in urban schools, the authors show how the concepts
reviewed in this paper are being applied in different ways in different schools. It is
hoped that this combination of conceptual analysis and practical examples will
prove useful for teachers and administrators impatient to rebuild their own schools.

ENDNOTES

1. Donald J. Willower, "Educational Change and Functional Equivalents," *Education and Urban Society,* August, 1970, p. 392; see also Alan Schick, "The Cybernetic State," *Trans-Action,* February, 1970, pp. 15–26.

2. Examples of other perspectives which it was not possible to include in this paper include Warren Bennis' writing on postbureaucratic, temporary organization and Kenneth Parsons' analysis of needs-cycling organizations.

3. Berton H. Kaplan, "Notes on a Non-Weberian Model of Bureaucracy: The Case of Development Bureaucracy," *Administrative Science Quarterly,* December, 1968, pp. 471–83.

4. *Ibid.,* p. 472.

5. *Ibid.,* p. 482.

6. Orion F. White, Jr., "The Dialectical Organization: An Alternative to Bureaucracy," *Public Administration Review,* January–February, 1969, p. 38.

7. *Ibid.,* pp. 36–37.

8. Eugene Litwak and Henry J. Meyer, "A Balance Theory of Coordination Between Bureaucratic Organizations and Community Primary Groups," *Administrative Science Quarterly,* June, 1966, pp. 31–58.

9. *Ibid.,* pp. 36, 58. In effect, Litwak and Meyer reject the arguments of social analysts such as Everett Riemer and Ivan Illich who suggest that noncognitive goals should have little place in the schools since they are more effectively achieved in primary-group settings (*Alternatives in Education, 1968–69.* Cuernavaca, Mexico: Central Intercultural Documentacion, 1970) and of psychologists like J. M. Stephens (*The Process of Schooling.* New York: Holt, Rinehart and Winston, 1967) who believe that schooling in modern educational bureaucracies is too far removed from real life to be effective in interesting more than a minority of the young in abstract academic studies. Although there is no space in this essay to weigh all the arguments for and against these points of view, it at least can be said that unless existing educational bureaucracies are significantly transformed and unless this rebuilding includes new mechanisms for coordination and communication with primary groups in the urban community, observers such as Riemer, Illich, and Stephens probably will be proved right by default.

10. *Ibid.,* pp. 51–52.

11. *Ibid.,* pp. 39, 42, 52, 53.

12. *Ibid.,* pp. 40, 41, 50, 53.

13. *Ibid.,* p. 57.

14. Fred A. Fiedler, "A Contingency Model of Leadership Effectiveness," in L. Berkowitz, ed., *Advances in Experimental Social Psychology.* New York: Academic Press, 1964, vol. 1.

15. Russell C. Doll, *Variations Among Inner City Elementary Schools.* Kansas City, Mo.: Center for the Study of Metropolitan Problems in Education, 1969.

Bureaucracy and the Lower Class

GIDEON SJOBERG
RICHARD A. BRYMER
BUFORD FARRIS

Bureaucratic structures, so our argument runs, not only encounter major difficulties in coping with the problems of the lower class but also serve to maintain and reinforce patterns that are associated with the "culture of poverty." Here we shall focus upon the relationships between client-centered bureaucracies[1] and the lower class in American society.

Sociologists have devoted little attention, on either the community or national level, to the impact of bureaucracy upon the stratification system. Yet our experience, based on research among lower-class Mexican-Americans in San Antonio,[2] points to the critical role of bureaucratic organizations in sustaining social stratification. Sociologists frequently compare lower- and middle-class culture patterns, but they fail to recognize that bureaucratic systems are the key medium through which the middle class maintains its advantaged position vis-à-vis the lower class.

Our analysis of the effect of the client-centered bureaucracy upon the lower class is cast in rather theoretical terms. However, illustrative materials from our research project and the writings of other scholars indicate the kinds of data that support our generalizations. After delineating the main elements of the bureaucratic model, we discuss the lower class from the perspective of the bureaucratic system and then bureaucracy from the viewpoint of the lower class. These materials set the stage for a consideration of various emergent organizational and political patterns in American society.

THE NATURE OF BUREAUCRACY

In the post-World War II era various sociologists[3] have questioned the utility of Weber's analysis of bureaucracy. Nevertheless, sociologists continue to assume that bureaucracy (as conceived by Weber) is positively associated with the continued

Reprinted from *Sociology and Social Research,* 50:325–327, 1966, by permission of the publisher.

development of an advanced industrial-urban order and that this bureaucracy is more or less inevitable.

Modern bureaucracies lay heavy stress upon rationality and efficiency. In order to attain these ends, men are called upon to work within a hierarchical system, with well-defined lines of authority, and within a differentiated social setting, with an elaborate division of labor that stresses the specialization of function. This hierarchy and division of labor are, in turn, sustained through a complex set of formalized rules which are to be administered in a highly impersonal and standardized manner. There is considerable centralization of authority, and as one moves from top to bottom there is greater specialization of function and adherence to the rules.

What is not as clearly recognized is that efficiency and rationality are predicated upon an explicit statement of the organization's goals. Only when an end is clearly stated can one determine the most efficient means for its attainment. Thus, because the corporate structure has had an explicit goal (*i.e.* profit), it has been quite successful in measuring the efficiency of its programs (*i.e.* means).

The corporate system has been the model that other bureaucracies have emulated. As a result, there has been considerable concern with efficiency within, say, the Federal Government. McNamara's reorganization of the U.S. Defense Department in the 1960's is a case in point. It is significant that McNamara has drawn heavily upon the work of Hitch and McKean[4] in developing his program, for Hitch and McKean argue that organizational goals must be spelled out in rather concrete terms in order to measure the effectiveness of various programs. An understanding of the interrelationships among measurement, objectification of goals, and efficiency and rationality is essential if we are to assess the impact of bureaucratic structures upon the lower class.

ORIENTATIONS OF BUREAUCRACIES TOWARDS THE LOWER CLASS

Bureaucratic organizations frequently reinforce the class structure of the community and the nation through their staffing procedures. When a bureaucracy serves both upper- and lower-class groups, as does the school, the poorly qualified teachers tend to drift into lower-class neighborhoods, or, as frequently occurs, beginning teachers are placed in "hardship" districts, and then the most capable move up and out into upper-status school districts where higher salaries and superior working conditions usually prevail. Thus, the advancement of lower-class children is impeded not only because of their cultural background but because of the poor quality of their teachers.

In welfare bureaucracies, social workers have struggled to escape from their traditional identification with the poor, either by redefining their functions in order to serve middle-class clients or by moving away from clients into administrative posts. Once again, evidence suggests that the lower class comes to be served by the least qualified personnel.

In addition to staffing arrangements, the bureaucracy's method of selecting clients reinforces the class system. At this point we must remember that bureaucracies are under constant pressure to define their goals so that the efficiency of their programs can be measured. But unlike corporate systems, client-centered bureaucracies experience grave difficulties in specifying their goals and evaluating their efficiency. The client-centered bureaucracies meet the demands placed upon them through the use of simplified operational definitions. Universities, for instance, do not judge their effectiveness in terms of producing "educated men" but according to the ratings of their students on national tests, the number of students who gain special awards, etc. These operational criteria reflect the orientation or view of persons in positions of authority within the bureaucracy and the broader society. In turn, these criteria become the basis for the selection of clients. Through this procedure, a bureaucratic organization can ensure its success, and it can more readily demonstrate to the power structure that the community or society is "getting something for its money." The bureaucracy's success is likely to lead to an increase in funds and expanded activities. It follows that client-centered bureaucracies often find it advantageous to avoid lower-class clients who are likely to handicap the organization in the attainment of its goals.[5]

Several illustrations should clarify our argument. The Federal Job Corps program has been viewed as one means for alleviating the unemployment problem among youth, especially those in the lower class. This program has sought to train disadvantaged youths in various occupational skills. The success of the Job Corps is apparently to be evaluated according to the number of trainees who enter the industrial labor force. Consequently, the organization has sought to select those youths who have internalized some of the middle-class norms of upward mobility and who are likely to succeed in the occupational system. The Job Corps by-passes many persons who in theory stand in greatest need of assistance; for example, potential "troublemakers"—young men with criminal records—are not accepted as trainees. Because of this selection process the Job Corps leadership will likely be able to claim success and to convince Congressmen that the program should be continued and perhaps broadened.

A more subtle form of client selection can be found in child guidance clinics. Here clients are often accepted in terms of their "receptivity" to therapy.[6] However, this criterion favors those persons who have been socialized into the middle-class value orientation held by, for example, the clinic staff and the social groups who pay the bill. The poor, especially the families from ethnic groups within the lower class, who according to the ideal norms of these agencies should receive the greatest amount of attention, are quietly shunted aside. Moreover, one study has indicated a positive association between the social status of the client and the social status of the professional worker handling the case in the agency.[7]

The procedures by which school systems cope with their clients are perhaps central to understanding the community and national class system, for the educational variable is becoming increasingly significant in sustaining or advancing one's status. At this point we are concerned with the differential treatment of clients by the organization once they have been accepted.

School systems frequently employ IQ tests and similar instruments in their evaluation of pupils. These tests, however, have been constructed in such a manner that they articulate with the values, beliefs, and knowledge of the middle class and the demands of the power elements of the society. That these tests are used to make early judgments on the ability of pupils serves to support the existing class system. Lower-class pupils often come to be defined as "dull," and, through a kind of self-fulfilling prophecy, this definition of the situation structures the students' future career. In fact, school counselors frequently interpret test scores according to their middle-class expectations; they, therefore, tend to discourage lower-class pupils from attending college even when their scores are relatively high.[8]

It is significant that the New York City school system has been forced to abandon the use of IQ tests.[9] It appears that the traditionally disadvantaged groups such as Negroes and Puerto Ricans have attained sufficient political power to challenge those methods that the school bureaucracy has used for determining success, methods that have been oriented to middle-class rather than lower-class norms.

Bureaucratized school systems place the lower-class clients at a disadvantage in still other ways. Various types of standardization or categorization, which are a product of middle-class expectations and which are viewed as essential for maintaining efficiency, limit the school's ability to adjust to the "needs" of lower-class pupils. We know of a special class, for example, that was established for the purpose of teaching lower-class and problem children, but in which the rules demanded that the teacher follow the same teaching plan employed in other classes in the school.

Actually, bureaucratic structures socialize the incumbents of roles in such a manner that they are frequently incapable of understanding the world-view of the lower-class client. Discussions of the bureaucratic personality, such as those by Merton and Presthus,[10] have given but scant attention to the difficulty of the bureaucrat's taking the role of the lower-class other. For as a result of his role commitment, the bureaucrat tends to impose his own expectations and interpretations of reality upon the client. He often comes to view the norms of the system as invariant. And bureaucrats in the lower echelons, those who have the greatest amount of contact with lower-class clients, are also the most bound by the rules. Faced with recalcitrant clients or clients having divergent value orientations, the typical office holder will say in effect, "If only clients would act properly, everything would be all right, and we could get on with our work."

The bureaucrat, oriented as he is to the middle- or upper-class life styles, usually lacks knowledge about the lower-class client's subculture. Moreover, he finds it difficult to step outside his formalized role. If he seeks to take the role of the client—in the sense of understanding the latter's belief and value system—he will ultimately have to challenge or at least question some of the rules that govern the operation of the system of which he is a part. For if he understands why clients act the way they do, he is likely to recognize that they have valid reasons for objecting to his conception of reality or, more specifically, to some of the bureaucratic regulations. Consequently, bureaucratic organizations tend to penalize those of their members who "overidentify" with clients.

Social workers who overidentify with their clients or teachers who overidentify with their students are considered to be indulging in nonprofessional action. Such action, so the reasoning runs, makes it impossible for the professional to adhere to the ideal norms of universalism and objectivity and thus to assist his clients effectively. Professional norms such as these reinforce those bureaucratic norms that impose barriers upon the lower-class person's advancement in the social order.

The controls exerted by the bureaucrats over members of the lower class are intensified because the office holders are constantly called upon to normalize and stabilize the system with an eye to maintaining the proper public image. One means of stabilizing and rationalizing the system's performance is to work within the context of established rules or categories. But to cope really effectively with such deviants as juvenile delinquents, the schools would have to alter radically their time-honored categories. Our experience suggests, however, that school systems stifle the grievances of deviant or lower-class groups, for these grievances, at least implicitly, challenge the bureaucratic norms that are supported by the groups that determine public policy.

The general insensitivity of bureaucracies to lower-class persons and their problems is highlighted in the "custodial function" adopted by many mental hospitals and even slum schools.[11] Because the bureaucracy's normative system runs counter to (or at best ignores) the norms and values of the lower class, a minimum of attention is given to socializing clients into the bureaucratic—or broader societal—norms. Bureaucratic systems adjust to this situation through the caretaker function.

ORIENTATIONS OF THE LOWER CLASS TOWARDS BUREAUCRACIES

Just as significant as the bureaucracy's orientation towards the lower class is the latter's orientation toward the bureaucracy. Our investigations, particularly in-depth interviews of Mexican-American families in San Antonio, support the conclusion of other social scientists—that members of the lower class encounter serious difficulties when they attempt to understand or to cope with the normative order of bureaucratic systems.

First and foremost, the lower-class person simply lacks knowledge of the rules of the game. Middle-class persons generally learn how to manipulate bureaucratic rules to their advantage and even to acquire special "favors" by working through the "private" or "backstage" (as opposed to the "public") sector of the bureaucratic organization. Middle-class parents teach by example as they intervene with various officials—e.g. the police or school teachers—to protect the family's social position in the community. In contrast, the lower-class person stands in awe of bureaucratic regulations and frequently is unaware that he has a legal and moral claim to certain rights and privileges. More often, however, it is the lack of knowledge of the system's technicalities and backstage regions that is responsible for the lower-class person's inability to manipulate a bureaucratic system to his advantage.

We mentioned earlier that in its lower echelons the bureaucracy is highly specialized and governed by numerous regulations. Therefore, the lower-class person, whose knowledge of the system is least adequate, must interact with the very officials who are most constrained by the formal rules. This situation is complicated by the fact that the problems the lower-class person faces are difficult to treat in isolation. The lack of steady employment, of education, and of medical care, for example, interlock in complex ways. Yet, the lower-class client encounters officials who examine only one facet of his difficulties and who, in the ideal, treat all cases in a similar fashion. After one agency (or official) has dealt with the special problem assigned it, the client is then referred to another agency which will consider another facet of the situation. It follows that no official is able to view the lower-class client as a whole person, and thus he is unable to point up to the client how he might use his strengths to overcome his weaknesses.

Middle-class persons, on the other hand, are in a position to deal with higher-status office holders, who are less encumbered by the rules and thus can examine their clients' problems in holistic terms. Delinquents from middle-class homes, for instance, are more apt than those from lower-class surroundings to be judged by officials according to their overall performance—both past and present.

The cleavage between modern bureaucracies and the lower class is intensified by various cultural differences. Gans,[12] for example, has found that lower-class persons typically relate to one another in a personal manner. Middle-class persons are better able to relate to others within an impersonal context. Thus, members of the lower class face a greater gulf when they attempt to communicate with middle-class bureaucrats who ideally must administer rules according to impersonal, universalistic norms.

This divergence between the lower class and bureaucratic officialdom in patterns of social interaction simply makes it more difficult for a lower-class person to acquire knowledge of how the system operates. It is not surprising that under these circumstances members of the lower class often experience a sense of powerlessness or alienation. This alienation in turn reinforces and is reinforced by the sense of fatalism that is an integral part of "the culture of poverty."[13] That is, those who live in the world of the lower class account for events in the social sphere in terms of spiritual forces, chance, luck, and the like; they have little or no sense of control over their own destiny.

Overall, the trends in the development of nonbureaucratic organizations suggest a close association between the system's internal structure and its relationships with clients. These trends also support our contention that bureaucratic systems have not been successful in working with lower-class clients.

POLITICAL IMPLICATIONS

The tensions generated by the bureaucratic solution to current social problems are highlighted by the efforts to resolve the difficulties encountered by the Negro lower class. The debate generated by the "Moynihan Report" is of special theoretical interest.[27] (This Report, issued by the U.S. Department of Labor, was written by Daniel P. Moynihan, although he is not formally listed as author.) Moynihan argues that the family structure of the lower-class Negro—which is mother-dominated and highly unstable by societal standards—must be revised if Negroes are to adapt to the industrial-urban order or the bureaucratic school systems, economic organizations, etc.

Elements of the Negro leadership have sharply attacked the Moynihan Report. They believe that instead of restructuring the lower-class Negro family we must remake modern bureaucratic systems so that these will be more responsive to the "needs" of the Negro lower class.

Moynihan's position is in keeping with that of many sociologists who accept present-day structural arrangements as more or less inevitable. Sociologists often argue that social problems arise because lower-class individuals or families are committed to sociocultural patterns that make it difficult for them to accommodate to the demands of industrial-urban organizations. Although some scholars have analyzed the dysfunctions of bureaucratic systems,[28] they rarely, if ever, assume that basic structural reorganization is necessary or possible. But the Weberian model may not be a rational or efficient organization for coping with many of the problems that have emerged (and will emerge) in an advanced industrial order where the problems of production have been resolved and the issues dealt with by client-centered organizations loom increasingly larger.

Sociologists must re-examine their basic premises if they are to grasp the nature of current social trends. For one thing, politics in a post-welfare, advanced industrial-urban order may become oriented around pro-bureaucratic and anti-bureaucratic ideologies. The rumblings of minorities (including some intellectuals in England, the United States, and Sweden) suggest that this type of political struggle may be in the offing. It is of interest, for example, that in the United States elements of the New Left—e.g. Students for a Democratic Society—share a common "devil"—the bureaucratic system—with elements of the right wing. We would hypothesize that some relationship exists between these ideological concerns and the problems of client-centered bureaucracies. Certainly, these developments are worthy of serious sociological investigation—and before, not after, the fact.

CONCLUSIONS

Evidence indicates that modern bureaucracies, especially client-centered ones, stand between lower-class and upper-status (particularly middle-class) persons. These groups do not encounter one another within a vacuum but rather within an organizational, bureaucratic context. Even when they meet in relatively informal situations, the bureaucratic orientation of the middle-class person structures his response to the lower-class individual. It is through their positions in the key bureaucracies that the higher-status groups maintain their social advantages and even at times foster bureaucratic procedures that impede the advancement of lower-class persons into positions of privilege. While our illustrative data are limited to the United States, many of our generalizations seem to hold for other industrial-urban orders as well.

The social and political implications of the dilemmas that face bureaucratic systems require far more attention than they have received. Weber's conception of bureaucracy may have deflected sociologists from some significant concerns. There are, after all, other intellectual traditions to draw upon. For example, Spencer's[29] analysis of how "military organizations" emphasize the contributions of individuals to the system and of how "industrial organizations" emphasize the contributions of the system to individuals is of considerable relevance for an understanding of the link between formal organizations and their clients and, ultimately, formal organizations and social stratification. But whatever one's source of inspiration, the study of the impact of different kinds of formal organizations upon social stratification is central to the sociologist's major concern—that of understanding the nature of order.

ENDNOTES

1. The term "client-centered bureaucracy" is derived from the classification scheme of Peter Blau and W. Richard Scott, *Formal Organizations* (San Francisco: Chandler Publishing Co., 1962). They employ the term "service organizations" for this type of structure.

2. Our main project, which focuses upon the evaluation of an action program for the prevention of juvenile delinquency, is supported by the National Institute of Mental Health: Grant No. R11-MH-1075-02 and 02SI. This project has, as a result of a grant from the Hogg Foundation, University of Texas, been broadened to include a study in depth of lower-class Mexican-American families.

3. Peter Blau, *The Dynamics of Bureaucracy* (rev. ed. Chicago: University of Chicago Press, 1963), and Alvin Gouldner, *Patterns of Industrial Bureaucracy* (New York: The Free Press, a Division of the Macmillan Co., 1965).

4. Charles J. Hitch and Roland N. McKean, *The Economics of Defense in the Nuclear Age* (Cambridge: Harvard University Press, 1960).

5. See e.g. Martin Rein, "The Strange Case of Public Dependency," *Transaction,* 2 (March-April, 1965), 16–23.

6. Based on the personal observations of Buford Farris who, as a social worker, has had extensive contact with these agencies.

7. Raymond G. Hunt, Orville Gurrslin, and Jack L. Roach, "Social Status and Psychiatric Service in a Child Guidance Clinic," *American Sociological Review,* 23 (February, 1959), 81–83.

8. Aaron Cirourel and John I. Kitsuse, *The Educational Decision-Makers* (Indianapolis: Bobbs-Merrill Co., 1963). For a general discussion of the bureaucratization of the school system see Dean Harper, "The Growth of Bureaucracy in School Systems," *American Journal of Economics and Sociology,* 23 (July, 1965), 261–71.

9. Fred M. Hechinger, "I.Q. Test Ban," *New York Times,* March 8, 1964, Section E, p. 7; Fred M. Hechinger, "Testing at Issue," *New York Times,* November 1, 1964, Section E, p. 9.

10. Robert K. Merton, *Social Theory and Social Structure* (rev. ed. New York: The Free Press, a Division of the Macmillan Co., 1957), 195–206 and Robert Presthus, *The Organizational Society* (New York: Vintage Books, 1965).

11. See e.g. Ivan C. Belknap, *Human Problems of a State Mental Hospital* (New York: McGraw-Hill Book Co., 1956); Fred M. Hechinger, "Poor Marks for Slum Schools," *New York Times,* December 12, 1965, Section E, p. 9; Kenneth Clark, *Dark Ghetto* (New York: Harper and Row, 1965), chap. 6.

12. Herbert Gans, *The Urban Villagers* (New York: The Free Press, a Division of the Macmillan Co., 1965).

13. See e.g. various essays in Frank Riessman, Jerome Cohen, and Arthur Pearl (eds.), *Mental Health of the Poor* (New York: The Free Press, a Division of the Macmillan Co., 1964).

14. U.S. Bureau of the Census, *Current Population Reprint Series P-60. No. 47, Income in 1964 of Families and Persons in the United States* (Washington, D.C.: U.S. Government Printing Office, 1965).

15. Gunnar Myrdal, *Economic Theory and Under-Developed Regions* (London: Gerald Duckworth and Co., 1957), 16–20.

16. Charles N. Cooper, "The Chicago YMCA Detached Workers: Current Status of an Action Program," Paper presented at a joint session of the annual meeting of the Society for the Study of Social Problems and American Sociological Association, Los Angeles, California, August, 1963.

17. Nathan Glazer, "The Good Society," *Commentary,* 36 (September, 1963), 226–34.

18. See e.g. Charles F. Grosser, "Community Development Programs Serving the Urban Poor," *Social Work,* 10 (July, 1965), 15–21.

19. There has been considerable interest in reorganizing corporate bureaucracy in recent years, but this material does not bear directly upon the problems at hand.

20. See e.g. Belknap, *op. cit.*

21. LaMar T. Empey and Jerome Rabow, "The Provo Experiment in Delinquency Prevention," *American Sociological Review,* 26 (October, 1961), 679–95.

22. Eugene Litwak, "Models of Bureaucracy Which Permit Conflict," *American Journal of Sociology,* 57 (September, 1961), 177–84.

23. From *Max Weber,* trans. and ed. by H.H. Gerth and C. Wright Mills (New York: Oxford University Press, 1946).

24. Research being carried out by James Otis Smith, J. Kenneth Benson and Gideon Sjoberg as part of the Timberlawn Foundation Research Project, Dallas, Texas, will bear directly upon this issue.

25. Gideon Sjoberg, "The Rise of the 'Mediator Society'," Presidential address delivered at the annual meeting of the Southwestern Sociological Association, Dallas, Texas, March, 1964, examines the overall role of mediators in modern society.

26. Harold L. Wilensky and Charles N. Lebeaux, *Industrial Society and Social Welfare* (New York: The Free Press, a Division of the Macmillan Co., 1965), 238–40.

27. U.S. Department of Labor, *The Case for National Action* (Washington, D.C.: U.S. Government Printing Office, 1965). For reactions to this essay see: "The Negro Family: Visceral Reaction," *Newsweek,* 60 (December 6, 1965), 39–40 and John Herbers, "Moynihan Hopeful U.S. Will Adopt a Policy of Promoting Family Stability," *New York Times,* December 12, 1965, 74.

28. See e.g. Harry Cohen, *The Demonics of Bureaucracy* (Ames, Iowa: Iowa State University Press, 1965).

29. Herbert Spencer, *The Principles of Sociology,* 3 vols. (New York: D. Appleton and Co., 1899).

▶ Part II

The Environment of the Urban School

In Part I we demonstrated that a host of social problems external to the schools nonetheless have an effect that is inescapable in the everyday existence of educators. These problems often constrict the ability of educators to critically and creatively reflect on the possibilities for equality of educational opportunity. In Part II we illustrate a variety of issues and problems within the school that impede equality of educational opportunity. In some respects, the connection between the external and internal problems is obvious, while in other instances the connections are more vague. One thing is certain; there are many forces at work in schools that either overtly or covertly influence the possibility of equality of educational opportunity.

During the 1970s and 1980s, a number of empirical studies emerged to illuminate the hidden dimensions of schooling. This rendered traditional views of the purposes for schooling and the causes and effects of school success opaque through a lens called "the hidden curriculum." The hidden curriculum was believed to be a powerful force on the schooling process. It was believed to function as a mechanism for the selection, preservation, and continuation of specific conceptions of social and cultural competence, ideological norms and values, and forms of knowledge and social practice that reproduced the advantages and disadvantages that children brought to the classroom. This view of education provided evidence of an ideological dimension of schooling that ran counter to the traditional beliefs in meritocracy and equality of educational opportunity. It also provided an analysis of the multiple problems in educational practice, school structures, and the context of teaching and learning. Issues of class, race, gender, and ethnicity were examined as they related to different interpretations of schools' success. Upon the messy terrain of public school practices, issues such as ability, testing, tracking, expectations, and dropping-out were no longer seen as neutral categories, simple organizational devices, or individual choices. The cultural capital that was exchanged in schools was no longer part of the taken-for-granted assumptions of middle-class, white society, but was critically interrogated to illuminate the relationship between school success and student characteristics.

For example, one of the earliest and most important empirical studies to emerge that demonstrated a relationship among school success, ability, expectations, and social class was initiated by Keddie (1971). Her study concerned the relationship among ability, social class, and classroom knowledge. This study examined how teachers define classroom experience and construct meaning for students differentially through "two principle organizing categories: ability and social class" (Keddie, 1971, p. 295). She went on to demonstrate how a category such as ability could be used not only to define the measure of success for students, but also to guarantee that some students would fail to attain it.

While teaching the same subject material to students differentiated through ability grouping, Keddie found that teachers adjusted their educational expectations, emphasis on content, modes of pedagogy, and criteria for evaluation to the perceived level of student competence. While the perceived competence levels of students were said to be based on the category of ability, the most significant expectations and responses of the teachers were implicitly based on social class criteria. Furthermore, teachers often appeared to use the categories of social class and ability interchangeably. Interestingly enough, the differences in the measure of success for students in the upper and lower tracks did not lie so much in superior qualities or intellectual skills. Instead, success was constituted by the student's ability to "take over" the teacher's categories and definitions, which usually conformed to middle-class expectations. This study suggests that the category of ability is more an indicator of social, economic, and cultural characteristics than of academic promise.

Through numerous other classroom studies it has been suggested that schools are organized differently around issues of class, race, gender, and ethnicity in such a way that students generally receive qualitatively and quantitatively different treatment. This differentiated organization and treatment functions as a form of occupational screening and selection. Furthermore, it results in the awarding of status based on inheritance. By resting on the common sense assumption that those who succeed are meritorious in the competitive educational market, the different value placed on the social and cultural capital students bring to the classroom and how that translates into academic ability and effort is obscured.

In Part II, the editors have selected articles that are broadly representative of the problems and issues that influence the ability of urban schools to achieve the goals of equality of educational opportunity from both inside and outside the schools. For example, insistence by educators that standardized tests are an integral part of the grouping process breeds the seeds of controversy. Some historians contend that testing and grouping procedures have their origin in the social fabric of the United States; they believe that schools are designed to sort students on the basis of ability. In this case, educators are influenced by larger societal pressures that expect schools to perform sorting functions in order to retain a rigid class system. So what appears to be a school-created problem is, in reality, a reflection of pressures emanating from the class structure of the nation.

If that argument is not acceptable, then one can suggest that the entire testing/grouping discussion is simply educators trying to group children to improve instruction, to channel children into the correct curriculum. Testing has been promoted to serve that function. However, if that function is performed correctly, why is it that elementary children who are in a low reading group become the general or vocational students in high school and most often the dropouts? In Chapter 5, the editors present articles addressing the issues of testing, tracking, expectations, and dropping-out as separate but related. The reader must personally determine the degree to which these relationships make sense in the everyday life of urban schools.

In Chapter 6, these issues are further muddled by the debate over the differences in school success of urban students in public and private education systems. Some argue that competition, privatization, and choice increase the possibilities of success in schools for all students. However, might the underlying reason for the purported success of poor and minority students in private schools be situated in the philosophic and cultural continuity that some schools are able to provide? Perhaps the ability of some schools to be more selective, while, in contrast, many public schools must admit all students, has an impact on the success of poor and minority children. Finally, as Kozol (1991) points out in *Savage Inequalities,* perhaps we need to examine the conditions under which students in urban schools are forced to function and the preparation and support teachers in those schools receive.

Chapter 7 looks at the issues of class, race, gender, and ethnicity as they relate to educational success. The issues of class, race, gender, and ethnicity have an enormous impact on the schooling process at both the overt and covert levels. An overwhelming majority of students want to learn when they enter school, regardless of race, class, gender, or ethnicity. However, from the moment many poor and minority children walk into schools they get a clear message that schools expect little from them and that society generally does not care about their education [National Coalition of Advocates for Students (NCAS), 1985]. If public schooling is the engine of democracy and represents what has been called the "last frontier" for mobility within the social and economic structure of society (Bowles and Gintis, 1976), a large percentage of the population is being systematically excluded from such possibilities. Educators must begin to raise questions concerning the contradictory nature of the schooling process and how it often functions to actively silence students, particularly those students representative of groups historically marginalized within dominant society.

While schools may serve the interest of some individuals or groups through the ideology of meritocracy and the promise of equality of opportunity, they also serve to reproduce the unequal economic, social, and cultural relations of the wider society. The meritocratic perspective does little to provide an accurate analysis of the production of inequality in the public schools or the larger social order. Furthermore, the ideology that informs this perspective has often prevented the realization of any notion of an egalitarian ideal, the elimination of inequality, or the improvement of those who are least well-off. Thus, equality of educational opportunity remains at best a dream deferred for poor and minority children in our urban schools. The opportunities that schools offer these children are quantitatively and qualitatively different from those experiences provided to students in suburbs or wealthy private schools. Could Joe Clark have survived using the same techniques, a bullhorn and a baseball bat, in an affluent suburban school?

REFERENCES

Bowles, S., and Gintis, H. (1976). *Schooling in Capitalist America.* New York: Basic Books.

Keddie, N. (1971). "Classroom knowledge." In M.F.D. Young, ed., *Knowledge and Control,* London: College Macmillan.

Kozol, J. (1991). *Savage Inequalities.* New York: Crown Publishers.

National Coalition of Advocates for Students (NCAS). (1985). *Our Children at Risk: An Inquiry into the Current Reality of American Public Education.* New York: NCAS.

gifted students or those with limited proficiency in English, for which there are no reliable figures. Nor does it include tests administered by private and parochial schools to their students. Information from sources outside the public schools also suggests that some school officials may have underreported test use in their districts. Finally, the FairTest survey counted each administration of a battery of tests as only one test, although some batteries included as many as five separate exams.

The FairTest survey revealed that the number of states that mandate testing has increased greatly in recent years. The survey also showed that standardized testing is most prevalent in the southern states and in large urban school systems—locales that tend to serve higher-than-average proportions of minority students and students from low-income families.

Those who favor standardized testing applaud these trends in the public schools. They see tests as "objective" methods of enforcing "accountability"—and thus of improving student achievement, staff competence, and educational quality. Indeed, standardized tests are an essential element of the "school reform movement."

In reality, however, these "objective" instruments often produce results that are inaccurate, inconsistent, and biased against minorities, females, and students from low-income families. By narrowing the curriculum, frustrating teachers, and driving students out of school, these standardized tests undermine school improvement instead of advancing its cause. Instead of promoting accountability, tests shift control and authority into the hands of an unregulated testing industry. Therefore, using standardized test scores as the primary criteria for making important educational decisions will lead to *less* public understanding of the schools and a *weaker* educational system.

The powerful negative effects of standardized multiple-choice tests leads us to emphasize the need to develop high-quality alternative assessment devices that yield educationally useful and accurate results, while strengthening the curriculum and making meaningful accountability possible.

THE INADEQUATE QUALITY OF STANDARDIZED TESTS

Standardized tests are consistently sold as scientifically developed instruments that objectively, simply, and reliably measure students' achievement, abilities, or skills.[2] In reality, however, the basic psychological assumptions undergirding the construction and use of standardized tests are open to question and often are clearly erroneous. In addition, the studies that are conducted to determine the reliability and validity of standardized tests are often inadequate. Many tests are administered in environments that erase their claims to being "standardized" or that discriminate against minority test-takers and those from low-income families. These flaws undermine the test makers' claims of objectivity and often produce test results that are inaccurate, unreliable, and ultimately invalid. As a result, standardized tests generally fail to provide effective and useful measures of test-takers' achievement, abilities, or skills.

False assumptions. The ability of standardized tests to accurately report students' knowledge, abilities, or skills is limited by the assumptions that these attributes can be isolated, sorted to fit on a linear scale, and reported in the form of a single score. Stephen Gould calls these assumptions fallacies of *reification* (treating "intelligence" as though it were a separable unitary thing underlying the complexity of human mental activity) and of *ranking* ("our propensity for ordering complex variation as a gradual ascending scale"). He concludes that "the common style embodying both fallacies of thought has been quantification, or the measurement of intelligence as a single number for each person."[3] As Les Levidow has noted, "Without anyone having to claim that I.Q. scores represent the quantity of a thing, it appears that way by virtue of assigning a number to each testee and then comparing those numbers through a distribution curve."[4]

Many of the assumptions and structures of achievement tests are based on I.Q. tests and operate in the same fashion. For example, assumptions regarding the linear sorting of students are common to both kinds of tests.[5] Such assumptions are at odds with contemporary research on child development, which emphasizes that considerable diversity exists in both the nature and pace of child development.[6] Ability or achievement tests that use a linear scale can label a student's performance as incorrect or substandard when it is really only a normal variation; such tests can also mask real differences.[7]

Test constructors not only assume—erroneously—that the knowledge, skill, or ability that they seek to measure is one-dimensional, but also that it tends to be distributed according to the "normal" bell-shaped curve. The bell-shaped curve is used for statistical convenience, not because any form of knowledge or ability is actually distributed in this manner.[8]

As is true of child development, modern theories emphasize the complexity of human intelligence. Researchers have observed that knowledge, learning, and thinking have multiple facets and that a high level of development in one area does not necessarily indicate a high level of development in others.[9] Unitary test scores and linear scaling of scores ignore the true complexity of human intelligence and thus provide a deceptive picture of individual achievement, ability, or skills. This fundamental problem underlies all standardized tests in education.

Test reliability. Claims that standardized tests exhibit a high level of reliability are usually taken to mean that test results for a given individual will be similar in successive administrations. But in fact, *reliability* is a technical term that encompasses several different concepts.

The type of reliability that is generally measured and reported for standardized tests is internal or inter-form reliability. Consistency over time, which many observers would consider of greater importance, is rarely measured and reported by test publishers. A study of consistency over time generally produces lower reliability coefficients and is more expensive to conduct.[10]

The level of a test's reliability (regardless of the type of reliability measured) is reported as a "reliability coefficient" that ranges from 0 to 1. For most standardized tests, the reported coefficients are very high—often exceeding .8 or .9.[11]

Yet, for an I.Q. test with a reliability coefficient of .89 and a standard deviation of 15, a student has a reasonable likelihood of having a "true score" that is up to 13 points higher or lower than his or her test score.[12] Thus a school system could, for example, bar a student who scores 117 from entering a program for the gifted and talented that requires participants to have I.Q.s of 130—even though that student's "true score" could well be 130.

Nonstandard procedures for administering tests and the impact of examiners on test-takers reduce the test reliability below the level that is reported in experimental settings. The scores of minority students and of students from low-income families are most likely to be negatively influenced by these factors. Such students are less apt to perform well when they do not know the person who administers the test—although an anonymous administrator does not affect the performance of middle-class white students.[13]

Because reliability is often much lower for subsections of achievement tests and for tests administered to children below grade 3, the chance for error increases when tests are used to place young children or when decisions are based on subtest scores.[14] Cautions against such potential misuses of tests are often buried in hard-to-read manuals.

No test has sufficient reliability to warrant making decisions *solely* or *primarily* on the basis of test scores. Such decisions disproportionately harm minorities, younger students, and those from low-income families.

Test validity. Validity tells us whether a test measures what it claims to measure, how well it measures it, and what can be inferred from that measurement. Test validity cannot be measured in the abstract; it can only be determined in the context of the relationship between the specific uses to which the test results will be put and the construct that is being measured. Thus information and conclusions regarding the validity of a given test in one context may not be relevant and applicable in other contexts.

As is the case with reliability, the term *validity* encompasses several concepts.

- Content validity determines whether the test items relate to the trait or traits the test purports to measure.
- Criterion validity compares test performance (for example, on a reading test) against a standard that independently measures the trait (such as reading ability) that the test purports to measure. Criterion validity takes two forms, concurrent and predictive.
- Construct validity examines how well a test actually correlates with the underlying theoretical characteristics of the trait it purports to measure. For example, does the test accurately measure "academic ability" or "competence" or "reading"? This form of validity is rarely reported by test makers, even though

knowledge of a test's construct validity is essential for assessing how useful and accurate that test will be in practice.[15]

Test developers (both commercial and governmental) generally validate the content of a test by asking subject-area experts to make qualitative judgments about the relationship between individual test items and the trait or traits that the test seeks to measure—a method occasionally referred to as BOGSAT (Bunch of Guys Sitting Around a Table). Unfortunately, many test developers do not go beyond content validity.[16] For example, even a widely used and highly respected test battery, such as the Iowa Tests of Basic Skills, "is somewhat lacking when it moves beyond content validity into other validity realms."[17] Reviewers of other standardized tests often make similar comments.[18]

Test developers who do go beyond content validity generally rely on other tests to demonstrate criterion or construct validity. For example, Blythe Mitchell demonstrated the predictive validity of the Metropolitan Readiness Tests and of the Murphy-Durrell Reading Readiness Analysis by correlating scores on those tests with scores on the Stanford Achievement Test. However, she failed to explain what the Stanford Achievement Test measures and how validly it does so.[19]

Another strategy for demonstrating criterion validity is to compare students' test scores and the grades their teachers give them. But this strategy undermines a major selling point of standardized tests: that they are objective substitutes for subjective teacher judgments.[20] If test scores and grades agree completely, why use the tests at all? If they differ significantly, which is better—and how do we know?

The question, then, is whether the test is more valid than teachers' judgments or some other plausible measure of ability or achievement.[21] This last point is important because test makers will argue that even tests with low validity can improve decision making over pure chance. But teachers' judgments and other high-quality alternatives are not equivalent to pure chance.

There are also serious doubts regarding the construct validity of standardized tests. Deborah Meier, for example, argues that reading tests do not measure reading, but "reading skills" (which are not the same thing).[22] In other words, the tests are based on a faulty understanding of reading and of learning to read. As we will discuss in detail later, teaching is directly and negatively influenced when the curriculum is driven by tests that lack construct validity.

Many tests are based on the assumption that the underlying trait (or "construct") being measured develops in a relatively consistent fashion among all individuals. Yet researchers who study human development generally agree that this is not the case.[23] The simple fact is that, as our knowledge of thinking, learning, teaching, and child development has grown over recent years, standardized tests have not changed accordingly. The WISC-R intelligence test, for example, "has remained virtually unchanged since its inception in 1949. . . . Developments in the fields of cognitive psychology and neuroscience have revolutionized our thinking about thinking, but the WISC-R remains the same."[24] The ability of standardized tests to validly measure growth and change in students' knowledge, abilities, or skills is seriously limited by the outdated and inaccurate views of child development and human learning that such tests still reflect.

As is the case with reliability, validity can be measured by statistical methods that produce numbers called validity coefficients. For many standardized multiple-choice tests, validity coefficients can be quite low. And even high coefficients can result in significant margins of error. As Lorrie Shepard and Mary Lee Smith have pointed out, various readiness tests are correlated with later school performance, but the predictive validities for all available tests are so low that some 30% to 50% of children who are identified as not ready to start first grade will have been placed in that category erroneously.[25]

Since tests are so often used for purposes for which they have not been validated, it is risky to base any decision about a child on a score from a single instrument. Increasingly, however, decisions are made solely on such a flawed basis.

Instead of indirectly measuring a construct that is often ill-defined and poorly analyzed, alternative assessments can use direct evidence of the trait itself, e.g., samples of writing on meaningful topics that have been collected over time (instead of an hour's worth of multiple-choice sentence corrections.) Rather than fitting tests to teacher observations, the observations themselves can be recorded in a systematic, standardized manner.[26] High-quality alternative methods of assessment would insure the use of a variety of forms of measurement—which, in turn, would produce more-valid and more-useful measures of competence, achievement, and ability.

BIAS IN STANDARDIZED TESTS

Levidow has noted:

> *The charge of "bias" understates the problem by suggesting that the test distorts the child's score from its otherwise true value, in the sense of inaccurately measuring a property residing in the testee. Yet there is no such "thing"—except as a mystification of a relation.*[27]

Nonetheless, a discussion of bias sheds further light on why testing has such limited validity.

Test makers claim that the lower test scores of racial and ethnic minorities and of students from low-income families simply reflect the biases and inequities that exist in American schools and American society. Biases and inequities certainly exist—but standardized tests do not merely reflect their impact; they compound them.

Researchers have identified several characteristics of standardized tests that could negatively bias the scores of minority students and of students from low-income families. These tests tend to reflect the language, culture, or learning style of middle- to upper-class whites. Thus scores on these tests are as much measures of race or ethnicity and income as they are measures of achievement, ability, or skill.[28]

To communicate their levels of ability, achievement, or skill, test-takers must understand the language of the test. Obviously, tests written in English cannot effectively assess the performance of those students for whom English is a second and only partially mastered language.[29]

Researchers have also discovered that the elaborated, stylized English commonly used in standardized tests prevents such tests from accurately measuring the achievement, ability, or skills of students who speak nonstandard (e.g., African-American, Hispanic, southern, Appalachian, working-class) dialects.[30]

A related type of bias stems from stylistic or interpretive language differences that are related to culture, income, or gender. For example, African-American students often associate the word *environment* with such terms as *home* or *people,* while white students tend to associate that word with *air, clean,* or *earth.* Neither usage is wrong. Yet only one of these two usages—generally the one reflecting the white perspective—will be acceptable on a standardized test.[31]

Similarly, researchers have discovered that individuals exhibit "different ways of knowing and problem solving" that reflect differing styles, not differing abilities. These differing styles are often related to race or ethnicity, income level, and gender. Yet standardized tests (and "standardized" instruction) assume that all individuals perceive information and solve problems in the same way. Again, assumptions about the universal applicability of a style that is exhibited primarily by middle- and upper-class white males limits the reliability of test results.[32]

Ironically, even an effort to decontextualize test content has been found to work against minority youths and those from low-income families. Middle-class whites are more apt to be trained (simply through cultural immersion) to respond to questions removed from context and to repeat information that they know the questioner already possesses. Shirley Brice Heath found that African-American children from working-class families were rarely asked, in their own communities, the kinds of questions to which questioners already knew the answers—the kinds found on tests.[33]

Another source of test bias shows up in questions that assume a cultural experience or perspective that is not shared by all children. The WISC-R, for example, asks, "What is the thing to do when you cut your finger?" According to the test makers, the best response is, "Put a Band-Aid on it." They give partial credit for the response, "Go to the hospital," but they award no credit for "Cry," "Bleed," or "Suck on it."

Minority children usually perform poorly on this item. A few years ago, a Baltimore sociologist asked several inner-city youths why they answered the question in the way they did. She found that many of these youngsters selected "Go to the hospital," because they thought that *cut* meant a big cut. Or they thought that *cut* meant a small cut—so they answered "Suck on it," since they didn't have Band-Aids in their homes. These youngsters received fewer or no points.[34] Giving the wrong answers to just a few such questions can cause a student's "I.Q." (or "achievement") to appear sharply lower than it really is, with possibly life-scarring results.

Students tend to perform better on tests when they identify with the topics covered by the test items. Research has shown this to be true of Mexican-Americans, of African-Americans, and of females.[35] Unfortunately, standardized tests continue to be dominated by questions about and for middle- or upper-class white males.

The timed format of tests can also be a source of bias. Several studies have found that time pressure accounts in part for lower scores among African-Americans and Hispanics.[36]

These and other forms of bias are reinforced by the procedures used to construct and norm tests. For example, questions that might favor minorities are apt to be excluded because they do not fit the "required" statistical properties of the test. Even when the samples on which tests are normed include minorities in proportions that accord with their representation in the total population, the samples remain at least 75% white. Moreover, a disproportionate number of African-Americans fall into the low-scoring group. In general, test makers discard those items on which low scorers do well but high scorers do poorly.[37] As a result, a test item on which African-Americans do particularly well but whites do not is likely to be discarded because of the interaction of two factors: African-Americans are a minority, and African-Americans tend to score low.

Nonetheless, test makers maintain that they effectively screen out biased questions. And they do subject items to review by experts who can supposedly detect bias—but such screening has low reliability.[38] Most major test makers also assess bias in test items through some form of statistical procedure—but, even when bias is found, items are not necessarily discarded. Moreover, the statistical procedures themselves are often problematic. Typically, they presume the independence of the part (the item) from the whole (the test). However, if the entire test is biased, item analysis will not reveal it.[39]

Since knowledge and language are culture-bound, there is no reason to believe that a "culture-free" test can be constructed. But the discriminatory impact of tests can be reduced by carefully selecting content that is more likely to be familiar to minorities or by using special techniques designed to reduce bias. One such procedure, called the "Golden Rule" principle, was included in an out-of-court settlement of a discrimination lawsuit in Illinois. Under the principle, test publishers must select—from among test items of equal validity—those items with the smallest differences between the correct-answer rates of minority and majority test-takers. The principle has caused substantial debate among psychometricians.[40]

It is important to note that advocates of standardized tests often defend their use because such tests are "objective." But *objective* merely means that the tests can be scored by machines, not by subjective human scorers.[41] Bias can still creep into the questions themselves. In fact, the purported objectivity of tests is often no more than the standardization of bias. The replacement of the potential bias of individual judgment with the numerical bias of an "objective" test is not progress.

IMPACT OF TEST USE ON SCHOOLS

Historically, standardized tests were one of several educational tools used to assess student achievement and to diagnose academic strengths and weaknesses. In recent years, however, standardized tests have become not only the primary criteria used by many schools for making decisions that affect students, but also major forces in shaping instruction and assessing the quality of teaching and of the schools.

The use of standardized test scores as the primary criteria for making decisions of any kind is reckless, given the erroneous assumptions that undergird standardized tests, the limited range of skills and knowledge that they measure, their limited reliability, their lack of validity, and the impact that race, ethnicity, family income, and gender exert on test results. Yet just such reckless decisions seriously damage student achievement, the curriculum, and education reform in many schools and school districts.

Impact on student progress. By controlling or compelling student placement in various educational programs, standardized tests perpetuate and even exacerbate existing inequities in educational services, particularly for minority students and those from low-income families. One clear example is tracking, which has been shown to harm the students placed in lower tracks without necessarily helping those placed in higher tracks to perform better then they would have performed in heterogeneous groupings. This is largely due to the fact that students whose test scores are low are presumed to be unable to master complex material and are thus subjected to a dumbed-down curriculum.[42]

The use of scores on standardized tests to determine placement in special education and remedial education programs also causes larger numbers of racial and ethnic minorities to be placed in those programs. In 1984, for example, 40% of African-American 5-year-olds in South Carolina failed the standardized tests used in that state to determine eligibility for kindergarten. Before their formal schooling had even begun, these youngsters were placed in remedial classes because of their scores on unreliable exams.[43]

The use of standardized test scores for sorting students also perpetuates the disproportional representation of white middle- and upper-class youngsters in "advanced" classes. Some local school districts in New York City use I.Q. test scores to place children in programs for the gifted and talented—thereby creating enclaves of white middle- and upper-class students in districts that primarily serve racial and ethnic minorities.[44] Overall, test use both narrows the educational opportunities available to many segments of our student population and maintains the isolation of racial and social groups and classes.

Particularly when they are used as promotional gates, standardized tests can act as powerful devices to exclude groups—and once again, minority students and those from low-income families are disproportionately affected. Research has shown that, when a student repeats a grade, the probability of that student dropping out prior to graduation increases by 20% to 40%.[45] In other words, students who are not promoted because they have failed to reach arbitrary cutoff scores on often unreliable, invalid, and biased standardized tests are more likely to drop out of high school.

The impact of standardized tests is particularly devastating when such tests are used to determine readiness for first grade. As we noted earlier, standardized tests for young children are among the least valid and least reliable exams; they are also among the most difficult tests to administer under relatively uniform conditions. Moreover, after examining 14 controlled studies on the effects of kindergarten retention, Shepard and Smith concluded that retention did not improve children's subsequent academic achievement but that it did impose a significant social stigma on the retained students.[46]

Nor does the use of standardized tests affect only low-achieving students. High-achieving students or those whose interests stray from the basics are likely to be frustrated by a narrowed curriculum that has been "dumbed down" in response to standardized tests, particularly minimum competency tests. Such students, too, are likely to drop out in greater numbers.[47]

Impact on educational goals and curricula. Children go to school not just to learn basic academic skills, but also to develop the personal, intellectual, and social skills that will enable them to become happy, productive members of a democratic society. Unfortunately, the current emphasis on standardized tests threatens to undermine these broad goals by forcing schools and teachers to focus on narrow, quantifiable skills at the expense of less easily quantifiable and more complex academic and nonacademic abilities.

This outcome is particularly noticeable in the very early grades. As the National Association for the Education of Young Children (NAEYC) recently noted:

> *Many of the important skills that children need to acquire in early childhood—self-esteem, social competence, desire to learn, self-discipline—are not easily measured by standardized tests. As a result, social, emotional, moral, and physical development and learning are virtually ignored or given minor importance in schools with mandated testing programs.*[48]

Many schools have embarked on a single-minded quest for higher test scores, even though this strategy severely constricts their curricula.[49] For example, Deborah Meier, the principal of Central Park East public school in Manhattan, testified at a 1981 National Institute of Education hearing on minimum competency testing that students in New York City read "dozens of short paragraphs about which they then answer questions"—an approach that duplicates the form of the tests that the students will take in spring.[50] Meanwhile, Gerald Bracey, former director of research, evaluation, and testing for the Virginia Department of Education, observed that some teachers did not teach their students how to add and subtract fractions, because Virginia's minimum competency test included questions on the multiplication and division—but not on the addition and subtraction—of fractions.[51]

Sometimes, as Arthur Wise has note, the curriculum is narrowed simply because "testing takes time, and preparing students for testing takes even more time. And all this time is taken away from real teaching."[52]

Unfortunately, a closer link between standardized tests and school curricula has become a conscious goal for some school systems. School systems in at least 13 states and the District of Columbia are seeking to "align" their curricula so that students do *not* spend hours studying materials on which they will never be tested—regardless of the value of those materials or the benefits that students might derive from studying them.[53] In other words, aligning curricula with tests subordinates the process of curriculum development to external testing priorities, and, for all intents and purposes, the test becomes the curriculum.

The educational price that is paid for allowing tests to dictate the curriculum can be high. Julia Palmer, executive director of the American Reading Council, recently noted that the major barrier to teaching reading in a commonsense and pleasurable way is the nationally normed, standardized second-grade reading test. Palmer went on to explain that the test questions force teachers and students in the early grades to focus on "reading readiness" exercises and workbooks instead of on reading. As a result, many students become disenchanted with reading.[54]

Mathematics instruction has also been harmed by the emphasis on testing. Constance Kamii notes that standardized tests cannot distinguish between students who understand underlying math concepts and students who are only able to perform procedures by rote (and who therefore cannot apply these procedures to new situations). Thus teaching to the test precludes teaching in a fashion that enables children to grasp the deeper logic.[55] The National Council of Teachers of Mathematics has concluded that, unless assessment is changed, the teaching of mathematics cannot improve.[56]

Just as curricula have been narrowed, so too have textbooks. Diane Ravitch argues that "textbooks full of good literature began to disappear from American classrooms in the 1920s, when standardized tests were introduced. Appreciation of good literature gave way to emphasis on the 'mechanics' of reading."[57] Similarly, a report by the Council for Basic Education (CBE) concluded that the emphases on standardized tests and on aligning curricula to match the tests were two major causes of the decline in the quality of textbooks.[58]

The narrowing of the curriculum is a virtually unavoidable by-product of placing our emphasis on multiple-choice instruments with limited construct validity. Not only do reading tests not test reading and math tests not test math, but the format militates against their ever being able to measure the essential constructs. As teaching becomes "coaching for the test" in too many schools, real learning and real thinking are crowded out. Among the instructional casualties are the higher-order thinking skills.

Standardized tests (including those that have been mandated by states as part of their school reform laws) focus on basic skills, not on critical thinking, reasoning, or problem solving. They emphasize the quick recognition of isolated facts, not the integration of information and the generation of ideas.[59] As Linda Darling-Hammond concluded, "It's testing for the TV generation—superficial and passive. We don't ask if students can synthesize information, solve problems, or think independently. We measure what they can recognize."[60]

Several studies have demonstrated that "teaching behaviors that are effective in raising scores on tests of lower-level cognitive skills are nearly the opposite of those behaviors that are effective in developing complex cognitive learning, problem-solving ability, and creativity."[61] Moreover, because children learn "higher skills" (the integration, use, and creation of knowledge) from the very start, there is no need to teach basic skills and higher skills sequentially.[62]

The effects of testing on the curriculum and on student placements lead to educational disaster for many young people. In an all-too-typical scenario, a child who does not test well (often due to cultural background, not academic capability) is tracked—sometimes prior to first grade—into a program for "slow learners" that rests on the assumption that participants cannot or will not learn. The tracking creates a self-fulfilling prophecy, as the child's "achievement" test scores come to correlate with his or her "ability" test scores.

Programs for "slow learners" emphasize the rote learning of basic skills. They also bore, frustrate, and alienate both students and teachers in a dialectic that fosters student resistance to the schooling that is offered.[63] Students who are forced to endure inappropriate teaching methods and a misplaced emphasis on basic skills do not learn. But when their test scores remain low, the commonly suggested solution is more "basics" and more testing in a program designed to raise the test scores. At best, these students graduate without having learned much save for dislike of school. At worst, they drop out of school and into the ranks of the chronically unemployed. This scenario most often affects minority students and those from low-income families.

Standardized testing is clearly not the only culprit in this disaster, but it plays a major role through its effects on texts, pedagogy, and educational goals. A continued emphasis on testing—and thus on learnings that tests can measure—will only make the situation worse and hinder any attempts at real reform.

Impact on local control. Because standardized tests increasingly determine what is taught and how it is taught, parents and other citizens are losing their traditional control over local schools to the state legislatures that mandate such testing. This, in turn, reduces "the responsiveness of schools to their clientele and so reduces the quality of education."[64]

Local control over the schools is also being lost to private organizations, namely the test developers. Despite the significant and growing role that their

products play in educational decisions, these testing companies face little government regulation or supervision. Unlike other industries that provide such services or
commodities as communications, food, drugs, and transportation, the billion-dollar-
a-year testing industry is governed by virtually no regulatory structures at either the
federal or the state levels.

States and school districts have neither the expertise nor the resources to
develop and validate the standardized tests that they need. Nor are states and school
districts equipped to adequately investigate the claims of test developers regarding
the validity of their products or to review the validation process.[65]

Even if the necessary expertise and resources were available, states and school
districts would probably be unable to conduct effective outside evaluations because
of the secrecy that characterizes the testing industry. As the late Oscar Buros, who
served as editor of the *Mental Measurement Yearbook,* lamented, "It is practically
impossible for a competent test technician or test consumer to make a thorough
appraisal of construction, validation, and use of standardized tests . . . because of
the limited amount of trustworthy information supplied by the test publishers."[66]

AN AGENDA FOR REFORM

Reflecting its concern about the misuse of standardized tests, FairTest has developed an agenda for testing reform. Making tests fair, accurate, open, and educationally relevant would require major changes in the instruments themselves and sharp
controls on their use.[67] However, reducing the most egregious offenses of standardized testing will not be sufficient.

The primary educational needs of the U.S. simply cannot be met by reliance on
standardized testing. Albert Shanker argues that education has "never worked well
for more than about 20% of our children."[68] To serve the rest, as education must do,
will require fundamental changes in curriculum, pedagogy, and management.

At best, standardized testing is hopelessly inadequate for promoting necessary
school reform. At worst, such testing will preclude reform. In either case, the
continued domination of testing will mean that millions of students—primarily
those most in need of improved education—will be dumped into dead-end tracks
and pushed out of school. To prevent damage to young people and to allow the
implementation of needed school reforms to proceed, testing must become an
occasional adjunct, used for obtaining certain basic but limited information about
education—and for nothing else.

Assessment, properly conducted, can be of great help to instruction and learning. Teachers can pinpoint not only what a given student knows, but how that
student learns best. Assessment can encourage critical thinking and creativity.
Across the country—in schools, school districts, state agencies, and research centers—alternatives to standardized testing are being designed. Most of these alternatives rely on some form of what Howard Gardner calls "process and product

portfolios."[69] But no matter how well-crafted it is, improved assessment is not a panacea that will reform education. Advocates of reform must remain vigilant: the more insightful and powerful the means of assessment, the more damage its misuse can cause.

Alternatives to standardizing testing must be carefully designed to avoid reproducing the biases, the inaccuracies, and the damage to students and curricula that standardized tests have wreaked. Replacing the biases inherent in standardized tests with the biases of individual teachers or schools would not be progress. Therefore, any alternatives to standardized testing must include methods of detecting bias and, when bias is found (as inevitably it will be), procedures to correct it. If, as we anticipate, the information provided by alternatives proves to be far richer, more complex, and more powerful than the information provided by standardized tests, that store of new information could be used in ways that harm students. Those most at risk will continue to be minorities and the poor. Proponents of alternatives must guard against their misuse.[70]

The problems of education are by no means limited to testing. Even the best alternative assessment, used in the most caring and helpful ways, will not resolve many of these problems, which predate the extensive use of standardized testing in the schools. Criticisms of testing and the development of alternatives must be rooted in the search for answers to lingering questions: Whom do we educate? How do we do so? And for what end?

ENDNOTES

1. Noe Medina and D. Monty Neill, *Fallout from the Testing Explosion: How 100 Million Standardized Exams Undermine Equity and Excellence in America's Public Schools* (Cambridge, Mass: FairTest, 1988). This report provides more detail on much of the information in this article.

2. As Les Levidow has observed, deciding which things to measure and which things not to measure is a socially determined act. See Les Levidow, "'Ability' Labeling as Racism," in Dawn Gill and Les Levidow, eds., *Anti-Racist Science Teaching* (London: Free Association Books, 1987), pp. 233–67.

3. Stephen J. Gould, *The Mismeasure of Man* (New York: Norton, 1981), p. 24.

4. Levidow, p. 239. He also observed that "the 'intelligence' of I.Q. testing is constructed by the testing process itself" (p. 235).

5. Birenda Singh, "Graded Assessments: Hijacking 'Process,'" in Gill and Levidow, pp. 219–32.

6. "NAEYC Position Statement on Developmentally Appropriate Practice in the Primary Grades, Serving 5- Through 8-Year-Olds," *Young Children*, January 1988, pp. 64–84.

7. Medina and Neill, p. 10. See also Orlando L. Taylor and Dorian L. Lee, "Standardized Tests and African-American Children: Communication and Language Issues," *Negro Educational Review*, April-July 1987, pp. 67–80.

8. Charlotte Ryan, *The Testing Maze* (Chicago: National PTA, 1979), p. 8.

Several related changes shaped the character of turn-of-the-century America: a switch from craftsman-based to industrial production, a population shift toward urban centers, a huge influx of poor, unskilled, and non-English-speaking immigrants, and the expansion of secondary schooling. Together they constituted a transformation of the economic, social, and political realities. All played a part in redefining the American conception of a democratic society. A central focus of this redefinition was establishing the prevailing 20th-century version of the relationship between equality and schooling. What resulted were the principles of equal educational opportunity outlined above.

The ideas undergirding these principles did not materialize from thin air. The air was thick with theories about the relationship of schooling to economic production and work, the value of a meritocracy, human evolution and the superiority of Anglo-Saxon cultures, and the unlimited potential of science and industry. A brief review of these ideas provides insight into the context of both turn-of-the-century and current definitions of educational equality.

School and Work. For the first time, students who would not become scholars, professionals, or gentlemen were attending secondary schools. The traditional academic curriculum seemed a mismatch, especially for immigrants who were difficult to keep in school. Yet it seemed important and humane to postpone these children's entry into the grind of factory life. At the same time industrial employers needed immigrants socialized with the work habits and attitudes required to "fit in" as factory workers (proper deportment, punctuality, willingness to be supervised and managed) and, perhaps less important, technical skills. Native-born youth needed a changed conception of work as well. The autonomy and complexity of a craftsman-based workforce were of the past. Work in the factory required respect for the industrial, in part to make the monotony of factory work tolerable. These requirements of industry coincided with the curricular vacuum in schools. Preparation for work became a central mission of secondary schools (Edson, 1982).

Social Darwinism and Differentiated Education. The misapplication of the theories of Charles Darwin to human society—social Darwinism—provided a *scientific* basis for viewing immigrant and minority groups as of lesser social and moral development than others. Their lives of squalor could be accounted for biologically, just as the disproportionate economic and social power held by men of Anglo stock could be justified by their "fitness." This misapplied social Darwinism, too, explained the disproportionate school failure and "retardation" rates of immigrant children. They failed because they were incapable, biologically unfit for an academic curriculum. The provision of different school content for these children— namely, industrial training—seemed not only democratic, but humane. Tracking into vocational or academic programs clearly provided equal opportunities for students with such inherently different capabilities (Hall, 1905).

Americanization and Anglo-Conformity. Not surprisingly, given social Darwinism, the languages and habits of the southern and eastern European immigrants were threatening to native-born Americans. They were numerous, strikingly different, and poor. There emerged a great concern about preserving the dominant WASP culture, eliminating the immigrants' "depraved" life style, and making the cities safe. It seemed absolutely necessary to bring the foreign-born into the American cultural mainstream by teaching them the Protestant American values of hard work, frugality, modesty, cleanliness, truthfulness, and purity of thought and action. The program to do so, closely aligned with preparation for work, was termed Americanization and located in the public schools. The rhetoric was one of an American melting pot, but in reality only certain people were to be melted. Americanization was driven both by a belief in the goodness of Anglo ways and by fear of the immigrants. Along with industrialism, Americanization provided much of the content of educational opportunities that were provided the children of the poor (Cremin, 1964).

Scientific Management. The concept of industrial efficiency shaped the *form* schooling would take to provide different but equal educations. The country had fallen in love with the idea of the factory busily engaged in a neatly standardized and controlled process of mass production. In went raw materials and, through the application of scientifically determined "best" methods and tools, out came ready-made goods and machinery—all designed to improve the quality of American life. The essence of the factory was efficiency. Human energies were controlled, coordinated, and channeled into machine-like parts, with little waste of material or duplication of effort. The "Taylor System" of scientific management made possible a system of production based on top-down decision making, a rigid division of labor, elaborate rules and regulations, and an attitude of impersonality toward the individual (Nelson, 1980). Schoolmen welcomed and often spearheaded the incorporation of "scientific management" into schools. Compared with the factory, schools seemed to be inefficient and unsuccessful. In an era of specifiable and measurable outcomes, what better way to manage the diversity of children's abilities and provide different educational opportunities than through the infusion of division of labor, standardization, specialization, and a division of labor into the schools?

Meritocracy. Fundamental to American conceptions of democracy is the principle that, while material rewards need not be distributed equally among citizens, the contest for these rewards must be fair. The American view of a "fair" contest is that it be won by effort and ability rather than by inherited status and privilege. Because of the central role of schools in preparing for work, educational opportunities determined by merit were seen as the fair and neutral means of providing access to economic rewards. The development of intelligence testing lent a "scientific objectivity" to the assignment of students to different curricula. Predictions about the appropriate futures of students could be made on the basis of their scores and then the requisite training could be provided.[2] It was clear from the beginning that the different educational opportunities were not equally valued. After all, they led to quite different social and economic outcomes. That poor and immigrant children consistently demonstrated the least merit and were consistently placed in the least-

collective muscles. The second half of the decade of the '70s was plagued with inflation, recession, and unemployment.

Two quite different responses to the ecological and economic crises were voiced by scientists, politicians, and economists. One stressed the acceptance of the reality of shrinking world resources and encouraged the development of a cooperative human society in harmony with nature toward a no-growth end (see, e.g., Boulding, 1973; Commoner, 1977; Heilbroner, 1974; Schumacher, 1973). The second denied the doomsday prediction and condemned the limited vision of its spokespersons (see, e.g., Kahn, Brown, & Martel, 1976; Lipset, 1979; Macrae, 1972).

With the defeat of Jimmy Carter and the election of Ronald Reagan, the American public turned over political power to the champions of this second response. Government tinkering with the free play of the marketplace and excessive spending on social programs were blamed for inhibiting expansion, suppressing productivity, providing an easy life on the public dole, and leading to the current economic woes. "Social tinkering" had had a destructive effect on the healing and generating forces of economic growth, i.e. personal incentive, thrift, and hard work.[3] Economic recovery required a return to the values and approaches—hard work, free enterprise, and American ingenuity—that had earlier accompanied growth and prosperity. Government action must be limited to two goals: (a) eliminating controls and restrictions on the marketplace and (b) providing incentives to those with the talent, skills, and resources to spearhead the new technological advances. Gains to all would result from the "trickling down" of economic benefits. Needless to say, this approach has had ramifications for the schools.

TRICKLE-DOWN EXCELLENCE

Schools, as Seymour Sarason has so insightfully commented, serve as both scapegoats and sources of salvation (Sarason, 1983). That, of course, is the most salient message of current reforms. Although there have been hundreds of reports and state reform initiatives during the past two years, the tenor of reform is still best articulated in the 1983 round of commission reports. Their tone and substance have become recurrent themes in the educational pronouncements of politicians. Most states have followed their recommendations quite consistently in their efforts to upgrade their schools.

As the reports make plain, the current reform movement both blames schools for our current post-industrial economic woes and places on them the hope for recovery. We are all by now quite familiar with the warning in *A Nation at Risk* that "the educational foundations of our society are presently being eroded by a rising tide of mediocrity that threatens our very future as a Nation and as a people" (NCEE, 1983, p. 5). The reassertion of American dominance of a world of diminishing resources, voiced in terms of keeping and improving the "slim competitive edge we still retain in world markets," (p. 5) will result from re-establishing educational excellence in schools. "Knowledge, learning, information, and skilled intelligence are the new raw materials of international commerce and are today spreading throughout the world as vigorously as miracle drugs, synthetic fertilizers, and blue jeans did earlier" (p. 7). Given this conception of education itself as the medium of economic exchange it is not surprising that the report *Action for Excellence* claims, "Our future success as a nation—our national defense, our social stability and well-being and our national prosperity—will depend on our ability to improve education and training" (TFEEG, 1983, p. 14).

Equality issues are central to both the diagnoses of current educational troubles and the prescriptions for educational reform. The theme consistent on the diagnoses and prescriptions is that we have made a grave error in trying to be all things to all people. We have "squandered the gains in student achievement made in the wake of the Sputnik challenge" (NCEE, 1983, p. 5). After noting that efforts during the '60s and '70s to improve educational opportunities resulted in increased achievement for black students, *Action for Excellence* continues with an indictment of that era: "The fact remains, however, that overall performance in higher-order skills . . . declined in the seventies. . . . This suggests that we may be regressing from the standard of literacy which was considered adequate 15 years ago" (TFEEG, 1983, p. 24). The clear implication is that the price of extending educational opportunities was a decline in educational quality. Furthermore, providing resources to improve achievement exacted a social and economic price greater than the benefits received. *Making the Grade* is blatant in this regard: "Its [the federal government's] emphasis on promoting equality of opportunity in the public schools has meant a slighting of its commitment to educational quality" (TCF, 1983, p. 6).

The thrust of educational reform, then, is toward economic recovery through increased productivity and technological growth. Schools are to provide salvation from the crises of the '70s. The road to this salvation is clearly reflective of these crises and the lingering spectre of scarcity—even in the face of optimistic presidential promises for the future. It is clear that the central problem viewed by the makers of the reform reports is not an educational one. Educational issues have meaning only as they bear upon the issues of "real life": jobs, security, stability, defense, prosperity, and so on. And equality is given even less concern; it is tolerable as a goal only to the degree it is not perceived to stand in the way of these more important issues. And since the "real life" issues are so inextricably tied to perceptions of scarcity and abundance, education itself has meaning largely in the context of its contributions to the "good (economic) life"—Sarason's "salvation." Conversely, to the degree that prosperity, economic well-being, and so on are found wanting, all of education is suspect—Sarason's "scapegoat." If education is primarily a means to the goal of material wellbeing, it is not surprising that equality in education would receive little attention—no one has proven how to make equality pay. Still further, if equality is perceived as operating *against* life's real purposes (abundance) then it is all the easier to lay equality to rest with the claims that

(a) we can't afford it, (b) it's bad for excellence, or (c) we solved the problem in the '60s.

It is in this context that current school reforms must be understood. Energy and resources for education are viewed as scarce. They must be expended judiciously and selectively with an eye toward maximizing economic returns. *Action for Excellence* seeks "more money *selectively invested* in efforts that promote quality" (TFEEG, 1983, p. 36). *Making the Grade* calls for public "report cards" assessing the effectiveness of funded programs (TCF, 1983, p. 18). Selective investment translates into extraordinary attention to preparing students for careers in scientific and technological fields and inattention to the worsening economic plight of the poor. This selectivity results in a reduced willingness to devote educational resources to poor and ethnic minority children. It is on those at the top that economic hopes, and therefore educational resources, are pinned.

It is in this regard that the College Board's report *Academic Preparation for College* (College Board, 1983) is of interest. The report focuses exclusively on the educational needs of the college-bound and is grounded in the view that improving college preparation is the first step toward educational reform. It is striking that a report so focused (and generated by an organization whose self-interest rests in the sale of SAT examinations) has assumed the status of a national report.[4] It symbolizes the current nearly exclusive attention on education for those students who can fulfill the hope for economic supremacy. In the current prevailing view, the provision of special opportunities or extra resources to those perceived as providing limited social and economic returns is a luxury permitted only in times of abundance. For these less promising students, financial stringency prohibits spending anything beyond what is required for preventing social disorganization (dropping out) and providing the minimum levels of competency required for low-level employment.

Still, those at the bottom are seen as benefiting educationally from this current emphasis. A more rigorously academic program at the top will create better programs for all students, it is claimed. Expanded course requirements and numbers of days and hours in school will benefit all—regardless of the differences that may exist inside their schools and classrooms. In this concentration of attention and resources on the best students there is clearly an expression of a "trickle-down" approach to educational excellence that parallels the prevailing mode of providing economic benefits. Emphasis on quality for those at the top will result in an enhanced quality of education for students throughout the system. This mood is made explicit by The College Board:

> *Better preparation for the college-bound will spill over and improve the schooling of those who are not college-bound. . . . Just as the Advanced Placement Program has "rubbed off" on other teaching and learning in the schools, so better college preparation will strengthen the education of those who go directly from high school into the world of work or into the military. (Bailey, 1983, p. 25)*

In all of this, little has really changed. The reform proposals are clearly shaped by the public response to scarcity. But the neglect of equality cannot be entirely explained as a response to the current economic crises. It must be viewed also in light of a neo-conservative reassertion of the turn-of-the-century values and beliefs considered earlier, beliefs that emerge virtually unaltered in the proposals for reform. The current crises have led to the stripping away of added-on programs that for a few years masked, but did not change, the fundamentally unequal structure of schooling.

Like the early 20th-century educational advocates, none of the current reformers state that equality should be sacrificed in the quest for excellence in schools. They even purport to uphold equality. But the view of equality presented—mostly by omission—is one firmly lodged in (a) a presumption of the neutrality of schools, (b) an Anglo-conformist perspective on educational excellence, and (c) faith in objective, quantifiable specifications of educational standards. From these proceeds a narrowly meritocratic allocation of educational opportunities and rewards. All of the above are simply variations on earlier themes—themes laid bare in times of crisis.

The Neutrality of Schools (Social Darwinism Revisited). In their general indictment of schools, the authors of the reform reports do not attach particular importance to the fact that schools fail to serve all students equally well. Consequently, they do not consider as targets for reform the school content and processes that limit school achievement for poor and minority students. Schools are seen as essentially neutral, and the reforms are presented as color-blind and affluence-blind. The failure of disadvantaged children (especially if they have had the additional benefits of remediation, free lunches, or other "compensatory" help) becomes a matter of their own deficiencies—social, economic, educational, or linguistic—and not of the schools' inadequate response to them. Social and economic inequalities are not seen as affecting students' access to high educational expectations or excellent treatment in school. All children are seen as entrants in an equal, fair, and neutral competition.

Current reform efforts do not address the unequal quality of school facilities, programs, materials, counseling, expectations, and instruction. No interest is shown, for example, in the unequal distribution of competent teachers. Neither do they address school organizational changes likely to equalize access to high-quality educational contexts—desegregation, the elimination of tracking, and reconceptualizing vocational education programs, for example. Even as an issue is made emphatically of increasing the skills and knowledge of teachers, the assumption is that teachers simply need to get better at what they've always done. There is little or no mention of the need for teachers to be more knowledgeable about how poverty, racism, and limited expectations affect the educational treatment of poor and minority children. The omission of these concerns makes clear the prevailing conviction that schools, *as they are now,* are neutral places. While many faults are found with schools, unfairness is not one.

Special resources are seen as necessary to provide separate and different schooling for those children with deficits that prevent them from succeeding in the neutral process of schooling. The assumption that poor and minority children are *unable* to learn lurks close to the surface of these recommendations. It certainly lies behind the assertion in *A Nation at Risk* that disadvantaged children (along with other "special needs" children—gifted and learning disabled) constitute a "thin-market area" in education. They are a group of students for whom *regular* instructional approaches are not suited. That these regular approaches themselves might be a source of disadvantage is unthinkable, given the assumption of school neutrality. And given this inattention to the race and class bias of schooling, *A Nation at Risk's* final admonition to students becomes a sad and painful message to the poor and non-white:

> *In the end it is* your *work that determines how much and how well you learn. When you work to your full capacity, you can hope to attain the knowledge and skills that will enable you to create your future and control your destiny. If you do not, you will have your future thrust upon you by others. Take hold of your life, apply your gifts and talents, work with dedication and self-discipline. Have high expectations for yourself and convert every challenge into an opportunity. (NCEE, 1983, pp. 35–36)*

A Single Standard of Excellence (Return to Anglo-Conformity). The elements proposed as the content and processes of excellent schooling are clearly reflective of Anglo-conformist values. Definitions of quality and standards are those that have historically served to discriminate against youngsters who are poor or members of ethnic minorities. There is nothing pluralistic or democratic about the educational content and processes that currently define "excellence." Perhaps *Making the Grade* is most straightforward in this regard. In a major section entitled "The Primacy of English," the report recommends that bilingual programs be replaced with programs "to teach non-English-speaking children how to speak, read, and write English" and calls the failure of bilingual programs to assert the primacy of English "a grave error" (TCF, 1983, p. 12). There is no recognition of the unique contributions of different cultures or of the special problems that arise from a history of discrimination and racism. There is not even a recognition that cultural differences are legitimate and can contribute to a broad general education for all American students.

Provisions of compensatory education are not to be interpreted as provisions for pluralism or, in the words of *Making the Grade,* "abandoning a single standard of excellence. There cannot be a white standard or black standard or a Hispanic standard when measuring educational performance" (TCF, 1983, p. 22). This statement ignores the fact that there is a single standard posed in the reports, and that standard is undeniably white and middle-class.

Listen also to Secretary of Education William Bennett's response to a Latino teacher who had pleaded for a multicultural, multi-ethnic perspective in California

schools. Bennett asserted, "I don't think it's the job of the public schools to introduce you to your grandparents" ("Bennett Says," 1985). Set next to Bennett's call
for a reemphasis on the history and thought of Western Civilization in undergraduate
collegiate education, the point becomes clear. Being introduced to your grandparents is an irrelevant educational matter—unless your grandparents represent the
dominant cultural tradition. The current move in the Department of Education to
dismantle bilingual education is a logical outgrowth of this perspective. Pluralism
is seen as an intolerable shift from current dominance of Anglo values and interests.

At the same time, it is clear that what is valued for students with little academic
promise is a quite different version of Anglo-conformity than that for the best
students. The current system of differentiated curricula through tracking and ability
grouping is clearly meant to be continued. The same subjects, the same "five new
basics" of *A Nation at Risk,* are to be learned by everyone. But whereas the favored
students will be helped to develop an *understanding* of science, mathematics,
technology, and foreign language, a very different and "minimum-competency"
education is envisioned for the rest who will be needed to fill low-status service jobs in
a post industrial economy. The emphasis for disadvantaged students is much as it has
been, an emphasis on low-level basic literacy and computation skills (Oakes, 1985).
There is no presumption that high-status knowledge is equally appropriate for all.

*The Commodification of Educational Opportunity (Scientific Management In-
tensified).* In the current push for productivity, education is increasingly treated as
a commodity, measurable by objective tests. Like the scientific managers early in
the century, current reformers appear to consider notions such as learning, knowledge, and experience to be soft and airy words unless they can be translated into
numbers. Quantification, as expressed in the reports, is used as a quality-control
check against the educational "factory workers" who might otherwise certify as
"safe" high-risk minorities and poor. This emphasis on quantitative measures, in
fact, signals a lack of trust in the responsibility of educators and their professional
judgment (see Sirotnik & Goodlad, 1985). A disturbing result is that quantitative
determinations of quality have a disproportionately negative effect on poor and
minority children (Gould, 1981; Wigdu, 1982). Witness the disproportionate placement of black males in classes for the educable mentally retarded based on standardized ability tests (Heller, Holtzman, & Messick, 1983).

*A Narrowed Meritocracy ("Opportunity . . . as will fit them equally well for
their particular life work").* As a marketable commodity, education is increasingly
subject to the same individualistic, competitive, acquisitive norms as are material
goods (Slaughter, 1985). These norms are all grounded in the presumption of
inequality. And in a period of perceived scarcity, there is likely to be a shift in how
the poor are provided for. In fact, the meager level of concern in the reports for those
on the bottom of the schooling hierarchy clearly indicates "stinginess" in the
distribution of educational goods. It is painfully clear that the least promising
students are expected to do least well. Staying in school, passing an eighth-grade
proficiency test, getting a job, not being a criminal, and staying off welfare become

"success" indicators. No report advocates substantive reforms to keep larger numbers of poor and minority students in schools or improve the quality of what they experience there. The expectations for poor and minority students, in other words, are far lower than in the reform proposals of a more abundant time.

The conception of school as a meritocracy is clearly reflective of the belief that some students can learn and others cannot or will not. In current reforms, promotion, assignment to various programs, graduation, and the kind of diploma received are all to be governed by merit in terms of objective measures of student learning. The fact that retention and low-track placement do not lead to increased student learning is irrelevant (see Larabee, 1984). As part of a meritocratic system, retention and low-track placement serve primarily to deny advancement in the educational system of those *not worthy.* "Student progress should be measured through periodic tests of general achievement and specific skills; promotion from grade to grade should be based on mastery, not age" (TFEE, p. 11).

Separate educations based on meritocratic selection within schools (tracking) or at different schools are recommended in several of the reports for students who do well or poorly on tests. *A Nation at Risk* suggests "placement and grouping . . . should be guided by the academic progress of students" (NCEE, 1983, p. 30) and proposes "alternative classrooms, programs, and schools" for those students who don't conform to expected standards of behavior (p. 29). *Making the Grade* calls for federal stipends to allow those "unable to learn in public schools" to attend "small-scale academies." "Such an experiment . . . would free up the substantial resources now being spent on remediation with so little to show for it" (p. 20).

Little attention is paid to rethinking classroom instruction or school organization in such a way as to promote the achievement of poor children. The only concern raised about the race/class consequences of tracking or testing criteria as standards of excellence is in a footnote of *Making the Grade* (TCF, 1983, p. 20). No concern is evidenced regarding the "dead-end" educational experiences of segregated groups of poor students with curricula aimed at passing minimum competency exams (see Darling-Hammond & Wise, 1985, for a review of this literature). Providing different curricula for different students, as at the turn of the century, is seen as the appropriate way of meeting "individual needs." These are individual needs seen in terms of intellectual limits, not as means of enabling students to develop higher-order knowledge and skills. One commission member contributing to *Making the Grade* asserts, "I believe the mixing in the same class of students with vastly differing abilities in the name of equality has been a retrogressive step" (TCF, 1983, p. 21). Funding for children with special needs—poverty or handicaps—is to be used to support separate programs. No provisions for special access to the best educational programs—such as open admission to enriched programs, cultural criteria for placement in special programs for the gifted and talented, or affirmative action programs—are suggested.

The retreat to this narrowly meritocratic approach to the allocation of school opportunities and rewards is justified in part by the perceived successes of prior equality efforts. Both *A Nation at Risk* and *Action for Excellence* laud the gains in opportunity and achievement over the last 30 years. It is as if past wrongs have been redressed and it is now fair to return to the real purpose of education: excellence.

REFORM AND EQUALITY

Of course, all of the current reform proposals acknowledge educational equity as a national interest. *Educating Americans for the 21st Century,* the report of the National Science Board (NSB, 1983), has equity as a major theme. But little in the current discussion suggests an interest in reaching beyond turn-of-the-century conceptions of social Darwinism and meritocracy to equality in access to knowledge, skills, and educational experiences. Where the reports call for equality as well as excellence, they seem to lack conviction, and they provide no strategies toward this end. As with the emergence in the '80s of economic policies of a much earlier era, the school reforms exhibit a retrenchment into the values of an earlier time. Priorities are set according to prevailing economic interests—which value most highly the kind of human capital development likely to lead to the biggest payoff in the current economic crisis. At the same time, these priorities are also consistent with the interests of the professional elite that dominates educational institutions. It would be a mistake to doubt the sincerity of most educational reformers. It is clearly too crass to suggest that they are setting out deliberately to perpetuate privilege. If overt, villainous intent were the culprit, these problems would be more easily solved. It is harder to engage the well-intended in the critical scrutiny of prevailing assumptions than to oust rascals from positions of influence.

Given the educational "reforms" of the '60s and early '70s (which may have been of considerable benefit to many minority and poor individuals, but did little to change their relative educational or economic position), we may conclude that in times of prosperity a good bit of money may be spent in efforts to create illusions of the fairest possible meritocracy. To the extent that disadvantaged individuals can be helped without jeopardizing the overall structure or control of society, so much the better. (In fact, whatever their motivation, such programs can and do change lives; they deserve a hard fight to retain even if the ground in which they are sown is so infertile as to produce only marginal yields.) In times of scarcity, however, the costs of these "equalizing" programs are deemed intolerable. Recipients of special help are perceived as responsible for the decline of not only their own well-being, but the well-being of the socio-economic class they supposedly aspire to join.

Only three years have passed since the nation's interest turned to educational reform, and it is too early for a full assessment. But reform has become national policy and the themes of the 1983 reports are sounded repeatedly in the statements of both the President and the Secretary of Education. Several states and hundreds of local school districts have rushed to implement reforms, and a number of scholars have assessed their likely effects. And, of course, many of the specific reforms were well underway at the time of the 1983 reports. In many respects the commissions only heralded and reiterated changes conceived in the economic crises and tax revolts of the 1970s.

Time adds conviction to the suspicion that the reforms will work largely to the advantage of those who are already well-off. Through differentiated schooling experiences, attention will be turned from the difficulties of those served less well by schools. Highly motivated, able students will be offered every opportunity to achieve in ways that will strengthen the US quest for technological, economic, and military supremacy. That the distribution of school achievement has racial and socio-economic dimensions is regrettable, but, as a consequence, there is little expectation that poor and minority children will contribute greatly to the national self-interest. While our humane and democratic ideology requires extending educational resources and opportunity to poor and minority children, the most pressing need at present is to cultivate those children with superior abilities, since they are seen as most likely to provide some relief from our national troubles.

All indications are that the current reform movement will produce success defined in its own terms: Children will spend more hours and days in school, more coursework will be taken in mathematics, science, and technology, and mean achievement test scores will probably rise. But beyond indicators of movement toward "excellence" (higher numbers) lies evidence of an ominous side of reform. We can already see a declining college attendance rate for minorities, increased underrepresentation of minorities in postgraduate and professional education, limited access of minority students to computers in schools and to instruction in programming, disproportionately large enrollment of minority students in low-track classes and high enrollment of whites in programs for the gifted, and disproportionately high failure rates on minimum competency tests for minority students.

The lack of evidence of advantages having "trickled down" is not unique to education. While those at the top have declared the recovery to be in full swing, those at the bottom of the economic hierarchy experience a different reality. Today 20 million Americans—two thirds of whom are children—are estimated to be hungry, a dramatic shift from the "virtual elimination" of hunger in the 1970s (Physicians Task Force on Hunger, 1985). In current policies, social justice programs are seen as harmful to economic growth, just as equitable schooling policies are seen as destructive to educational excellence. For tangible benefits in either sphere, children who are poor and nonwhite must continue to wait.

NOTES

1. A Study of Schooling was a comprehensive inquiry into a national sample of schools. Results of the study are reported in Goodlad (1984).

2. As an aside, it should be noted that "scientifically" normed intelligence tests spearheaded the rationale for *all* testing even to the point of schoolwide testing and grade-level testing—even into the classroom. So, much of the "real work" of intelligence testing quickly

passed down to schools and teachers, where poorer performance on tests, "scientific" or otherwise, justified the daily reinforcement of merit.

3. See Kuttner (1984) for a fascinating counter-argument to the negative influence of social justice programs on economic health.

4. It needs to be noted, however, that the College Board's Equality Project, from which the report came, pays far more attention to the provision of both opportunities and improved educational treatment for minority students than do most current proposals. See, for example, the report *Equality and Excellence: The Educational Status of Black Americans* (College Board, 1985).

REFERENCES

Bailey, A.Y. (1983). The educational equality project: Focus on results. *Kappan, 65* (September), 22–25.

Banks, J.R. (Ed.) (1981). *Education in the '80s: Multiethnic education.* Washington, DC: National Education Association.

Bell, D. (1973). *The coming of post-industrial society.* New York: Basic Books.

Bennett says he is "consumer advocate." (1985). *Los Angeles Times,* March 3, p. 1.

Boulding, K.E. (1973). The shadow of a stationary state. *Daedalus, 102,* 93.

Cagan, E. (1978). Individualism, collectivism, and radical educational reform. *Harvard Educational Review, 48,* 227–266.

Cheng, C.W., Brizendine, E., & Oakes, J. (1979). What is an "equal chance" for minority children. *Journal of Negro Education, 48,* 267–287.

College Board. (1983). *Academic preparation for college: What students need to know and be able to do.* New York: College Board.

College Board. (1985). *Equality and excellence: The educational status of black Americans.* New York: College Board.

Commoner, B. (1977). *The poverty of power.* New York: Bantam.

Cremin, L.A. (1964). *The transformation of the school.* New York: Random House.

Darling-Hammond, L., & Wise, A. (1985). Beyond standardization: State standards and school improvement. *Elementary School Journal, 85,* 315–336.

Edson, C.H. (1982). Schooling for work and working at school: Perspectives on immigrant and working-class education in urban America, 1880–1920. In R.B. Everhart (Ed.), *The public school monopoly.* Cambridge, MA: Ballinger.

Goodlad, J.I. (1984). *A place called school.* New York: McGraw-Hill.

Gould, S.J. (1981). *The mismeasure of man.* New York: W.W. Norton.

Grant, C. (Ed.) (1977). *Multicultural education: Commitments, issues, and applications.* Washington, DC: ASCD.

Hall, G.S. (1905). *Adolescence: Its psychology and its relations to physiology, anthropology, sociology, sex, crime, religion, and education.* New York: D. Appleton.

Heilbroner, R.L. (1974). *An inquiry into the human prospect.* New York: W.W. Norton.

Heiler, K., Holtzman, W., & Messick, S. (Eds.) (1983). *Placing children in special education: Strategies for equity.* Washington, DC: National Academy Press.

Kahn, H., Brown, W., & Martel, L. (1976). *The next 200 years: A scenario for America and the world.* New York: Morrow.

Kuttner, R. (1984). *The economic illusion: False choices between prosperity and social justice.* Boston: Houghton Mifflin.

Larabee, D.F. (1984). Setting the standard: Alternative policies for student promotion. *Harvard Educational Review,* 54, 67–87.

Lazerson, M. (1974). *Origins of the urban school.* Cambridge: Harvard University Press.

Lipset, S.M. (1978). Growth, affluence, and the limits of futurology. In *From abundance to scarcity: Implications for the American tradition.* Columbus: Ohio State University Press.

Macrae, N. (1972). The future of international business. *Economist,* 22 (January), 5–7.

NCEE (National Commission on Excellence in Education). (1983). *A nation at risk: The imperative for educational reform.* Washington, DC: Government Printing Office.

NSB (National Science Board Commission on Precollege Education in Mathematics, Science, and Technology). (1983). *Educating Americans for the 21st century.* Washington, DC: National Science Foundation.

Nelson, D. (1980). *Frederick W. Taylor and the rise of scientific management.* Madison: University of Wisconsin Press.

Oakes, J. (1985). *Keeping track: How schools structure inequality.* New Haven: Yale University Press.

Physician's Task Force on Hunger report. (1985). Cambridge, MA: Harvard University Press.

Ryan, W. (1976). *Blaming the victim.* New York: Vintage Books.

Sarason, S.B. (1983). *Schooling in America: Scapegoat and salvation.* New York: The Free Press.

Schumacher, E.F. (1973). *Small is beautiful.* New York: Harper & Row.

Sirotnik, K.A., & Goodlad, J.I. (1985). The quest for reason amidst the rhetoric of reform: Improving instead of testing our schools. In W.J. Johnson (Ed.), *Education on trial: A midterm report.* San Francisco: Institute for Contemporary Studies.

Slaughter, S. (1985). *The pedagogy of profit: National commission reports on education.* Unpublished manuscript, State University of New York, Buffalo.

TCF (Twentieth Century Fund). (1983). *Making the grade: Report of the task force on federal elementary and secondary education policy.* New York: Twentieth Century Fund.

TFEEG (Task Force on Education and Economic Growth). (1983). *Action for excellence.* Washington, DC: Economic Commission of the States.

Wigder, S. (1982). *Ability-testing, uses and consequences.* Washington, DC: National Academy Press.

The Self-Fulfillment of the Self-Fulfilling Prophecy

SAMUEL S. WINEBURG

In the fall of 1948, a 17-page essay appeared in *The Antioch Review* that altered how we speak about social life. It did so by inventing a term to describe a widespread yet poorly understood social phenomenon. The man who coined the term was Robert K. Merton; the term was also the title of his paper, "The Self-Fulfilling Prophecy."

What began as a neologism of theoretical sociology has become common parlance. Sportswriters hurl the self-fulfilling prophecy from their columns; legislators issue it from the rostrums of Congress; and even a president has been known to invoke it, hoping thereby to find a verbal tonic for an ailing economy (Richard Nixon, 1971, quoted in Merton, 1981). Thousands of scholarly papers employing the term have appeared in sociology, social psychology, economics, political science, anthropology, public administration, and social work. But the self-fulfilling prophecy has wielded greatest influence—and doubtless stirred the most controversy—in education.

In its original form, the self-fulfilling prophecy scarcely seemed controversial. The notion that a false but widely-believed prediction could become true simply because enough people believed in it was neither new nor original. Merton, in fact, saw the term as convenient shorthand for W. I. Thomas's famous dictum that "if men define situations as real, they are real in their consequences." But the idea predated Thomas, finding roots in Bishop Bossuet's defense of Catholic orthodoxy in the 17th century; in Marx's critique of the Hegelian dialectics of change; and in Freud's work in places too numerous to count.

The self-fulfilling prophecy was a uniquely social idea with no corollary in the physical or natural sciences. Predictions of earthquakes may set Californians on edge, but words do not make the ground tremble. But in the social sphere, self-ful-

From *Educational Researcher*, 16:28–37, 1987. Copyright 1987 by the American Educational Research Association. Reprinted by permission of the publisher.

filling prophecies abounded. So, for example, rumors about the insolvency of banks, when widely believed and acted upon, brought doom to otherwise flourishing financial institutions. Although the term "self-fulfilling prophecy" was new, the idea was not, and Merton wove it into his text with no claim of originality. Indeed, he abjured pretenses of innovation: "So common is the pattern of the self-fulfilling prophecy that each of us has his favored specimen" (p. 195).

The self-fulfilling prophecy begins, according to Merton, with the false definition of a situation, which in turn engenders behavior that brings the situation into conformity with the definition. "The Negro is a strikebreaker and a traitor to the working class," claimed union officials in barring blacks from labor unions prior to World War II. Hungry and out-of-work, thousands of blacks couldn't resist the invitation by strike-bound employers to take jobs otherwise closed to them. Did blacks become scabs because of their "inability to participate in collective bargaining," or because, excluded from union membership, they had no choice but to accept what was offered? For Merton, the final arbiter in cases of the self-fulfilling prophecy was *time:*

> *History creates its own test of the theory of self-fulfilling prophecies. That Negroes were strikebreakers because they were excluded from unions (and from a large range of jobs) rather than excluded because they were strikebreakers can be seen from the virtual disappearance of Negroes as scabs in industries where they have gained admission to unions in the last decades. (p. 197)*

Quoting de Tocqueville, Merton asserted that self-fulfilling prophecies were rooted in a social structure created by humans and thus open to change by them: "What we call necessary institutions are often no more than institutions to which we have grown accustomed" (p. 210).

THE SELF-FULFILLING PROPHECY, DESEGREGATION, AND TEACHERS' EXPECTATIONS

America on the eve of the 20th century was a land that had grown accustomed to its social institutions, especially its system of separate schools for children of different colors. But by this century's midpoint much had changed, and claims that the "necessary institutions" of separate schools were no more than "mere customs"—and inhumane customs at that—were heard with greater frequency. Separating children on the basis of skin color, claimed critics, flouted the ideals of a democratic society. This was not all. Segregation's effects extended beyond institutional spheres—more was at stake than inequality of *social* opportunity. Segregation, according to these claims, caused *psychological* damage to its victims, engendering maladaptive internal states that left the personality scarred. These were new and serious charges, and their documentation became a social priority. Society looked to the universities for evidence, and the universities looked to the social sciences.

The research program of Kenneth B. Clark stands out above the rest. In Clark's work (e.g., Clark, 1955/1963; Clark & Clark, 1939) black youngsters between the ages of 3 and 7 were presented with two dolls, one black and one white, and asked by an adult experimenter which doll they wanted to play with. At each age level, the majority of children rejected the black doll. Sometimes youngsters showed extreme reactions, as did one little girl who, after choosing the white doll, called the black one "ugly" and "dirty." This girl sobbed uncontrollably when the researcher asked her to identify herself with one of the two dolls. Clark, a black social psychologist then at the City College of New York, summarized the implications of such an episode:

> As minority-group children learn the inferior status to which they are assigned and observe that they are usually segregated and isolated from the more privileged members of their society, they react with deep feelings of inferiority and with a sense of personal humiliation. . . . Like all other human beings, they require a sense of personal dignity and social support for positive self-esteem. . . . Under these conditions, minority-group children develop conflicts with regard to their feelings about themselves and about the values of the group with which they are identified. (1955/1963, p. 63)

Not fleeting or easily healed, this feeling of inferiority was "enduring or lasting as the situation endured, changing only in its form and in the way it manifested itself" (*Brown v. Board of Education*, 1954, pp. 89–90). Taught by society to be inferior, black children learned to feel and act inferior. Aided by the mechanism of the self-fulfilling prophecy, the effects of racism moved from "out there" in society to inside people's heads, and became, in Clark's terms, "embedded in the personality" (1955/1963, p. 50).

In his role as social science consultant to the NAACP in *Brown v. Board of Education* (1954), Clark was as instrumental as any other social scientist in swaying the court to dismantle this country's system of separate schools. But as many of the promised benefits of desegregation failed to materialize (cf. Cohen & Weiss, 1977; Gerard, 1983; St. John, 1975; Weinberg, 1975), the task of solving the problems of disadvantaged youth came to be seen as one that required more than mixing children of different colors in the same school. According to one explanation, it was not ghetto youth but their teachers who were the problem, and the self-fulfilling prophecy, as an explanation for differential achievement between white and black students, came to be used with ever greater frequency. Simply changing the social organization of schools would have little effect on the achievement of minority students unless a concomitant change occurred in the minds of their teachers. Therefore, because of the "importance of the role of teachers in the developing self-image, academic aspirations and achievements of their students," Kenneth Clark (1963, p. 148) began a study of teacher attitudes in ten inner-city schools.

In a report describing this research (Clark, 1963), the term "self-fulfilling prophecy" first appeared in the educational literature. Foreshadowing controversies that would rage a few years later, the term appeared in the context of a discussion of IQ tests. The argument was straightforward. Because teachers thought minority children were dumb, they didn't waste their time on them, and teachers' expectations were later borne out by students' low test scores. Clark wrote:

> *If a child scores low on an intelligence test because he cannot read and then is not taught to read because he has a low score, then such a child is being imprisoned in an iron circle and becomes the victim of an* educational self-fulfilling prophecy *[italics added]. (p. 150)*

By the late 1950s and early 1960s, this view struck a responsive chord among educational researchers and practitioners. Clark's ideas about educational self-fulfilling prophecies filtered down to schoolpeople and became part of in-service training programs. In 1957, superintendents and school board members of 14 of the largest school districts in the country convened in Atlantic City to discuss the problems of urban schools. Emerging from the deliberations of the "Great Cities School Improvement Project" was a master plan for improving schools, the first plank of which called for the "development of a program of education adapted to the needs of these children" (Marburger, 1963, p. 302).

Carl Marburger, director of Detroit's Great Cities project, outlined how his city responded to the first plank of the master plan: "One major approach is our work with teachers. Improvement of schooling depends to a great extent upon more effective teaching" (Marburger, 1963, p. 303). But effective teaching in the early 1960s meant something much different from what that term means today. At issue was not how teachers made transitions from one part of the lesson to another (Anderson, Evertson, & Brophy, 1979), or how they reviewed math homework at the beginning of each lesson (Good & Grouws, 1979). The spotlight again sought the inner recesses of the mind: "At this point . . . we conceive the formula that teacher expectations have surprising impact on pupil achievement. Indeed we might even say that teacher expectations have a similar impact on pupil intelligence scores" (Marburger, 1963, p. 306).

These were bold claims, and in making them, Marburger ignored the traditional distinction between intelligence and achievement, a tenet of educational psychology since the days of E.L. Thorndike. Achievement was customarily seen as a reflection of school learning, malleable and open to training (Franzen, 1920; Gregory, 1922). Intelligence, on the other hand, was thought partially innate and partially fixed by environmental factors during the earliest years of life. Thus, one could grant the possibility that teachers' expectations affected student achievement, because expectations guided what teachers chose to teach and consequently what students learned. But the claim that *intelligence* could be raised or lowered by teacher expectations contradicted a long-standing research tradition that had shown IQ to be a relatively stable construct after the early years of childhood.

Lacking empirical data to array before the participants at a conference on "Education in Depressed Areas" at Columbia University in 1962, Marburger did the next best thing. He borrowed data and argued by analogy. Citing an unpublished manuscript by a professor of psychology at the University of North Dakota, Marburger described an experiment that showed that when psychology students thought their albino rats were either "maze-bright" or "maze-dull," the rats, after a week of maze-running, fulfilled their experimenters' expectations. The designer of this experiment was unfamiliar to most schoolpeople. But five years later there would scarcely be an educator who did not recognize the name of Robert Rosenthal.

A FINDING IN SEARCH OF DATA

By the mid-1960s, the notion that teachers' expectations for minority students caused them to do poorly in school was well-established in people's minds. But one problem remained. If children who did poorly in school were expected by their teachers to do poorly, it could always be argued that expectations were based, not on self-fulfilling prophecies, but on students' past performance. Thus viewed, the educational self-fulfilling prophecy became a chicken or egg problem, something to be puzzled over endlessly but never known with certainty. That is, unless this alternative hypothesis could be ruled out.

Robert Rosenthal, by the early 1960s, had moved from the University of North Dakota to Harvard. Rosenthal (1966) had earned a reputation for a series of ingenious experiments that demonstrated how researchers influenced the results of their seemingly dispassionate investigations. By 1963, Rosenthal had already begun to wonder if the expectancy effects he discovered with psychology students and albino rats (Rosenthal & Fode, 1963) might not also operate with doctors and their patients, psychotherapists and their clients, bosses and their employees, and teachers and their students. As Rosenthal (1985), in a retrospective essay on the course of his research program, put it, "If rats became brighter when expected to then it should not be farfetched to think that children could become brighter when expected to by their teachers" (p. 44).

Rosenthal's idea to test the self-fulfilling prophecy in a school, rather than in a hospital, a factory, or a mental health clinic, was not wedded, it seems, to any deep educational interest. Among the requests he received for a copy of an article on experimenter effects was one from Lenore Jacobson, an elementary school principal in South San Francisco. Rosenthal sent her the article along with a stack of unpublished papers and "thought no more about it" (Rosenthal, 1985, p. 44). But Lenore

Jacobson did. She dashed off a second note to the Harvard psychologist and in it presented a challenge. "If you ever 'graduate' to classroom children," she wrote, "please let me know whether I can be of assistance" (p. 44). From this challenge *Pygmalion in the Classroom* was born.

Rosenthal and Jacobson's experiment was unabashedly simple, elegant, and arch. Their research site was the "Oak School," located in a low-income South San Francisco neighborhood, and, in order for the experiment to work, the researchers had to violate the good faith of teachers. First, children in this elementary school were administered a little-known IQ test. Rosenthal described the procedure: "We had special covers printed for the test; they bore the high-sounding title 'Test of Inflected Acquisition.' The teachers were told that the testing was part of an undertaking being carried out by investigators from Harvard University" (Rosenthal & Jacobson, 1968c, p. 21). An information sheet given to the teachers explained that the "Harvard Test of Inflected Acquisition" could identify children who could be expected to "bloom," or experience an intellectual growth spurt, during the ensuing academic year. The test was actually Flanagan's Test of General Ability (TOGA), a group administered IQ test. The bloomers had been chosen by means of a table of random numbers.

The subject of the "bloomers" was brought up casually at a faculty meeting during which each teacher was given a list of about 2–7 bloomers in each classroom as identified by the "Harvard Test of Inflected Acquisition." Four months later, and again at the end of the school year, the test was readministered. The findings of the study, as reported in the full-length book about it, were striking. "We find increasing expectancy advantage as we go from the sixth to the first grade; the correlation between grade level and magnitude of expectancy advantage ($r = -.86$) was significant at the .03 level" (1968a, p. 74).[1] Elsewhere, Rosenthal and Jacobson wrote, "The results indicated strongly that children from whom teachers expected greater intellectual gains showed such gains" (1968c, p. 22).

The finding of "an increasing expectancy advantage as we go from the sixth grade to the first grade" seemed to mean two things: First, that the treatment conferred an "advantage" upon the children who received it (the bloomers) and, second, that there was some kind of progression in the data, with the magnitude of effect decreasing linearly as children became older. But did the data support this claim? Not exactly. Table 7.1 (1968a, p. 75) showed statistically significant results (or "expectancy advantages") only for children in the first and second grades. In the other four grades, the treatment either conferred a statistically nonsignificant advantage (4th grade), no difference at all (3rd grade), or a statistically nonsignificant *disadvantage* (5th and 6th grades). In other words, the null hypothesis could not be ruled out in 66% of the grade levels.

Odd, then, were statements like "when teachers expected that certain children would show greater intellectual development, those children did show greater intellectual development" (Rosenthal & Jacobson, 1968a, p. 82). The lack of qualifications in the assertions was even more striking in light of the mixed results of a replication experiment in two Midwestern schools by Evans and Rosenthal (1969). Described in a footnote on Page 96 of *Pygmalion,* the results of this study showed that in these two schools, control-group girls gained about 15 points on the reasoning subscale of the IQ test, whereas the treatment-group girls gained just over 5 points, a statistically significant advantage in favor of the control-group girls.

Rosenthal and Jacobson's assertions about the effects of expectations on IQ did not go unnoticed by the research community. Scholarly reviews of the book appeared in the American Psychological Association's review journal, *Contemporary Psychology,* and in AERA's main publication, *American Educational Research Journal.* Neither took kindly to *Pygmalion.*

Writing in *Contemporary Psychology,* Richard Snow, a differential psychologist at Stanford University, pointed out that TOGA was inadequately normed for children in the youngest grades. In one classroom, a group of 19 normal children had a mean IQ score of 31 on the reasoning subscale of the test (Rosenthal & Jacobson, 1968a, p. 189). Like most IQ tests, TOGA was normed to have a mean of 100. Thus, the 19 children in the "C" track of the first grade were hardly the type of children one would expect at this run-of-the-mill school. Snow asked pointedly, "Were these children actually functioning at imbecile and low moron levels?" "More likely," he hypothesized, "the test was not functioning at this grade level . . . to obtain IQ scores as low as these, given reasonably distributed ages, raw scores would have to represent random or systematically incorrect responding" (Snow, 1969, p. 198). In other words, even if some students marked their tests at random the raw scores would have been higher than those obtained. In order to score so low, some students must have refused to put pen to paper. Snow criticized other features of the book, such as the fact that additional mental ability information (readily available at the school) was not used in the analysis, the reliance on simple gain scores "even though many mean pretest differences between treatment groups equal or exceed obtained posttest differences" (p. 198), and the use of "microscopic scales to overemphasize practically insignificant differences" (p. 199). Snow concluded: "*Pygmalion,* inadequately and prematurely reported . . . has performed a disservice to teachers and schools, to users and developers of mental tests, and perhaps worst of all, to parents and children whose newly gained expectations may not prove quite so self-fulfilling" (p. 198).

Robert Thorndike, an expert in educational and psychological testing at Columbia University and the coauthor of a widely used IQ test, was no kinder to *Pygmalion.* Like Snow's criticisms, Thorndike's had less to do with the theory behind the study or even with the design employed, than with an IQ test that produced uneven and wildly unpredictable results. Thorndike (1968) questioned the validity of a measure that would yield a mean of 150.17 among the six bloomers in class 2A, an extraordinarily high score that could only be obtained if most students received a perfect score on the subtest. But because the standard deviation for these six scores was 40 points, Thorndike wondered about the students who fell above the mean.

Pygmalion, he wrote, "is so defective technically that one can only regret that it ever got beyond the eyes of the original investigators!" (p. 708).

Not only did *Pygmalion* get past the eyes of the original investigators but, even before the book hit the streets, headlines about it splashed over the front page of the August 14, 1967 *New York Times* (Leo, 1967). (Details of the experiment's failure to replicate, however, received a scant column inch in the continuation of the story on page 20.) Robert Rosenthal appeared on national television telling the Today Show's Barbara Walters that "teachers shouldn't be allowed to teach students who they know won't learn" (NBC, May 28, 1969). And reviews of *Pygmalion* in the media hailed it as a major contribution to understanding the problems of disadvantaged students.

Robert Coles, a Harvard psychiatrist, writing in the *New Yorker* (Coles, 1969), declared that *Pygmalion's* lesson was clear: "All sorts of young children did very much better in school than others like them, presumably because their teachers *expected* them to become 'bloomers,' and TOGA's putative prophecy was fulfilled so conclusively that even hard-line social scientists were startled" (p. 174). Who were these "startled" social scientists, and in what forum did they shake their heads in wonderment? Coles did not say, but it was certainly not at the 1966 American Psychological Association symposium in which Rosenthal presented the study and listened to his discussant, N. L. Gage, a Stanford University expert on teaching methods, criticize it roundly (Gage, 1966). Equally reticent was Coles on the fact that in four of six grade levels there were no statistically significant differences between the bloomers and the regular pupils; nor did he have anything to say about the failure of the experiment to replicate. Although these points eluded Coles's analysis, the opportunity to point his finger at the real culprits in the American educational system did not: "The prejudices of teachers—and the effects the prejudices have on learning—come across on almost every page of this book" (p. 175).

The reports of *Pygmalion* in the press showed how the study came to stand for whatever people wanted it to, regardless of the original research questions asked by Rosenthal and Jacobson. *Pygmalion* tested the hypothesis that teachers who believe their students are due for an intellectual growth spurt will, in fact, score higher on an IQ test than a group of comparable students for whom no expectations are held. But an article in *Time* reported that "a new book called *Pygmalion in the Classroom*" demonstrated that "many children *fail to learn* simply because their teachers do not expect them to" (September 20, 1968, p. 62, emphasis added). Not only was such an effect not documented, it was never even addressed in Rosenthal and Jacobson's study. *Time* went on to claim that the findings of *Pygmalion* "raise some fundamental questions about teacher training" and "cast doubt on the wisdom of assigning children to classes according to presumed ability" (p. 62).

One might think that only writers in the popular press would leap so quickly from the findings of a field-experiment to questions of reforming teacher education and the organization of schooling. But the idea that *Pygmalion* had direct implications for teacher training, compensatory education, and the ways in which this nation dealt with its poorest students was not the media's invention. Rosenthal and Jacobson themselves set the stage by forging links between *Pygmalion's* findings and questions about how to train our teachers and run our schools.

Writing in the *Scientific American* (1968c), they questioned the wisdom of federal programs that had been trying to come up with ways to overcome the educational handicaps of disadvantaged children. They argued that such programs rested on the assumption that disadvantaged children possessed some problem, or deficit, that must be remedied. Rosenthal and Jacobson asserted that such thinking was, at best, misguided:

> *Our experiment rested on the premise that at least some of the deficien-cies—and therefore at least some of the remedies—might be in the schools, and particularly in the attitudes of teachers toward disadvantaged chil-dren. In our experiment nothing was done directly for the child. There was no crash program to improve his reading ability, no extra time for tutoring, no program of trips to museums and art galleries. The only people affected directly were the teachers. (p. 23)*

What conclusions were readers to draw from such statements? That compensa-tory education had been a waste? That changing teachers' expectancies might prove more cost-effective than programs sponsored under the Elementary and Secondary Education Act? "More attention in educational research should be focused on the teacher," the authors continued. And once researchers learned how the Oak School teachers were able to accomplish what they did, training packages could be de-signed so that "other teachers could be taught to do the same." This might even lead to the development of psychological instruments for earmarking teachers who could produce similar effects and weeding out those unable to do so. *Pygmalion* would thus play a role in the "sophisticated selection of teachers" (p. 23). Given enough time, it seemed, *Pygmalion's* findings would revolutionize American education.

PYGMALION'S FOLLOWERS

The scholarly community witnessed the next major event in the history of the educational self-fulfilling prophecy when, in 1970, the *Harvard Educational Re-view* published an article by Ray Rist, a sociologist then at Washington University. The essay was entitled, "Student social class and teacher expectations: The self-ful-filling prophecy in ghetto education." Running to 40 pages, Rist's work received more space in Volume 40 of *HER* than any other article that year, save for a study by Marshall Smith and Joan Bissell on the impact of Head Start. By 1970, the self-fulfilling prophecy had lost all vestiges of technical terminology, and Rist wove it into the early pages of his article with no citation.[2] Shedding quotation marks, the self-fulfilling prophecy had emerged as the common coin of educational discourse.

Rist studied a cohort of black children in an urban school from their entry into kindergarten until the beginning of second grade. Much of the article detailed the day-to-day activities in the kindergarten classroom of Mrs. Caplow, a black woman who, on the eighth day of the school year, assigned her kindergartners to three reading groups and sat them at different tables. Rist noticed a systematic pattern in the groupings. At table 1, closest to Mrs. Caplow, sat children with clean clothes, "processed" hair, and fluency in standard English. At the other two tables, and especially at table 3, the children came to class unwashed, smelling of "body odor" (p. 419), had "unprocessed" hair, and responded to the teacher's questions in black dialect. Rist described this seating arrangement, which endured in classroom groupings throughout the study, in no uncertain terms: "The group perceived as slow learners were ascribed a caste position that sought to keep them apart from the other students" (p. 444).

Mrs. Caplow's classroom organization became internalized by the youngsters, and soon they began to enact their status differences among themselves. Rist's field notes offer: "The children are rehearsing a play, Little Red Riding Hood. Pamela [table 1] tells the observer, 'The teacher gave me the best part.' The teacher overheard this comment, smiled, and made no verbal response." On another occasion, Betty, poorly dressed, left class, and hid behind a door. In an authoritarian voice, Mrs. Caplow commanded her to return. Again, Rist's field notes observe: "When the child returns, Mrs. Caplow seizes her by the right arm, brings her over to the group, and pushes her down to the floor. Betty begins to cry" (p. 428).

The self-fulfilling prophecy was "in its final stages" by May of the school year (p. 425), catapulting some kindergartners to success while sentencing others to failure. In Rist's analysis, Mrs. Caplow was not a good-hearted, if ill-informed, black woman trying to do her best given the conditions of the urban school, but a woman who taught her students that "it was acceptable to act in an aggressive manner towards those from low-income and poorly educated backgrounds" (p. 430). Like other teachers in the school, Mrs. Caplow served as an "agent of the larger society," who vigilantly monitored the social interactions among her students "to ensure that proper 'social distance' was maintained between the various strata of the society as represented by the children" (p. 444). Not background experience, nutrition, parental involvement, or even the impoverished home and community environments of children at table 3 accounted for their lower school performance. The expectations of Mrs. Caplow and her colleagues doomed these children.[3]

By the final pages of Rist's analysis, Mrs. Caplow as person faded into Mrs. Caplow as symbol. Notions that schools created opportunity were naive. Schools existed not to mitigate the effects of poverty but to reconfirm them, to shackle society's least able with "ascribed labels" that took on, through the mechanism of the self-fulfilling prophecy, "objective dimensions" (p. 431). Far from being a mirror of social inequity, the school "strongly shares in the complicity of maintaining the organizational perpetuation of poverty and unequal opportunity" (p. 447). In sum, Rist limned a portrait of schools that had gained wider and wider credence since the 1950s: Behind the failure of minority children lurked the bigotry of teachers.

PYGMALION IN THE COURTS

To policy makers, legislators, and jurists, the findings of social science constitute a well-stocked arsenal. It was only a matter of time before the self-fulfilling prophecy was being hurled back and forth in legal salvos over educational equity, desegregation, ability tracking, testing, and busing. When social science findings become embroiled in the adversarial system of the courts—a system that educates judges by persuading them—strange things happen. Two cases shed light on this process.

The public school system in the District of Columbia was on trial in *Hobson v. Hansen.* Issuing his opinion in June 1967, Judge J. Skelly Wright ordered Carl Hansen, D.C.'s Superintendent of Schools, to eliminate district "optional school zones" (which had allowed white students to cross neighborhood lines to attend predominantly white schools) and mandated busing to desegregate the schools. Further, Judge Wright ordered Hansen to dismantle ability tracks because of bias in the selection process. Throughout the five months of the trial, Judge Wright listened to pages of testimony from both sides' expert witnesses, with each side claiming a monopoly on scientific truth. At one point, Judge Wright remarked, "The unfortunate if inevitable tendency has been to lose sight of the disadvantaged young students . . . in an overgrown garden of numbers and charts and jargon like 'standard deviation of the variable' . . . 'statistical significance' and 'Pearson product-moment correlations' " (quoted in Wolf, 1981, p. 265). Growing weary of arcane statistical analyses, Judge Wright found himself relying on a tried-and-true source of knowledge. The court, he wrote, "has been forced back to its own common sense" (quoted in Cohen & Weiss, 1977, p. 96).

Common sense goes hand in hand with the zeitgeist; today's common sense—like the right of women to vote and hold public office—is often yesterday's nonsense (cf. Geertz, 1983). Despite Judge Wright's reservations about the tangles of social science research, the idea of the educational self-fulfilling prophecy not only made sense but had the warrant of science behind it. A portion from his decision read:

> *Studies have found that a teacher will commonly tend to underestimate the abilities of disadvantaged children and will treat them accordingly—in the daily classroom routine, in grading, and in evaluating these students' likelihood of achieving in the future. The horrible consequence of a teacher's low expectation is that it tends to be a self-fulfilling prophecy. The unfortunate students, treated as if they were subnormal, come to accept as a fact that they are subnormal. (* Hobson v. Hansen, *p. 484)*

To substantiate these claims, Judge Wright cited two studies: one by Clark (1963), which presented no data directly bearing on the self-fulfilling prophecy, and an edited chapter on the *Pygmalion* study (Rosenthal & Jacobson, 1968b). But unbeknownst to him, *Pygmalion* dealt with the overestimation, not underestimation, of children's abilities. Moreover, it presented no observational data of teachers and students, so there was no information on how teachers "treated" students. Further, no interviews were conducted with students to see whether they accepted their "subnormal" status. Although all of the points raised by Judge Wright may in fact be true, *Pygmalion* did not provide the evidence.

The educational self-fulfilling prophecy also played a significant role in *Bradley v. Milliken* (1971), a suit charging the Detroit Public School System with *de jure* segregation. The trial was not yet a day old when a former school board member testified that the gap in performance between black and white students could be explained by the fact that teachers "didn't have the expectations for the students that would be necessary if you were expecting the student to perform at his best" (quoted by Wolf, 1981, p. 112). The testimony of the plaintiff's expert witness on education, Dr. Robert Green, set in bold relief what can happen when social science research is used in the courts. The following excerpt is drawn from that testimony:

Q: Can you describe the experiment? I believe it was done in California, was it not, with elementary children?

Green: In a nutshell, what Rosenthal did was to allow teachers to begin to believe that one group of youngsters in the classroom [was] bright, and another in a classroom or, say, in a school, [was] not quite as bright, when, in fact, the data indicated there was very little difference between the youngsters in terms of socio-economic status and past educational achievement. With this kind of background information, it was found that teachers who were given youngsters who were alleged to be not quite as bright, the youngsters' ability was quite different than those who were alleged to be brighter, which was reflected by actual achievement of the youngsters.

Q: In other words, if the teacher was told these children were bright children, they tended to perform in that fashion?

Green: Yes. . . . Teachers were also told in this particular study that those youngsters categorized as being bright, that in mid-year . . . there would be a spurt upwards in terms of academic achievement. This did, in fact, occur with the bright youngsters, not with those . . . described as being dull. In terms of systematically observing the behavior of teachers, it was discovered that at mid-year . . . the teachers with the so-called bright youngsters spent more time with the class and presented them with more information, more educational data, and they did, in fact, cause the spurt. (quoted in Wolf, 1981, p. 112–113)

This testimony was entered into the court record without note of the inaccuracies it contained. In *Pygmalion,* teacher expectations were created only for bloomers; other students (the control group) were regarded as normal, not "less bright" and never "dull." Moreover, *Pygmalion* presented no systematic data about the socio-economic status of individuals, and there was actually a 4-point difference on the pretest in favor of the 1st- and 2nd-grade bloomers (a seemingly minor point that looms large when one remembers that these were the grade levels in which an effect was found).[4] Not only was there no "systematic" observation of teachers in *Pygmalion,* there was no observation. This fact made it impossible to know if teachers "spent more time" with the bloomers, "presented them with more information," or taught them "more educational data." Beliefs about *Pygmalion* had become nearly as important as its actual findings, and separating fact from fancy would prove to be no easy task.[5]

PYGMALION RECONSIDERED IN EDUCATIONAL RESEARCH

Pygmalion's influence on educational research is nothing short of remarkable— since the original study there have been, by one estimate (Meyer, 1985), between 300 and 400 published reports related to the educational self-fulfilling prophecy (for reviews see Brophy, 1983; Brophy & Good, 1974; Cooper & Good, 1983; Dusek, 1975, 1985). A research tradition that began by inducing teachers to form false expectations based on experimental manipulation quickly progressed to the study of expectations as they naturally occurred in ordinary classrooms. In the course of this work, researchers built and refined elaborate models for the communication of expectations (Brophy & Good, 1974; Cooper, 1979; Cooper & Good, 1983; West & Anderson, 1976) and developed finely-tuned observation systems for analyzing complex classroom interactions (Brophy & Good, 1970b).

Brophy and Good (1970a) were among the first to study naturally occurring expectations. They asked four 1st-grade teachers to rank their students in order of expected achievement and then observed high- and low-expectation students in their respective classrooms. Interesting patterns emerged. High-expectation students volunteered more answers, initiated more contacts with their teachers, raised their hands more often, and had fewer reading problems than their low expectation peers, findings which led Brophy and Good to the realization that many "teacher expectation effects" are best understood as student effects on teachers. But other findings were less easy to explain this way. For instance, when low-expectation students gave wrong answers they were less likely to receive specific feedback, and when they gave right answers they were less likely to receive praise. Although all four teachers in this study displayed relatively similar behavior patterns, a follow-up study (Evertson, Brophy, & Good, 1972, cited in Brophy & Good, 1974) yielded less uniform results. Here, only three of nine teachers resembled those in the first study; three others displayed few differences in their interactions with high- and low-expectation students; and the final three showed the opposite pattern from the first—often seeking out lows for extra help and giving them more of a chance to get the right answer. These early studies set the tone for much of the research that followed—expectations in the classroom were phenomena far more complex and multi-dimensional than most had imagined (Dusek, 1985).

As research on teacher expectancies began to accumulate, teachers looked less like the villains portrayed in the earlier studies. True, some teachers ignored information from students and hewed to rigid expectations, distributing turns unfairly in reading groups (Allington, 1980), criticizing some students more harshly than others (Brophy & Good, 1970b; Good, Sikes, & Brophy, 1973), and smiling at some while reacting coolly toward others (Babad, Inbar, & Rosenthal, 1982). Every profession includes those who do it a disservice, and teaching is no exception. But for the most part, teachers' expectations proved to be based on the best evidence in their possession (Borko, Cone, Russo, & Shavelson, 1979; Shavelson, Cadwell, & Izu, 1977), and most teachers were willing to abandon initial expectations when more dependable evidence became available. Indeed, a recent study suggests that those *least* acquainted with classroom life are often most influenced by the background information they receive about students (Carter, Sabers, Cushing, Pinnegar, & Berliner, 1987). Experienced teachers tend to disregard such information, preferring to form judgments based on their own firsthand experience with students. Summarizing much research over the years on educational self-fulfilling prophecies, Brophy (1983) concluded:

> *Although there are relationships between teacher expectations, teacher-student interaction, and student achievement, most of these are more accurately construed as student effects on teachers rather than as teacher expectation effects on students. Most differential teacher expectations are accurate and reality-based, and most differential teacher interaction with students represents either appropriate, proactive response to differential student need, or at least understandable reactive response to differential student behavior . . . although the potential for teachers' expectations to function as self-fulfilling prophecies always exists, the extent to which they actually do so in typical classrooms is probably limited . . . (p. 634)*

One might assume that somewhere amidst all of these subsequent studies lay the vindication of *Pygmalion,* proving once and for all that teacher expectations boost (or lower) students' IQs. If one were to rely on Rosenthal's reading of the literature, it would seem this way. Indeed, he has claimed that in the process of examining the results of 345 studies of the interpersonal self-fulfilling prophecy "some clear conclusions have emerged. The reality of the phenomenon is beyond doubt" (Rosenthal & Rubin, 1978, p. 385). To arrive at this conclusion, Rosenthal and Rubin combined studies of the self-fulfilling prophecy in areas as diverse as animal learning, ink-blot reading, reaction times, interpersonal interviews, and classroom learning.

Within education, the issue had never been whether teachers form expectancies or whether these expectancies affect students in sundry subtle and not-so-subtle ways. Acknowledging as much in his preface to Elashoff and Snow's book-length reanalysis of the *Pygmalion* data, Gage (1971) noted that previous research had not only provided support for the existence of teacher expectancies but that expectancies influenced what "teachers try to teach and thus what students learn, how students feel about themselves, how they get along with the teacher and their fellow students" (p. 5). But regarding the dispute that has come to be known as the "*Pygmalion* controversy" such questions missed the point.

Obscured and long forgotten, the heart of the *Pygmalion* controversy was the bold claim that *intelligence* was affected by teacher expectations. It was this claim that was heralded by the media and influenced the Los Angeles School Board to ban IQ testing in the elementary grades (cf. McCurdy, 1969). But years of replications and follow-up studies have shown that strong claims about the relationship between expectations and intelligence were unwarranted. For example, Rosenthal and his associates tried several times to replicate the expectation-IQ linkage they reported in *Pygmalion.* Evans and Rosenthal (1969) found no significant differences in total IQ after a year between the treatment and control groups. A study by Conn, Edwards, Rosenthal, and Crowne (1968) yielded no statistically significant differences between the treatment and control groups in total IQ after 4 months (though there was a 1.46 point gain score advantage to the bloomers). After 3 semesters the effect faded in total IQ, with slight nonsignificant differences favoring the control groups. In another study, Anderson and Rosenthal (1968) manipulated the expectations of counselors at a day camp for retarded boys and administered an IQ test at the beginning and end of the eight-week experimental period. The only significant IQ change was a decrease on the reasoning subscale for the boys who were expected to bloom, a finding that clearly ran contrary to predicted results. In a meta-analysis based on 18 studies, Raudenbush (1984) found a small mean effect size in IQ-expectation studies ($\Delta = .11$), a finding that either achieved or failed to achieve statistical significance depending on the test employed. In Smith's (1980) meta-analysis, sizeable effects were found for teacher expectancies on student achievement, class participation, and social competence. But a meta-analysis of 22 teacher expectancy/IQ studies showed that the "effect of teacher expectations on pupil IQ was quite low. . . . Pupil intellectual ability is minimally affected by the labelling information about this intellectual potential" (p. 54).

Yet such evidence often does little to dislodge beliefs about the expectation/intelligence linkage. Thus, when *Pygmalion's* critics (e.g., Snow, 1986) try to refute claims that the self-fulfilling prophecy is responsible for enduring intellectual gains (Jones, 1986), their letters to the editor are rejected for "lack of space." Perhaps this response is understandable given the almost mythic proportions *Pygmalion* has assumed in some college textbooks. When material from the study appeared in a chapter on "Prejudice and Discrimination" in Kenneth and Mary Gergen's *Social Psychology* (1981), the data for grades 3, 4, 5, and 6 (the grade levels in which there were no significant effects) mysteriously vanished, leaving a chart containing only the *positive* effects for grades 1 and 2. It seems that, in Pygmalion's old age, she doesn't develop wrinkles—but loses them.

PYGMALION AS A CULTURAL IDEAL

Most new ideas in education have a pitifully short half-life, but occasionally an idea captures the popular imagination and takes hold. In one form or another, the self-fulfilling prophecy had been in the educational literature since the late 1950s, but it wasn't until *Pygmalion in the Classroom* that its popularity soared. Why?

Pygmalion represented not merely an idea, but an *ethos,* a uniquely American way of looking at ourselves and understanding what we saw. *Pygmalion* used empirical research to document what we believed as a people: That not our social class, our previous experiences, or even the test scores in our academic files limited our ability to bloom. An ad in *Reader's Digest* put it thus: "Self-Fulfilling Prophecy—A key to success. Actual experiments prove this mysterious force can heighten your intelligence, your competitive ability, your will to succeed. The secret: just make a prediction" (quoted in Good & Brophy, 1977, p. 383). In intelligence, as in so many other spheres of American life, the road to success was paved with the power of positive thinking.

Not only was *Pygmalion* born in the right country, but her timing was impeccable. Bewildered by a far-off war and rocked by the civil rights movement, busing, and racial disturbances at home, America readily laid blame. Teachers, sufficiently powerless and disorganized, were convenient candidates.[6] Graphic portrayals of teacher negligence poured from all quarters—especially from bookstores where Jonathan Kozol's *Death at an Early Age* (the 1967 National Book Award winner) and Herbert Kohl's *36 Children* (1967) became best-sellers. Reviewing *Pygmalion* for the *New York Review of Books,* Kohl (1968) claimed the book's findings were consistent with what critics of schools had long been saying. Indeed, before the nation had ever heard of the Oak School or the Harvard Test of Inflected Acquisition, the educational self-fulfilling prophecy was a *social truth,* a familiar explanation of how schools undermined the intellectual performance of the disadvantaged. By the time *Pygmalion* arrived, her numbers were of less importance than her message. Her data did not substantiate a theory as much as a theory substantiated her.

Events within the educational community also spread *Pygmalion's* popularity. By the late 1960s, Arthur Jensen's ideas about the heritability of IQ were being noted (Jensen, 1969). Jensen proposed that the average difference in "IQ scores between black and white people may be attributable as much to heredity as environment" (1973, p. 80). To these claims, *Pygmalion* provided a powerful counter, asserting that intelligence was as much a function of our social situation as anything in our genes. For years, Arthur Jensen and Robert Rosenthal squared off in perennial, sometimes acrimonious debates (e.g., Edson, 1969; Jensen, 1969, 1980; Rosenthal, 1980, 1985; Rosenthal & Rubin, 1971). But divisiveness between two psychologists is of less interest to us here than the impressions about this conflict picked up by the popular press and the public. *Pygmalion,* matching the beliefs of jurists, journalists, and the public at large, came to symbolize the American ideal (cf. Cronbach, 1975). As the cover of the May, 1970, *Family Circle* proclaimed: "Your Child's IQ Can Be Improved—New Findings."

Educational researchers are naturally drawn to studying variables they can control, and obviously teachers' expectations are much easier to manipulate than students' social class or parents' educational attainments. In *Pygmalion's* trail, teacher expectations became an educational growth industry. The "Teacher Expectancy and Student Achievement" (TESA) training program of the Los Angeles County Unified School District (cf. Kerman, 1979; Columbus Public Schools, 1982) has emerged as one of the most widely distributed in-service programs in this country, in addition to its distribution in Western Europe, Puerto Rico, England, Panama, Australia, and Saudi Arabia (Kerman, personal communication, June 15, 1987). Workshops that bring teachers' biases to the surface and heighten their awareness of classroom behavior can only be viewed positively. But when distinctions between what expectations can and cannot do become blurred, when all differences among students are cast as a function of their teachers' expectations, a dangerous trend is set. As Fein (1971) noted of such thinking:

> [It] makes educational equality seem much easier to attain. No longer are we required to worry centrally about . . . environmental disadvantage; simply create a system which can provide teachers who will say to their students, in effect, that they are getting better in every way, every day and, eureka, the gap will vanish. (p. 114)

Training programs and courses in teacher education programs notwithstanding, the painful gap in school performance between children of different colors and social classes remains. This is not to dismiss the contributions made by research on the educational self-fulfilling prophecy. But *writ large,* the attempt to solve the ills of American schools by changing the expectations of teachers diverts attention from basic social inequities by claiming that the central, if not the entire, cause of school failure rests in the minds of teachers.

The process by which schools inherit the responsibility for social inequity is not well understood. Yet one thing is certain—creating high expectations for schoolchildren costs less than building new housing or funding new jobs. The omnipotence of schooling is a compelling idea in a democracy, but sometimes popularity obscures falseness. Ironically, in the same article in which Robert Merton (1948) introduced the self-fulfilling prophecy, he expressed doubts about education's ability to solve the problems caused by it: "The appeal to 'education' as a cure-all for the most varied social problems is rooted deep in the mores of America. Yet it is nonetheless illusory for all that" (p. 197).

ENDNOTES

1. This "ecological correlation," based on group as opposed to individual data, is almost certainly not equal to its corresponding individual correlation. See Robinson (1950).

2. When the self-fulfilling prophecy is cited today in the educational (e.g., Schmida, Katz, & Cohen, 1987) or psychological (e.g., Jussim, 1986) literatures, it is often Rosenthal, not Merton, who is given credit for the term.

3. Early in the paper, Rist noted, "The basic position to be presented in this paper is that the development of expectations by the kindergarten teacher as to the differential academic potential and capability of any student was significantly determined by a series of subjectively interpreted attributes and characteristics of that student. The argument may be succinctly stated in five propositions. First, the kindergarten teacher possessed a roughly constructed 'ideal type' as to what characteristics were necessary for any given student to achieve 'success' both in the public school and in the larger society. These characteristics appeared to be, in significant part, related to social class criteria. Secondly, upon first meeting her students at the beginning of the school year, subjective evaluations were made of the students as to possession or absence of the desired traits necessary for anticipated 'success.' On the basis of the evaluation, the class was divided into groups expected to succeed (termed by the teacher 'fast learners') and those anticipated to fail (termed 'slow learners'). Third, differential treatment was accorded to the two groups in the classroom, with the group designated as 'fast learners' receiving the majority of the teaching time, reward-directed behavior, and attention from the teacher. Those designated as 'slow learners' were taught infrequently, subjected to more frequent control-oriented behavior, and received little if any supportive behavior from the teacher. Fourth, the interactional patterns between the teacher and the various groups in her class became rigidified, taking on caste-like characteristics, during the course of the school year, with the gap in completion of academic material between the two groups widening as the school year progressed. Fifth, a similar process occurred in later years of schooling, but the teachers no longer relied on subjectively interpreted data as the basis for ascertaining differences in students. Rather, they were able to utilize a variety of informational sources related to past performance as the basis for classroom grouping" (pp. 413–414).

4. Regarding pretest scores Elashoff and Snow (1971) remarked, "The fact that Grade 1 and 2 experimental children have total scores averaging 4.9 IQ points higher, and reasoning scores averaging 13.2 IQ points higher than the control group does cast doubt on the effects of randomization" (p. 158).

5. *Pygmalion* was also used by the plaintiffs in *Larry P. v. Riles* (1979), but this time the defense assembled its own team of experts, including R. L. Thorndike. Judge Peckham, perhaps because of the negative comments about the study, had little to say about the

educational self-fulfilling prophecy in his decision. For an account of this case see Elliots (1987).

6. Teachers did not take all of this lying down. See Alexander Visser's letter to the editor in the June 29, 1965 *Boston Globe* (reprinted in Kozol, 1967) as well as Albert Shanker's objections to the *Pygmalion* study (Shanker, 1971, p. 13).

REFERENCES

Allington, R. (1980). Teacher interruption behaviors during primary-grade oral reading. *Journal of Educational Psychology, 72,* 371–377.

Anderson, D.F., & Rosenthal, R. (1968). Some effects of interpersonal expectancy and social interaction on institutionalized retarded children. *Proceedings of the 76th Annual Convention of the American Psychological Association, 3,* 479–480.

Anderson, L.M., Evertson, C.M., & Brophy, J.E. (1979). An experimental study of effective teaching in first-grade reading groups. *Elementary School Journal, 79,* 193–222.

Babad, E.Y., Inbar, J., & Rosenthal, R. (1982). Pygmalion, Galatea, and the Golem: Investigations of biased and unbiased teachers. *Journal of Educational Psychology, 74,* 459–474.

Borko, H., Cone, R., Russo, N., & Shavelson, R. (1979). Teachers' decision making. In P. Peterson & H. Walberg (Eds.), *Research on teaching: Concepts, findings, and implications.* Berkeley, CA: McCutchan.

Bradley v. Milliken, 338 F. Supp. (E.D. Michigan, 1971).

Brophy, J.E. (1983). Research on the self-fulfilling prophecy and teacher expectations. *Journal of Educational Psychology, 75,* 631–661.

Brophy, J.E., & Good, T.L. (1970a). Teachers' communication of differential expectations for children's classroom performance: Some behavioral data. *Journal of Educational Psychology, 61,* 365–374.

Brophy, J.E., & Good, T.L. (1970b). The Brophy-Good dyadic interaction system. In A. Simon & E. Boyer (Eds.), *Mirrors for behavior: An anthology of observation instruments continued, 1970 supplement. Volume A.* Philadelphia: Research for Better Schools.

Brophy, J.E., & Good, T.L. (1974). *Teacher-student relationships: Causes and consequences.* New York: Holt, Rinehart, & Winston.

Brown v. Board of Education, 347 U.S. 483 (1954).

Carter, K., Sabers, D., Cushing, K., Pinnegar, S., & Berliner, D.C. (1987). Processing and using information about students: A study of expert, novice, and postulant teachers. *Teaching & Teacher Education, 3,* 147–157.

Clark, K.B. (1955/1963). *Prejudice and your child.* Boston: Beacon Press.

Clark, K.B. (1963). Educational stimulation of racially disadvantaged children. In A. H. Passow (Ed.), *Education in depressed areas.* New York: Bureau of Publications, Teachers College of Columbia University.

Clark, K.B., & Clark, M. (1939). Development of consciousness and the emergence of racial identification in Negro children. *Journal of Social Psychology, 10,* 591–599.

Cohen, D.K., & Weiss, J.A. (1977). Social science and social policy: Schools and race. In R.C. Rist & R.J. Anson (Eds.), *Education, social science, and the judicial process* (pp. 72–96). New York: Teachers College Press.

Coles, R. (1969, April). What can you expect? [Review of *Pygmalion in the classroom*]. *The New Yorker,* pp. 169–177.

Columbus Public Schools. (1982). *TESA News, 1*(1).

Conn, L.K., Edwards, C.N., Rosenthal, R., & Crowne, D. (1968). Perception of emotion and response to teachers' expectancy by elementary school children. *Psychological Reports, 22,* 27–34.

Cooper, H.M. (1979). Pygmalion grows up: A model for teacher expectation communication and performance influence. *Review of Educational Research, 49,* 389–410.

Cooper, H.M., & Good, T.L. (1983). *Pygmalion grows up: Studies in the expectation communication process.* New York: Longman.

Cronbach, L.J. (1975). Five decades of public controversy over mental testing. *American Psychologist, 30,* 1–14.

Dusek, J.B. (1975). Do teachers bias children's learning? *Review of Educational Research, 45,* 661–684.

Dusek, J.B. (1985). *Teacher expectancies.* Hillsdale, NJ: Lawrence Erlbaum Associates.

Edson, L. (1969, August 31). Jensenism, *n.* The theory that I.Q. is largely determined by the genes. *New York Times Magazine,* pp. 10–11, 40–45.

Elashoff, J.D. & Snow, R.E. (1971). *Pygmalion reconsidered.* Worthington, OH: Jones.

Elliots, R. (1987). *Litigating intelligence: IQ tests, special education, and social science in the courtroom.* Dover, MA: Auburn.

Evans, J.T., & Rosenthal, R. (1969). Interpersonal self-fulfilling prophecies: Further extrapolation from the laboratory to the classroom. *Proceedings of the 77th Annual Convention of the American Psychological Association, 4,* 371–372.

Fein, L.J. (1971). *The ecology of the public schools: An inquiry into community control.* New York: Pegasus.

Franzen, R. (1920). The accomplishment quotient: A school mark in terms of individual capacity. *Teachers College Record, 21,* 432–440.

Gage, N.L. (1966, September). *Discussion of the symposium on "Teachers' expectations as an unintended determinant of pupils' intellectual reputation and competence."* Paper presented on the program of Divisions 15 and 8 of the American Psychological Association, New York.

Gage, N.L. (1971). Preface. In J.D. Elashoff & R.E. Snow (Eds.), *Pygmalion reconsidered* (pp. 4–5). Worthington, OH: Jones.

Gerard, H.B. (1983). School desegregation: The social science role. *American Psychologist, 38,* 869–877.

Geertz, C. (1983). Common sense as a cultural system. In C. Geertz (Ed.), *Local knowledge.* New York: Basic Books.

Gergen, K.J., & Gergen, M.M. (1981). *Social psychology.* New York: Harcourt, Brace, & Jovanovich.

Good, T.L., & Brophy, J.E., (1977). *Educational psychology: A realistic approach.* New York: Holt, Rinehart, & Winston.

Good, T.L., & Grouws, D.A. (1979). The Missouri mathematics effectiveness project. *Journal of Educational Psychology, 71,* 353–362.

Good, T.L., Sikes, J., & Brophy, J. (1973). Effects of teacher sex and student sex on classroom interaction. *Journal of Educational Psychology, 65,* 74–87.

Gregory, C.A. (1922). *Fundamentals of educational measurement.* New York: Appleton.

Hobson v. Hansen, 269 F. Supp. 401 (1967).

Jensen, A.R. (1969). How much can we boost IQ and scholastic achievement? *Harvard Educational Review, 39,* 1–123.

Jensen, A.R. (1973, December). The differences are real. *Psychology Today,* 80–86.

Jensen, A.R. (1980). *Bias in mental testing.* New York: Free Press.

Jones, E.E. (1986). Interpreting interpersonal behavior: The effects of expectancies. *Science, 234,* 41–46.

Jussim, L. (1986). Self-fulfilling prophecy: A theoretical and integrative review. *Psychological Review, 93,* 429–445.

Kerman, S. (1979). Teacher expectations and student achievement. *Phi Delta Kappan, 60,* 716–718.

Kohl, H. (1967). *36 children.* New York: New American Library.

Kohl, H. (1968, September 12). Great expectations [Review of *Pygmalion in the classroom*]. *The New York Review of Books,* p. 31.

Kozol, J. (1967). *Death at an early age.* New York: Houghton Mifflin.

Larry P. v. Riles, 495 F. Supp. 926 (N.D. Cal. 1979).

Leo, J. (1967, August 8). Study indicates pupils do well when teacher is told they will. *New York Times,* pp. 1, 20.

Marburger, C.L. (1963). Considerations for educational planning. In A. H. Passow (Ed.). *Education in depressed areas* (pp. 298–321). New York: Bureau of Publications, Teachers College of Columbia University.

McCurdy, J. (1969, January 31). Testing of IQs in L.A. primary grades banned. *Los Angeles Times,* p. 1.

Merton, R.K. (1948). The self-fulfilling prophecy. *Antioch Review, 8,* 193–210.

Merton, R. K. (1981, November). Our sociological vernacular. *Columbia: The magazine of Columbia University.*

Meyer, W.J. (1985). Summary, integration, and prospective. In J.B. Dusek (Ed.), *Teacher expectancies* (pp. 353–370). Hillsdale, NJ: Lawrence Erlbaum Associates.

Raudenbush, S.W. (1984). Magnitude of teacher expectancy effects on pupil IQ as a function of the credibility of expectancy induction: A synthesis of findings from 18 experiments. *Journal of Educational Psychology, 76,* 85–97.

Rist, R.C. (1970). Student social class and teacher expectations: The self-fulfilling prophecy in ghetto education. *Harvard Educational Review, 40,* 411–451.

Robinson, W.S. (1950). Ecological correlations and the behavior of individuals. *American Sociological Review, 15,* 351–357.

Rosenthal, R. (1966). *Experimenter effects in behavioral research.* New York: Appleton-Century-Crofts.

Rosenthal, R. (1980). Error and bias in the selection of data. *The Behavioral and Brain Sciences, 3,* 352–353.

Rosenthal, R. (1985). From unconscious experimenter bias to teacher expectancy effects. In J.B. Dusek (Ed.), *Teacher expectancies* (pp. 37–65). Hillsdale, NJ: Lawrence Erlbaum Associates.

Rosenthal, R., & Fode, K.L. (1963). The effect of experimenter bias on the performance of the albino rat. *Behavioral Science, 8,* 183–189.

Rosenthal, R., & Jacobson, L. (1968a). *Pygmalion in the classroom: Teacher expectation and pupils' intellectual development.* New York: Holt, Rinehart, & Winston.

Rosenthal, R., & Jacobson, L. (1968b). Self-fulfilling prophecies in the classroom: Teachers' expectations as unintended determinants of pupils' intellectual competence. In M. Deutsch, I. Katz, & A.R. Jensen (Eds.), *Social class, race, and psychological development* (pp. 219–253). New York: Holt, Rinehart, & Winston.

Rosenthal, R., & Jacobson, L. (1968c). Teacher expectations for the disadvantaged. *Scientific American, 218,* 19–23.

Rosenthal, R., & Rubin, D.B. (1971). *Pygmalion* reaffirmed. In J.D. Elashoff & R.E. Snow (Eds.), *Pygmalion reconsidered* (139–155). Worthington, OH: Jones.

Rosenthal, R., & Rubin, D.B. (1978). Interpersonal expectancy effects: The first 345 studies. *The Behavioral and Brain Sciences, 3,* 377–415.

Schmida, M., Katz, Y.J., & Cohen, A. (1987). Ability grouping and students' social orientations. *Urban Education, 21,* 421–431.

Shanker, A. (1971, May 23). False research vs. the public schools. *The New York Times.* p. 13.

Shavelson, R., Cadwell, J., & Izu, T. (1977). Teachers' sensitivity to the reliability of information in making pedagogical decisions. *American Educational Research Journal, 14,* 83–97.

Smith, M. L. (1980). Teacher expectations. *Evaluation in Education: An International Journal, 4,* 53–55.

Snow, R.E. (1969). Unfinished Pygmalion [Review of *Pygmalion in the classroom*]. *Contemporary Psychology, 14,* 197–200.

Snow, R.E. (1986). *Letter to the editor of Science.* Unpublished manuscript, Stanford University, Stanford, CA.

St. John, N.H. (1975). *School desegregation.* New York: John Wiley & Sons.

Teachers: Blooming by deception. (1968, September 20). *Time,* p. 62.

Thorndike, R.L. (1968). Review of *Pygmalion in the classroom. American Educational Research Journal, 5,* 708–711.

Weinberg, M. (1975). The relationship between school desegregation and academic achievement: A review of the research. *Law and Contemporary Problems, 39,* 240–270.

West, C., & Anderson, T. (1976). The question of preponderant causation in teacher expectancy research. *Review of Educational Research, 46,* 185–213.

Wolf, E.P. (1981). *Trial and error: The Detroit school segregation case.* Detroit: Wayne State University Press.

High School Dropouts: A Review of Issues and Evidence

RUSSELL W. RUMBERGER

Dropping out of high school has long been viewed as a serious educational and social problem. By leaving high school prior to completion, most dropouts have serious educational deficiencies that severely limit their economic and social well-being throughout their adult lives. The individual consequences lead to social costs of billions of dollars.

Over the last 40 years, the proportion of young people who have failed to finish high school has decreased substantially. In 1940, more than 60% of all persons 25 to 29 years old had not completed high school; by 1980, that proportion had dropped to less than 16% (U.S. Bureau of the Census, 1985, Table 215).

Despite these long-term declines in dropout rates, interest in the dropout issue among educators, policymakers, and researchers has increased substantially in recent years. State and local education officials are currently devoting more time and resources to measuring the extent of the problem, to examining its causes, and setting up programs for dropout prevention and recovery. Policymakers are promoting and supporting these efforts and passing legislation to fund them. More research has appeared on the problem of dropouts in the last 2 years than in perhaps the previous 15.

If the long-term incidence of dropping out is declining, why has the concern for this problem increased of late? Several explanations could account for this increased concern. First, although the long-term trend of dropping out has declined, the short-term trend has remained steady and even increased, especially for some groups. The proportion of white male dropouts, for example, increased from 14% to 17% between 1968 and 1978, and then declined to 16% in 1984 (Table 5-1).

A second reason for the increased attention to dropouts is that minority populations, who have always had higher dropout rates than the white population, are

From *Educational Researcher,* 57:101–121, 1987. Copyright 1987 by the American Educational Research Association. Reprinted by permission of the publisher.

TABLE 5-1 Dropout Rates by Age, Sex, Race, and Ethnicity: Selected Years, 1968–1984 (percentages)

Cohort	1968	1978	1980	1982	1984
3 to 34-year-olds	18.3	12.9	12.7	12.7	12.6
white males	17.1	12.2	12.2	12.4	12.5
white females	17.3	12.4	11.9	11.9	11.7
black males	25.8	17.2	16.5	16.7	15.7
black females	25.6	16.2	16.2	14.9	15.0
Hispanic males	—	28.1	28.3	26.9	27.0
Hispanic females	—	29.0	27.3	27.3	26.7
18 to 19-year-olds	15.7	16.7	15.7	16.7	15.2
white males	14.3	16.3	16.1	16.6	15.8
white females	14.6	15.0	13.8	14.9	14.0
black males	23.8	25.8	22.7	26.4	19.7
black females	24.7	22.8	19.8	18.1	14.5
Hispanic males	—	36.6	43.1	34.9	26.2
Hispanic females	—	39.6	34.6	31.1	26.0
16 to 17-year-olds	7.8	8.8	8.8	7.3	6.8
white males	6.9	9.6	9.3	7.3	7.3
white females	7.6	8.7	9.2	8.0	6.9
black males	10.1	5.2	7.2	6.4	5.5
black females	14.2	9.4	6.6	5.5	4.9
Hispanic males	—	15.6	18.1	12.2	13.6
Hispanic females	—	12.2	15.0	15.9	12.7

Note: Dropout rates represent the percent of each cohort who are dropouts. Dropouts are defined as persons of a given cohort who are not enrolled in school in October of the year in question and have not received a high school diploma or an equivalent high school certificate. Source: U.S. Department of the Census, *School Enrollment,* Current Population Reports, Series P-20, various issues (Washington, D.C.: U.S. Government Printing Office, various years).

increasing in public schools. In 1982, racial and ethnic minorities represented the majority of students enrolled in most large U.S. cities and more than 90% of all students in such cities as Newark, Atlanta, and San Antonio (Plisko & Stern, 1985, Table 1.5). And the proportions will increase in the future; this alone could drive up high school dropout rates.

A third reason for increased concern about dropouts is that many states have recently passed legislation to raise academic course requirements for high school graduation. Although increasing academic demands could help to motivate some students, others—especially those who already have a tenuous commitment to school—might be more inclined to drop out (McDill, Natriello, & Pallas, 1985, 1986). Major efforts will be required to prevent more students in this high-risk population from dropping out, efforts that have often not been included in the initial round of educational reforms (Levin, 1986).

A fourth reason for the increased concern about dropouts is a widespread belief that the educational requirements of work will increase in the future. Most of the recent state reform efforts and the national reports on education that prompted them have been predicated on a belief that the increased use of new technologies and structural changes in the composition of jobs in the economy will require more educational skills (e.g., National Commission on Excellence in Education, 1983; Task Force on Education for Economic Growth, 1983). While these visions of the future have yet to be substantiated (Levin & Rumberger, in press), they do suggest that dropouts will be even more disadvantaged in the future job market than they have been in the past (National Academy of Sciences, 1984).

A final reason for increased concern about dropouts is political. Leading education officials at the state and federal levels have recently initiated the idea of using a series of "indicators" to judge the performance of the nation's and states' school systems. These efforts began with the U.S. Department of Education's publishing a series of education "wall charts" that compared state systems of education along a series of dimensions, including the high school completion rates. Now the states themselves, through the efforts of the Council of Chief State School Officers and the U.S. Department of Education, are beginning to define and collect comparable data that can be used for such comparisons. This requirement has prompted increased attention not only to the problem of how to define and measure dropouts (Wittebols, 1986) but also how to reduce the incidence of dropping out and improve this indicator of school performance.

Whatever the reasons for this heightened concern, the dropout issue is likely to command increased attention from researchers, policymakers, and educators at the local, state, and national levels for some time to come. The purpose of this paper is to begin to examine the many issues involved in trying to understand and solve this complex social and educational problem.

In the remainder of the paper, I will briefly analyze four major facets of this problem: its (a) incidence; (b) causes, including social, economic, psychological, and educational factors; (c) individual and social consequences; and (d) solutions. For each facet, I will identify the important issues involved, the current state of research on the issues, and considerations for future research. I will also attempt to identify the various academic disciplines—such as psychology, sociology, and economics— that are useful in understanding the nature of this problem and its solutions.

THE INCIDENCE OF THE PROBLEM

Before this or any perceived social problem can be fully understood, it is important to know the magnitude or incidence of the problem. What is the incidence of dropping out of high school? Is the incidence increasing or decreasing? How do the incidence of dropping out and trends in the dropout rate vary among different social groups and different educational settings?

The Incidence of Dropping Out

The first question is the most important in understanding the nature of this problem, yet it is also the most difficult to answer. In fact, no one knows what the high school dropout rate really is in the United States. That is because there is no consensus definition of a high school dropout, nor is there a standard method for computing the dropout rate. At the national level, the two most widely cited dropout statistics—the dropout rate computed from U.S. Census data and the high school attrition rate computed from state-level school enrollment data—show widely different dropout rates and probably represent lower and upper limits to the true rate.

The U.S. Census Bureau computes the dropout rate as the proportion of a given age cohort that is not enrolled in school and has not completed high school. The latest figures available are for October 1984. They show a dropout rate of 6.8% for persons 16 and 17 years old and a dropout rate of 15.2% for persons 18 and 19 years old (Table 5-1).

The other widely cited national dropout statistic is based on attrition data. It shows the proportion of a given entering high school class, usually the ninth grade, that graduates 4 years later. The latest figures show an average attrition rate of 29.1% for high school class of 1984 in the U.S., with state-level attrition rates varying from a low of 10.7% in Minnesota to a high of 43.3% in Louisiana (Table 5-2).

One reason these two statistics are so different is that they were designed to answer different questions about dropouts. The Census statistic is designed to determine the number and proportion of persons from a given demographic cohort who are dropouts. State attrition data, which are constructed from enrollment and graduation information, are designed to reveal how well the educational system is doing in graduating students. But beyond differences in purpose, differences in these statistics can be traced to six factors that must be considered in computing any dropout rate: (a) choice of cohort, (b) initial membership in cohort, (c) definition of dropout, (d) time for determining dropout status, (e) source of information, and (f) level of determination.

The first factor is the choice of cohort to be used as a base for determining the dropout rate. The Census figure is based on an age cohort, while the education figure is based on a class cohort. Neither one is necessarily superior to the other, although the latter creates more problems because it requires measuring a cohort's status over an interval of time—first as a member in the cohort and then as a dropout—while the former can be determined at one point in time. In either case it is necessary to determine the particular age or class cohort to use in computing a dropout rate. One problem with using the entering ninth grade class is that it ignores those students who have dropped out in earlier grades.

TABLE 5-2 Attrition Rates by State (Percentages)

State	1972	1982	1984	State	1972	1982	1984
U.S. average	22.8	27.2	29.1	Missouri	22.5	24.6	33.8
Alabama	34.6	32.9	37.9	Montana	21.0	17.8	17.9
Alaska	20.7	29.0	25.3	Nebraska	14.1	16.4	13.7
Arizona	26.2	27.6	35.4	Nevada	25.0	24.7	33.5
Arkansas	31.1	25.3	24.8	New Hampshire	19.3	21.7	25.8
California	20.1	31.1	36.8	New Jersey	20.3	21.9	22.3
Colorado	15.2	23.7	24.6	New Mexico	23.1	28.4	29.0
Connecticut	16.6	28.8	20.9	New York	25.3	33.7	37.8
Delaware	22.0	18.2	28.9	North Carolina	31.4	31.6	30.7
District of Columbia	45.2	44.2	44.8	North Dakota	11.0	12.7	13.7
Florida	27.9	34.6	37.8	Ohio	19.7	22.5	20.0
Georgia	35.2	—	36.9	Oklahoma	20.7	22.4	26.9
Hawaii	10.9	15.8	26.8	Oregon	20.8	28.3	26.1
Idaho	15.3	23.1	24.2	Pennsylvania	15.0	21.2	22.8
Illinois	22.0	25.2	25.5	Rhode Island	18.9	27.1	31.3
Indiana	23.9	23.1	23.0	South Carolina	30.8	35.7	35.5
Iowa	10.5	14.2	14.0	South Dakota	9.5	16.1	14.5
Kansas	17.2	19.1	18.3	Tennessee	27.6	31.1	29.5
Kentucky	29.6	33.1	31.6	Texas	29.8	31.8	35.4
Louisiana	33.5	36.0	43.3	Utah	16.7	18.6	21.3
Maine	19.1	27.9	22.8	Vermont	29.1	22.3	16.9
Maryland	19.8	24.4	22.2	Virginia	23.6	25.0	25.3
Massachusetts	22.1	24.1	25.7	Washington	16.1	23.1	24.9
Michigan	19.0	27.3	27.8	West Virginia	28.1	25.2	26.9
Minnesota	8.5	10.8	10.7	Wisconsin	10.9	16.5	15.5
Mississippi	42.4	37.0	37.6	Wyoming	16.9	21.7	24.0

Note: Attrition rates were calculated by subtracting graduation rates from 100%. Graduation rates were calculated by dividing the number of public high school graduates by the public 9th-grade enrollment four years earlier. 1984 data were adjusted for migration and unclassified students. Source: U.S. Department of Education, *State Education Statistics* (Washington, DC: U.S. Department of Education, January 1984 and January 1986).

The second factor is determining a person's initial status as a member of the cohort. It is not difficult to determine one's status in an age cohort, but it is in a class cohort. In the latter case it is necessary to determine which students should be included as members of the cohort, such as students in special education or in juvenile and mental institutions, as well as when membership in the cohort is determined (Wittebols, 1986). At the school or district level this may be particularly problematic because some students shop around for schools or are transients (such as the children of migrant workers), which means they could be "enrolled" in more than one school or district at any one time (California State Department of Education, 1986, p. 26–27). Students who are counted twice as members of a given class cohort (including students held back a grade) would overstate enrollment figures and therefore overstate the attrition rate.

The third, and most critical, factor in measuring dropout rates is determining whether or not a person is a high school dropout. Currently, local and state education agencies employ widely different methods for defining dropouts (Wittebols, 1986). "Dropout" is generally defined as a residual status, indicating someone who has not graduated from, or is not currently enrolled in, a full time, state-approved education program. That is, most states recognize only persons who are studying for, or who have received, regular high school diplomas. Persons who have completed the General Education Development (GED) examination or receive a high school equivalency certificate from the state are often considered dropouts. So too are persons still enrolled in school at the time dropout status is determined (usually 4 years after entering the ninth grade).

The Census Bureau uses a much narrower definition of dropouts. Persons who have a regular or equivalent high school certificate or who are still attending school are not considered dropouts. This method also raises questions. First, is an alternative high school certificate equivalent to a regular high school diploma? Some recent research suggests that GED holders do not do as well as regular high school graduates in the labor market or further educational opportunities, which may indicate that the two credentials are not equivalent (Fields, 1986; Quinn & Haberman, 1986).

Second, how should subsequent enrollment status be determined? Some students who are officially enrolled in school may not be attending regularly and at some point should be considered dropouts rather than students. A more difficult problem concerns students who transfer from one institution to another. Most states require some official verification that a student has enrolled in another state-approved institution, such as an official request for the student's transcript received within a specified number of days (Wittebols, 1986). Surveys of individual school districts show that many school leavers cannot be easily traced, and even those who reenter may not have their transcripts requested (California State Department of Education, 1986; Hammack, 1986). Thus, this procedure not only could overstate the number of dropouts but also puts schools and districts with large proportions of school leavers and transient students at a disadvantage, in that they would have a greater proportion of students to follow up.

A fourth factor that must be considered in computing any dropout rate is the time interval for determining dropout status. Currently, state-level attrition data are based on graduation rates of a ninth-grade class 4 years later. Dropouts include not only persons who may receive a regular or equivalent high school certificates at that time but also persons who may receive a regular or equivalent high school diploma at a later point in time.

A recent study of 1980 high school sophomores who later dropped out of school shows that 38% had received a regular or equivalent high school diploma by 1984 (Kolstad & Owings, 1986, Table 1). A 1985 survey found that almost 50% of young Americans who did not complete the 12th grade had studied for the GED, and 40% of those had received it (Kirsch & Jungeblut, 1986, Figure 3). The current 30% attrition rate in California could be reduced to 20% if adjustments were made for those persons who are likely to receive regular or equivalent high school diplomas by the time they are 30 years of age (California State Department of Education, 1986, pp. 30–31).

The issue of determining an appropriate time interval may become more important in the future if more students opt to finish high school at a later time or through alternative means. This, in fact, could be happening as more students become aware of, and have, the opportunity to finish their high school diplomas at community colleges, at night school programs, or through other means.

A fifth factor that must be considered in computing any dropout rate is the source of information on enrollment and graduation status. The Census Bureau uses population data collected in October of each year as part of the ongoing Current Population Survey. Census enumerators obtain enrollment information about each member of the sample household. This information, which can come secondhand, should be inaccurate because parents, for example, might not know the actual enrollment graduation status of their children, or they may not want to reveal it.

Dropout rates computed with official education data at a state or local level are also subject to error because of current differences in measuring and collecting dropout data. Some of these differences may be overcome by current efforts to define and collect comparable data by states and localities. But it appears unlikely that all these differences will be overcome because of the inherent difficulties in collecting and sharing information among schools, districts, and state education agencies over an extended period of time.

The final factor to consider in measuring dropout rates is the level of determination. Currently, Census data are used to compute a dropout rate at a national and regional level. Attrition rates are currently computed at a state level and averaged across states to compute a national figure. Dropout rates are also computed for schools and districts in some states, with more likely to be computed in the future.

Dropout statistics, computed at any level of the educational system, are clearly appropriate for measuring the number of students who are failing to finish high school and for measuring, in part, how well the educational system is performing. However, the existence of these statistics, even if they were comparably defined and measured, inevitably leads to inappropriate comparisons between schools, districts, and states. Such comparisons are inappropriate because school systems enroll different types of students who have very different propensities to drop out of school. One remedy to this problem is to produce "adjusted" or disaggregated statistics that reflect differences in the kinds of students attending different school systems, although appropriate procedures have yet to be established (Toles, Shulz, & Rice, 1986).

This discussion has pointed out the numerous factors that must be considered in deriving suitable and accurate dropout statistics. Additional research can help to illuminate these issues further, but ultimately policymakers and educators must decide on an appropriate definition of dropping out before accurate data can be collected. Such efforts are currently under way through cooperative work between the U.S. Department of Education and the Council of Chief State School Officers

(Wittebols, 1986). But even with such cooperation, differences in official dropout rates are likely to continue because different dropout measures are used to address different questions and are computed by different organizations.

Trends in Dropout Rates

A second major question about the incidence of dropping out concerns trends: Is the dropout rate getting better or worse? Since there is no consensus on an appropriate dropout measure, it is difficult to assess trends in the dropout rate.

Census data, which have been computed on a yearly basis for more than 20 years, show no long-term increase in the aggregate dropout rate, only short-term increases. The dropout rate for persons 16 and 17 years old increased from 7.8% in 1968 to 8.8% in 1980 and then declined to 6.8% in 1984. The dropout rate for persons 18 and 19 years old increased from 15.7% to 16.7% between 1968 and 1982, and then dropped to 15.2% in 1984 (Table 1).

State-level attrition data show that average dropout rates for the nation increased from 22.8% in 1972 to 27.2% in 1982 and then remained steady between 1982 and 1984 (Table 2). These same data show that dropout rates increased in most states between 1972 and 1984, but decreased quite substantially in some states, such as Arkansas and Vermont.

Some of the observed increases in dropout rates could have come about from changes in the school participation patterns. California enrollment data show that the proportion of 9th-, 10th-, and 11th-grade students failing to enroll in school the following year actually went down between 1977 and 1983, while the proportion of 12th-grade students who failed to graduate went up dramatically (California Assembly Office of Research, 1985, Figure 4). This shift could have come about from an increasing number of high school seniors deciding to finish high school at a later time, such as through night school programs or through community colleges.

Variations Among Social Groups and School Systems

A third major question about the incidence of dropping out concerns variations among social groups and school systems. It is well-known that dropout rates vary widely among social groups. Dropout rates are higher for members of racial, ethnic, and language minorities, for men, and for persons from lower socioeconomic status. A national survey of 1980 high school sophomores shows an overall dropout rate of 13.6%. But dropout rates computed with these data varied from 12.2% for whites to 18.7% for Hispanics, from 12.6% for women to 14.6% for men, and from 8.9% for students from the highest socioeconomic levels to 22.3% for students from the lowest socioeconomic levels (Kolstad & Owings, 1986, Tables 1, 2, and 3). Census data show dropout rates for 18- and 19-year-olds varying from 14.0% for white females to 26.2% for Hispanic males (Table 1). Dropout rates are also higher for

American Indians and particular Hispanic subgroups, particularly Cubans and Mexican Americans (Brown, Rosen, Hill, & Olivas, 1980, Table 2.31; LaFromboise & Rudes, 1983, Table 12.1).

Trends in dropout rates based on Census data also show variations among social groups. Dropout rates for persons 18 and 19 years old declined from 23.8% in 1968 to 19.7% in 1984 for black males, from 24.7% to 14.5% for black females, and from 14.6% to 14.0% for white females. For white males, the dropout rate *increased* from 14.3% in 1968 to 17.9% in 1981, although it declined to 15.8% in 1984. Dropout rates for Hispanics show little change over the last decade, except for Hispanic males 18 to 19 years old, for whom the rate declined from 35.5% in 1972 to 26.2% in 1984 (Table 1).

These data suggest that some racial and ethnic minorities, particularly blacks, who traditionally have always had much higher dropout rates than whites, have shown marked improvements in their propensity to finish high school. The increasing dropout rates for white males could be related to changing patterns of school participation mentioned earlier and therefore may not indicate that the problem is actually getting worse for this group.

Dropout rates vary widely among school systems as well as social groups. Not only are there widespread variations in dropout rates among state educational systems, as the earlier data clearly show, but there are also widespread variations among school districts and even among schools within the same district.

In Chicago, for example, dropout rates for the 63 Chicago high schools range from 10% to 62% (Toles, Shulz, & Rice, 1986, Table 1). Of course, some of these differences are due to differences in the populations of students enrolled in the educational systems. But even after controlling for differences in student populations, widespread differences among school systems remain, differences that more clearly illustrate the ability of schools to educate and graduate their students. In the Chicago schools, observed dropout rates were 50% higher to 50% lower than the rate expected given the composition of the students in the schools (Toles, Shulz, & Rice, Table 1).

THE CAUSES OF THE PROBLEM

No one really knows what causes students to drop out of high school. Dropouts themselves report a number of different reasons for leaving school, with marked differences reported by different social groups (Table 5-3). Almost one half of all dropouts and more than half of white and black males cite school-related reasons for leaving school, such as disliking school or being expelled or suspended. Twenty percent of of all dropouts, but almost 40% of Hispanic males, cite economic reasons for leaving school. A third of all female dropouts report personal reasons for leaving school, such as pregnancy or marriage. While these reasons suggest that students drop out of school for a variety of reasons, they are unable to reveal the underlying, causal factors that lead to dropping out. Many reasons, such as getting a job or

TABLE 5-3 **Primary Reason High School Dropouts Left School, By Sex, Race, and Ethnicity: 1979 (percentage distribution)**

Reason	Males White	Males Black	Males Hispanic	Females White	Females Black	Females Hispanic	Total
School-related:							
Poor performance	9	9	4	5	5	4	7
Disliked school	36	29	26	27	18	15	29
Expelled or suspended	9	18	6	2	5	1	7
School too dangerous	1	0	0	2	1	1	1
Economic:							
Desired to work	15	12	16	5	4	7	10
Financial difficulties	3	7	9	3	3	9	4
Home responsibilities	4	4	13	6	8	8	6
Personal:							
Pregnancy	0	0	0	14	41	15	17
Marriage	3	0	3	17	4	15	9
Other	20	21	23	19	11	25	19
TOTAL	100	100	100	100	100	100	100

Note: Data are for persons 14 to 21 years of age. Source: "Dropping out of high school: The influence of race, sex, and family background" by R.W. Rumberger, 1983, *American Educational Research Journal, 20, p. 201.*

getting pregnant, should probably be considered symptoms rather than causes of dropping out.

Factors Associated With Dropping Out

A large body of empirical research has identified a wide range of factors that are associated with dropping out. The factors can be grouped into several major categories: demographic, family-related, peer, school-related, economic, and individual. Within each of these categories there can be a large number of specific factors. Some are well-known and widely documented in numerous studies; others have not been well-explored in relation to this particular problem. Some of these factors can be manipulated through policy interventions within the outside of the schools; others cannot.

The demographic factors associated with dropping out are well-known and were cited earlier. Members of racial and ethnic minorities are much more likely to drop out of school than white, Anglo students, and males are somewhat more likely to drop out of school than females.

A large number of factors associated with family background and structure have also been identified in the research literature. Perhaps the most important is socioeconomic status. Numerous studies have found that dropout rates are higher for students from families of low socioeconomic status, no matter what particular factors are used to measure socioeconomic status (e.g., Kolstad & Owings, 1986; Rumberger, 1983a). Particular family-related factors associated with dropping out include low educational and occupational attainment levels of parents, low family income, speaking a language other than English in the home, single-parent families, and the absence of learning materials and opportunities in the home (e.g., Ekstrom, et al., 1986; Rumberger, 1983a; Steinberg, Blinde, & Chan, 1984).

The influence of peers has not received much attention in previous research on this problem, although it is a subject of considerable interest in other areas of educational achievement (Bridge, Judd, & Moock, 1979, chapter 8). Many dropouts have friends who are also dropouts, just as friends' educational aspirations and expectations are related more generally. But it is not clear to what extent and in what ways a student's friends and peers influence the decision to leave school.

School-related factors associated with dropping out have received considerable attention, particularly because many of these factors are ones that can be manipulated through practice and policy. It is fairly well-documented that poor academic achievement in school, as measured by grades, test scores, and grade retention, is associated with dropping out (Borus & Carpenter, 1984; Ekstrom, et al., 1986; Wehlage & Rutter, 1986). It is also known that behavioral problems in school are also associated with dropping out, including absenteeism, truancy, and discipline problems (Bachman, Green, & Wirtanen, 1971; Wehlage & Rutter).

Most research on school-related factors has focused on students' behaviors and performance in school. Little attention has been given to the influences of schools themselves—their organization, leadership, teachers—on students' decisions to drop out. Yet many dropouts attend schools with very poor facilities and inadequate teaching staffs, conditions that could affect their performance in school and ultimately their decision to leave (Fine, 1986). School-level dropout rates vary widely even controlling for differences in student populations; this further suggest that school-related factors exert a powerful influence on students' decisions to leave school (Toles, Schulz, & Rice, 1986).

Economic factors also influence students' decisions to leave school. About 20% of dropouts report that they left school because they wanted to or felt they had to work to help out their families (Table 5-3). But as with other reasons students report, it is unclear to what extent work is initially seen as a desirable or necessary alternative to school before a student drops out or whether students first decide to leave school and then decide to find a job.

Finally, there are a host of individual factors associated with dropping out. Dropouts have lower levels of self-esteem and less sense of control over their lives than other students. They have poor attitudes about school and low educational and occupational aspirations (Ekstrom et al., 1986; Wehlage & Rutter, 1986). Finally, many dropouts report that they leave school to get married or because they're pregnant (Ekstrom et. al., 1986; Rumberger, 1983a).

Developing a More Comprehensive Model

While previous research on the causes of dropping out has been helpful in identifying the wide range of factors associated with this behavior, the empirical literature is still lacking. Many studies have focused on only a few of the many factors known to be associated with this problem, and many are based on correlational models that simply identify the direct relationship between one factor and dropout behavior, sometimes controlling for the influence of other factors.

What is needed is a more comprehensive, causal model of the dropout process. Such a model should successfully identify the full range of proximal and distal influences, the interrelationships among them, and their long-term, cumulative effects. Developing such a model should be the goal of researchers working in this area. In pursuit of this goal, researchers should consider the following factors.

First, they should attempt to uncover the processes that underlie and lead to this problem. Many of the factors known to be associated with this problem are structural in nature and reveal little of the underlying processes. For example, why do Hispanics or children from socioeconomically poor families have higher dropout rates? Some possible explanations include the use of language in the home, the amount of time that parents spend with their children, and the type of "parenting" style used in the home (Dornbush et al., in press; Liebowitz, 1977; Steinberg, Blinde, & Chan, 1984).

Understanding school processes also deserves further attention (Natriello, Pallas, & McDill, 1986). In fact, dropping out itself might better be viewed as a process of disengagement from school, perhaps for either social or academic reasons (Catterall, 1986), that culminates in the final act of leaving. Identifying and understanding the processes within homes and schools is an area where ethnographic studies can make important contributions (e.g., Fine, 1986).

Second, future research efforts need to explore the interrelationships among the various factors associated with dropping out. This is particularly important in trying to separate actual causes of this problem from correlates such as attitudes and behaviors. For example, while many female dropouts say they leave school because they are pregnant, both getting pregnant and leaving school may be caused by a number of other, related factors (Hofferth & Moore, 1979). Similarly, poor attitudes and disruptive behavior in school might be better considered symptoms of underlying problems than actual causes of dropping out.

Third, researchers should attempt to measure the long-term, cumulative effects of the various influences on dropping out. This is particularly important given the influences of family background and early school achievement. Family background can have a powerful, cumulative influence on school achievement through its effects on such things as kinds of schools children attend, their attitudes about school, and learning that takes place in the home. These influences affect a student's achievement at an early age, which, in turn, influences subsequent attitudes and performance in school (e.g., Stroup & Robins, 1972). Yet the cumulative influence of family background and early school achievement has not been fully explored either generally or with respect to the problem of dropping out.

Finally, a comprehensive model of dropout behavior should address the notion that there are different types of dropouts who leave school for different reasons.

That is, there is no "typical" dropout. A poor, urban black may drop out of school because he is doing badly, his school is understaffed, and he believes his economic prospects are poor whether or not he finishes school. A suburban, middle-class white may drop out of school because he is bored although doing reasonably well in school, he wants to spend some time with his friends, and he knows he can finish school later on at the community college. The causes and the nature of dropping out are very different for these two types of teenagers. Such differences should be explored further and used to develop separate models of dropping out for different types of students (Grant & Sleeter, 1986).

A more comprehensive model of dropout behaviors should help identify the actual causes of dropping out and their relative influence. The result would be of immediate use to educators and policymakers. It would help identify potential dropouts at an early age, when effective interventions could be designed and implemented. It would also help identify the kinds of educational interventions, both academic and psychological in nature, that could be most effective in addressing this problem. And it would help identify the mix of both educational and social interventions that could be effective in helping potential and actual dropouts.

THE CONSEQUENCES OF THE PROBLEM

Concern for dropouts is predicated on the belief that leaving high school before graduation is bad for the individual and for society. Dropping out of high school is generally viewed as a visible form of academic failure in the same way that high school graduation is seen as a visible form of academic success at the secondary level. Yet neither act may reveal much about educational achievement. A recent study of the Chicago school system found, for example, that 47% of students enrolled in the ninth grade in 1980–81 graduated by 1984, but only 15% graduated who could read at or above the national average (Designs for Change, 1985). Similarly, not all dropouts are behind in school and have poor test scores (Fine, 1986).

In fact, dropping out could be beneficial for some kids as well as for the schools they attend. Some students are not able or willing to get anything out of school; others choose other alternatives over going to school, alternatives that in some cases can be more fulfilling and rewarding. And some students who remain in school can be very disruptive to those students who want to be there and to learn. A recent study of high school graduates and dropouts found, for example, that dropouts showed equal or greater improvements in self-esteem and a sense of control than high school graduates (Wehlage & Rutter, 1986).

Overall, however, most evidence supports the notion that dropping out has negative individual and social consequences. Individual dropouts suffer because many have difficulty finding steady, well-paying jobs not just when they first leave school but over their entire lifetimes. Society suffers as well because unemployment and lost earnings lower tax revenues and increase demands on social services. But the consequences of dropping out go beyond simple economic losses, no matter how large they may be. They cover a wide range of individual and social outcomes that need to be better understood.

The most immediate individual consequence of dropping out of school is a low level of academic skills. While graduating from high school does not ensure that a person has sufficient academic skills for successful employment and further education, failing to graduate usually ensures that a person does not. Recent studies confirm that dropouts, on average, have lower academic skills than high school graduates generally and even those graduates of similar personal characteristics (e.g., Alexander, Natriello, & Pallas, 1985).

Because of their low levels of academic skills, many high school dropouts find it difficult to secure steady employment and an adequate income. These economic effects are sizable and are well-documented with published government statistics. In the fall of 1982, for example, dropouts from the 1981–82 school year had unemployment rates almost twice as high as 1982 high school graduates, 42% versus 23% (Table 5-4). Even those dropouts who are able to secure year-round, full-time employment still earn from 12% to 18% less than workers who complete high school (Table 5-4).

Dropouts' lower level of educational achievement does not just have an immediate economic consequence, it becomes an even bigger disadvantage over time because dropouts have fewer opportunities to obtain additional education and training needed to remain even relatively competitive in the job market. For example, Census data reveal that the difference in expected lifetime earnings from ages 18 to 64 between a male high school graduate and a male high school dropout in 1979 was more than $250,000 (U.S. Bureau of the Census, 1983, Table 1).

Of course, the economic consequences of dropping out of school are not the same for all social groups. The relative economic disadvantage of dropping out is larger for whites than for Hispanics or blacks. In the fall of 1982, for example, white dropouts had unemployment rates almost twice as large as white high school graduates, while the unemployment rates for Hispanics and blacks were only one fourth to one third as high (Table 5-4). Thus, there may be less economic incentive for minorities to stay in school than whites, especially when black high school graduates still experience an unemployment rate of over 50%.

While the educational and economic consequences of dropping out are generally well-documented, much less attention has been focused on trying to identify and measure other individual consequences. These would include effects on psychological well-being and health. It is possible that dropping out of school leads to poorer mental and physical health either directly or indirectly through its effects on employment and income. One study found, for example, that increased unemployment was associated with increases in total mortality, suicides, and admissions to state mental hospitals (Brenner, 1976). Since dropouts have higher rates of unem-

TABLE 5-4 Unemployment Rates (percentages) and Annual Earnings (in dollars) for High School Dropouts and High School Graduates, By Sex, Race, and Ethnicity

| | 1976 | | 1982 | |
Cohort	Level	Ratio Dropouts/ Graduates	Level	Ratio Dropouts/ Graduates
Unemployment[a]				
Total		1.78		1.85
Dropouts	30.9		41.6	
Graduates	17.4		22.5	
Males		1.75		2.05
Dropouts	28.3		43.4	
Graduates	16.2		21.2	
Females		1.96		1.60
Dropouts	36.9		38.3	
Graduates	18.8		23.9	
Whites		1.90		1.89
Dropouts	27.5		36.0	
Graduates	14.5		19.0	
Blacks		1.24		1.35
Dropouts	56.9		71.4	
Graduates	45.8		53.0	
Hispanics		2.01		1.23
Dropouts	27.9		42.2	
Graduates	13.9		34.3	
Annual earnings[b]				
Males		.82		.84
Dropouts	7,351		10,964	
Graduates	9,004		13,088	
Females		.87		.82
Dropouts	5,758		8,414	
Graduates	6,620		10,235	

[a]Unemployment rates in October of each year for persons 16 to 24 years old who either graduated or dropped out of high school in the preceding academic year.
[b]Annual earnings for year-round, full-time workers who were 18 to 24 years old as of March of the following year.
Sources: Unemployment data from A.M. Young, "Students, graduates and dropouts in the labor market," *Monthly Labor Review, 100* (July 1977), Table 3, and A.M. Young, "Youth labor force marked turning point in 1982," *Monthly Labor Review, 106* (August 1983), Table 4. Earnings data from U.S. Bureau of the Census, *Current Population Reports,* Series P-60, No. 114 (July 1978), Table 48, and No. 142 (February 1984), Table 48.

ployment than other persons, this study would suggest that they would also suffer greater rates of mortality, suicide, and mental disorders. Yet the causal relationship between dropping out of school and subsequent mental and physical health has not been fully explored.

Social Consequences

Dropping out of high school affects not only those who leave school but also society at large. Moreover, the social consequences go beyond the economic and psychological impacts that befall individual high school dropouts. In the only comprehensive study that has ever been done on this facet of the dropout problem, Levin (1972) identified seven social consequences of inadequate education, which he defined as the failure to complete high school:

1. Forgone national income;
2. Forgone tax revenues for the support of government services;
3. Increased demand for social services;
4. Increased crime;
5. Reduced political participation;
6. Reduced intergenerational mobility; and
7. Poorer levels of health. (p. 10)

For each of these areas he examined the research literature and summarized what was known about the relationship between education and that particular social outcome. He then estimated the social costs associated with the first four outcomes.

Forgone income is perhaps the most often cited social consequence of dropping out of high school. It is also the most widely documented. Levin estimated that the forgone income from a cohort of males 25 to 34 in 1969 who failed to finish high school amounted to $237 billion. This forgone income resulted in forgone government revenues of $71 billion (Levin, 1972, p. ix). A more recent study estimated the forgone income of both male and female dropouts from the national high school class of 1981 at $228 billion and forgone government revenues at more than $68 billion (Catterall, 1985, Table 2).

The social consequences and social costs of dropping out go beyond forgone income and revenues, however. As Levin documented, high school dropouts are more likely to require a wide range of social services, including welfare, medical assistance, and unemployment assistance. They are also more likely to engage in crime, have poorer health, have lower rates of intergenerational mobility, and lower rates of political participation. Based on the research literature and cost data available at that time, he estimated the social costs of providing social services and fighting crime associated with dropping out at $6 billion per year (Levin, 1972, p. ix). Today, of course, the figures would be much higher.

Levin's study is remarkably useful in helping to identify a wide range of social consequences that are due to dropping out. However, the study and the literature it reviews are more than 14 years old. Given the large amount of research that has been undertaken in the last 14 years in the areas of crime, health, and welfare, it would be useful to once again examine this large body of literature to try to ascertain the many social consequences of dropping out.

It is likely, for example, that the social consequences are greater today than in the past. That definitely appears to be the case with respect to earnings and unemployment. The earnings differential between male high school dropouts and male high school graduates increased from $73,000 in 1968 to $260,000 in 1979, a much greater increase than the increase in consumer prices over the same period (Levin, 1972, Table 8; U.S. Bureau of the Census, 1983, Table 1). Unemployment rates for high school dropouts were 20% higher than overall unemployment rates in 1950, but 100% higher in 1979 (Rumberger, 1983b, Table 5).

Yet the economic consequences of dropping out may not be changing similarly for all racial and ethnic groups. In 1976, for example, Hispanic dropouts had unemployment rates twice as high as Hispanic high school graduates, but by 1982 unemployment rates for Hispanic dropouts were 25% higher (Table 4). These differences need to be better documented and linked to students' decisions to drop out of school.

In the future, the relative economic disadvantage of dropping out of high school could be even greater than today. The skill requirements of many jobs could be altered in the future because of the increased use of new technologies. Without a sound, basic education, dropouts will be less able to learn new skills and adapt to a changing work environment (National Academy of Sciences, 1984). Therefore they could become even less employable.

The consequences of dropping out of high school deserve more attention from researchers and policy analysts. An attempt should be made to document more fully the wide range of impacts, both good and bad, resulting from dropping out of high school, as well as differences in these impacts among racial and ethnic groups. And more comprehensive estimates should be prepared on the total social costs of this major problem. Such estimates could be valuable in rallying political support to fund dropout prevention and recovery programs.

SOLUTIONS TO THE PROBLEM

Not all students can or should be expected to finish high school. Yet many students want to finish school and could be helped through effective policy interventions. Without such interventions the dropout rate could easily increase due to the rising proportion of minorities in the school-age population and increased academic requirements for high school graduation. Whereas further research on the causes of dropping out will help to better identify and measure the influence of the many factors associated with this problem, the search for effective solutions cannot wait.

Concerted efforts are currently being made in finding and promoting solutions to the dropout problem throughout the United States. At least 15 state-level commissions have been convened in the last couple of years to address the problems of at-risk students (Smith & Hester, 1985). Many districts, especially those with large at-risk populations, have enacted a variety of programs designed to reduce the incidence of dropping out. And new studies have been undertaken to identify and characterize successful dropout programs around the country (e.g., Bullis, 1986; National Foundation for the Improvement of Education, 1986; Stern et al., 1985).

Toward Effective Interventions

Recent reviews of dropout programs and the vast literature on the causes of dropping out, although far from complete, do suggest some of the elements needed to develop a successful strategy of dropout prevention and recovery. Some of these elements include: (a) different programs designed for different types of dropouts; (b) an appropriate mix of educational and noneducational services in each program; (c) accurate and timely identification of students with a high risk of dropping out; and (d) programs designed for early prevention, late prevention, and recovery.

The first element follows from the discussion of the causes of dropping out. Different kinds of students drop out for different reasons. Some are related to problems in school, such as a lack of interest or poor performance; others are related to factors outside of the school, such as the need to find the work or having a child. A comprehensive strategy will need to address all of these factors, providing programs for different children with different needs. For example, recovery programs for teenage mothers will have to serve their needs for child care as well as for an education; prevention programs for similar kinds of students should include birth control information and services as well as educational services.

Beyond these apparent needs, there are a host of other needs that effective programs must address. They must first address the particular academic needs of the students, by providing an appropriate type of curriculum, teaching staff, instructional progress, and even schedule and location (Stern, 1986). For example, reviews of dropout programs suggest that successful programs often mix academic and vocational studies, provide more individualized instruction, and use a teaching staff more sensitive and responsive to the needs of the students (Bullis, 1986; Olsen & Edwards, 1982; Stern, 1986).

Besides these educational elements, successful programs need to address other needs of students. Perhaps the most important is their psychological need for someone to care about them individually, a need that is often met through the provisions of counseling (Bullis, 1986; Olsen & Edwards, 1982: Treadway, 1985).

The third element is crucial if dropout prevention programs are to be successful. That is, the schools must be able to successfully identify those students who are most likely to drop out of school if they hope to do something about it. A recent study of California dropouts found that half of the dropouts interviewed did not discuss their decision with anyone at school before they left (Olsen & Edwards, 1982, p. 32).

Timely identification is equally important. The earlier a student with a high risk of dropping out is identified, the more likely it is that a sustained effort at dropout prevention will be successful. Research has shown that some dropouts begin showing signs of academic failure and disengagement in school in the early elementary grades (Lloyd, 1978; Stroup & Robins, 1972). Successful identification of high-risk students in elementary and junior high schools would provide more time to intervene and address the needs of these kids at an early age.

The final element follows from the third. If students with a high risk of dropping out can be identified at an early age, prevention programs should be started at an early age as well. Even if accurate, early identification is not possible, it still makes sense to initiate early interventions for disadvantaged kids who generally have a high probability of dropping out. A recent evaluation of one preschool program for the disadvantaged found that it reduced the incidence of dropping out (Schweinhart et al., 1985).

Many current efforts to address the problem of dropouts are premised on a belief that dropouts constitute a relatively small percentage of the school population. In this case, special, supplemental programs can be set up to target these at-risk populations while schools continue to serve other students with regular programs. But such a strategy is insufficient in school systems, such as those in New York, Boston, and Chicago, where close to half of the students drop out. In this case, where dropping out is often the rule rather than the exception, more fundamental and systematic changes will be needed to address the problem (Hess, 1986).

The Need of Systematic Evaluations

While descriptive reviews of programs are helpful in helping to design effective interventions, systematic evaluations are needed to determine both the effectiveness of dropout prevention and recovery programs and their costs (Rossi, Freeman, & Wright, 1979). Evaluations of program effectiveness determine the extent to which programs are effective in producing their desired outcomes. In dropout prevention programs, for example, desired outcomes may be a reduced incidence of dropping out among the target population or improvements in some of the known correlates of dropping out, such as student involvement or academic performance. Evaluations must be able to determine whether the outcome was actually caused by the program or caused by something else.

Evaluations of costs involve determining all the resources used in the program, not only so that the full cost of the program can be determined, but so that the program can be properly implemented in another setting (Levin, 1983). Information on program effects and costs can be compared in two ways. Cost-benefit studies determine whether a program's benefits exceed its costs; cost-effectiveness studies determine whether one program is more effective for each dollar spent than other, alternative programs.

Although some early cost-benefit studies of dropout programs were done in the 1960s (e.g., Weisbrod, 1965), to my knowledge there have been no recent studies where both the effectiveness and the costs of dropout programs have been fully evaluated (U.S. Government Accounting Office, 1986). Yet only by considering both the costs and the effectiveness of dropout programs will it be possible to produce the greatest improvement in the dropout problem at the lowest social cost.

One of the problems that plagues even modest efforts to identify effective programs is a lack of suitable information on program features and outcomes (Stern et al., 1985, p. 34).

There have been some attempts to measure the effectiveness of some regular school programs is keeping students in school. Vocational education in high schools, for example, is often said to make schooling more relevant for certain kinds of kids and thus increase their likelihood of staying in school. Other kinds of alternative educational programs, such as alternative or continuation schools or employment training programs, are thought to have similar effects (Stern, et al., 1985). Yet the effectiveness of such programs on reducing the likelihood of dropping out has not been demonstrated (Catterall & Stern, 1986; U.S. Government Accounting Office, 1986).

While no cost-effectiveness evaluations of dropout programs have been undertaken, there have been attempts to compare the costs of dropout prevention to the economic benefits associated with the completion of high school. In his earlier study, Levin estimated that each dollar of social investment in dropout prevention would produce $6 in national income and almost $2 in tax revenues over the lifetime of the 25- to 34-year-old males he examined (Levin, 1972, p. 30). A more recent study estimated that the costs of dropout prevention in Chicago would be less than 1% of the economic benefits derived from increased tax revenues, reduced welfare payments, and savings from the costs of crime (Hess & Lauber, 1985, p. 7).

CONCLUSIONS

Dropping out of high school is considered to be an important educational and social problem. As such, it has commanded to the attention of researchers, policymakers, and educators who are trying both to better understand the nature of the problem and to do something about it. Part of the difficulty in pursuing these efforts is that this problem, like many others, is complex and multifaceted. Each of the four major facets discussed in this review—the incidence of the problem, its causes, consequences, and remedies—requires attention. And each requires a broad, interdisciplinary approach that acknowledges not only the educational aspects of the problem, but the social, economic, and psychological ones as well.

Because dropping out of school has been a long-standing problem, there is considerable research literature on this topic, especially from the 1960s (e.g., Bachman, Green, & Wirtanen, 1971). This earlier literature, although useful in exploring the wide range of factors associated with this problem, in general suffers from several shortcomings. First, many of the studies were largely correlational in nature and are able to show only bivariate relationships between dropping out and a host of antecedents or outcomes. Second, at best they explore the longitudinal nature of the problem over a short period of time, such as from an early high school to a later high school period. Third, many of the factors associated with this problem, especially those related to the family background, focus on structural characteristics rather than processes.

Current and future research efforts need to move beyond these earlier efforts while building on them. Much recent research on dropouts has simply replicated the descriptive nature of earlier studies with more recent data. Such efforts are necessary and useful as a first step, but to move beyond them will require overcoming the limitations of these earlier studies. That is, new research efforts should focus on developing multivariate, longitudinal, and comprehensive models of the causes and consequences of dropping out. Additional research effort is also needed in conducting systematic evaluations of dropout prevention and recovery programs.

The dropout problem is unlikely ever to go away. But concerted and cooperative efforts by educators, policymakers, and educational researchers can improve our understanding of the problem and help reduce its incidence.

REFERENCES

Alexander, K.L., Natriello, G., & Pallas, A.M. (1985). For whom the school bell tolls: The impact of dropping out on cognitive performance. *American Sociological Review, 50,* 409–420.

Bachman, J.G., Green, S., & Wirtanen, I.D. (1971). *Dropping out: Problem or symptom?* Ann Arbor: Institute for Social Research, University of Michigan.

Borus, M.E., & Carpenter, S.A. (1984). Choices in education. In M.E. Borus (Ed.), *Youth and the labor market* (81–110). Kalamazoo, MI: W.E. Upjohn Institute for Employment Research.

Brenner, M.H. (1976). *Estimating the costs of national economic policy.* Study prepared for the Joint Economic Committee, U.S. Congress, 94th Congress, 2nd Session. Washington, DC: U.S. Government Printing Office.

Bridge, R.G., Judd, C.M., & Moock, P.R. (1979). *The determinants of educational outcomes.* Cambridge, MA: Ballinger.

Brown, G.H., Rosen, N.L., Hill, S.T., and Olivas, M.A. (1980). *The condition of education for Hispanic Americans.* Washington, DC: U.S. Government Printing Office.

Bullis, B.M. (1986). *Dropout Prevention.* Berkeley, CA: Policy Analysis for California Education.

California Assembly Office of Research. (1985). *Dropping out, losing out: The high cost for California.* Sacramento: Assembly Office of Research.

California State Department of Education. (1986). *California dropouts: A status report.* Sacramento: California State Department of Education.

Catterall, J.S. (1985). *On the social costs of dropping out of high school* (Report 86–SEPI–3). Stanford, CA: Stanford Education Policy Institute, Stanford University.

Catterall, J.S. (1986), A process model of dropping out of school. Unpublished paper, University of California, Los Angeles.

Catterall, J.S., & Stern, D. (1986). The effects of alternative school programs on high school completion and labor market outcomes. *Educational Evaluation and Policy Analysis, 8,* 77–86.

Designs for Change. (1985). *The bottom line: Chicago's failing schools and how to save them.* Chicago: Author.

Dornbusch, S.M., Ritter, P.L., Leiderman, P.H., Roberts, D.F., & Fraleigh, M.J. (in press). The relation of parenting style to adolescent school performance. *Child Development.*

Ekstrom, R.B., Goertz, M.E., Pollack, J.M., & Rock, D.A. (1986). Who drops out of high school and why? Findings from a national study. *Teachers College Record, 87,* 356–373.

Fields, C.M. (1986, May 14). Value of high-school-equivalency certificates for dropouts is questioned in Wisconsin study. *Education Week,* p. 30.

Fine, M. (1986). Why urban adolescents drop into and out of public high school. *Teachers College Record, 87,* 393–409.

Grant, C.A., & Sleeter, C.E. (1986). Race, class, and gender in education research: An argument for integrative analysis. *Review of Educational Research, 565,* 195–211.

Hammack, F.M. (1986). Large school systems' dropout reports: An analysis of definitions, procedures, and findings. *Teachers College Record, 87,* 324–341.

Hess, G.A., Jr. (1986). Educational triage in an urban school setting. *Metropolitan Education, 2,* 39–52.

Hess, G.A., Jr., & Lauber, D. (1985). *Dropouts from the Chicago public schools.* Chicago: Chicago Panel on Public School Finances.

Hofferth, S.L., & Moore, K.A. (1979). Early childbearing and later economic well-being. *American Sociological Review, 44,* 784–815.

Kirsch, I., & Jungeblut, A. (1986). *Literacy: Profiles of America's young adults.* Princeton, NJ: Educational Testing Service.

Kolstad, A.J., & Owings, J.A. (1986, April). *High school dropouts who change their minds about school.* Paper presented at the annual meeting of the American Educational Research Association, San Francisco.

LaFramboise, T., & Rudes, B. (1983). Student attendance and retention. In Development Associates (Ed.), *The evaluation of the impact of the Part A entitlement program funded under Title IV of the Indian Education Act.* Washington, DC: U.S. Department of Education.

Levin, H.M. (1972). *The costs to the nation of inadequate education.* Study prepared for the Select Committee on Equal Educational Opportunity, U.S. Senate. Washington, DC: U.S. Government Printing Office.

Levin, H.M. (1983). *Cost-effectiveness: A primer.* Beverly Hills, CA: Sage.

Levin, H.M. (1986). *Education reform for disadvantaged students: An emerging crisis.* West Haven, CT: National Education Association.

Levin, H.M., & Rumberger, R.W. (in press). Educational requirements for new technologies: Visions, possibilities, and current realities. *Educational Policy.*

Liebowitz, A, (1977). Parental inputs and children's achievement. *Journal of Human Resources, 12,* 242–251.

Lloyd, D.N. (1978). Prediction of school failure from third-grade data. *Educational and Psychological Measurement, 38,* 1192–1200.

McDill, E.L., Natriello, G., and Pallas, A.M. (1985). Raising standards and retaining students: The impact of the reform recommendations on potential dropouts. *Review of Educational Research, 55,* 415–433.

McDill, E.L., Natriello, G., and Pallas, A.M. (1986). A population at risk: Potential consequences of tougher school standards for student dropouts. *American Journal of Education, 94,* 135–181.

National Academy of Sciences. (1984). *High schools and the changing workplace: The employers' view.* Report of the Panel on Secondary Education for the Changing Workplace. Washington, DC: National Academy Press.

National Commission on Excellence in Education. (1983). *A nation at risk.* Washington, DC: U.S. Government Printing Office.

National Foundation for the Improvement of Education. (1986). *Operation rescue: A blueprint for success.* Washington, DC: National Foundation for the Improvement of Education.

Natriello, G., Pallas, A.M., & McDill, E.L. (1986). Taking stock: Renewing our research agenda on the causes and consequences of dropping out. *Teachers College Record, 87,* 430–440.

Olsen, L., & Edwards, R. (1982). *Push out, step out: A report on California's public school drop-outs.* Oakland, CA: Citizens Policy Center.

Plisko, V.W., & Stern, J.D. (1985). *The condition of education: 1985 edition.* Washington, DC: U.S. Government Printing Office.

Quinn, L., & Haberman, M. (1986). Are GED certificate holders ready for postsecondary education? *Metropolitan Education, 2,* 72–82.

Rossi, P.H., Freeman, H.E., & Wrights, S.R. (1979). *Evaluation: A systematic approach.* Beverly Hills, CA: Sage.

Rumberger, R.W. (1983a). Dropping out of high school: The influence of race, sex, and family background. *American Educational Research Journal, 20,* 199–220.

Rumberger, R.W. (1983b). Education, unemployment, and productivity (Project Report No. 83-A14). Stanford, CA: Institute for Research on Educational Finance and Governance, Stanford University.

Schweinhart, L.J., Berrueta-Clement, J.R., Barnett, W.S., Epstein, A.S., & Weikart, D.P. (1985). The promise of early childhood education. *Phi Delta Kappan, 66,* 548–553.

Smith, R.C., & Hester, E.L. (1985). *Who's looking our for at-risk youth?* New York: MDC.

Steinberg, L., Blinde, P.L., & Chan, K.S. (1984). Dropping out among language minority youth. *Review of Educational Research, 54,* 113–132.

Stern, D. (1986). *Dropout prevention and recovery in California.* Unpublished paper, University of California, Berkeley.

Stern, D., Catterall, J., Alhabeff, D., & Ash, M. (1985). *Reducing the high school dropout rate in California.* Report to the California Policy Seminar. Berkeley: University of California.

Stroup, A.L., & Robins, L.N. (1972). Elementary school predictors of high school dropout among black males. *Sociology of Education, 45,* 212–222.

Task Force on Education for Economic Growth. (1983). *Action for excellence.* Denver, CO: Education Commission of the States.

Toles, T., Schulz, E.M., & Rice, W.K., Jr. (1986). A study of variation in dropout rates attributable to effects of high schools. *Metropolitan Education, 2,* 30–38.

Treadway, P.G. (1985, November). *Beyond statistics: Doing something about dropping out of school.* Paper presented at the School Drop-out Prevention Conference. Aptos, CA.

U.S. Bureau of the Census. (1983). *Lifetime earnings estimates for men and women in the United States: 1979.* Current Population Reports Series P-60, No. 139. Washington, DC: U.S. Government Printing Office.

U.S. Bureau of the Census. (1985). *Statistical abstract of the United States, 1986* (196th ed.). Washington, DC: U.S. Government Printing Office.

U.S. Government Accounting Office. (1986). *School dropouts: the extent and nature of the problem*. Washington, DC: U.S. Government Printing Office.

Wehlage, G.G. & Rutter, R.A. (1986). Dropping out: How much do schools contribute to the problem? *Teachers College Record, 87,* 374–392.

Weisbrod, B.A. (1965). Preventing high school dropouts. In R. Dorfman (Ed.), *Measuring benefits of government investments* (pp. 117–171). Washington, DC: The Brookings Institution.

Wittebols, J.H. (1986). *Collecting national dropout statistics*. Washington, DC: Council of Chief State School Officers, State Education Assessment Center.

▶ 6

Schools of Choice and Private Education

Due to widespread displeasure with the quality of public education and its traditional organization and curriculum, a number of urban parents have sought alternatives in securing increased educational opportunities for their children. Such arrangements are described by Raywid (1984) as "schools of choice." The organization of these schools is quite varied and includes both elementary and secondary schools. They might appear as a school within a school or as a magnet plan that attempts to capitalize on the talents of teacher and pupil. We are cautiously encouraged that these organizations demonstrate an effort by public educators to balance learning and provide meaningful alternatives for poor and minority students. However, the different uses of choice and their purported purposes raise questions about the interests that are served.

Some parents have decided to exercise their prerogatives and send their children to private schools. In the 1960s this would almost always mean a Catholic school. Today, less than one-half of the children who attend private schools are in Catholic schools. However, these schools, for the most part, are located in dioceses in the northeastern United States, where urban change resulted in problems described earlier. Correctly or incorrectly, many urban parents decided that private education was the alternative that they had to select. Is such an education superior?

Coleman (1981) and associates, using national data from the *High School and Beyond* study (National Opinion Research Center, 1980), reported higher academic achievement in basic cognitive skills, particularly reading comprehension, vocabulary, and mathematics for children in Catholic schools when compared with public school students with similar family backgrounds. Since that time, the debate over whether this conclusion is valid has continued unabated.

We have selected one of Coleman's earliest articles dealing with this subject. He also offers various implications relative to America's ideals concerning the common school, local control, financing, and *in loco parentis*. He argues for abandonment of school assignments by residence and new models of financial support that might include schools in the private sector.

Since one of Coleman's findings focused on higher achievement for minority students in Catholic schools, we selected the Keith and Page (1985) reanalysis of the *High School and Beyond* data. Using path analysis, they agree that minority students in Catholic schools have "slightly higher achievement," but probably not as high as earlier claims.

It is not unusual for critics of these findings to complain about "selectivity bias"; that is, parents choose to send their children to Catholic schools often at a financial sacrifice. Consequently, because of this decision, they participate and cooperate in school programs and support teachers regarding such matters as behavior, attendance, homework, and academic achievement. Furthermore, Catholic schools have selective enrollment policies and expel disruptive students. Therefore, the positive differences in achievement favoring Catholic students are caused not by curriculum and teaching practices, but by selection and retention policies.

Although Coleman attempted to control for family background, an unmeasured variable could make a difference. However, Catholic schools have become much less exclusive about who they accept. Financial pressures caused by hiring more lay teachers have forced them to be less exclusive in admissions (including increasing numbers of non-Catholics) and more willing to retain students—for example, 3.4% dropouts versus 14.3% in public schools (Coleman, 1991). A recent Rand study in New York addressed the selectivity issue in New York City (Gill, Foster, and Gendler, 1990).

Many inner-city schools are dedicated to education of the poor. "They consciously accept below-average students and expel fewer than 3 percent of their students each year. . . . Catholic schools traditionally accept troubled students and give them many classes to turn their basic skills around" (p. 58). The Rand report offers a somewhat neutral explanation on selectivity bias. "The fact that selection bias is an admissible explanation does not always make it a plausible one" (p. 60). There really hasn't been a thorough study that documents the impact of such a parental choice. An inner-city parent who is given the opportunity of an educational option that might improve a child's educational opportunity would be foolish to refuse. After all, didn't the middle class, which fled to the suburbs, create new schools with their own type of selectivity bias? They could afford the choice and leave the lower class to declining inner-city public schools. However, when the lower class take alternative measures to achieve equal educational opportunity and succeed because the schools serve them, it's called selectivity bias. Rather than debate the selectivity bias issue, Chubb and Moe have analyzed structural factors that appear to impede the smooth functioning of public schools. In a time when *site-based management* is a current education buzzword, it is clear that that is the administrative model in most private schools. Because the private school principal often has greater control over the hiring and firing of teachers, he or she is more secure and willing to involve teachers in governance, while the public sector is characterized by "weak principals and tenured, unionized teachers, struggle for power" (Chubb and Moe, 1988). Bureaucratic solutions in the public sector are added costs that are not present in private schools. Chubb and Moe offer persuasive arguments that conclude that the greater success of private school students is driven by a competitive market that forces teachers and administrators "to organize their schools in ways that are most sensitive to and most effective in meeting parent and student demands" (Chubb and Moe, 1991). Ernest Boyer said that: "The education system is diminished every time a Catholic school is closed because it shuts off another option for good education in the inner city" ("Of more than," 1989).

Obviously, this is an emotionally charged issue. Data gathered by Coleman, Keith, and Page in the early 1980s remain important benchmarks when comparing public and private schools. More recent research by Chubb and Moe and the Rand Corporation, with a somewhat different focus, offers reinforcement to the earlier findings. All educators, especially in city schools, need to concentrate their efforts on evaluating what constitutes successful educational practice, irrespective of setting, then move toward constructive change.

REFERENCES

Chubb, J.E., and Moe, T.M. (1988). "Politics, markets and the organization of schools." *American Political Science Review,* 82:1084.

Chubb, J.E., and Moe, T.M. (1991, July 26). "The private vs. public school debate." *The Wall Street Journal,* p. A8.

Coleman, J.S. (1981). "Quality and equality in American education: Public and Catholic schools." *Phi Delta Kappan,* 63:159–164.

Gill, P.T., Foster, G.E., and Gendler, T. (1990). *High Schools with Character.* Santa Monica: Rand Corporation.

Keith, T.Z., and Page, E.B. (1985). "Do Catholic high schools improve minority student achievement?" *American Educational Research Journal,* 22:337–349.

National Opinion Research Center. (1980). *High School and Beyond—Information for Users: Base Year Data.* Chicago: Author.

"Of more than parochial interest." (1989, May 22). *U.S. News and World Report,* 61.

Raywid, M.A. (1984). "Synthesis of research on schools of choice." *Educational Leadership,* 41:70–77.

Synthesis of Research on Schools of Choice

MARY ANNE RAYWID

Among the educational innovations introduced during the 1960s, alternatives—or schools of choice—have proved one of the most durable and are increasingly finding support from research. This support may be one reason why schools of choice continue to proliferate.

When looking at the research on schools of choice, it is necessary to understand that it is multifaceted. This is because schools of choice are multifaceted: they are not a curricular *or* an instructional *or* an organizational proposal, but all of these in combination. Since both interest and explanations of success have focused as often on the organizational features of alternative schools as on their programs, this review includes both.

A recent survey located 2,500 secondary-level alternative schools, but the estimated national total is several times this number (Raywid, 1982). The survey omitted elementary school alternatives and there is reason to believe that large numbers of magnet schools at all levels were also omitted. Simultaneously, however, another survey identified 1,019 magnet schools and programs in the nation[1] (Fleming et al., 1982). The magnet investigators concluded that one-third of our urban districts offer such programs and that they enroll up to 31 percent of each district's youngsters.

Perhaps a characterization of alternative schools is a good place to begin. We shall purposely sidestep a definition since definitional attempts have proved troublesome. What seems common to most is an emphasis on choice, on responsiveness, on broadly construed educational aims, and on alternatives as grass roots or "home grown" programs (Deal, 1975; Smith et al., 1976; Parrett, 1981). It may be impossible to establish definitional accord, but it is possible to identify a series of characteristics common to most alternatives, albeit not all:

From *Educational Leadership,* 41:70–77, 1984. Reprinted by permission of the Association for Supervision and Curriculum Development and the author. Copyright © 1984 by ACSD. All rights reserved.

1. The alternative constitutes a distinct and identifiable administrative unit, with its own personnel and program. Moreover, substantial effort is likely to be addressed to creating a strong sense of affiliation with the unit.

2. Structures and processes generative of school climate are held important and receive considerable attention within the unit.

3. Students as well as staff enter the alternative as a matter of choice rather than assignment.

4. The alternative is designed to respond to particular needs, desires, or interests not otherwise met in local schools, resulting in a program that is distinctly different from that of other schools in the area.

5. The impetus to launching the alternative, as well as its design, comes from one or more of the groups to be most immediately affected by the program: teachers, students, and parents.

6. Alternative schools generally address a broader range of student development than just the cognitive or academic. Typically, the sort of person the learner is becoming is a matter of first concern.

Many view magnet schools simply as alternatives developed to the purpose of desegregation. So viewed, it seems clear that they are currently the largest subtype of schools of choice. And they also seem to differ from the parent group in some important ways. The 1982 magnet school survey (Fleming and others) found that these programs are designed to "promote desegregation; develop an image of a 'high quality' public education; provide unique (or alternative) curricula or educational structures; retain public school students and draw nonpublic school students." The survey also found that, unlike other types of alternatives, magnets are located almost exclusively in large school districts or urban centers. Like other alternatives, they may consist of separate schools or schools-within-schools.

ORGANIZATIONAL FORMS AND STRUCTURES

Schools of choice differ as to organizational type, although most are small in relation to conventional schools. Over half have fewer than 100 students, and 69 percent enroll fewer than 200 (Raywid, 1982). Some alternatives occupy the entire school building in which they are housed, while other smaller programs enjoy a comparable separateness by being placed in storefronts or other small quarters. Some are schools-within-schools, usually assigned a limited contiguous set of rooms within the comprehensive high school. During the early 70s, a number of comprehensive high schools were transformed into sets of mini-schools, with Quincy High School in Illinois and Haaren High in New York being two of the better known. Individual schools-within-schools and mini-schools have both been successful, but their main challenge seems to lie in meeting two particular conditions of success: (1) enough separateness to sustain a distinct climate and ethos, and

(2) enough autonomy so that staff can develop and implement their own vision of schooling (Raywid, 1982; Wehlage and others, 1982).

There are numerous types of alternatives in addition to magnets—learning centers, continuation schools, schools without walls, street academies—each identifiable in terms of a particular student target group or a particular type of program. Not since the mid-70s have alternatives been associated with any specific ideological tendencies. Many of the early public schools of choice tended toward the informality and unstructured quality of free or open schools; but as early as 1973, some California parents began to assert that schools of choice ought to include some that are more conservative than the usual, as well as those which are less so. Thus, alternatives came to run the ideological gamut in education, ranging from relatively free schools to fundamentalist types, with even a military academy or two.

Alternatives are found at all school levels, K–12, although there are probably more at the secondary than at the elementary level. The situation appears to be reversed with magnet schools, with 59 percent at the elementary level (Fleming and others, 1982). Elementary school alternatives, including magnets, are most likely to define themselves in terms of a particular pedagogical style, such as open, basics, or Montessori. High school magnets tend to define themselves according to curricular specialities, while most other high school level alternatives seem to focus more on climate-related features than on curriculum. For instance, in the recent alternatives survey, 63 percent of respondents indicated that their foremost point of departure from other schools lay in interpersonal relationships within the school, rather than in curricular distinctiveness (Raywid, 1982).

Internally, the more conservative alternatives have tended to depart very little in structural terms from conventional schools (Zusman and Guthrie, n.d.). And magnet schools have sometimes focused on modifying little but their curricular orientation (Fleming and others, 1982). Other alternatives, however, have pioneered some novel organizational forms and have attracted considerable research attention by virtue of that. Perhaps one of their greatest, though less commonly recognized, contributions was to institutionalize a means for introducing variety into school systems. In the language of David Tyack (1974), alternatives represent a clear departure from the "one best system" approach that undergirded public schooling throughout the century. They presuppose, that is, that there is no one best way of educating all youngsters; instead, different learner needs and parent preferences call for a variety of educations. Alternative schools came to represent the mechanism for introducing departures—the means of institutionalizing diversity within a system highly resistant to novelty and change (Metz, 1981; Warren, 1978). They were also recognized by some as a means whereby school systems could inform, as well as reform, themselves: the demand for a new alternative would serve as an important indicator of community needs and interests, as would underenrollment in an existing option.

At least some alternatives modeled arrangements that have been elaborated as school-based or site-based management and budgeting plans. Schools of choice provided early opportunities to see what happens when typical central district control patterns are relaxed and greater control reverts to the individual school level (Duke, 1976; Nirenberg, 1977; Rand, 1981). They have also facilitated study of novel social control arrangements (Metz, 1978; Swidler, 1979); of human interaction patterns in nonbureaucratic institutions (Argyris, 1974; Wilson, 1976); and of the impacts of school structure on both program (Gracey, 1972), and behavior (Gitlin, 1981).

ORGANIZATIONAL PROCESSES

Schools of choice are noticeably different from conventional schools with respect to their feel and flavor. They elicit quite different responses and behavior from the human beings within them—and a considerable amount of organizational research has sought to explain that and identify its elements. A number of aspects of the way alternatives are put together and operate daily have been singled out as major contributors to their unique climates.

Many analysts have pointed to the importance of choice in this regard (deCharms, 1977; Fantini, 1973; Grant, 1981). It not only provides an initial advantage to the chooser, but it serves to heighten one's investment in what has been chosen (Erickson, 1982; Nault, 1975–76). The choice arrangement also has the advantage of yielding a group of human beings who are similar or united in some educationally significant way. They are agreed upon a particular type of educational mission or environment. Thus, collectively the choosers constitute a more coherent group than do the students, staff, and parents of a comprehensive high school deliberately planned to bring all preferences and persuasions under a common roof. The importance of this likemindedness and cohesion have been underscored recently in both the private school literature (Erickson, 1982; Grant, 1981) and in the effective schools research (Rutter, 1979; Schneider, 1982–83).

Analysts have often named smallness as a key ingredient of the type of environment alternatives provide. Where numbers are limited, it is possible to run schools in such ways that the presence of thousands simply renders out of the question. One of the consequences of smallness is, of course, that everyone knows everyone else—an important ingredient of the personalization discussed below. Another consequence is that the limited number of staff make bureaucratic controls, with their tiers of formal authority, unnecessary. Limited numbers also make bureaucracy's elaborate divisions of labor impossible, and as a result, the responsibilities and prerogatives of everyone within an alternative school are likely to be much broader than in a conventional school. This means that the roles of both staff and students differ notably in schools of choice, and tend to be more expanded and diffuse—for instance, with teachers sharing administrative and counseling functions, and students and administrators sharing in more typical teaching roles.

As this suggests, the social order of schools of choice differs considerably from that in other schools, and is typically maintained in quite different ways (Metz, 1978; Swidler, 1979). Staff as well as students share a sense of substantial autonomy. Teachers feel they exert considerable control over their own programs, and students feel much less like pawns than in other schools (deCharms, 1977; Gladstone and Levin, 1982). The experience of autonomy is important since feelings of control over one's own fate are associated with a sense of ownership and affiliation; with teacher satisfaction (Wehlage, 1982); and, in the case of students, with educational achievement (Coleman, 1966). But the reason for the autonomy feelings is not always apparent, since alternatives students sometimes report such feelings even though their teachers describe the program as highly structured!

A number of early alternative schools sought to function as participatory democracies, with students and staff reaching decisions together in town meetings (Miller, n.d.). There are probably fewer alternatives making just that sort of attempt today (Raywid, 1982), yet students in schools of choice nevertheless often reflect a strong sense of power. This may stem from several causes. First, alternatives, as smaller organizations have less need for restricting students and hence have fewer rules and regulations (Duke and Perry, 1978). And many tend to permit a considerable amount of freedom with respect to clothes, language, and personal style. Second, students do retain the considerable final power to opt out if they are sufficiently dissatisfied. This right alone tends to make for a community of civility and respectful interaction. Third, as is commonly reported by youngsters who have rejected conventional schools, alternatives differ most by virtue of their "caring" teachers. Where teachers are so perceived, and relationships are marked by trust, formal enfranchisement may appear less vital to having one's concerns taken into consideration.

As the above suggests, the climate and the culture or ethos of schools of choice differ considerably from that of other schools. As Erickson (1982) noted, it is the difference between *Gesellschaft* and *Gemeinschaft*—between a formally constituted group held together by regulations, and a genuine community bound by common, mutual sentiments and understandings.

These distinctive elements in the climate of schools of choice seem closely tied to the remarkable levels of satisfaction of both students and their parents. Student attitudes toward school are widely reported to change for the better in alternative schools (Barr and others, 1977; Doob, 1977; Duke and Muzio, 1978), and the attitudes of parents toward these schools is consistently reported as unusually positive (Fleming and others, 1982; Metz, 1981). What is more, post-graduation surveys of former students of the alternative school suggest that they continue to regard it very positively, as a place where they received help that has proved relevant and adequate to their post-high school pursuits (Nathan, 1981; Phillips, 1977).

GOALS

Most schools of choice demonstrate concern with multiple sorts of development in their students, not solely with cognitive growth or intellectual achievement. Although conventional practice in public education narrows the school's focus quite sharply from 1st to 12th grade—with the elementary school's interest in "the whole child" giving way to the high school's concern primarily with the academic—alternative schools continue to acknowledge and actively foster various kinds of student growth over this entire period. Even in back-to-basics, or fundamentalist alternatives initiated for more intense concentration on the academic, there is much explicit concern with molding character; that is, with shaping values, pervasive dispositions, and other personal characteristics (Zusman and Guthrie, n.d.).

The broad concern with the sort of person each youngster is becoming yields several tendencies common to many schools of choice. One is a program consciously designed to abet social growth and such personal development as decision-making ability, moral maturity, and self-knowledge. The pursuit of such goals may be integrated with more traditional learning or stand as separate activities. Either way, such development tends to be viewed as an integral part of the school's mission.

A second consequence of the alternative school's developmental orientation is often a stronger preoccupation with realizing individual potential than with achievement in relation to group norms. This does not mean an indifference to standards; many alternative school students report working far harder in the alternative than ever before. It does mean, however, that these standards are not likely to be imposed or regulated by standardized tests.

A third tremendously important consequence of the developmental orientation of many schools of choice is the personalization it yields. Quite simply, systematic efforts to help someone grow require extensive knowledge of that individual. This requisite alone calls for a personalized education in the sense that students must become known as individual human beings to school staff. They cannot remain uni-dimensional consumers of instruction. Furthermore, activities then built on this knowledge yield the responsiveness to individuals that developmental purposes require. Thus it is no accident that teachers and students both find alternative schools uniquely successful at meeting student needs (Gregory and Smith, 1983). This personalization feature seems strongly associated with the appeal of schools of choice to students, and to parents and teachers as well. It may also be an important factor in the other forms of success achieved by these schools.

INSTRUCTIONAL METHODS

Alternative school staff report instructional methods to be one of their main points of departure from conventional school practice (Raywid, 1982) and several studies

better transition from the dependency of adolescence to the independence and self-responsibility of adulthood. Still another curricular emphasis has been that of the "Just Community" schools inspired by the moral development theory of Lawrence Kohlberg. Just Community alternatives emphasize reasoning related to moral situations, as well as student participation in decision making (Kuhmerker, 1981). As popular as these particular examples have been, however, and as often used for inspiration and a source of ideas, it appears that most schools of choice develop their own curricula.

Highlights from Research on Schools of Choice

- For all types of students, from the neediest to the most outstanding, alternatives seem to produce significant growth and achievement: cognitive, social, and affective.
- Both attendance and student behavior improve in schools of choice.
- Alternative schools prove highly attractive to those who are associated with them—staff, students, and parents. In various ways, all three groups show unusual satisfaction and approval rates.
- The success of alternative schools is variously attributed to the benefits of smallness, choice, climate, and degree of staff autonomy.
- Alternatives manage to "personalize" the school environment and to make it a genuine community of individuals.
- The two instructional modes most distinctive of alternative schools are independent study and experiential learning.
- Alternatives have institutionalized diversity. They exist in varying types and appear to be a well-established component of school districts across the country.

THE PEOPLE IN ALTERNATIVES AND HOW THEY ARE AFFECTED

Although 73 percent of 1982 survey respondents indicated that their districts associate alternatives with all kinds of students (Raywid), a large number of schools of choice have been established to deal with groups posing special problems. The early success of a number of alternatives probably made it inevitable that they would be embraced as solutions for the most educationally challenging groups (the turned-off, disruptive, underachieving, dropout-prone), as well as the means for resolving wider social problems (segregation, crime, youth, unemployment). Thus, today there are large numbers of alternatives targeted for dealing with particular groups and problems, as well as others reflecting a representative cross-section of local youngsters. Programs targeted for disruptive youngsters, underachievers, dropouts, and other varieties of "at risk" youngsters have provided instances of impressive success. They appear particularly effective at improving student attitudes toward school and learning (Foley and McConnaughy, 1982; Mann and Gold, 1980), self-concept and self-esteem (Arnove and Strout, 1978), attendance (Foley and McConnaughy, 1982; Wehlage, 1982), and behavior (Berger, 1974; Duke and Perry, 1978; Wehlage, 1982). They also lead to greater academic accomplishment on the part of those students variously known as "marginal," "resistant," and simply "at risk" (Arnove and Strout, 1978; Foley and McConnaughy, 1982).

The evidence suggests that similar benefits accrue also to quite different kinds of students in alternatives not targeted for "special needs" groups. Average and above-average students also profit from schools of choice. However, fewer investigations and comparative studies have been undertaken in these kinds of schools of choice and indeed, almost all of the evidence regarding impacts comes from individual program evaluations. There have, however, been three careful analyses of multiple evaluations (Barr and others, 1977; Doob, 1977; Duke and Muzio, 1978), and based on these it seems clear that the attitudes of students toward themselves and toward school are markedly enhanced in the alternative setting. Attendance and school involvement increase, and dropout rates decline. Higher grade-point averages and test scores, and gains in math and reading levels are common, although academic impacts are less clear and consistent in these evaluations than are other sorts of outcomes. The academic evidence seems positive, even though it remains tentative and somewhat scant.

In contrast to aggregate studies of many schools—which average out and thus obscure dramatic accomplishment along with dismal failure—there is now at least one individual school study with a highly credible and extensive comparative base. It demonstrates remarkable academic success. It was done in Pennsylvania where a state-administered quality assessment program not only yields statewide percentile rankings, but also assesses achievement levels in relation to reasonable expectations for a particular school. In the spring of 1982, the Alternative Program in State College ranked at the 99th percentile for its students' performance in reading, writing, math, knowledge of law and government, and analytic thinking. The percentile fell to 90 on humanities and science, but returned to the 99 level with respect to student self-esteem, interest in school and learning, understanding of others, sense of societal responsibility, and appreciation of human accomplishment. In eight of these 11 measures of school quality, the Alternative Program scored above what the state deemed appropriate expectations.[2]

There is no way to know at this point how typical such success may someday be found to be. The evidence is already clear enough that not all alternative schools are successful—so schools of choice are not the elusive model guaranteeing success under any and all circumstances. But perhaps subsequent research will further clarify the requisites of success and identify the pitfalls to avoid.

Meanwhile, however, there is one more group that needs attention in our review of the effects of schools of choice: this is their teachers, for there is evidence of considerable impact of alternatives on those who work within them. A number of the findings already mentioned would predict that such schools are pleasant places to be: the absence of discipline problems and the trust of students augur less adolescent-adult conflict as the tussle between student and staff subcultures evaporates. Furthermore, the amount of autonomy teachers enjoy and the unusual control over their own programs would suggest distinct professional rewards. Such predictions are borne out. Alternative school teachers report unusually high levels of satisfaction (Gladstone and Levin, 1982; Nirenberg, 1977), which they attribute to increased collegiality, and to greater professional autonomy and personal agency in their work. Although many report working harder in the alternative than in their previous school, morale is clearly enhanced.

The benefits to the school of such teacher satisfaction are reported by one researcher to fulfill the organizational idealist's dream, wherein staff become sufficiently identified with the school to find personal fulfillment, or self-actualization, in doing its work (Nirenberg, 1977).

CONCLUSION

It would appear, then, that schools of choice offer heightened satisfactions to the several groups most immediately associated with them: staff, students, and parents. They also claim other advantages with respect to climate and productivity. Although not all such schools succeed, the number of positive instances brings real promise to the diversification and choice arrangement reviewed here. Challenges and reservations that have been expressed have not been reviewed, since these have not been subjected to systematic investigation and thus remain speculative. But commentators and observers have wondered whether the diversification would prove culturally divisive (Broudy, 1973), whether it would increase social class isolation (Arnove and Strout, 1978), whether it would yield "skimming and dumping" (removal of the most desirable students from neighborhood schools, and concentration of the least desirable in separate programs), and whether it would in consequence diminish the quality of non-choice schools (Fleming and others, 1982). Investigation of these questions is certainly needed, along with much more extensive study of the correlates of success in schools of choice. We need much more of that kind of evidence, which will help practitioners to decide just which features are vital for such schools and which can and should be omitted.

ENDNOTES

1. Definitions are cloudy, so that whether magnets are a first cousin to alternatives—or a variety of alternative, or vice versa—may depend on no more than who happens to be speaking. Here, we shall view magnets as one type of alternative and we shall use "alternatives" and "schools of choice" synonymously. This makes for fairly broad and inclusive usage, but it does exclude the punitive programs that in the South are called alternatives.

2. Unpublished study. For further information, contact Rick Lear, Director, Alternative Program, 411 S. Fraser Street, State College, PA 16801.

REFERENCES

Agnew, J.C. "Better Education Through Application." *Synergist* (Winter 1982): 44–48.

Argyris, Chris. "Alternative Schools: A Behavioral Analysis." *Teachers College Record* (May 1974): 429–452.

Arnove, Robert, and Strout, Toby. *Alternative Schools for Disruptive Youth.* Prepared for the National Institute of Education, Grants P-76–0217 and P-77–0254 (September 1978).

Baker, Thomas. *An Investigation of Teachers and Students Perceptions of Instructional Practices in Selected Conventional and Alternative Public Schools.* Unpublished dissertation, Indiana University, 1976.

Barr, Robert; Colston, Bruce; Parrett, William. "The Effectiveness of Alternative Public Schools: An Analysis of Six School Evaluations." *Viewpoint* (July 1977): 1–30.

Berger, Michael. *Violence in the Schools.* Bloomington, Ind.: Phi Delta Kappan, 1974.

Broudy, Harry. "Educational Alternatives—Why Not? Why *Not*" *Phi Delta Kappan* (March 1973): 438–440.

Center for New Schools, "Some Conclusions and Questions About Decision-Making in Alternative Secondary Schools." In *Alternative Schools.* Edited by T. Deal and R. Nolan. (Chicago: Nelson-Hall, 1978), pp. 301–306.

Coleman, James. *Equality of Educational Opportunity.* Washington: Government Printing Office, 1966.

Coleman, James S. "The Children Have Outgrown the Schools." *Psychology Today* (February 1972): 72–75.

Conrad, Dave, and Hedin, Diane. "National Assessment of Experiential Education: Summary and Implications." *Journal of Experiential Education* 4 (1982): 6–20.

Deal, Terrence. "An Organizational Explanation of the Failure of Alternative Secondary Schools." *Educational Researcher* (April 1975): 10–16.

deCharms, Richard. "Pawn or Origin? Enhancing Motivation in Disaffected Youth." *Educational Leadership* (March 1977): 444–448.

Doob, Heather. *Evaluations of Alternative Schools.* Arlington, Va: Educational Research Service, 1977.

Duke, Daniel Linden. "Challenge to Bureaucracy: The Contemporary Alternative School." *Journal of Educational Thought* (May 1976): 34–48.

Duke, Daniel Linden, and Muzio, Irene. "How Effective Are Alternative Schools? A Review of Recent Evaluations and Reports." *Teachers College Record* (February, 1978): 461–483.

Duke, Daniel Linden, and Perry, Cheryl. "Can Alternative Schools Succeed Where Benjamin Spock, Spiro Agnew, and B.F. Skinner Have Failed?" *Adolescence* (Fall, 1978): 375–395.

Erickson, Don. *The British Columbia Story: Antecedents and Consequences of Aid to Private Schools.* Los Angeles: Institute for the Study of Private Schools, 1982.

Fantini, Mario. *Public Schools of Choice.* New York: Simon and Schuster, 1973.

Fleming, Patricia; Blank, Rolf; et al. *Survey of Magnet Schools: Interim Report.* Washington: James H. Lowry and Associates, September 1982.

Foley, Eileen M., and McConnaughy, Susan. *Towards School Improvement: Lessons from Alternative High Schools.* New York: Public Education Association, 1982.

Gitlin, Andrew. "School Structure Affects Teachers." *Educational Horizons* (Summer 1981): 173–178.

Gladstone, F., and Levin, Malcolm. *Public Alternative School Teacher Study.* Toronto: Ontario Institute of Educational Studies, Mimeo, 1982.

Gracey, Harry L. *Curriculum or Craftsmanship: Elementary School Teachers in a Bureaucratic System.* Chicago: University of Chicago Press, 1972.

Grant, Gerald. "The Character of Education and the Education of Character." *Daedalus* (Summer 1981): 135, 149.

Gregory, Thomas, and Smith, Gerald. "Differences Between Alternative and Conventional Schools in Meeting Students' Needs." Paper presented to the American Educational Research Association, Montreal, April 11, 1983. Mimeo, 16 pp.

Hedin, Diane. "The Impact of Experiential Learning on Academic Learning: A Summary of the Theoretical Foundations and Review of Recent Research." Mimeo, n.d. (1983).

Kuhmerker, Lisa, ed. *Moral Education Forum* (Winter 1981) (Issue devoted largely to Just Community Schools).

Mann, David W., and Gold, Martin. *Alternative Schools for Disruptive Secondary Students: Testing a Theory of School Processes, Students' Responses, and Outcome Behaviors.* Institute for Social Research, University of Michigan, December 1980.

Metz, Mary H. *Classrooms and Corridors: The Crisis of Authority in Desegregated Secondary Schools.* Berkeley: University of California Press, 1978.

Metz, Mary H. "Magnet Schools in Their Organizational and Political Context." Paper presented at the American Sociological Association. Toronto, August 23–28, 1981.

Miller, Lynne. "Patterns of Decision Making in Public Alternative Schools." National Alternative Schools Program, University of Massachusetts, n.d. (1974).

Nathan, Joe. *Attitudes Toward High School Education Held by Graduates of a Traditional and an Alternative Public School in St. Paul, Minnesota.* Unpublished dissertation, University of Minnesota, 1981.

Nault, Richard. "School Affiliation and Student Commitments." *Administrator's Notebook.* Chicago: Midwest Administration Center, University of Chicago, 1975–76.

Nault, Richard, and Uchitelle, Susan. "School Choice in the Public Sector: A Case Study of Parental Decision Making." Edited by Michael E. Manley-Casimir. In *Family Choice in Schooling.* Lexington. Mass: D.C. Health, 1982, pp. 85–98.

Nirenberg, John. "A Comparison of the Management Systems of Traditional and Alternative Public High Schools." *Educational Administration Quarterly* (Winter 1977): 86–104.

Parrett, William. "Alternative Schools: What's Really Happening in the Classrooms." Paper presented to the American Educational Research Association, Los Angeles, April, 1981. Mimeo, 40 pp.

Phillips, Gary. *Descriptive Study of the Impact of a High School Alternative Learning Environment on Post High School Lives by a Group of Resistant Learners.* Unpublished dissertation, Ball State University. 1977.

Raywid, Mary Anne. *The Current Status of Schools of Choice in Public Secondary Education.* Hempstead, N.Y.: Project on Alternatives in Education, Hofstra University, 1982.

Rutter, Michael, and others. *Fifteen Thousand Hours: Secondary Schools and Their Effects on Children.* Cambridge: Harvard University Press, 1979.

Schneider, Joseph. "Stop the Bandwagon, We Want to Get Off." *R & D Report* (Winter 1982–83): 7–11.

Sitton, Thad. "Bridging the School-Community Gap: The Lessons of Foxfire." *Educational Leadership* (December 1980): 248–250.

Smith, Vernon; Barr, Robert; and Burke, Daniel. *Alternatives in Education.* Bloomington, Ind.: Phi Delta Kappan, 1976.

A Study of Alternatives in American Education, Vol. VII: Conclusions and Policy Implications. Santa Monica: The Rand Corporation, August 1981.

Swidler, Ann. *Organization Without Authority: Dilemmas of Social Control in Free Schools.* Cambridge: Harvard University Press, 1979.

Tyack, David B. *The One Best System.* Cambridge: Harvard University Press, 1974.

Warren, Constancia. "The Magnet School Boom: Implications for Desegregation." *Equal Opportunity Review,* ERIC Clearinghouse on Urban Education. Columbia: Teachers College, Spring 1978.

Wehlage, Gary, et al. *Effective Programs for the Marginal High School Student.* Madison: University of Wisconsin Center for Education Research, 1982.

Wilson, Stephen. "You Can Talk to Teachers: Student-Teacher Relations in an Alternative High School." *Teachers College Record* (September 1976): 77–100.

Zahorik, John. "Teaching Practices and Beliefs in Elementary Specialty Schools." *Elementary School Journal* (January 1980): 145–157.

Zusman, Ami, and Guthrie, James W. "Back to Basics: The 'New' Tradition in Public High Schools?" Berkeley: University of California, Mimeo, n.d.

Quality and Equality In American Education: Public and Catholic Schools

JAMES S. COLEMAN

The report, "Public and Private Schools," of which I was an author, has raised some questions about certain fundamental assumptions and ideals underlying American education.[1] In this article, I shall first describe briefly the results that raise these questions. Then I shall examine in greater detail these fundamental assumptions and ideals, together with changes in our society that have violated the assumptions and made the ideals increasingly unattainable. I shall then indicate the negative consequences that these violations have created for both equality of educational opportunity in U.S. public schools and for the quality of education they offer. Finally, I shall suggest what seems to me the direction that a new set of ideals and assumptions must take if the schools are to serve American children effectively.

A number of the results of "Public and Private Schools" have been subjected to intense reexamination and reanalysis. The report has occasioned a good deal of debate and controversy, as well as a two-day conference at the National Institute of Education and a one-day conference at the National Academy of Sciences, both in late July. Part of the controversy appears to have arisen because of the serious methodological difficulties in eliminating bias due to self-selection into the private sector. Another part appears to have arisen because the report was seen as an attack on the public schools at a time when tuition tax credit legislation was being proposed in Congress.

I shall not discuss the controversy except to say that all the results summarized in the first portion of this article have been challenged by at least one critic; I would not report them here if these criticisms or our own further analyses had led me to have serious doubts about them. Despite this confidence, the results could be incorrect because of the extent of the methodological difficulties involved in an-

Reprinted from *Phi Delta Kappan*, 63:159–164, 1981, by permission of the author and the publisher.

swering any cause-and-effect question when exposure to the different treatments (that is, to the different types of schools) is so far from random. Most of my comparisons will be between the Catholic and the public schools. The non-Catholic private schools constitute a much more heterogeneous array of schools; our sample in those schools is considerably smaller (631 sophomores and 551 seniors in 27 schools), and the sample may be biased by the fact that a substantial number of schools refused to participate. For these reasons, any generalizations about the non-Catholic private sector must be tenuous. Fortunately, the principal results of interest are to be found in the Catholic schools.

There are five principal results of our study, two having to do with quality of education provided in both the public and private sectors and three related to equality of education.

First, we found evidence of higher academic achievement in basic cognitive skills (reading comprehension, vocabulary, and mathematics) in Catholic schools than in public schools for students from comparable family backgrounds. The difference is roughly one grade level, which is not a great difference. But, since students in Catholic schools take, on the average, a slightly greater number of academic courses, the difference could well be greater for tests more closely attuned to the high school curriculum. And the higher achievement is attained in the Catholic schools with a lower expenditure per pupil and a slightly higher pupil/teacher ratio than in the public schools.

The second result concerning educational quality must be stated with a little less certainty. We found that aspirations for higher education are higher among students in Catholic schools than among comparable students in public schools, despite the fact that, according to the students' retrospective reports, about the same proportion had planned to attend college when they were in the sixth grade.

The first two results concerning equality in education are parallel to the previous two results; one concerns achievement in cognitive skills and the other plans to attend college. For both of these outcomes of schooling, family background matters less in the Catholic schools than in the public schools. In both achievement and aspirations, blacks are closer to whites, Hispanics are closer to Anglos, and children from less well-educated parents are closer to those from better-educated parents in Catholic schools than in public schools. Moreover, in Catholic schools the gap narrows between the sophomore and senior years, while in the public schools the gap in both achievement and aspirations widens.

It is important to note that, unlike the results related to educational quality, these results related to equality do not hold generally for the public/private comparison. That is, the results concerning equality are limited to the comparison between public schools and Catholic schools. Within other segments of the private sector (e.g., Lutheran schools or Jewish schools) similar results for educational differences might well hold (though these other segments have too few blacks and Hispanics to allow racial and ethnic comparisons), but they are not sufficiently represented in the sample to allow separate examination.

The final result concerning educational equality is in the area of racial and ethnic integration. Catholic schools have, proportionally, only about half as many black students as do the public schools (about 6% compared to about 14%); but internally they are less segregated. In terms of their effect on the overall degree of racial integration in U.S. schools, these two factors work in opposing directions; to a large extent they cancel each other out. But of interest to our examination here, which concerns the internal functioning of the public and Catholic sectors of education, is the lesser internal segregation of blacks in the Catholic sector. Part of this is due to the smaller percentage of black students in Catholic schools, for a general conclusion in the school desegregation literature is that school systems with smaller proportions of a disadvantaged minority are less segregated than those with larger proportions. But part seems due to factors beyond the simple proportions. A similar result is that, even though the Catholic schools in our sample have slightly higher proportions of Hispanic students than the public schools they have slightly less Hispanic/Anglo segregation.

These are the results from our research on public and private schools that raise questions about certain fundamental assumptions of American education. Catholic schools appear to be characterized by *both* higher quality, on the average, *and* greater equality than the public schools. How can this be when the public schools are, first, more expensive, which should lead to higher quality, and, second, explicitly designed to increase equality of opportunity? The answer lies, I believe, in the organization of public education in the United States, and that organization in turn is grounded in several fundamental assumptions. It is to these assumptions that I now turn.

FOUR BASIC IDEALS AND THEIR VIOLATION

Perhaps the ideal most central to American education is the ideal of the common school, a school attended by all children. The assumption that all social classes should attend the same school contrasted with the two-tiered educational systems in Europe, which reflected their feudal origins. Both in the beginning and at crucial moments of choice (such as the massive expansion of secondary education in the early part of this century), American education followed the pattern of common, or comprehensive, schools, including all students from the community and all courses of study. Only in the largest eastern cities were there differentiated, selective high schools, and even that practice declined over time, with new high schools generally following the pattern of the comprehensive school.

One implication of the common-school ideal has been the deliberate and complete exclusion of religion from the schools. In contrast, many (perhaps most) other countries have some form of support for schools operated by religious groups. In many countries, even including very small ones such as the Netherlands and Israel, there is a state secular school system, as well as publicly supported schools under the control of religious groups. But the melting-pot ideology that shaped American education dictated that there would be a single set of publicly supported schools, and the reaction to European religious intolerance dictated that these be free of religious influence.[2]

The absence of social class, curriculum, or religious bases for selection of students into different schools meant that, in American schooling, attendance at a given school was dictated by location of residence. This method worked well in sparsely settled areas and in towns and smaller cities, and it was a principle compatible with a secular democracy. Two factors have, however, led this mode of school assignment to violate the assumptions of the common school. One is the movement of the U.S. population to cities with high population densities, resulting in economically homogeneous residential areas. The other is the more recent, largely post-World War II expansion of personal transportation, leading to the development of extensive, economically differentiated suburbs surrounding large cities.

The combined effect of these two changes has been that in metropolitan areas the assumptions of the common school are no longer met. The residential basis of school assignment, in an ironic twist, has proved to be segregative and exclusionary, separating economic levels just as surely as do the explicitly selective systems of European countries and separating racial groups even more completely. The larger the metropolitan area, the more true this is, so that in the largest metropolitan areas the schools form a set of layers of economically stratified and racially distinct schools, while in small cities and towns the schools continue to approximate the economically and racially heterogeneous mix that was Horace Mann's vision of the common school in America.

In retrospect, only the temporary constraints on residential movement imposed by economic and technological conditions allowed the common-school ideal to be realized even for a time. As those constraints continue to decrease, individual choice will play an increasing role in school attendance (principally through location of residence), and the common-school assumption will be increasingly violated. Assignment to school in a single publicly supported school system on the basis of residence is no longer a means of achieving the common-school ideal. And, in fact, the common-school ideal may no longer be attainable through *any* means short of highly coercive ones.

The courts have attempted to undo the racially segregative impact of residential choice, reconstituting the common-school ideal through compulsory busing of children into different residential areas.[3] These attempts, however, have been largely thwarted by families who, exercising that same opportunity for choice of school through residence, move out of the court's jurisdiction. The unpopularity and impermanence of these court-ordered attempts to reinstitute the common school suggest that attempts to reimpose by law the constraints that economics and technology once placed upon school choice will fail and that, in the absence of those naturally imposed constraints, the common-school ideal will give way before an even stronger ideal—that of individual liberty.

It is necessary, then, to recognize the failure of school assignment by residence and to reexamine the partially conflicting ideals of American education in order to determine which of those ideals we want to preserve and which to discard. For example, in high schools distinguished by variations in curriculum—one form of which is a type of magnet school and another form of which is the technical high school—a more stable racial mix of students is possible than in comprehensive high schools. As another example, Catholic schools are less racially and economically segregated than are U.S. public schools; this suggests that, when a school is defined around and controlled by a religious community, families may tolerate more racial and economic heterogeneity than they would in a school defined around a residential area and controlled by government officials.

A second ideal of American education has been the concept of local control. This has meant both control by the local school board and superintendent and the responsiveness of the school staff to parents. But these conditions have changed as well. The local school board and superintendent now have far less control over education policy than only 20 years ago. A large part of the policy-making function has shifted to the national level; this shift was caused primarily by the issue of racial discrimination, but it has also affected the areas of sex discrimination, bilingual education, and education for the handicapped, among others. Part of the policy-making power has shifted to the school staff or their union representatives, as professionalization and collective bargaining have accompanied the growth in size of school districts and the breakdown of a sense of community at the local level.

The loss of control by school boards and superintendents has been accompanied by a reduced responsiveness of the school to parents. This too has resulted in part from the breakdown of community at the local level and the increasing professionalization of teachers, both of which have helped to free the teacher from community control. The changes have been accompanied and reinforced by the trend to larger urban agglomerates and larger school districts. And some of the changes introduced to overcome racial segregation—in particular, busing to a distant school—have led to even greater social distances between parent and teacher.

A result of this loss of local control has been that parents are more distant from their children's school, less able to exert influence, less comfortable about the school as an extension of their own child rearing. Public support for public schools, as evidenced in the passage of school tax referenda and school bond issues and in the responses to public opinion polls, has declined since the mid-1960s, probably in part as a result of this loss of local control. Even more recently, in a backlash against the increasingly alien control of the schools, some communities have attempted to counter what they see as moral relativism in the curriculum (e.g., the controversy over the content in *Man: A Course of Study*) and have attempted to ban the teaching of evolution.

Technological and ecological changes make it unlikely that local control of education policy can be reconstituted as it has existed in the past, that is, through a local school board controlling a single public school system and representing the consensus of the community. Individuals may regain such local control by moving ever farther from large cities (as the 1980 census shows they have been doing), but the educational system as a whole cannot be reconstituted along the old local-control lines. Again, as in the case of the common-school ideal, present conditions (and the likelihood that they will persist) make the ideal unrealizable. One alternative is to resign ourselves to ever-decreasing public support for the public schools as they move further from the ideal. Another, however, is to attempt to find new principles for the organization of American education that will bring back parental support.

A third fundamental assumption of American public schooling, closely connected to local control, has been local financing of education. Some of the same factors that have brought about a loss of local control have shifted an increasing portion of education financing to the state and federal levels. Local taxes currently support only about 40% of expenditures for public schooling; federal support amounts to about 8% or 9% and state support, slightly over half of the total. The shift from local to state (and, to a lesser extent, federal) levels of financing has resulted from the attempt to reduce inequalities of educational expenditures among school districts. Inequalities that were once of little concern come to be deeply felt when local communities are no longer isolated but interdependent and in close social proximity. The result has been the attempt by some states, responding to the *Serrano* decision in California, to effect complete equality in educational expenditures for all students within the state. This becomes difficult to achieve without full statewide financing, which negates the principle of local financing.

Yet the justification for student assignment to the schools within the family's taxation district has been that the parents were paying for the schools *in that district*. That justification vanishes under a system of statewide taxation. The rationale for assignment by residence, already weakened by the economic and racial differences among students from different locales, is further weakened by the decline in local financing.

A fourth ideal of American public education has been the principle of *in loco parentis*. In committing their child to a school, parents expect that the school will exercise comparable authority over and responsibility for the child. The principle of *in loco parentis* was, until the past two decades, assumed not only at the elementary and secondary levels but at the college level as well. However, this assumption vanished as colleges abdicated the responsibility and parents of college students shortened the scope of their authority over their children's behavior from the end of college to the end of high school.

Most parents, however, continue to expect the school to exercise authority over and responsibility for their children through the end of high school. Yet public schools have been less and less successful in acting *in loco parentis*. In part, this is due to the loss of authority in the society as a whole, manifested in high school by a decreasing willingness of high school-age youths to be subject to *anyone's* authority in matters of dress and conduct. In part, it is due to the increasing dissensus among parents themselves about the authority of the school to exercise discipline over their children, sometimes leading to legal suits to limit the school's authority. And, in part, it is due to the courts, which, in response to these suits, have expanded the scope of civil rights of children in school, thus effectively limiting the school's authority to something less than that implied by the principle of *in loco parentis.*

There has been a major shift among some middle-class parents—a shift that will probably become even more evident as the children of parents now in their thirties move into high school—toward an early truncation of responsibility for and authority over their adolescent children. This stems in part from two changes— an increase in longevity and a decrease in number of children—which, taken together, remove child rearing from the central place it once held for adults. Many modern adults who begin child rearing late and end early are eager to resume the leisure and consumption activities that preceded their child-rearing period; they encourage early autonomy for their young. But the high school often continues to act as if it has parental support for its authority. In some cases it does; in others it does not. The community consensus on which a school's authority depends has vanished.

An additional difficulty is created by the increasing size and bureaucratization of the school. The exercising of authority—regarded as humane and fair when the teacher knows the student and parents well—comes to be regarded as inhumane and unfair when it is impersonally administered by a school staff member (teacher or otherwise) who hardly knows the student and seldom sees the parents. Thus there arises in such large, impersonal settings an additional demand for sharply defined limits on authority.

This combination of factors gives public schools less power to exercise the responsibility for and authority over students that are necessary to the school's functioning. The result is a breakdown of discipline in the public schools and, in the extreme, a feeling by some parents that their children are not safe in school. Again, a large portion of the change stems from the lack of consensus that once charac- terized the parental community about the kind and amount of authority over their children they wished to delegate to the school—a lack of consensus exploited by some students eager to escape authority and responded to by the courts in limiting the school's authority. And, once again, this raises questions about what form of reorganization of American education would restore the functioning of the school and even whether it is possible to reinstate the implicit contract between parent and school that initially allowed the school to act *in loco parentis.*

The violation of these four basic assumptions of American education—the common school, local control, local financing, and *in loco parentis*—together with our failure to establish a new set of attainable ideals, has hurt both the quality and the equality of American education. For this change in society, without a corre- sponding change in the ideals that shape its educational policies, reduces the capability of its schools to achieve quality and equality, which even in the best of circumstances are uncomfortable bedfellows.

Next I shall give some indications of how the pursuit of each of these goals of quality and equality is impeded by policies guided by the four assumptions I have examined, beginning first with the goal of equality.

The organization of U.S. education is assignment to school by residence, guided by the common-school, local-control, and local-financing assumptions, despite those elements that violate these assumptions. In a few locations, school assignment is relieved by student choice of school or by school choice of student. But, in general, the principle observed in American education (thus making it different from the educational systems of many countries) has been that of a rigid assignment by residence, a practice that upholds the common-school myth and the local-control and local-financing myths.

It is commonly assumed that the restriction of choice through rigid assignment by residence is of relative benefit to those least well off, from whom those better off would escape if choice were available. But matters are not always as they seem. Assignment by residence leaves two avenues open to parents: to move their residence, choosing a school by choice of residence; or to choose to attend a private school. But those avenues are open only to those who are sufficiently affluent to choose a school by choosing residence or to choose a private school. The latter choice may be partially subsidized by a religious community operating the school, or, in rare cases, by scholarships. But these partial exceptions do not hide the central point: that the organization of education through rigid assignment by residence hurts most those without money (and those whose choice is constrained by race or ethnicity), and this increases the inequality of educational opportunity. The reason, of course, is that, because of principles of individual liberty, we are unwilling to close the two avenues of choice: moving residence and choosing a private school. And although economic and technological constraints once kept all but a few from exercising these options, that is no longer true. The constraints are of declining importance; the option of residential change to satisfy educational choice (the less expensive of the two options) is exercised by larger numbers of families. And in that exercise of choice, different economic levels are sorted into different schools by the economic level of the community they can afford.

We must conclude that the restrictions on educational choice in the public sector and the presence of tuition costs in the private sector are restrictions that operate to the relative disadvantage of the least well off. Only when these restrictions were reinforced by the economic and technological constraints that once existed could they be regarded as effective in helping to achieve a "common school." At present, and increasingly in the future, they are working to the disadvantage of the least well off, increasing even more the inequality of educational opportunities.

One of the results of our recent study of public and private schools suggests these processes at work. Among Catholic schools, achievement of students from less-advantaged backgrounds—blacks, Hispanics, and those whose parents are poorly educated—is closer to that of students from advantaged backgrounds than is true for the public sector. Family background makes much less difference for achievement in Catholic schools than in public schools. This greater homogeneity of achievement in the Catholic sector (as well as the lesser racial and ethnic segregation of the Catholic sector) suggests that the ideal of the common school is more nearly met in the Catholic schools than in the public schools. This may be because a religious community continues to constitute a functional community to a greater extent than does a residential area, and in such a functional community there will be less stratification by family background, both within a school and between schools.

At the same time, the organization of American education is harmful to quality of education. The absence of consensus, in a community defined by residence, about what kind and amount of authority should be exercised by the school removes the chief means by which the school has brought about achievement among its students. Once there was such consensus, because residential areas once were communities that maintained a set of norms reflected in the schools' and the parents' beliefs about what was appropriate for children. The norms varied in different communities, but they were consistent within each community. That is no longer true at the high school level, for the reasons I have described. The result is what some have called a crisis of authority.

In our study of high school sophomores and seniors in both public and private schools, we found not only higher achievement in the Catholic and other private schools for students from comparable backgrounds than in the public schools, but also major differences between the functioning of the public schools and the schools of the private sector. The principal differences were in the greater academic demands made and the greater disciplinary standards maintained in private schools, even when schools with students from comparable backgrounds were compared. This suggests that achievement increases as the demands, both academic and disciplinary, are greater. The suggestion is confirmed by two comparisons: Among the public schools, those that have academic demands and disciplinary standards at the same level as the average private school have achievement at the level of that in the private sector (all comparisons, of course, involving students from comparable backgrounds). And, among the private schools, those with academic demands and disciplinary standards at the level of the average public school showed achievement levels similar to those of the average public school.

The evidence from these data—and from other recent studies—is that *stronger academic demands and disciplinary standards produce better achievement.* Yet the public schools are in a poor position to establish and maintain these demands. The loss of authority of the local school board, superintendent, and principal to federal policy and court rulings, the rise of student rights (which has an impact both in shaping a "student-defined" curriculum and in impeding discipline), and, perhaps most fundamental, the breakdown in consensus among parents about the high schools' authority over and responsibility for their children—all of these factors put the average public school in an untenable position to bring about achievement.

Many public high schools have adjusted to these changes by reducing their academic demands (through reduction of standards, elimination of competition, grade inflation, and a proliferation of undemanding courses) and by slackening their disciplinary standards (making "truancy" a word of the past and ignoring cutting of classes and the use of drugs or alcohol).

These accommodations may be necessary, or at least they may facilitate keeping the peace, in some schools. But the peace they bring is bought at the price of lower achievement, that is, a reduced quality of education.

One may ask whether such accommodations are inevitable or whether a different organization of education might make them unnecessary. It is to this final question that I now turn.

ABANDONING OLD ASSUMPTIONS

The old assumptions that have governed American education all lead to a policy of assignment of students to school by place of residence and to a standard conception of a school. Yet a variety of recent developments, both within the public sector and outside it, suggest that attainment of the twin goals of quality and equality may be incompatible with this. One development is the establishment, first outside the public sector and then in a few places within it as well, of elementary schools governed by different philosophies of education and chosen by parents who subscribe to those philosophies. Montessori schools at the early levels, open education, and basic education are examples. In some communities, this principle of parental choice has been used to maintain more stable racial integration than occurs in schools with fixed pupil assignment and a standard educational philosophy. At the secondary level, magnet schools, with specialized curricula or intensive programs in a given area (e.g., music or performing arts), have been introduced, similarly drawing a clientele who have some consensus on which a demanding and effective program can be built. Alternative schools have flourished, with both students and staff who accept the earlier autonomy to which I have referred. This is not to say, of course, that all magnet schools and all alternative schools are successful, for many are not. But if they were products of a well-conceived pluralistic conception of modes of secondary education, with some policy guidelines for viability, success would be easier to achieve.

Outside the public sector, the growth of church-operated schools is probably the most prominent development, reflecting a different desire by parents for a non-standard education. But apart from the religious schools, there is an increasingly wide range of educational philosophies, from the traditional preparatory school to the free school and the parent-run cooperative school.

I believe that these developments suggest an abandonment of the principle of assignment by residence and an expansion of the modes of education supported by public funds. Whether this expansion goes so far as to include all or part of what is now the private sector or is instead a reorganization of the public sector alone is an open question. The old proscriptions against public support of religious education should not be allowed to stand in the way of a serious examination of this question. But the elements of successful reorganization remain, whether it stays within the public sector or encompasses the private: a pluralistic conception of education, based on "communities" defined by interests, values, and educational preferences rather than residence; a commitment of parent and student that can provide the school a lever for extracting from students their best efforts; and the educational choice for all that is now available only to those with money.

Others may not agree with this mode of organizing education. But it is clear that the goals of education in a liberal democracy may not be furthered, and may in fact be impeded, by blind adherence to the ideals and assumptions that once served U.S. education—some of which may be unattainable in modern America—and by the mode of school organization that these ideals and assumptions brought into being. There may be extensive debate over what set of ideals is both desirable and attainable and over what mode of organization can best attain these ideals, but it is a debate that should begin immediately. Within the public sector, the once-standard curriculum is beginning to take a variety of forms, some of which reflect the search for a new mode of organizing schooling. And an increasing (though still small) fraction of youngsters are in private schools, some of which exemplify alternative modes of organizing schooling. These developments can be starting points toward the creation of an educational philosophy to guide the reorganization of American schooling in ways fruitful for the youth who experience it.

ENDNOTES

1. The other two authors are Thomas Hoffer and Sally Kilgore. A first draft of "Public and Private Schools" was completed on 2 September 1980. A revised draft was released by the National Center for Education Statistics (NCES) on 7 April 1981. A final draft is being submitted to NCES this fall. A revised version of the April 7 draft, together with an epilogue and prologue examining certain broader issues, is being published this fall by Basic Books as *Achievement in High School: Public and Private Schools Compared.*

2. It has nevertheless been true that in many religiously homogeneous communities, ordinarily Protestant, religious influence did infiltrate the schools. Only since the Supreme Court's ban on prayer in the schools has even nonsectarian religious influence been abolished.

3. The legal rationale for these decisions has been past discriminatory practices by school systems; but, in fact, the remedies have constituted attempts to overcome the effects of residential choice.

Do Catholic High Schools Improve Minority Student Achievement?

TIMOTHY Z. KEITH   ELLIS B. PAGE

There has been already considerable debate concerning the efficiency of Catholic (and other private) schools in producing student achievement (cf., Coleman, Hoffer, & Kilgore, 1981; Hallinan & Olneck, 1982; Page & Keith, 1981; Walberg & Shanahan, 1983). With current arguments over tuition tax credits, and with charges of "a rising tide of mediocrity" by the National Commission on Excellence in Education (1983, p. 5), it seems likely that such debate will continue.

Contained in the overall question of private schooling is the issue of the effects of Catholic schooling on *minority* achievement. Recent research has purported to show that Catholic schools produce higher achievement in minorities (black and Hispanic students) than do public schools, even when those students' background characteristics are "controlled" (Greeley, 1982). In his analysis, Father Greeley used the massive High School and Beyond (HSB) data set to test whether Catholic schooling had an impact on high school minority students' achievement. There were controls for family and student background characteristics, such as parental education and possessions in the home. Greeley's analyses stated that there was a considerable effect of Catholic over public schooling on minority achievement (Greeley, 1982).

Greeley's analyses and conclusions were quite similar to those of Coleman et al. (1981) in their claims for U.S. students in private schools. Yet others (Page & Keith, 1981) have argued that the models used by Coleman and colleagues, controlling only for SES characteristics, were misspecified, since the Coleman analysis made no correction for student intellectual ability, an omission that has been shown to lead to major fallacies in school effects (Alexander, Pallas, & Cook, 1981). When

From *Educational Researcher,* 22:337–348, 1985. Copyright 1985 by the American Educational Research Association. Reprinted by permission of the publisher.

the HSB public/private data were reanalyzed with controls for both family background and ability, the difference between public and private high school seniors' achievement was trivial; the effect Coleman claimed to be an *outcome* of private schooling appeared to be, rather, a criterion for selection *into* private schools![1] Thus one may question whether the Catholic school effect reported for minorities (Greeley, 1982) might also be an artifact of selection into Catholic schools rather than an outcome of school type. Here, we also have used the HSB data with explicit path techniques to compare the achievement of black and Hispanic high school seniors enrolled in Catholic schools with those enrolled in public schools, using models explicitly designed to attempt to control for such possible student selection.

METHOD

Subjects

Subjects for the present study were again drawn from the first wave (1980) of the HSB longitudinal study. As documented elsewhere (National Opinion Research Center, 1980), HSB is a stratified, two-stage probability sample of 58,270 sophomores and seniors from 1,015 high schools across the United States. Subjects for these analyses were all those black and Hispanic high school seniors who were attending either Catholic or public high schools. Thus the sample consisted of 3,922 black high school seniors (3,552 from public schools and 370 from Catholic schools) and 3,146 Hispanic high school seniors (2,661 public and 485 Catholic).

Variables

Family Background
This is a composite socioeconomic status variable computed for HSB for each student. Family Background includes responses to questions concerning parental occupational status and education, income, and certain possessions in the home.

Ability
The HSB seniors were given a series of short tests (each requiring from 3 to 15 minutes to complete). Such tests may be divided into relatively school-related, or achievement, and relatively school-free, or ability, measures based on their content in comparison to traditional tests of achievement and intellectual ability (Page & Keith, 1981). The Ability variable is a factor score from factor analysis of six HSB verbal and nonverbal ability, or relatively school-free, tests. Scores on Vocabulary I and II, Mosaic Comparisons I and II, Picture Number, and Visualization in Three Dimensions were factor analyzed for the entire HSB senior sample, with each subject weighed by his or her design weight (a variable designed to reproduce the U.S. high school population according to major demographic variables) as recorded

on the HSB tape. The factor score coefficients for the unrotated first principal factor from this analysis were used to create a general ability factor score for each subject in the present analysis (cf., Keith, 1982a; Page & Keith, 1981; Roberson, Keith, & Page, 1983).

School Type

This is a dummy variable coded 0 for subjects attending public schools and 1 for Catholic high school students.

Achievement

Achievement is a composite of the more school-related of the HSB senior tests. Scores on the Reading, Mathematics I, and Mathematics II tests were summed, with the composite weighted to be $\frac{1}{2}$ reading and $\frac{1}{2}$ math.[2]

Structure of the Models

The path models (each was analyzed once for blacks and once for Hispanics) are displayed in Figures 6-1 and 6-2. The models displayed are simple, recursive, just-identified path models, with arrows representing a weak causal ordering, drawn from presumed causes (exogenous variables) to presumed effects (endogenous variables). Such models may be estimated using standard multiple regression analysis (Kenny, 1979, chap. 4); we used the SPSS package (Hull & Nie, 1981). For statistical purposes, students attending Catholic schools were weighted to produce apparently equal frequencies of public and Catholic school students.[3]

Figure 1 displays a simplified model explaining student achievement only as a product of Family Background and School Type; this model, loosely based on Greeley's (1982) research, is shown for comparison with other models presented here.[4] We assume that this model is seriously misspecified, that an important common cause of both Catholic schooling and achievement—intellectual ability—has been left out of the model. Therefore, Figure 6-2 presents a more complete model, incorporating intellectual ability as an additional influence on student achievement.

INITIAL ANALYSES TO EXPLAIN MINORITY STUDENT ACHIEVEMENT

Table 6-1 presents the means, standard deviations, and the weighted zero-order correlations among the variables used in the analyses for black seniors. Data for Hispanic seniors are shown in Table 6-2. Figure 6-1 shows the results of the simpler model in explaining black seniors' achievement in public versus Catholic schools. Without controls for the selection variable of student ability, we note that Catholic schools seem to have a powerful effect on black students' achievement (path, or *p*, of .277).

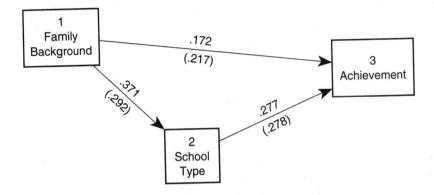

FIGURE 6-1. The apparent benefits of school type on black high school seniors' achievement, without controls for student ability. Paths for the same model for Hispanic seniors are shown in parentheses. All paths are standardized coefficients, where complete influence would be ± 1.00.

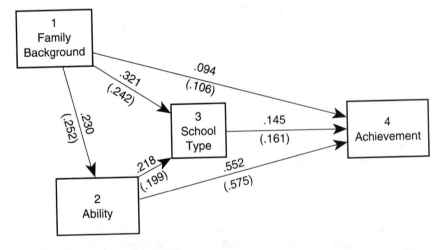

FIGURE 6-2. A fuller model to explain black student achievement. Here both family background and intellectual ability are included. Path coefficients for Hispanics are in parentheses.

TABLE 6-1 Weighted Correlations, Means, and Standard Deviations for Black Seniors

Variables	1	2	3	4	5	6
1. Family background	1.00					
2. Ability	.230	1.00				
3. School type	.371	.292	1.00			
4. Achievement	.275	.616	.341	1.00		
5. Educational aspiration	.249	.220	.242	.271	1.00	
6. Academic courses	.302	.454	.381	.594	.304	1.00
M	−.291	60.463	.500	45.616	.583	3.044
SD	.772	8.595	.500	7.233	.493	2.030

The path coefficients for Hispanic seniors are displayed in Figure 6-1 in parentheses. Again, Catholic schooling appears to exert a powerful influence on Hispanic achievement ($p = .278$). Indeed, with this kind of analysis, moving from public to Catholic school should increase achievement by more than one-half a standard deviation![5]

Figure 6-2 displays the solved path model to explain black seniors' achievement, with controls for both family background characteristics and student ability. For black students, Ability has, as expected, a very strong effect on Achievement (as symbolized by the path of .552). The path from Ability to School Type (.218) is also substantial, clearly illustrating the importance of Ability for selection into Catholic schools for these minority students. And, as expected, the incorporation of Ability into the path model substantially reduced the path from Catholic schooling to Achievement (from .277 in Figure 6-1 to .145). Despite inclusion of both Background and Ability controls in the causal model, however, Catholic schooling still appears to exert a moderate, meaningful (defined here as a path $\geq .05$) influence on black seniors' achievement.

Figure 6-2 also shows (in parentheses) the path coefficients for the same model for Hispanic seniors. For Hispanics as well as blacks, the inclusion of Ability into the causal model greatly reduced the apparent effect of Catholic schooling, yet for both minority groups, the paths from Catholic schooling to achievement *were still meaningful* ($p = .145$ for blacks and .161 for Hispanics).[6]

SELECTION BY-PRODUCT OR SCHOOL EFFECT?

Results of the analyses of the model displayed in Figure 6-2 suggest that Catholic schools do indeed have a meaningful effect on minority students' achievement. Yet the analyses do not reveal whether this apparent Catholic school effect is the spurious by-product of yet another uncontrolled selection variable, or whether these paths represent a true product of some aspect of Catholic schooling. Furthermore, if these paths do represent a Catholic school effect, it seems important to determine *how* this effect is achieved, whether through increased work loads, curricular differences, or tighter discipline.

The recent report of the National Commission on Excellence in Education (1983) has stirred much media interest by citing current problems in education and presenting possible solutions. One finding of the Commission was too little substance in the curricula of many schools. These and other findings (e.g., Alexander & Pallas, 1984; Walberg & Shanahan, 1983) suggest that curriculum could well be a means for producing higher minority achievement. On the other hand, perhaps minority students who choose Catholic schools are already more committed to their education, and have higher educational aspirations, than their public school peers. In that case, more academic coursework and higher achievement could both be products of this greater interest.

Figure 6-3 displays a model that incorporates the earlier variables, but adds student aspiration and academic coursework:

Educational Aspiration is a dummy variable based on students' answers to the question "Did you expect to go to college when you were in the eighth grade?" A "yes" was coded as 1; all other responses ("no," "hadn't thought about it," and "was not sure") were coded 0.[7]

Academic Courses is the sum of responses to questions concerning basic academic coursework taken by the student, including courses in advanced or honors English, Algebra I, Algebra II, Geometry, Trigonometry, Calculus, Physics, and Chemistry.

As indicated above, this model assumes that the apparent Catholic school effect found in the initial analyses might be a product of the background (including Family Background and Ability) and interests of minority students choosing to attend Catholic schools, and of Catholic schools themselves, through the demanding coursework they require their students to take.

Figure 6-3 displays the solution to this path model for black high school seniors. As can be seen from the very strong path from Academic Courses to Achievement ($p = .356$), the amount of such coursework seems to have a powerful effect on achievement, even when achievement is measured with only basic reading and math tests. In fact, the only direct influence stronger than that from Academic Courses was that from Ability ($p = .418$). Furthermore, Academic Courses not only had a powerful direct effect on Achievement, but its inclusion in the model (along with Educational Aspirations) substantially reduced the direct effect of School Type, from a path of .145 in Figure 6-2 to a path of .057 in Figure 6-3. Such results, along with the strong path from School Type to Academic Courses ($p = .205$), suggest that the small but meaningful Catholic school effect found for black seniors is at least in part due to the more academic coursework they take in Catholic schools.

Educational Aspirations had only a small direct effect on Achievement ($p = .047$); however, it appears that such expectations influence black students to attend Catholic schools ($p = .126$) and to take more advanced courses than their peers ($p = .154$).

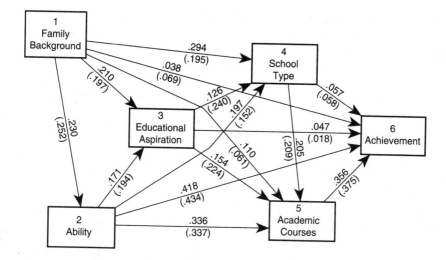

FIGURE 6-3. Model explaining black high school seniors' achievement as a result of family background, ability, educational aspirations, Catholic schooling, and academic coursework. Paths for Hispanic seniors are shown in parentheses.

In fact, it appears that the *indirect* effects of Educational Aspirations, primarily through Academic Courses, are greater than their direct effects on Achievement (indirect effect through Academic Courses = .154 × .356 = .055).

The results for Hispanic seniors (Figure 6-3, in parentheses) suggest that similar influences apply for their achievement. The strongest effect on Hispanics' achievement was still from Ability ($p = .434$), with Academic Courses also exerting a powerful influence on Achievement ($p = .375$). In fact, the primary difference between the models for Hispanics and for blacks is that for Hispanics, Educational Aspirations appears to have even less *direct* effect on Achievement than for blacks, while its *indirect* influence is somewhat stronger (and even these minor differences are probably insignificant).

DISCUSSION AND SUMMARY

Our results, then, suggest that reports of a powerful impact for Catholic high school attendance on minority achievement were largely the result of the inadequate models used to study these effects. Yet even when more adequate models were used, incorporating controls for selection into Catholic school based on student ability, there still remained a meaningful, albeit smaller, Catholic school effect. But such results, while interesting, seem of limited utility unless they can point to the *reason* for this apparent effect—additional "selection variables" or true Catholic school effects. Additional analyses, incorporating both selection variables and potential school effects, have shown that Catholic schools do indeed seem to have *real influence* on minority high school seniors' academic achievement, and that this effect is largely accomplished through the more stringent curricular demands of Catholic schools. Thus our analyses have not only helped to explain the Catholic school "advantage," but have also pointed to a possible method for public schools to improve minority achievement.

In some ways, however, these analyses raise many questions. These results are, for example, quite inconsistent with Page and Keith's (1981) results showing that the reported *private* (mostly Catholic) school effect for students in general (both minority and majority) was almost entirely a product of selection into private schools based on ability. To address this question, we also analyzed the model shown in Figure 6-2 for white students in Catholic and public schools. The results were consistent with Page and Keith's (1981) results; when Family Background and Ability were controlled, School Type had *no meaningful effect* on white seniors' achievement (as suggested by the resulting path of .010 from School Type to Achievement). Thus it appears that the positive impact found for Catholic schools is confined to *minority* seniors.[8]

Another question concerns the nature of the Academic Courses variable, heavily laden with science and mathematics courses. Despite its inadequacies, this variable seems the best composite for assessing the number of academic courses taken by each student. While other questions concerning numbers of courses (e.g., number of English or Math courses taken) were available in the HSB data, there was no indication of the level of those courses; that is, there is no way to tell which of the math courses were, for example, Consumer Math and which were basic academic courses such as Algebra. On the other hand, the nature of this variable raises the question of whether its effect is due only to its influence on the mathematics portion of the achievement measure. Analyses separating Reading and Math Achievement suggest that *both* are influenced, although Math more than Reading. It is also possible that the path from Academic Courses to Achievement is in part spurious, that it is simply a by-product of inadequate measurement of other variables in the model, such as Aspiration, or even Ability. Yet our results are quite consistent with those of others (e.g., Alexander & Pallas, 1984), using different data and different conceptualizations of the same constructs, in showing the relative importance for coursework, and the relative lack of *direct* influence for aspirations, on achievement.

The nature of the Achievement variable is also open to question in that it measures only basic reading and math skills, rather than achievement in high school subject matter. In other words, perhaps our Achievement variable is too loaded with ability to serve as a useful criterion for school differences. To examine this possibility, we analyzed models similar to those shown in Figures 6-1 through 6-3 using data from the HSB sophomores, who were administered Civics, Writing, and Science, in addition to Reading and Math, tests. Unfortunately, neither Ability nor Academic Courses were well measured for the sophomores; we could use only a single Vocabulary test for Ability (thus reflecting only verbal ability, which is much more school-related than our general ability variable for seniors). Academic Courses was the sum of two questions asking whether the student had taken advanced or honors English and Math. We constructed two different Achievement measures for the sophomores, one measuring basic achievement (Reading and Math, similar to the seniors), and one measuring more advanced skills (Civics, Writing, and Science). Analyses of our models separately for each of these achievement measures yielded very similar results for basic and advanced achievement, thus suggesting that the reading and math composite used for the seniors is a reasonable measure of achievement, even at this level. In fact, the only substantial difference suggested that academic coursework (at least as measured for the sophomores) had more effect on *basic* than advanced achievement for the black sophomores.

Our analyses with the HSB sophomores also speak to the stability of these results. Even with the necessary changes in the measurement of some constructs in the models, the results for the first two sets of analyses were quite consistent with those shown in Figures 6-1 and 6-2. Catholic schooling appeared to have a major effect on Achievement when Ability was uncontrolled, but there still remained a smaller, yet still meaningful, effect when Ability was controlled (although of course this effect was smaller for sophomores, with Ability measured only by a verbal test). The results of analysis 3 were less conclusive. Academic Courses still had a meaningful effect on Achievement, although this effect was considerably smaller for sophomores than for seniors ($p = .079$ for blacks, $.128$ for Hispanics). Yet there was no meaningful influence for School Type on Academic Courses for black sophomores ($p = -.040$), while *public* school Hispanics more often took advanced or honors courses than did those in Catholic schools ($p = -.097$). Although interpretation of these results must be tempered by suspicion about the Courses variable (we wonder, for example, if Catholic and public school students define "advanced or honors" courses differently), one plausible interpretation is that is is the differentiation in coursework taken *during,* rather than before, high school that has the greatest impact on high school achievement.

Finally, readers may wonder whether the small Catholic school effect found here could be explained equally well by other selection variables or potential school effects, as has been suggested elsewhere (e.g., Coleman et al., 1981; Greeley, 1982; Peng, Owings, & Fetters, 1982; Walberg & Shanahan, 1983). Additional analyses incorporating some of these potential influences along with Family Background, Ability, and School Type suggested that potential school effects (such as student ratings of the quality of teaching or the disciplinary climate) had little effect on Achievement and even less effect on the path from School Type to Achievement. Several variables representing stronger background controls (e.g., Family Size, Parental Monitoring) and student characteristics (e.g., Locus of Control, Self-Concept, Handicapped/Nonhandicapped, Catholic/Other Religion) also showed little effect. A product (or "interaction term"; cf. Cohen, 1978) of Family Background and School Type was also added to the model to test claims that Catholic schools are most effective with the lowest SES minorities (Greeley, 1982, chap. 8). Such interactions, however, did not contribute to Achievement when Ability was controlled. Additional analyses suggest that, while Catholic Schools may admit very low SES minorities, those low SES minority students admitted are also quite intellectually able. On the other hand, homework (cf. Keith, 1982b; Keith & Page, in press; Page & Keith, 1981), possibly related to extra effort required from advanced coursework, and program of study (college preparatory, general, or vocational; cf. Peng et al., 1982), which are both obviously related to courses taken but are more confounded with School Type, also help explain the Catholic school effect.

These results, then, indicate that Catholic schools do produce slightly higher achievement in minority students than do public schools, and that they do this through a strong academic curriculum requiring more advanced coursework and, presumably, more effort. And while such results are fascinating in their support of the conclusions of the recent report of the National Commission on Excellence in Education, caution is still needed. The school effects found here, both for Catholic schooling and advanced coursework, could be the product of other unspecified causes, such as previous achievement. That is, minorities' previous achievement might well cause not only their selection into Catholic schools, but also their coursework taken *and* their current achievement, to a greater extent than we control for with Ability alone.[9] Thus, further analysis, including longitudinal methods using the HSB follow-ups, is still needed if we intend to understand these important questions of school effect at a yet deeper level.

ENDNOTES

1. We use the term selection in the broad sense, referring not only to the selection of students *by* private schools, but also to the process by which students and their parents make decisions concerning public versus private school attendance.

2. For more information concerning the HSB tests, see Heyns and Hilton (1982), National Opinion Research Center (1980), or Page and Keith (1981). Keith (1982a), Page and Keith (1981), and Page (1981) discuss in more detail the justification for dividing the senior tests into Ability and Achievement components.

3. Equal weighting of public and Catholic school students was done to maximize the correlations and paths associated with School Type. We did not use the HSB design weights in these analyses. As additional variables were added, such heavy weighting resulted in instability of the results. Results of the earlier analyses, however, were very similar with or without the design weights. We used pairwise deletion of missing data. To use regression to estimate the paths, it must be assumed that the disturbances are uncorrelated with the exogenous variables, an assumption that further implies that there are *no* unmeasured common causes of the variables in the model (Kenny, 1979, chap. 4).

4. Greeley's (1982) analyses were a good deal more complicated than the model presented here. The Family Background composite was not used and controls were made for some student characteristics (although not ability); these and other differences (noted in Keith, 1982a) make Greeley's analyses difficult to reproduce.

5. Due to the weighting used, the dummy variable School Type had both a mean and a standard deviation of .50, so that moving from a public (coded 0) to a Catholic (coded 1) school would represent a change of two standard deviations in School Type. Thus, for this model, such a move should result in $2 \times .278$, or .556, or a standard deviation increase in Achievement.

6. Some readers may question the apparent decrease in the influence of Family Background on Achievement as our models become more complex. This happens structurally since, when more intervening variables are added to the model, Family Background's effects become indirect rather than direct. While the direct effects are represented by the paths, indirect effects are calculated by multiplying and summing several paths. For example, for Figure 2 for Hispanics, the indirect effect of Background on Achievement, through Ability, is $.252 \times .575$, or .140. In fact, the total (direct and indirect) effect of Background on Achievement is the same across all of the models presented here.

7. We realize that intention to go to college might well be confounded with School Type. Yet eighth grade was the earliest time this question was asked of seniors. Also, we assume that such a variable points to educational interests and aspirations that are fairly stable over time. Still, this variable is only a weak measure of aspirations.

8. These results, in fact, illuminate the fallacy of one criticism of the Page and Keith analysis—that their Ability Factor score was not separable from achievement (Coleman, 1981; see also Page, 1981). Here, Ability did not totally explain Achievement; school effects are also involved. Such controlling for ability when studying achievement, then, is *not* "throwing out the baby with the bath." The variables are *not* the same thing.

9. Such a possibility could be studied using longitudinal data or using nonrecursive path models with Achievement both affecting and being affected by School Type. Our analyses of such nonrecursive models (using both two-stage least squares regression and LISREL [Jöreskog & Sörbom, 1981]) have yielded equivocal and sometimes highly unlikely results, but have tended toward support of Catholic school effects on Achievement as stronger than Achievement on Catholic school selection.

REFERENCES

Alexander, K.L., & Pallas, A.M. (1984, April). Curriculum reform and school performance: An evaluation of the "New Basics." In E.B. Page (Chair), *How much can research improve the schools? Hypotheses and findings for "A Nation at Risk."* Symposium at the annual meeting of the American Educational Research Association, New Orleans.

Alexander, K.L., Pallas, A.M., & Cook, M.A. (1981). Measure for measure: On the use of the endogenous ability data in school-process research. *American Sociological Review, 46,* 619–631.

Cohen, J. (1978). Partialed products *are* interactions; partialed powers *are* curve components. *Psychological Bulletin, 85,* 858–866.

Coleman, J.S. (1981). Response to Page and Keith. *Educational Researcher, 10* (7), 18–20.

Coleman, J., Hoffer, T., & Kilgore, S. (1981). *Public and private schools.* Chicago: University of Chicago. (ERIC Document Reproduction Service No. ED 197 503)

Greeley, A.M. (1982). *Catholic high schools and minority students.* New Brunswick, NJ: Transaction.

Hallinan, M.T., & Olneck, M.R. (Eds.). *Sociology of Education, 36.*

Heyns, B., & Hilton, T.L. (1982). The cognitive tests for High School and Beyond: An assessment. *Sociology of Education, 55,* 89–102.

Hull, C.H., & Nie, N.H. (Eds.). (1981). *SPSS update 7–9.* New York: McGraw-Hill.

Jöreskog, K.G., & Sörbom, D. (1981). *LISREL V: Analysis of linear structural relationships by the method of maximum likelihood: User's guide.* Chicago: International Educational Services.

Keith, T.Z. (1982a). *Academic achievement of minority students enrolled in Catholic and public high schools* (Doctoral dissertation, Duke University, 1982). *Dissertation Abstracts International, 43,* 402A.

Keith, T.Z. (1982b). Time spent on homework and high school grades: A large-sample path analysis. *Journal of Educational Psychology, 74,* 248–253.

Keith, T.Z., & Page, E.B. (1982, August). Minority issues in Catholic schooling. In M.O. Chandler (Chair), *School characteristics and student performance: Evidence from national longitudinal surveys.* Symposium at the American Psychological Association convention, Washington, DC.

Keith, T.Z., & Page, E.B. (in press). Homework works at school: National evidence for policy changes. *School Psychology Review.*

Kenny, D.A. (1979). *Correlation and causality.* New York: Wiley.

National Commission on Excellence in Education. (1983). *A nation at risk: The imperative for educational reform.* Washington, DC: U.S. Government Printing Office.

National Opinion Research Center. (1980). *High school and beyond information for users: Base year (1980) data.* Chicago: Author.

Page, E.B. (1981). The media, technical analysis, and the data feast: A response to Coleman. *Educational Researcher, 10*(7), 21–23.

Page, E.B., & Keith, T.Z. (1981). Effects of U.S. private schools: A technical analysis of two recent claims. *Educational Researcher, 10*(7), 7–17.

Page, E.B., & Keith, T.Z. (1982, March). Private and public schools: Still another look. In W.M. Mathews (Chair), *Distinguished papers from the regional research associations.* Symposium at the annual meeting of the American Educational Research Association, New York.

Peng, S.S., Owings, J.A., & Fetters, W.B. (1982, August). Effective high schools: What are their attributes? In M.O. Chandler (Chair), *School characteristics and student performance: Evidence from national longitudinal surveys.* Symposium at the American Psychological Association convention, Washington, DC.

Roberson, S.D., Keith, T.Z., & Page, E.B. (1983). Now who aspires to teach? *Educational Researcher, 12*(6), 13–21.

Walber, H.J., & Shanahan, T. (1983). High school effects on individual students. *Educational Researcher, 12*(7), 4–9.

▶ 7

The Context
of Teaching
and Learning

Educational research and theory have identified many problems that face educational practice in urban schools. Classroom studies have been conducted that illuminate practices capable of overcoming many of these problems. In fact, it has been argued that we presently know enough about the techniques of "best practice in education" to be able to implement such practice. However, technique is not sufficient to overcome a number of educational problems that often lurk beneath the surface structure of public schools.

The context of teaching and learning in urban schools is partially structured by the beliefs and expectations that teachers hold. Unfortunately, these beliefs are most often based on biases and stereotypical attitudes concerning class, race, gender, and ethnicity. The climate of the classroom and the expectations of teachers for student learning are clearly related to the social, economic, and cultural characteristics of the student population. While the social and economic class position of the school most often determines the amount of support that that school receives, it also has a deep effect on the form and content of the curricular, pedagogical, and evaluation practices that take place in that school.

Many studies suggest that schools are organized around issues of class, race, gender, and ethnicity in such a way that students generally receive quantitatively and qualitatively different treatment. Anyon (1980) provides evidence that there are qualitative differences in the type of schooling children have access to based on social class differences. She argues that schools reproduce the unequal social relations found in society-at-large so that children are prepared differently based on the perceived workplace roles of their present class position. Simply stated, poor and minority students go to poor and minority schools and receive an education designed to prepare them for their role as poor and minority adults.

Banks (1988) provides a different perspective concerning the low academic achievement of poor and minority youths. He poses a different set of questions that illuminate the effects of ethnicity, race, and gender, as well as class, regarding learning problems of students. Does family socialization across social class make a difference? Does generational middle-class status make a difference? That is, when a poor black is upwardly mobile to middle class, what behavioral and attitudinal differences are there between this person and a fourth generation Caucasian who is also middle class? Banks concludes that teachers need to understand these issues and others in order to teach in a multicultural environment and that teachers need to reach beyond their own cultural barriers and recognize the diversity present in the students they teach.

Vasquez (1988) provides an overview of the problems associated with the context in which learning takes place from a psychological perspective. The issues of classroom climate and teacher expectations and their relationship to the social, economic, and cultural characteristics of students are important factors for teachers of poor and minority students to consider. He provides suggestions for developing an equitable psychological context that presupposes that teachers understand student differences to create classroom balance. Teachers must recognize and legitimate the multiple cultures found in the classroom and create a democratic environment through strategies such as cooperative learning and attitudes of caring.

REFERENCES

Anyon, J. (1980). "Social class and the hidden curriculum of work." *Journal of Education,* 162:67–92.

Banks, J.A. (1988). "Ethnicity, class, cognitive, and motivational styles: Research and teaching implications." *Journal of Negro Education,* 57:452–466.

Vasquez, J.A. (1988). "Contexts of learning for minority students." *The Educational Forum,* 52:243–253.

Social Class
and the Hidden
Curriculum of Work

JEAN ANYON

Scholars in political economy and the sociology of knowledge have recently argued that public schools in complex industrial societies like our own make available different types of educational experience and curriculum knowledge to students in different social classes. Bowles and Gintis (1976), for example, have argued that students from different social class backgrounds are rewarded for classroom behaviors that correspond to personality traits allegedly rewarded in the different occupational strata—the working classes for docility and obedience, the managerial classes for initiative and personal assertiveness. Basil Bernstein (1977), Pierre Bourdieu (Bourdieu and Passeron 1977), and Michael W. Apple (1979), focusing on school knowledge, have argued that knowledge and skills leading to social power and reward (e.g., medical, legal, managerial) are made available to the advantaged social groups but are withheld from the working classes, to whom a more "practical" curriculum is offered (e.g., manual skills, clerical knowledge). While there has been considerable argumentation of these points regarding education in England, France, and North America, there has been little or no attempt to investigate these ideas empirically in elementary or secondary schools and classrooms in this country.[1]

This article offers tentative empirical support (and qualification) of the above arguments by providing illustrative examples of differences in student work in classrooms in contrasting social class communities. The examples were gathered as part of an ethnographical study of curricular, pedagogical and pupil evaluation practices in five elementary schools. The article attempts a theoretical contribution as well, and assesses student work in the light of a theoretical approach to social class analysis. The organization is as follows: the methodology of the ethnographi-

Reprinted from *Journal of Education,* 162:67–92, 1980, by permission of the publisher and the author.

Jean Anyon is an Associate Professor and Chair of the Education Department of Rutgers University.

cal study is briefly described; a theoretical approach to the definition of social class is offered; income and other characteristics of the parents in each school are provided, and examples from the study that illustrate work tasks and interaction in each school are presented; then the concepts used to define social class are applied to the examples in order to assess the theoretical meaning of classroom events. It will be suggested that there is a "hidden curriculum" in school work that has profound implications for the theory—and consequence—of everyday activity in education.

METHODOLOGY

The methods used to gather data were classroom observation; interviews of students, teachers, principals, and district administrative staff; and assessment of curriculum and other materials in each classroom and school. All classroom events to be discussed here involve the fifth grade in each school. All schools but one departmentalize at the fifth grade level. Except for that school where only one fifth grade teacher could be observed, all the fifth grade teachers (that is, two or three) were observed as the children moved from subject to subject. In all schools the art, music, and gym teachers were also observed and interviewed. All teachers in the study were described as "good" or "excellent" by their principals. All except one new teacher had taught for more than four years. The fifth grade in each school was observed by the investigator for ten three-hour periods between September 15, 1978 and June 20, 1979.

Before providing the occupations, incomes, and other relevant social characteristics of the parents of the children in each school, I will offer a theoretical approach to defining social class.

SOCIAL CLASS

One's occupation and income level contribute significantly to one's social class, but they do not define it. Rather, social class is a series of relationships. A person's social class is defined here by the way that person relates to the process in society by which goods, services, and culture are produced.[2] One relates to several aspects of the production process primarily through one's work. One has a relationship to the system of ownership, to other people (at work and in society) and to the content and process of one's own productive activity. One's relationship to all three of these aspects of production determines one's social class; that is, all three relationships are necessary and none is sufficient for determining a person's relation to the process of production in society.

Ownership Relations. In a capitalist society, a person has a relation to the system of private ownership of capital. Capital is usually thought of as being derived from physical property. In this sense capital is property which is used to produce profit, interest, or rent in sufficient quantity so that the result can be used to produce more profit, interest, or rent—that is, more capital. Physical capital may be derived from money, stocks, machines, land, or the labor of workers (whose labor, for instance, may produce products that are sold by others for profit). Capital, however, can also be symbolic. It can be the socially legitimated knowledge of how the production process works, its financial, managerial, technical, or other "secrets." Symbolic capital can also be socially legitimated skills—cognitive (e.g., analytical), linguistic, or technical skills that provide the ability to, say, produce the dominant scientific, artistic, and other culture, or to manage the systems of industrial and cultural production. Skillful application of symbolic capital may yield social and cultural power, and perhaps physical capital as well.

The ownership relation that is definitive for social class is one's relation to physical capital. The first such relationship is that of capitalist. To be a member of the capitalist class in the present-day United States, one must participate in the ownership of the apparatus of production in society. The number of such persons is relatively small: while one person in ten owns some stock, for example, a mere 1.6 percent of the population owns 82.2 percent of *all* stock, and the wealthiest one-fifth owns almost all the rest (see New York Stock Exchange, 1975; Smith and Franklin, 1974; Lampman, 1962).

At the opposite pole of this relationship is the worker. To be in the United States working class a person will not ordinarily own physical capital; to the contrary, his or her work will be wage or salaried labor that is either a *source* of profit (i.e., capital) to others, or that makes it possible for others to *realize* profit. Examples of the latter are *white*-collar clerical workers in industry and distribution (office and sales) as well as the wage and salaried workers in the institutions of social and economic legitimation and service (e.g., in state education and welfare institutions).[3] According to the criteria to be developed here, the number of persons who presently comprise the working class in the United States is between 50 percent and 60 percent of the population (see also Wright, 1978; Braverman, 1974; Levison, 1974).

In between the defining relationship of capitalist and worker are the middle classes, whose relationship to the process of production is less clear, and whose relationship may indeed exhibit contradictory characteristics. For example, social service employees have a somewhat contradictory relationship to the process of production because, although their income may be at middle-class levels, some characteristics of their work are working-class (e.g., they may have very little control over their work). Analogously, there are persons at the upper income end of the middle class, such as upper-middle-class professionals, who may own quantities of stocks and will therefore share characteristics of the capitalist class. As the next criterion to be discussed makes clear, however, to be a member of the present-day capitalist in the United States, one must also participate in the social *control* of this capital.

Relationships Between People. The second relationship which contributes to one's social class is the relation one has to authority and control at work and in society.[4] One characteristic of most working-class jobs is that there is no built-in mechanism by which the worker can control the content, process or speed of work. Legitimate decision making is vested in personnel supervisors, in middle or upper management, or, as in an increasing number of white-collar working-class (and most middle-class) jobs, by bureaucratic rule and regulation. For upper-middle-class professional groups there is an increased amount of autonomy regarding work. Moreover, in middle- and upper-middle-class positions there is an increasing chance that one's work would also involve supervising the work of others. A capitalist is defined within these relations of control in an enterprise by having a position which participates in the direct control of the entire enterprise. Capitalists do not directly control workers in physical production and do not directly control ideas in the sphere of cultural production. However, more crucial to control, capitalists make the decisions over how resources are used (e.g., where money is invested) and how profit is allocated.

Relations Between People and Their Work. The third criterion which contributes to a person's social class is the relationship between that person and his or her own productive activity—the type of activity that constitutes his or her work. A working-class job is often characterized by work that is routine and mechanical and that is a small, fragmented part of a larger process with which workers are not usually acquainted. These working-class jobs are usually blue-collar, manual labor. A few skilled jobs such as plumbing and printing are not mechanical, however, and an increasing number of working-class jobs are *white*-collar. These white-collar jobs, such as clerical work, may involve work that necessitates a measure of planning and decision making, but one still has no built-in control over the content. The work of some middle- and most upper-middle-class managerial and professional groups is likely to involve the need for conceptualization and creativity, with many professional jobs demanding one's full creative capacities. Finally, the work that characterizes the capitalist position is that this work is almost entirely a matter of conceptualization (e.g., planning and laying-out) that has as its object management and control of the enterprise.

One's social class, then, is a result of the relationships one has, largely through one's work, to physical capital and its power, to other people at work and in society, and to one's own productive activity. Social class is a lived, developing process. It is not an abstract category, and it is not a fixed, inherited position (although one's family background is, of course, important). Social class is perceived as a complex of social relations that one develops as one grows up—as one acquires and develops certain bodies of knowledge, skills, abilities, and traits, and as one has contact and opportunity in the world.[5] In sum, social class describes relationships which we as adults have developed, may attempt to maintain, and in which we participate every working day. These relationships in a real sense define our material ties to the world.

An important concern here is whether these relationships are developing in children in schools within particular social class contexts.

THE SAMPLE OF SCHOOLS

With the above discussion as a theoretical backdrop, the social class designation of each of the five schools will be identified, and the income, occupation, and other relevant available social characteristics of the students and their parents will be described. The first three schools are in a medium-sized city district in northern New Jersey, and the other two are in a nearby New Jersey suburb.

The first two schools I will call *Working-class Schools.* Most of the parents have blue-collar jobs. Less than a third of the fathers are skilled, while the majority are in unskilled or semiskilled jobs. During the period of the study (1978–1979) approximately 15 percent of the fathers were unemployed. The large majority (85 percent) of the families are white. The following occupations are typical: platform, storeroom, and stockroom workers; foundrymen, pipe welders, and boilermakers; semiskilled and unskilled assembly-line operatives; gas station attendants, auto mechanics, maintenance workers, and security guards. Less than 30 percent of the women work, some part-time and some full-time, on assembly lines, in storerooms and stockrooms, as waitresses, barmaids, or sales clerks. Of the fifth grade parents, none of the wives of the skilled workers had jobs. Approximately 15 percent of the families in each school are at or below the federal "poverty" level[6]; most of the rest of the family incomes are at or below $12,000, except some of the skilled workers whose incomes are higher. The incomes of the majority of the families in these two schools (i.e., at or below $12,000) are typical of 38.6 percent of the families in the United States (U.S. Bureau of the Census, 1979, p. 2, table A).

The third school is called the *Middle-class School,* although because of neighborhood residence patterns, the population is a mixture of several social classes. The parents' occupations can be divided into three groups: a small group of blue-collar "rich," who are skilled, well-paid workers such as printers, carpenters, plumbers, and construction workers. The second group is composed of parents in working-class and middle-class white-collar jobs: women in office jobs, technicians, supervisors in industry, and parents employed by the city (such as firemen, policemen, and several of the school's teachers). The third group is composed of occupations such as personnel directors in local firms, accountants, "middle management," and a few small capitalists (owners of shops in the area). The children of several local doctors attend this school. Most family incomes are between $13,000 and $25,000 with a few higher. This income range is typical of 38.9 percent of the families in the United States (U.S. Bureau of the Census, 1979, p. 2, table A).

The fourth school has a parent population that is at the upper income level of the upper middle class, and is predominantly professional. This school will be called the *Affluent Professional School.* Typical jobs are: cardiologist, interior designer, corporate lawyer or engineer, executive in advertising or television. There are some families who are not as affluent as the majority (e.g., the family of the superintendent of the district's schools, and the one or two families in which the fathers are skilled workers). In addition, a few of the families are more affluent than the majority, and can be classified in the capitalist class (e.g., a partner in a prestigious Wall Street stock brokerage firm). Approximately 90 percent of the children in this school are white. Most family incomes are between $40,000 and $80,000. This income span represents approximately 7 percent of the families in the United States.[7]

In the fifth school the majority of the families belong to the capitalist class. This school will be called the *Executive Elite School* because most of the fathers are top executives, (e.g., presidents and vice presidents) in major U.S.-based multinational corporations—for example, ATT, RCA, City Bank, American Express, U.S. Steel. A sizable group of fathers are top executives in financial firms on Wall Street. There are also a number of fathers who list their occupations as "general counsel" to a particular corporation, and these corporations are also among the large multinationals. Many of the mothers do volunteer work in the Junior League, Junior Fortnightly, or other service groups; some are intricately involved in town politics; and some are themselves in well-paid occupations. There are no minority children in the school. Almost all family incomes are over $100,000 with some in the $500,000 range. The incomes in this school represent less than 1 percent of the families in the United States (see Smith and Franklin, 1974).

Since each of the five schools is only one instance of elementary education in a particular social class context, I will not generalize beyond the sample. However, the examples of school work which follow will suggest characteristics of education in each social setting that appear to have theoretical and social significance and to be worth investigation in a larger number of schools.

SOCIAL CLASS AND SCHOOL WORK

There are obvious similarities among United States schools and classrooms. There are school and classroom rules, teachers who ask questions and attempt to exercise control and who give work and homework. There are textbooks and tests. All of these were found in the five schools. Indeed, there were other curricular similarities as well: all schools and fifth grades used the same math book and series (*Mathematics Around Us,* Scott Foresman, 1978); all fifth grades had at least one boxed set of an individualized reading program available in the room (although the variety and amounts of teaching materials in the classrooms increased as the social class of the school population increased); and, all fifth grade language arts curricula included aspects of grammar, punctuation and capitalization.[8]

This section provides examples of work and work-related activities in each school that bear on the categories used to define social class. Thus, examples will be provided concerning students' relation to capital (e.g., as manifest in any symbolic capital that might be acquired through school work); students' relation to persons and types of authority regarding school work; and students' relation to their own productive activity. The section first offers the investigator's interpretation of what school work is for children in each setting, and then presents events and interactions that illustrate that assessment.

The *Working-class Schools.* In the two working-class schools, work is following the steps of a procedure. The procedure is usually mechanical, involving rote behavior and very little decision making or choice. The teachers rarely explain why the work is being assigned, how it might connect to other assignments, or what the idea is that lies behind the procedure or gives it coherence and perhaps meaning or significance. Available textbooks are not always used, and the teachers often prepare their own dittoes or put work examples on the board. Most of the rules regarding work are designations of what the children are to do; the rules are steps to follow. These steps are told to the children by the teachers and often written on the board. The children are usually told to copy the steps as notes. These notes are to be studied. Work is often evaluated not according to whether it is right or wrong, but according to whether the children followed the right steps.

The following examples illustrate these points. In math, when two-digit division was introduced, the teacher in one school gave a four-minute lecture on what the terms are called (i.e., which number is the divisor, dividend, quotient, and remainder). The children were told to copy these names in their notebooks. Then the teacher told them the steps to follow to do the problems, saying, "This is how you do them." The teacher listed the steps on the board, and they appeared several days later as a chart hung in the middle of the front wall: "Divide; Multiply; Subtract; Bring Down." The children often did examples of two-digit division. When the teacher went over the examples with them, he told them for each problem what the procedure was, rarely asking them to conceptualize or explain it themselves: "3 into 22 is 7; do your subtraction and one is left over." During the week that two-digit division was introduced (or at any other time), the investigator did not observe any discussion of the idea of grouping involved in division, any use of manipulables, or any attempt to relate two-digit division to any other mathematical process. Nor was there any attempt to relate the steps to an actual or possible thought process of the children. The observer did not hear the terms dividend, quotient, etc., used again. The math teacher in the other working-class school followed similar procedures regarding two-digit division, and at one point her class seemed confused. She said, "You're confusing yourselves. You're tensing up. Remember, when you do this, it's the same steps over and over again—and that's the way division always is." Several weeks later, after a test, a group of her children "still didn't get it," and she made no attempt to explain the concept of dividing things into groups, or to give them manipulables for their own investigation. Rather, she went over the steps with them again and told them that they "needed more practice."

In other areas of math, work is also carrying out often unexplained, fragmented procedures. For example, one of the teachers led the children through a series of steps to make a one-inch grid on their paper *without* telling them that they were making a one-inch grid, or that it would be used to study scale. She said, "Take your ruler. Put it across the top. Make a mark at every number. Then move your ruler down to the bottom. No, put it across the bottom. Now make a mark on top of every number. Now draw a line from. . . . " At this point a girl said that she had a faster way to do it and the teacher said, "No, you don't; you don't even know what I'm making yet. Do it this way, or it's wrong." After they had made the lines up and down and across, the teacher told them she wanted them to make a figure by connecting some dots and to measure that, using the scale of one inch equals one mile. Then they were to cut it out. She said, "Don't cut until I check it."

In both working-class schools, work in language arts is mechanics of punctuation (commas, periods, question marks, exclamation points), capitalization, and the four kinds of sentences. One teacher explained to me, "Simple punctuation is all they'll ever use." Regarding punctuation, either a teacher or a ditto stated the rules for where, for example, to put commas. The investigator heard no classroom discussion of the aural context of punctuation (which, of course, is what gives each mark its meaning). Nor did the investigator hear any statement or inference that placing a punctuation mark could be a decision-making process, depending, for example, on one's intended meaning. Rather, the children were told to follow the rules. Language arts did not involve creative writing. There were several writing assignments throughout the year, but in each instance the children were given a ditto, and they wrote answers to questions on the sheet. For example, they wrote their "autobiography" by answering such questions as "Where were you born?" "What is your favorite animal?" on a sheet entitled, "All About Me."

In one of the working-class schools the class had a science period several times a week. On the three occasions observed, the children were not called upon to set up experiments or to give explanations for facts or concepts. Rather, on each occasion the teacher told them in his own words what the book said. The children copied the teacher's sentences from the board. Each day that preceded the day they were to do a science experiment, the teacher told them to copy the directions from the book for the procedure they would carry out the next day, and to study the list at home that night. The day after each experiment, the teacher went over what they had "found" (they did the experiments as a class, and each was actually a class demonstration led by the teacher). Then the teacher wrote what they "found" on the board, and the children copied that in their notebooks. Once or twice a year there are science projects. The project is chosen and assigned by the teacher from a box of three-by-five-inch cards. On the card the teacher has written the question to be answered, the books to use, and how much to write. Explaining the cards to the observer, the teacher said, "It tells them exactly what to do, or they couldn't do it."

Social studies in the working-class schools is also largely mechanical, rote work that was given little explanation or connection to larger contexts. In one school, for example, although there was a book available, social studies work was to copy the teacher's notes from the board. Several times a week for a period of several months, the children copied these notes. The fifth grades in the district were to study U.S. history. The teacher used a booklet she had purchased called "The Fabulous Fifty States." Each day she put information from the booklet in outline form on the board and the children copied it. The type of information did not vary: the name of the state, its abbreviation, state capital, nickname of the state, its main products, main business, and a "Fabulous Fact" (e.g., "Idaho grew 27 billion potatoes in one year. That's enough potatoes for each man, woman and . . ."). As the children finished copying the sentences, the teacher erased them and wrote more. Children would occasionally go to the front to pull down the wall map in order to locate the states they were copying, and the teacher did not dissuade them. But the observer never saw her refer to the map; nor did the observer ever hear her make other than perfunctory remarks concerning the information the children were copying. Occasionally the children colored in a ditto and cut it out to make a stand-up figure (representing, for example, a man roping a cow in the Southwest). These were referred to by the teacher as their social studies "projects."

Rote behavior was often called for in classroom oral work. When going over math and language arts skills sheets, for example, as the teacher asked for the answer to each problem, he fired the questions rapidly, staccato, and the scene reminded the observer of a sergeant drilling recruits: above all, the questions demanded that you stay at attention: "The next one? What do I put here? . . . Here? Give us the next." Or "How many commas in this sentence? Where do I put them . . . The next one?"

The (four) fifth grade teachers observed in the working-class schools attempted to control classroom time and space by making decisions without consulting the children and without explaining the basis for their decisions. The teacher's control thus often seemed capricious. Teachers, for instance, very often ignored the bells to switch classes—deciding among themselves to keep the children after the period was officially over, to continue with the work, or for disciplinary reasons, or so they (the teachers) could stand in the hall and talk. There were no clocks in the rooms in either school, and the children often asked, "What period is this?" "When do we go to gym?" The children had no access to materials. These were handed out by teachers and closely guarded. Things in the room "belonged" to the teacher: "Bob, bring me my garbage can." The teachers continually gave the children orders. Only three times did the investigator hear a teacher in either working-class school preface a directive with an unsarcastic "please," or "let's" or "would you." Instead, the teachers said, "Shut up," "Shut your mouth," "Open your books," "Throw your *gum* away—if you want to rot your teeth, do it on your *own* time." Teachers made every effort to control the movement of the children, and often shouted, "Why are you out of your *seat*??!!" If the children got permission to leave the room they had to take a written pass with the date and time.

The control that the teachers have is less than they would like. It is a result of constant struggle with the children. The children continually resist the teachers' orders and the work itself. They do not directly challenge the teachers' authority or legitimacy, but they make indirect attempts to sabotage and resist the flow of assignments:

Teacher: I will put some problems on the board. You are to divide.

Child: We got to divide?

Teacher: Yes.

Several children: (Groan) Not again. Mr. B, we done this yesterday.

Child: Do we put the date?

Teacher: Yes. I hope we remember we work in silence. You're supposed to do it on white paper. I'll explain it later.

Child: Somebody broke my pencil. (Crash—a child falls out of his chair.)

Child: (repeats) Mr. B., somebody broke my *pencil!*

Child: Are we going to be here all morning?

(Teacher comes to the observer, shakes his head and grimaces, then smiles.)

The children are successful enough in their struggle against work that there are long periods where they are not asked to do any work, but just to sit and be quiet.[9] Very often the work that the teachers assign is "easy," that is, not demanding, and thus receives less resistance. Sometimes a compromise is reached where, although the teachers insist that the children continue to work, there is a constant murmur of talk. The children will be doing arithmetic examples, copying social studies notes, or doing punctuation or other dittoes, and all the while there is muted but spirited conversation—about somebody's broken arm, an afterschool disturbance of the day before, etc. Sometimes the teachers themselves join in the conversation because, as one teacher explained to me, "It's a relief from the routine."

Middle-class School. In the middle-class school, work is getting the right answer. If one accumulates enough right answers one gets a good grade. One must follow the directions in order to get the right answers, but the directions often call for some figuring, some choice, some decision making. For example, the children must often figure out by themselves what the directions ask them to do, and how to get the answer: what do you do first, second, and perhaps third? Answers are usually found in books or by listening to the teacher. Answers are usually words, sentences, numbers, or facts and dates; one writes them on paper, and one should be neat. Answers must be in the right order, and one can not make them up.

The following activities are illustrative. Math involves some choice: one may do two-digit division the long way, or the short way, and there are some math problems that can be done "in your head." When the teacher explains how to do two-digit division, there is recognition that a cognitive process is involved; she gives several ways, and says, "I want to make sure you understand what you're doing—so you get it right"; and, when they go over the homework, she asks the *children* to tell how they did the problem and what answer they got.

In social studies the daily work is to read the assigned pages in the textbook and to answer the teacher's questions. The questions are almost always designed to check on whether the students have read the assignment and understood it: who did so-and-so; what happened after that; when did it happen, where, and sometimes, why did it happen? The answers are in the book and in one's understanding of the book; the teacher's hints when one doesn't know the answer are to "read it again," or to look at the picture or at the rest of the paragraph. One is to search for the answer in the "context," in what is given.

Language arts is "simple grammar, what they need for everyday life." The language arts teacher says, "They should learn to speak properly, to write business letters and thank-you letters, and to understand what nouns and verbs and simple subjects are." Here, as well, the actual work is to choose the right answers, to understand what is given. The teacher often says, "Please read the next sentence and then I'll question you about it." One teacher said in some exasperation to a boy who was fooling around in class, "If you don't know the answers to the questions I ask, then you can't stay in this *class!* (pause) You *never* know the answers to the questions I ask, and it's not fair to me—and certainly not to you!"

Most lessons are based on the textbook. This does not involve a critical perspective on what is given there. For example, a critical perspective in social studies is perceived as dangerous by these teachers because it may lead to controversial topics; the parents might complain. The children, however, are often curious, especially in social studies. Their questions are tolerated, and usually answered perfunctorily. But after a few minutes the teacher will say, "All right, we're not going any farther. Please open your social studies workbook." While the teachers spend a lot of time explaining and expanding on what the textbooks say, there is little attempt to analyze how or why things happen, or to give thought to how pieces of a culture, or, say, a system of numbers or elements of a language fit together or can be analyzed. What has happened in the past, and what exists now may not be equitable or fair, but (shrug) that is the way things are, and one does not confront such matters in school. For example, in social studies after a child is called on to read a passage about the pilgrims, the teacher summarizes the paragraph and then says, "So you can see how strict they were about everything." A child asks, "Why?" "Well, because they felt that if you weren't busy you'd get into trouble." Another child asks, "Is it true that they burned women at the stake?" The teacher says, "Yes, if a woman did anything strange, they hanged them. [sic] What would a woman do, do you think, to make them burn them? [sic] See if you can come up with better answers than my other [social studies] class." Several children offer suggestions, to which the teacher nods but does not comment. Then she says, "OK, good," and calls on the next child to read.

Work tasks do not usually request creativity. Serious attention is rarely given in school work to *how* the children develop or express their own feelings and ideas, either linguistically or in graphic form. On the occasions when creativity or self-expression is requested, it is peripheral to the main activity, or it is "enrichment," or "for fun." During a lesson on what similes are, for example, the teacher explains what they are, puts several on the board, gives some other examples herself, and then asks the children if they can "make some up." She calls on three children who give similes, two of which are actually in the book they have open before them. The teacher does not comment on this, and then asks several others to choose similes from the list of phrases in the book. Several do so correctly, and she says, "Oh *good!* You're picking them out! See how *good* we are?" Their homework is to pick out the rest of the similes from the list.

Creativity is not often requested in social studies and science projects, either. Social studies projects, for example, are given with directions to "find information on your topic," and write it up. The children are not supposed to copy, but to "put it in your own words." Although a number of the projects subsequently went beyond the teacher's direction to find information and had quite expressive covers and inside illustrations, the teacher's evaluative comments had to do with the amount of information, whether they had "copied," and if their work was neat.

The style of control of the three fifth grade teachers observed in this school varied from somewhat easygoing to strict, but in contrast to the working-class schools, the teachers' decisions were usually based on external rules and regulations, for example, on criteria that were known or available to the children. Thus, the teachers always honor the bells for changing classes, and they usually evaluate children's work by what is in the textbooks and answer booklets.

There is little excitement in school work for the children, and the assignments are perceived as having little to do with their interests and feelings. As one child said, what you do is "store facts in your head like cold storage—until you need it later for a test, or your job." Thus, doing well is important because there are thought to be *other* likely rewards: a good job, or college.[10]

Affluent Professional School. In the affluent professional school, work is creative activity carried out independently. The students are continually asked to express and apply ideas and concepts. Work involves individual thought and expressiveness, expansion and illustration of ideas, and choice of appropriate method and material. (The class is not considered an open classroom, and the principal explained that because of the large number of discipline problems in the fifth grade this year they did not departmentalize. The teacher who agreed to take part in the study said she is "more structured" this year than she usually is.) The products of work in this class are often written stories, editorials and essays, or representations of ideas in mural, graph, or craft form. The products of work should not be like everybody else's and should show individuality. They should exhibit good design, and (this is important), they must also fit empirical reality. Moreover, one's work should attempt to interpret or "make sense" of reality. The relatively few rules to be followed regarding work are usually criteria for, or limits on, individual activity. One's product is usually evaluated for the quality of its expression and for the appropriateness of its conception to the task. In many cases one's own satisfaction with the product is an important criterion for its evaluation. When right answers are called for, as in commercial materials like SRA (Science Research Associates) and math, it is important that the children decide on an answer as a result of thinking about the idea involved in what they're being asked to do. Teacher's hints are to "think about it some more."

The following activities are illustrative. The class takes home a sheet requesting each child's parents to fill in the number of cars they have, the number of television sets, refrigerators, games, or rooms in the house, etc. Each child is to figure the average number of a type of possession owned by the fifth grade. Each child must compile the "data" from all the sheets. A calculator is available in the classroom to do the mechanics of finding the average. Some children decide to send sheets to the fourth grade families for comparison. Their work should be "verified" by a classmate before it is handed in.

Each child and his or her family has made a geoboard. The teacher asks the class to get their geoboards from the side cabinet, to take a handful of rubber bands, and then to listen to what she would like them to do. She says, "I would like you to design a figure and then find the perimeter and area. When you have it, check with your neighbor. After you've done that, please transfer it to graph paper and tomorrow I'll ask you to make up a question about it for someone. When you hand it in, please let me know whose it is, and who verified it. Then I have something else for you to do that's really fun. (pause) Find the average number of chocolate chips in three cookies. I'll give you three cookies, and you'll have to *eat* your way through, I'm afraid!" Then she goes around the room and gives help, suggestions, praise, and admonitions that they are getting noisy. They work sitting, or standing up at their desks, at benches in the back, or on the floor. A child hands the teacher his paper and she comments, "I'm not accepting this paper. Do a better design." To another child she says, "That's fantastic! But you'll never find the area. Why don't you draw a figure inside [the big one] and subtract to get the area?"

The school district requires the fifth grades to study ancient civilizations (in particular, Egypt, Athens, and Sumer.) In this classroom, the emphasis is on illustrating and re-creating the culture of the people of ancient times. The following are typical activities: The children made an 8mm film on Egypt, which one of the parents edited. A girl in the class wrote the script, and the class acted it out. They put the sound on themselves. They read stories of those days. They wrote essays and stories depicting the lives of the people and the societal and occupational divisions. They chose from a list of projects, all of which involved graphic representations of ideas: for example, "Make a mural depicting the division of labor in Egyptian society."

Each child wrote and exchanged a letter in hieroglyphics with a fifth grader in another class, and they also exchanged stories they wrote in cuneiform. They made a scroll and singed the edges so it looked authentic. They each chose an occupation and made an Egyptian plaque representing that occupation, simulating the appropriate Egyptian design. They carved their design on a cylinder of wax, pressed the wax into clay, and then baked the clay. Although one girl did not choose an occupation, but carved instead a series of gods and slaves, the teacher said, "That's all right, Amber, it's beautiful." As they were working the teacher said, "Don't cut into your clay until you're satisfied with your design."

Social studies also involves almost daily presentation by the children of some event from the news. The teacher's questions ask the children to expand what they say, to give more details, and to be more specific. Occasionally she adds some remarks to help them see connections between events.

The emphasis on expressing and illustrating ideas in social studies is accompanied in language arts by an emphasis on creative writing. Each child wrote a rhebus story for a first grader whom they had interviewed to see what kind of story the child liked best. They wrote editorials on pending decisions by the school board, and radio plays, some of which were read over the school intercom from the office, and one of which was performed in the auditorium. There is no language arts textbook because, the teacher said, "The principal wants us to be creative." There is not much grammar, but there is punctuation. One morning when the observer arrived the class was doing a punctuation ditto. The teacher later apologized for using the ditto. "It's just for review," she said. "I don't teach punctuation that way. We use their language." The ditto had three unambiguous rules for where to put commas in a sentence. As the teacher was going around to help the children with the ditto, she repeated several times, "Where you put commas depends on how you say the sentence; it depends on the situation and what you want to say." Several weeks later the observer saw another punctuation activity. The teacher had printed a five-paragraph story on an oak tag and then cut it into phrases. She read the whole story to the class from the book, then passed out the phrases. The group had to decide how the phrases could best be put together again. (They arranged the phrases on the floor.) The point was not to replicate the story, although that was not irrelevant, but to "decide what you think the best way is." Punctuation marks on cardboard pieces were then handed out and the children discussed, and then decided, what mark was best at each place they thought one was needed. At the end of each paragraph the teacher asked, "Are you satisfied with the way the paragraphs are now? Read it to yourself and see how it sounds." Then she read the original story again, and they compared the two.

Describing her goals in science to the investigator, the teacher said, "We use ESS (Elementary Science Study). It's very good because it gives a hands-on experience—so they can make *sense* out of it. It doesn't matter whether it [what they find] is right or wrong. I bring them together and there's value in discussing their ideas."

The products of work in this class are often highly valued by the children and the teacher. In fact, this was the only school in which the investigator was not allowed to take original pieces of the children's work for her files. If the work was small enough, however, and was on paper, the investigator could duplicate it on the copying machine in the office.

The teacher's attempt to control the class involves constant negotiation. She does not give direct orders unless she is angry because the children have been too noisy. Normally, she tries to get them to foresee the consequences of their actions and to decide accordingly. For example, lining them up to go see a play written by the sixth graders, she says, "I presume you're lined up by someone with whom you want to sit. I hope you're lined up by someone you won't get in trouble with." The following two dialogues illustrate the process of negotiation between student and teacher.

Teacher: Tom, you're behind in your SRA this marking period.

Tom: So what!

Teacher: Well, last time you had a hard time catching up.

Tom: But I have my [music] lesson at 10:00.

Teacher: Well, that doesn't mean you're going to sit here for twenty minutes.

Tom: Twenty minutes! OK. (He goes to pick out a SRA booklet and chooses one, puts it back, then takes another, and brings it to her.)

Teacher: OK, this is the one you want, right?

Tom: Yes.

Teacher: OK, I'll put tomorrow's date on it so you can take it home tonight or finish it tomorrow if you want.

Teacher: (to a child who is wandering around during reading) Kevin, why don't you do *Reading for Concepts?*

Kevin: No, I don't like *Reading for Concepts.*

Teacher: Well, what are you going to do?

Kevin: (pause) I'm going to work on my DAR. (The DAR had sponsored an essay competition on "Life in the American Colonies.")

One of the few rules governing the children's movement is that no more than three children may be out of the room at once. There is a school rule that anyone can go to the library at any time to get a book. In the fifth grade I observed, they sign their name on the chalkboard and leave. There are no passes. Finally, the children have a fair amount of officially sanctioned say over what happens in the class. For example, they often negotiate what work is to be done. If the teacher wants to move on to the next subject, but the children say they are not ready, they want to work on their present projects some more, she very often lets them do it.

Executive Elite School. In the executive elite school, work is developing one's analytical intellectual powers. Children are continually asked to reason through a problem, to produce intellectual products that are both logically sound and of top academic quality. A primary goal of thought is to conceptualize rules by which elements may fit together in systems, and then to apply these rules in solving a problem. School work helps one to achieve, to excel, to prepare for life.

The following are illustrative. The math teacher teaches area and perimeter by having the children derive formulae for each. First she helps them, through discussion at the board, to arrive at $A = W \times L$ as a formula (not *the* formula) for area. After discussing several, she says, "Can anyone make up a formula for perimeter? Can you figure that out yourselves? (pause) Knowing what we know, can we think of a formula?" She works out three children's suggestions at the board, saying to two, "Yes, that's a good one," and then asks the class if they can think of any more. No one volunteers. To prod them, she says, "If you use rules and good reasoning, you get many ways. Chris, can you think up a formula?"

She discusses two-digit division with the children as a decision-making process. Presenting a new type of problem to them, she asks, "What's the *first* decision you'd make if presented with this kind of example? What is the first thing you'd *think?* Craig?" Craig says, "To find my first partial quotient." She responds, "Yes, that would be your first decision. How would you do that?" Craig explains, and then the teacher says, "OK, we'll see how that works for you." The class tries his way. Subsequently, she comments on the merits and shortcomings of several other children's decisions. Later, she tells the investigator that her goals in math are to develop their reasoning and mathematical thinking and that, unfortunately, "there's no *time* for manipulables."

While right answers are important in math, they are not "given" by the book or by the teacher, but may be challenged by the children. Going over some problems in late September the teacher says, "Raise your hand if you do not agree." A child says, "I don't agree with 64." The teacher responds, "OK, there's a question about 64. (to class) Please check it. Owen, they're disagreeing with you. Kristen, they're checking yours." The teacher emphasized this repeatedly during September and October with statements like, "Don't be afraid to say if you disagree. In the last [math] class, somebody disagreed, and they were right. Before you disagree, check yours, and if you still think we're wrong, then we'll check it out." By Thanksgiving, the children did not often speak in terms of right and wrong math problems, but of whether they agreed with the answer that had been given.

There are complicated math mimeos with many word problems. Whenever they go over the examples, they discuss how each child has set up the problem. The children must explain it precisely. On one occasion the teacher said, "I'm more— just as interested in *how* you set up the problem as in what answer you find. If you set up a problem in a good way, the answer is *easy* to find."

Social studies work is most often reading and discussion of concepts and independent research. There are only occasional artistic, expressive, or illustrative projects. Ancient Athens and Sumer are, rather, societies to analyze. The following questions are typical of those which guide the children's independent research: "What mistakes did Pericles make after the war?" "What mistakes did the citizens of Athens make?" "What are the elements of a civilization?" "How did Greece build an economic empire?" "Compare the way Athens chose its leaders with the way we choose ours." Occasionally the children are asked to make up sample questions for their social studies tests. On an occasion when the investigator was present the social studies teacher rejected a child's question by saying, "That's just fact. If I asked you that question on a test, you'd complain it was just memory! Good questions ask for concepts."

In social studies—but also in reading, science, and health—the teachers initiate classroom discussions of current social issues and problems. These discussions occurred on every one of the investigator's visits, and a teacher told me, "These children's opinions are important—it's important that they learn to reason things through." The classroom discussions always struck the observer as quite realistic and analytical, dealing with concrete social issues like the following: "Why do workers strike?" "Is that right or wrong?" "Why do we have inflation, and what can be done to stop it?" "Why do companies put chemicals in food when the natural ingredients are available?" etc. Usually the children did not have to be prodded to give their opinions. In fact, their statements and the interchanges between them struck the observer as quite sophisticated conceptually and verbally, and well-informed. Occasionally the teachers would prod with statements such as, "Even if you don't know [the answers], if you think logically about it, you can figure it out." And "I'm asking you [these] questions to help you think this through."

Language arts emphasizes language as a complex system, one that should be mastered. The children are asked to diagram sentences of complex grammatical construction, to memorize irregular verb conjugations (he lay, he has lain, etc. . . .), and to use the proper participles, conjunctions, and interjections, in their speech. The teacher (the same one who teaches social studies) told them, "It is not enough to get these right on tests; you must use what you learn [in grammar classes] in your written and oral work. I will grade you on that."

Most writing assignments are either research reports and essays for social studies, or experiment analyses and write-ups for science. There is only an occasional story or other "creative writing" assignment. On the occasion observed by the investigator (the writing of a Halloween story), the points the teacher stressed in preparing the children to write involved the structural aspects of a story rather than the expression of feelings or other ideas. The teacher showed them a filmstrip, "The Seven Parts of a Story," and lectured them on plot development, mood setting, character development, consistency, and the use of a logical or appropriate ending. The stories they subsequently wrote were, in fact, well-structured, but many were also personal and expressive. The teacher's evaluative comments, however, did not refer to the expressiveness or artistry, but were all directed toward whether they had "developed" the story well.

Language arts work also involved a large amount of practice in presentation of the self and in managing situations where the child was expected to be in charge. For example, there was a series of assignments in which each child had to be a "student teacher." The child had to plan a lesson in grammar, outlining, punctuation, or other language arts topic and explain the concept to the class. Each child was to prepare a worksheet or game and a homework assignment as well. After each presentation, the teacher and other children gave a critical appraisal of the "student teacher's" performance. Their criteria were: whether the student spoke clearly; whether the lesson was interesting; whether the student made any mistakes; and whether he or she kept control of the class. On an occasion when a child did not maintain control, the teacher said, "When you're up there, you have authority, and you have to use it. I'll back you up."

The teacher of math and science explained to the observer that she likes the ESS program because "the children can manipulate variables. They generate hypotheses and devise experiments to solve the problem. Then they have to explain what they found."

The executive elite school is the only school where bells do not demarcate the periods of time. The two fifth grade teachers were very strict about changing classes on schedule, however, as specific plans for each session had been made. The teachers attempted to keep tight control over the children during lessons, and the children were sometimes flippant, boisterous, and occasionally rude. However, the children may be brought into line by reminding them that "it is up to you." "You must control yourself," "you are responsible for your work," you must "set your priorities." One teacher told a child, "You are the only driver of your car—and only you can regulate your speed." A new teacher complained to the observer that she had thought "these children" would have more control.

While strict attention to the lesson at hand is required, the teachers make relatively little attempt to regulate the movement of the children at other times. For example, except for the kindergartners, the children in this school do not have to wait for the bell to ring in the morning; they may go to their classroom when they arrive at school. Fifth graders often came early to read, to finish work, or to catch up. After the first two months of school the fifth grade teachers did not line the children up to change classes or to go to gym, etc., but, when the children were ready and quiet, they were told they could go—sometimes without the teachers.

In the classroom, the children could get materials when they needed them and took what they needed from closets and from the teacher's desk. They were in charge of the office at lunchtime. During class they did not have to sign out or ask permission to leave the room; they just got up and left. Because of the pressure to get work done, however, they did not leave the room very often. The teachers were very polite to the children, and the investigator heard no sarcasm, no nasty remarks, and few direct orders. The teachers never called the children "honey," or "dear," but always called them by name. The teachers were expected to be available before school, after school, and for part of their lunch time to provide extra help if needed.

DISCUSSION AND CONCLUSION

One could attempt to identify physical, educational, cultural, and interpersonal characteristics of the environment of each school that might contribute to an empirical explanation of the events and interactions. For example, the investigator could introduce evidence to show that the following *increased* as the social class of the community increased (with the most marked differences occurring between the two districts): increased variety and abundance of teaching materials in the classroom; increased time reported spent by the teachers on preparation; higher social class background and more prestigious educational institutions attended by teachers and administrators; more stringent board of education requirements regarding teaching methods; more frequent and demanding administrative evaluation of teachers; increased teacher support services such as in-service workshops; increased parent expenditure for school equipment over and above district or government funding; higher expectations of student ability on the part of parents, teachers, and administrators; higher expectations and demands regarding student achievement on the part of teachers, parents, and administrators; more positive attitudes on the part of the teachers as to the probable occupational futures of the children; an increase in the children's acceptance of classroom assignments; increased intersubjectivity between students and teachers; and increased cultural congruence between school and community.

All of these—and other—factors may contribute to the character and scope of classroom events. However, what is of primary concern here is not the immediate causes of classroom activity (although these are in themselves quite important). Rather, the concern is to reflect on the deeper social meaning, the wider theoretical significance, of what happens in each social setting. In an attempt to assess the theoretical meaning of the differences among the schools, the work tasks and milieu in each will be discussed in light of the concepts used to define social class.

What potential relationships to the system of ownership of symbolic and physical capital, to authority and control, and to their own productive activity are being developed in children in each school? What economically relevant knowledge, skills, and predispositions are being transmitted in each classroom, and for what future relationship to the system of production are they appropriate? It is of course true that a student's future relationship to the process of production in society is determined by the combined effects of circumstances beyond elementary schooling. However, by examining elementary school activity in its social class context in the light of our theoretical perspective on social class, we can see certain potential relationships already developing. Moreover, in this structure of developing relationships lies theoretical—and social—significance.

The *working-class* children are developing a potential *conflict* relationship with capital. Their present school work is appropriate preparation for future wage labor that is mechanical and routine. Such work, insofar as it denies the human capacities for creativity and planning, is degrading; moreover, when performed in industry, such work is a source of profit to others. This situation produces industrial conflict over wages, working conditions, and control. However, the children in the working-class schools are not learning to be docile and obedient in the face of present or future degrading conditions or financial exploitation. They are developing abilities and skills of resistance. These methods are highly similar to the "slowdown," subtle sabotage and other modes of indirect resistance carried out by adult workers in the shop, on the department store sales floor, and in some offices.[11] As these types of resistance develop in school, they are highly constrained and limited in their ultimate effectiveness. Just as the children's resistance prevents them from learning socially legitimated knowledge and skills in school and is therefore ultimately debilitating, so is this type of resistance ultimately debilitating in industry. Such resistance in industry does not succeed in producing, nor is it intended to produce, fundamental changes in the relationships of exploitation or control. Thus, the methods of resistance that the working-class children are developing in school are only temporarily, and *potentially,* liberating.

In the *middle-class* school the children are developing somewhat different potential relationships to capital, authority, and work. In this school the work tasks and relationships are appropriate for a future relation to capital that is *bureaucratic.* Their school work is appropriate for white-collar working-class and middle-class jobs in the supportive institutions of United States society. In these jobs one does the paperwork, the technical work, the sales and the social service in the private and state bureaucracies. Such work does not usually demand that one be creative, and one is not often rewarded for critical analysis of the system. One is rewarded, rather, for knowing the answers to the questions one is asked, for knowing where or how to find the answers, and for knowing which form, regulation, technique, or procedure is correct. While such work does not usually satisfy human needs for engagement and self-expression, one's salary can be exchanged for objects or activities that attempt to meet these needs.

In the *affluent professional* school the children are developing a potential relationship to capital that is instrumental and expressive and involves substantial negotiation. In their schooling these children are acquiring *symbolic capital:* they are being given the opportunity to develop skills of linguistic, artistic, and scientific expression and creative elaboration of ideas into concrete form. These skills are those needed to produce, for example, culture (e.g., artistic, intellectual, and scientific ideas and other "products"). Their schooling is developing in these children skills necessary to become society's successful artists, intellectuals, legal, scientific, and technical experts and other professionals. The developing relation of the children in this school to their work is creative and relatively autonomous. Although they do not have control over which ideas they develop or express, the creative act in itself affirms and utilizes the human potential for conceptualization and design that is in many cases valued as intrinsically satisfying.

Professional persons in the cultural institutions of society (in, say, academe, publishing, the nonprint media, the arts, and the legal and state bureaucracies) are in an expressive relationship to the system of ownership in society because the ideas and other products of their work are often an important means by which material relationships of society are given ideological (e.g., artistic, intellectual, legal, and scientific) expression. Through the system of laws, for example, the ownership relations of private property are elaborated and legitimated in legal form; through individualistic and meritocratic theories in psychology and sociology, these individualistic economic relations are provided scientific "rationality" and "sense." The relationship to physical capital of those in society who create what counts as the dominant culture or ideology also involves substantial negotiation. The producers of symbolic capital often do not control the socially available physical capital nor the cultural uses to which it is put. They must therefore negotiate for money for their own projects. However, skillful application of one's cultural capital may ultimately lead to social (for example, state) power and to financial reward.

The *executive elite* school gives its children something that none of the other schools do: knowledge of and practice in manipulating the socially legitimated tools of analysis of systems. The children are given the opportunity to learn and to utilize the intellectually and socially prestigious grammatical, mathematical, and other vocabularies and rules by which elements are arranged. They are given the opportunity to use these skills in the analysis of society and in control situations. Such knowledge and skills are a most important kind of *symbolic capital*. They are necessary for control of a production system. The developing relationship of the children in this school to their work affirms and develops in them the human capacities for analysis and planning and helps to prepare them for work in society that would demand these skills. Their schooling is helping them to develop the abilities necessary for ownership and control of physical capital and the means of production in society.

The foregoing analysis of differences in school work in contrasting social class contexts suggests the following conclusion: the "hidden curriculum" of school work is tacit preparation for relating to the process of production in a particular way. Differing curricular, pedagogical, and pupil evaluation practices emphasize different cognitive and behavioral skills in each social setting and thus contribute to the development in the children of certain potential relationships to physical and symbolic capital, to authority, and to the process of work. School experience, in the sample of schools discussed here, differed qualitatively by social class. These differences may not only contribute to the development in the children in each social class of certain types of economically significant relationships and not others, but would thereby help to *reproduce* this system of relations in society. In the contribution to the reproduction of unequal social relations lies a theoretical meaning, and social consequence, of classroom practice.

The identification of different emphases in classrooms in a sample of contrasting social class contexts implies that further research should be conducted in a large number of schools to investigate the types of work tasks and interactions in each, to see if they differ in the ways discussed here, and to see if similar potential relationships are uncovered. Such research could have as a product the further elucidation of complex but not readily apparent connections between everyday activity in schools and classrooms and the unequal structure of economic relationships in which we work and live.

ENDNOTES

1. But see, in a related vein, Apple and King (1977) and Rist (1973).

2. The definition of social class delineated here is the author's own, but it relies heavily on her interpretation of the work of Eric Olin Wright (1978), Pierre Bourdieu (Bourdieu and Passeron, 1977) and Raymond Williams (1977).

3. For discussion of schools as agencies of social and economic legitimation see Althusser (1971); see also Anyon (1978; 1979).

4. While relationships of control in society will not be discussed here, it can be said that they roughly parallel the relationships of control in the workplace, which will be the focus of this discussion. That is, working-class and many middle-class persons have less control than members of the upper-middle and capitalist classes do, not only over conditions and processes of their work, but over their nonwork lives as well. In addition, it is true that persons from the middle and capitalist classes, rather than workers, are most often those who fill the positions of state and other power in United States society.

5. Occupations may change their relation to the means of production over time, as the expenditure and ownership of capital change, as technology, skills, and the social relations of work change. For example, some jobs which were middle-class, managerial positions in 1900 and which necessitated conceptual laying-out and planning are now working-class and increasingly mechanical: e.g., quality control in industry, clerical work, and computer programming (see Braverman, 1974).

6. The U.S. Bureau of the Census defines "poverty" for a nonfarm family of four as a yearly income of $6,191 a year or less. U.S. Bureau of the Census, *Statistical Abstract of the United States: 1978* (Washington, D.C.: U.S. Government Printing Office, 1978, p. 465, table 754).

7. This figure is an estimate. According to the Bureau of the Census, only 2.6 percent of families in the United States have money income of $50,000 or over. U.S. Bureau of the Census, *Current Population Reports,* series P-60, no. 118, "Money Income in 1977 of Families and Persons in the United States." (Washington, D.C.: U.S. Government Printing Office, 1979, p. 2, table A). For figures on income at these higher levels, see Smith and Franklin (1974).

8. For other similarities alleged to characterize United States classrooms and schools, but which will not be discussed here, see Dreeben (1968), Jackson (1968), and Sarasan (1971).

9. Indeed, strikingly little teaching occurred in either of the working-class schools; this curtailed the amount that the children were taught. Incidentally, it increased the amount of time that had to be spent by the researcher to collect data on teaching style and interaction.

10. A dominant feeling, expressed directly and indirectly by teachers in this school, was boredom with their work. They did, however, in contrast to the working-class schools, almost always carry out lessons during class times.

11. See, for example, discussions in Levison (1974), Aronowitz (1978), and Benson (1978).

REFERENCES

Althusser, L. Ideology and ideological state apparatuses. In L. Althusser, *Lenin and philosophy and other essays.* Ben Brewster, Trans. New York: Monthly Review Press, 1971.

Anyon, J. Elementary social studies textbooks and legitimating knowledge. *Theory and Research in Social Education,* 1978, 6, 40–55.

Anyon, J. Ideology and United States history textbooks. *Harvard Educational Review,* 1979, 49, 361–386.

Apple, M.W. *Ideology and curriculum.* Boston: Routledge and Kegan Paul, 1979.

Apple, M.W., & King, N. What do schools teach? *Curriculum Inquiry,* 1977, 6, 341–358.

Aronowitz, S. Marx, Braverman, and the logic of capital. *The Insurgent Sociologist,* 1978, 8, 126–146.

Benson, S. The clerking sisterhood: rationalization and the work culture of saleswomen in American department stores, 1890–1960. *Radical America,* 1978, 12, 41–55.

Bernstein, B. *Class, codes and control, Vol. 3. Towards a theory of educational transmission.* 2nd ed. London: Routledge and Kegan Paul, 1977.

Bourdieu, P. and Passeron, J. *Reproduction in education, society, and culture.* Beverly Hills, Calif.: Sage, 1977.

Bowles, S. & Gintis, H. *Schooling in capitalist America: educational reform and the contradictions of economic life.* New York: Basic Books, 1976.

Braverman, H. *Labor and monopoly capital: the degradation of work in the twentieth century.* New York: Monthly Review Press, 1974.

Dreeben, R. *On what is learned in school.* Reading, Mass.: Addison-Wesley, 1968.

Jackson, P. *Life in classrooms.* Holt, Rinehart & Winston, 1968.

Lampman, R.J. *The share of top wealth-holders in national wealth, 1922–1956:* A study of the National Bureau of Economic Research. Princeton, N.J.: Princeton University Press, 1962.

Levison, A. *The working-class majority.* New York: Penguin Books, 1974.

New York Stock Exchange. *Census.* New York: New York Stock Exchange, 1975.

Rist, R.C. *The urban school: a factory for failure.* Cambridge, Mass.: MIT Press, 1973.

Sarasan, S. *The culture of school and the problem of change.* Boston: Allyn and Bacon, 1971.

Smith, J.D. and Franklin, S. The concentration of personal wealth, 1922–1969. *American Economic Review,* 1974, 64, 162–167.

U.S. Bureau of the Census. *Current population reports.* Series P-60, no. 118. Money income in 1977 of families and persons in the United States. Washington, D.C.: U.S. Government Printing Office, 1979.

U.S. Bureau of the Census. *Statistical abstract of the United States: 1978.* Washington, D.C.: U.S. Government Printing Office, 1978.

Williams, R. *Marxism and literature.* New York: Oxford University Press, 1977.

Wright, E.O. *Class, crisis and the state.* London: New Left Books, 1978.

Ethnicity, Class, Cognitive, and Motivational Styles: Research and Teaching Implications*

JAMES A. BANKS

ETHNIC MINORITIES AND ACADEMIC ACHIEVEMENT

The low academic achievement of some ethnic minority youths, such as Afro-Americans, Mexican Americans, and Puerto Rican Americans, is a major national problem that warrants urgent action at the local, state, and national levels. The problem is complex and difficult to diagnose because there is substantial disagreement among educational researchers, practitioners, and the lay community about what causes the wide discrepancies in the academic achievement of groups such as Blacks and mainstream White youths, and between Mexican American and Japanese American students. The writer has reviewed and discussed elsewhere the conflicting explanations and paradigms that have emerged since the civil rights movement of the 1960s to explain the low academic achievement of ethnic youths.[1]

The Cultural Deprivation and Cultural Difference Hypotheses

When national attention focused on the underachievement of poor and ethnic minority youths in the 1960s, cultural deprivation emerged as the dominant paradigm to explain their educational problems.[2] Cultural deprivation theorists stated

*Based on a paper prepared for presentation at the Annual Meeting of the American Educational Research Association, Washington, D.C., April 20–24, 1987.

Reprinted from *The Journal of Negro Education*, 57:452–466, 1988, by permission of the author and the publisher.

that lower-income and minority students were not achieving well in school because of the culture of poverty in which they were socialized. The cultural deprivation paradigm was harshly attacked in the late 1960s and during the 1970s.[3] Its critics argued that it promoted assimilationism and violated the cultural integrity of students from diverse income and cultural groups.

Researchers who rejected the cultural deprivation paradigm created a conception of the cultures and educational problems of lower-income and minority youths based on a different set of assumptions. They argued that these students, far from being culturally deprived, have rich and elaborate cultures. Their rich cultural characteristics are evident in their languages and communication styles, behavioral styles, and values.[4] These theorists also contended that the cognitive, learning, and motivational styles of ethnic minorities such as Afro-Americans and Mexican Americans are different from those fostered in the schools.[5] These students, therefore, achieve less well in school because the school culture favors the culture of White mainstream students and places students from other backgrounds and cultures at a serious disadvantage. The school environment consequently needs to be reformed substantially so that it will be sensitive to diverse learning, cognitive, and motivational styles.

The Social Class Hypothesis

While the cultural difference paradigm has provided rich insights with implications for practice, it has devoted little attention to variation within ethnic groups. Learning and other social science theories should accurately reflect the tremendous diversity within ethnic groups such as Afro-Americans and Mexican Americans. While these cultures share a number of overarching beliefs, values, and behavioral styles, there are enormous within-group differences caused by factors such as region, gender, and social class. Diversity within ethnic groups has received insufficient attention within the social science literature and in the popular imagination.

While variables such as region, religion, gender, and social class create intragroup variation within ethnic groups, social class is presumably one of the most important of these variables. Wilson's important and controversial book—in which he argues that the importance of race in the United States has declined and that class has created important divisions among Blacks—evoked a stimulating and acid debate about race and class in the United States.[6] Wilson believes that class is a major factor that stratifies the Afro-American community. Gordon also hypothesizes that class has a strong influence on ethnic behavior.[7] He writes, "With regard to cultural behavior, differences of social class are more important and decisive than differences of ethnic group. This means that people of the same social class tend to act alike and to have the same values even if they have different ethnic backgrounds."[8]

My aim in this article is to examine the social class hypothesis and to determine the extent to which ethnicity is class sensitive. I will do this by reviewing studies on cognitive styles, learning styles, and motivational styles which include social class as a variable. If social class is as powerful a variable as Wilson and Gordon state, then middle-class Black and White students should not differ significantly in their cognitive, learning, and motivational styles. However, middle-class and lower-class Blacks should differ significantly on these variables. Another, and perhaps more likely possibility, is that social class and ethnicity interact in complex ways to influence learning, motivation, and cognitive styles.

PROBLEMS IN STUDYING
CLASS AND ETHNICITY

Several intractable problems confront the scholar who tries to determine the relationship between social class, ethnicity, and cognitive and motivational styles. Most of the literature that describes the cognitive and motivational styles of ethnic students includes little or no discussion of social class or other factors that might cause within-group variations, such as gender, age, or situational aspects. Social class is often conceptualized and measured differently in studies that include class as a variable; this makes it difficult to compare results from different studies. Researchers frequently use different scales and instruments to measure variables related to cognitive, learning, and motivational styles. To operationally define social class, especially across different ethnic and cultural groups, is one of the most difficult tasks facing social scientists today.

The nature of social class is changing in the United States. Behavior associated with the lower-class fifteen years ago—such as single-parent families—is now common among the middle class. Social class is a dynamic and changing concept. This makes it difficult to study social class over time and across different cultural and ethnic groups. Many of the studies reviewed in this article used Warner's Index of Status Characteristics which was published almost forty years ago.[9]

Cognition and Learning Studies

Lesser, Fifer, and Clark studied the patterns of mental abilities in six- and seven-year-old children from different social-class and ethnic backgrounds.[10] They studied verbal ability, reasoning, number facility, and space conceptualization among Chinese, Jewish, Black, and Puerto Rican students in New York City. They found that the four ethnic groups were markedly different in both the level of each mental ability and the pattern among these abilities. In a replication study, Lesser, Fifer, and Clark studied middle- and lower-class Chinese, Black, and Irish Catholic first-grade students in Boston.[11] The replication data for Chinese and Black students were similar to the data on these groups from their earlier study. However, the data for the Irish Catholic students showed neither a distinctive ethnic-group pattern nor similarity of patterns for the two social classes.

Burnes studied the pattern of WISC (Wechsler Intelligence Scale for Children) scores of Black and White students who were upper-middle and lower class.[12] She found significant social-class differences in the scores of the students but no significant racial differences. No interaction effects were found for social class and race. The scores on the subtests for Blacks and Whites did not show a pattern by race or cultural group.

Beckman studied six mental ability factors among 2,925 twelfth-grade students who had participated in Project TALENT.[13] She examined how the six mental abilities were related to ethnicity, social class, and sex. Sex accounted for a much larger proportion of the variance than did either ethnicity or social class. Sex was related significantly to both the shape and the level of the patterns of mental ability. It accounted for 69 percent of the total variance in the shape of the patterns. Ethnicity was the only other variable that showed a significant effect on the patterns. It accounted for 13 percent of the total variance: 9 percent associated with shape and 4 percent with level. The patterns of mental abilities of the social-class groups differed significantly in both shape and level. However, these differences accounted for only 2 percent of the variance and were considered by the investigator too small to be important.

A number of researchers have examined a variety of learning variables and cognitive functions related to ethnicity and social class. However, it is difficult to derive clear-cut generalizations from these studies. Siegel, Anderson, and Shapiro examined the categorization behavior of lower- and middle-class Black preschool children.[14] The children were presented with sorting objects, colored pictures, and black-and-white pictures. Lower-class and middle-class children differed in their ability to group only on the pictures. They used different types of categories. Lower-class children preferred to form groups based on use and interdependence of items. Middle-class children preferred to group items on the basis of common physical attributes.

Orasanu, Lee, and Scribner investigated the extent to which category clustering in recall is dependent on preferred organization of the to-be-recalled items and whether preferred organization or recall are related to ethnic or economic group membership.[15] Social-class status was related to the number of high-associate pairs the subjects produced in sorting. Middle-income children produced significantly more pairs than low-income children. Ethnicity was related to the number of taxonomic categories; White children sorted taxonomically more often than did Black children, who showed a preference for functional sorting. Ethnicity and social-class status were unrelated to amount recalled on the pairs-list tasks or to the amount of clustering. Although Black and White children showed differences in organizational preferences, there were no differences in recall.

Rychlak investigated the role of social class, race, and intelligence on the affective learning styles of 160 lower- and middle-income seventh-grade children who were equally divided by sex and race (White and Black).[16] The researchers hypothesized and found that, for all subjects, moving from positive to negative reinforcement value across lists resulted in less nonspecific transfer than does moving from negative to positive reinforcement across successive lists. They hypothesized that this general pattern would be more apparent for Blacks than for Whites and for lower-class than for middle-class subjects. Their hypotheses were confirmed. The White subjects reflected positive non-specific transfer across the lists regardless of whether they were moving from positive to negative or negative to positive levels of reinforcement value. However, Black subjects reflected a negative transfer when moving from positive to negative and a positive transfer when moving from negative to positive lists.

Family Socialization

Some evidence indicates that the socialization and intellectual environment of the homes of different racial groups vary even when they are members of the same social class as determined by an index such as Warner's Index of Status Characteristics.[17] Trotman compared the home environment ratings of fifty Black and fifty White middle-class families of ninth-grade girls to the girls' Otis-Lennon Mental Ability Test results, Metropolitan Achievement Test scores and grade point averages.[18] She found that the home environments of middle-class White families showed a significantly higher level of intellectuality than did those of middle-class Black families. There was an overall positive relationship between the family's home environment and the child's score on the Otis-Lennon Mental Ability Test. This relationship was stronger for Black than for White families. Trotman believes that there is a cultural difference in the home experience and parent-child interactions in Black and White families of the same social class, and that this difference may help to explain the variation in intelligence test performance by members of the two cultural groups.

Research by Moore supports the hypothesis that family socialization practices related to intelligence test performance is different within Black and White families of the same social class.[19] She compared the intelligence test performances of a sample of Black children adopted by Black and by White middle-class parents. She hypothesized that Black children adopted by Black families would achieve significantly lower WISC scores than Black children adopted by White families. Her hypothesis was confirmed. The children adopted by the White families scored significantly higher on the WISC than did those adopted by Black families. The 13.5-point difference in performance between the two groups is the level usually observed between Black and White children.

The studies by Trotman and by Moore support the hypothesis that the socialization practices of Black and White middle-class parents, at least as they relate to intelligence test performance, differ significantly. However, it cannot be inferred from these findings that family socialization practices do not vary within different social classes in the Black community. A study by Kamii and Radin indicates that the socialization practices of lower-lower and middle-class Black mothers differ in significant ways.[20] These researchers directly observed how the mothers interacted with their preschool children and conducted interviews with the mothers in their homes. While they found that lower-lower and middle-class mothers differed significantly in some socialization practices, "not all mothers demonstrated the characteristics of their strata. Social class is thus not a determinant of behavior but a statement of probability that a type of behavior is likely to occur."[21]

Cognitive Styles

Theorists and researchers who support the cultural difference hypothesis, such as Ramírez and Castañeda, Hilliard, White, and Hale-Benson,[22] have been heavily influenced by the "cognitive style" concept pioneered by Witkin.[23] Witkin hypothesizes that the learning styles of individuals vary; some are field independent in their learning styles, while others are field dependent. Learners who are field independent easily perceive a hidden figure on the Embedded Figures Test, while field-dependent learners find it difficult to perceive because of the obscuring design.[24]

Ramírez and Castañeda used Witkin's concept in their work with Mexican American students. They substituted "field sensitive" for "field dependent," which they believe has negative connotations. Field-independent and field-sensitive students differ in some significant ways in their learning styles and behaviors. Field independent learners prefer to work independently, while field-sensitive learners like to work with others to achieve a common goal. Field-independent learners tend to be task-oriented and inattentive to their social environment when working. Field-sensitive learners tend to be sensitive to the feelings and opinions of others.[26] Ramírez and Castañeda found that Mexican American children tend to be field sensitive in their learning styles, while teachers usually prefer field-independent students and assign them higher grades. The teaching styles of most teachers and the school curriculum also tend to reflect the characteristics of field-independent students. Mainstream Anglo students tend to be more field independent than ethnic minorities such as Mexican American and Black students. Although field-independent students tend to get higher grades than do field-dependent students, researchers have found that cognitive style is not related to measured intelligence or IQ.

Cohen,[27] who has influenced the works of Hale-Benson and Hilliard, has conceptualized learning styles similar to those formulated by Witkin. She identifies two conceptual styles, analytic and relational. The analytic style is related to Witkin's field-independent concept. The relational is similar to his field-dependent concept. Cohen found that these styles of thinking are produced by the kinds of families and groups into which students are socialized. Family and friendship groups in which functions are periodically performed or widely shared by all members of the group, which she calls "shared function" groups, tend to socialize students who are relational in their learning styles. Formal styles of group organization are associated with analytic styles of learning.

Several researchers have tested the hypothesis that ethnic minority students tend to be more field-dependent or relational in their learning styles than mainstream students, even when social-class status is held constant. Ramírez and Price-Williams studied 180 fourth-grade children to determine whether Mexican American and Black students were more field dependent than Anglo students.[28] Both the Black and the Mexican American students scored in a significantly more field-dependent direction than did the Anglo children. The social-class effect was not significant. Ramírez found that most teachers are significantly more field independent than are Mexican American students. However, their level of field independence does not differ significantly from that of Anglo students.[29]

Perney studied field dependence-independence among suburban Black and White sixth-grade students.[30] No information is given about the social-class status of the community. She found that the Black students were significantly more field dependent than were the White students. However, it was the scores of the Black females that accounted for most of the difference between the races. Black females were the most field-dependent subjects in the study. The females in the study, as a group, were significantly more field dependent than the males. Perney's study reveals that there are significant field-dependence differences between Black and White students and between males and females. However, it does not help us determine the extent to which field dependence is related or sensitive to social-class status.

Locus of Control and Motivation

Researchers have devoted considerable attention to locus of control and its influence on learning and motivation.[31] This psychological construct is related to how individuals perceive the relationship between their action and its consequences. Individuals who believe that consequences are a direct result of their actions are said to have internal locus of control or internality. Persons who believe that there is little or no relationship between their behavior and its consequences are said to have an external locus of control.

Researchers have found that internality is positively related to academic achievement.[32] Students who believe that their behavior can determine consequences tend to achieve at higher levels than students who believe that their behavior is determined by external forces such as luck, fate, or other individuals. Researchers have found that internality is related to social class and to socialization practices.[33] Higher-socioeconomic-status students tend to be more internal in their orientations than are lower-socioeconomic-status students.

Some researchers interested in minority education have devoted considerable attention to locus of control because of the percentage of ethnic minority students who are lower-class and consequently tend to be external in their psychological orientations.[34] Research rather consistently indicates a relationship between social-class status, internality, and academic achievement. A study by Garner and Cole indicates that while both field dependence and locus of control are related to academic achievement, field dependence is the more important factor; the achievers in their study were more field independent.[35] However, when locus of control and field dependence were combined, locus of control dominated. The achievement of the groups ranged from high to low as follows: internal and field independent, internal and field dependent, external and field independent, external and field dependent. A study by Battle and Rotter supports the well-established principle that locus of control is related primarily to social class rather than to race or ethnicity.[36]

THE PERSISTENCE OF ETHNICITY

As the above review of research indicates, our knowledge of the effect of social-class status on cognitive and motivational styles among ethnic minorities is thin and fragmentary. My review of such studies is representative but not exhaustive. This research does not give a clear and unmixed message about how sensitive ethnicity is to social-class status. Some researchers, such as Lesser, Fifer, and Clark, Trotman, and Moore, have found that ethnicity has a powerful effect on behavior related to learning and intellectual performance when social class is varied or controlled. Other researchers, such as Orasanu, Lee, and Scribner and Burnes, have derived findings that reveal the effects of social class on learning behavior or the effects of both class and ethnicity.

Collectively, the studies reviewed in this article provide more support for the cultural difference than for the social-class hypothesis. They indicate that ethnicity continues to have a significant influence on the learning behavior and styles of Afro-American and Mexican American students, even when these students are middle class. *In other words, the research reviewed in this article indicates that while ethnicity is to some extent class sensitive, its effects persist across social-class segments within an ethnic group.* However, the research also indicates that social class causes within-ethnic-group variation in behavior. Middle-class Afro-Americans and middle-class Whites differ in some significant ways, as do middle-class and lower-class Afro-Americans.

While the research reviewed herein indicates that cognitive and learning styles are influenced by ethnicity across social classes within ethnic groups, it suggests that locus of control is primarily a class variable. Whether students believe that they can exert control over their environment appears to be related more to their socioeconomic status than to their ethnic socialization or culture.

Why Does Ethnicity Persist Across Social Classes?

In his important and influential publication, Gordon hypothesizes that social-class differences are more important and decisive than ethnic-group differences.[37] He also states that people of the same social class will share behavioral similarities. Gordon emphasizes the importance of social class in shaping behavior. His "ethclass" hypotheses need to be revised and made more consistent with the research and thinking that have taken place during the last two decades.[38]

Gordon's hypotheses are not consistent with many of the studies reviewed in this paper. His ethclass hypotheses predict that social class has a stronger effect on behavior than ethnicity has on behavior. However, this does not seem to be the case for behavior related to the learning and cognitive styles of Afro-Americans and Mexican Americans. We need to examine why there is an inconsistency between Gordon's hypotheses and the research reviewed in this article.

I believe that this inconsistency results primarily from a major problem in social science research in the United States related to the conceptualization and study of social classes within non-White populations such as Afro-Americans and Mexican Americans. The tendency in social science is to use standard indices such as occupation, income, and educational level to identify lower-class and middle-class populations within these groups and to compare them with White populations with similar occupational, income, and educational characteristics. The assumption is made that social-class groups within the non-White populations and those within the White population are equivalent.

The comparative study of social classes across ethnic groups in the United States creates problems in both theory construction and in the formulation of valid generalizations because significant differences often exist between Blacks and Whites with similar income, educational, and occupational characteristics. The study of the Black middle class is a case in point. Most middle-class White families live in a middle-class community, have middle-class relatives and friends, and send their children to middle-class schools. This may or may not be true of a middle-class Black family. Approximately 55 percent of Blacks in the United States are members of the lower class.[39] Many Black middle-class families have relatives who are working class or lower class. Black middle-class families often live in mixed-class neighborhoods, participate in community organizations and institutions that have participants from all social-class groups, and often visit relatives who live in the inner city.[40]

Many Blacks are also members of an extended family, which often includes lower- and working-class relatives. Lower-class relatives often play an important role in the socialization of their children. These relatives may serve as babysitters for short and long periods for the middle-class family. There is a strong expectation within the Black extended family that the individual who becomes middle class will not forsake his or her family and should help it financially when necessary.[41] Unlike many middle-class White families, which tend to function highly independently within a largely middle-class world, the middle-class Black family is often a first-generation middle-class family that exists within an extended family and a community network that have definite group expectations for it and strongly influence its behaviors and options. Many of the generalizations made here about Black families are also true for Mexican American and Puerto Rican American middle-class families.[42]

THE PERSISTENCE OF ETHNICITY: THEORY AND RESEARCH IMPLICATIONS

To reformulate Gordon's ethclass hypotheses to make them more consistent with research that has taken place in the last two decades, we need to recognize the persistence of ethnicity when social-class mobility takes place. This is especially the case when an ethnic group is non-White and is a part of a group that has a disproportionately large working-class or lower-class population. Significant differences exist for the individual who is middle class but functions within a community that is primarily working class or lower class, and for the individual who is middle class but who functions within a predominantly middle-class community. Taking these factors into account, we may reformulate one of Gordon's hypotheses to read: With regard to cultural behavior, ethnicity continues to influence the behavior of members of ethnic groups within certain characteristics when social mobility occurs. This means that while people of the same social class from different ethnic groups will exhibit some similar behaviors, they will have some significant behavioral differences caused by the persistence of ethnicity.

When studying race, class, and ethnicity, social scientists need to examine *generational middle-class status* as a variable. There are often important behavioral and attitudinal differences between a Black individual who grew up poor and became middle class within his or her adulthood and a Black who is fourth-generation middle class. Many of the middle-class Afro-Americans and Mexican Americans described in existing research studies are probably first-generation middle class. Such individuals are sometimes compared with Whites who have been middle class for several generations. Generational social-class status needs to be varied systematically in research studies so that we can learn more about the tenacity of ethnicity across generations.

Other Research Implications

We need more replications of studies related to race, class, and cognitive styles. One of the major problems with the research is that various researchers formulate different questions, study subjects of different ages who attend different kinds of schools, use different statistical analysis techniques, and use different instruments to measure the same variables. Important lines of inquiry on problems related to ethnic groups and cognitive styles are begun but not pursued until valid generalizations and theories have been formulated. Lesser, Fifer, and Clark published a pathbreaking study that described the patterns of mental abilities of ethnic minorities in 1967. However, we know little more about patterns of mental abilities in ethnic groups today than we knew in 1967. Neither the original researchers nor other students have pursued this line of inquiry in any systematic way. As a result, the research on learning patterns among ethnic minorities remains thin and fragmented, and provides few insights that can guide practice.

THE PERSISTENCE OF ETHNICITY: IMPLICATIONS FOR PRACTICE

Teachers and other practitioners reading the review of research in this article are likely to be disappointed by the fragmentary nature of the research that exists on ethnicity, social class, and cognitive styles. It is difficult to find such studies. Nevertheless, we can glean some guidelines for practice from the research.

The research suggests that students will come to the classroom with many kinds of differences, some of which may be related to their ethnic group, their social-class status, or social class and ethnicity combined. Research suggests that Afro-American and Mexican American students tend to be more field sensitive in their learning styles than are mainstream Anglo-American students. This means that Mexican American and Afro-American students are more likely to be motivated by curriculum content that is presented in a humanized or story format than are mainstream Anglo students. The research also suggests that middle-class students tend to be more internal than are lower-class students. This suggests that teachers will need to work with many lower-class students to help them to see the relationship between their effort and their academic performance.

It is important for teachers to understand that the characteristics of ethnic groups and socioeconomic classes can help us to understand groups but not individual students. All types of learning and motivational styles are found within all ethnic groups and social classes. Many Afro-American students are field independent and analytic; many White students are field dependent and relational. The teacher cannot assume that every Mexican American student is field dependent and that every Anglo student is field independent. These kinds of assumptions result in new stereotypes and problems. There is a delicate and difficult balance between using generalizations about groups to better understand and interpret the behavior of groups, and using that knowledge to interpret the behavior of a particular student. Cox and Ramírez have described some of the difficulties that resulted when practitioners applied their research on cognitive styles:

> *The dissemination of research information on cognitive styles has also had a negative effect in some cases, arising primarily from common problems associated with looking at mean differences; that is, by using averages to describe differences between groups, the dangers of stereotyping are more likely. The great diversity within any culture is ignored, and a construct which should be used as a tool for individualization becomes yet another label for categorizing and evaluating.*[43]

Teachers should recognize that students bring a variety of learning, cognitive, and motivational styles to the classroom, and that while certain characteristics are associated with specific ethnic and social-class groups, these characteristics are distributed throughout the total student population. This means that the teacher should use a variety of teaching styles and content that will appeal to diverse students. Concepts should be taught when possible with different strategies so that students who are relational in their learning styles as well as those who are analytic will have an equal opportunity to learn. Researchers such as Slavin and Cohen have documented that cooperative learning strategies appeal to ethnic-group students and foster positive intergroup attitudes and feelings.[44]

Teachers should also select content from diverse ethnic groups so that students from various cultures will see their images in the curriculum.[45] Educational equity will exist for all students when teachers become sensitive to the cultural diversity in their classrooms, vary their teaching styles so as to appeal to a diverse student population, and modify their curricula to include ethnic content. This is a tall but essential order in an ethnically and racially diverse nation that is wasting so much of its human potential.

ENDNOTES

1. J.A. Banks, "Multicultural Education: Developments, Paradigms, and Goals," in J.A. Banks and J. Lynch, eds., *Multicultural Education in Western Societies* (New York: Praeger, 1986), pp. 2–28.

2. F. Reissman, *The Culturally Deprived Child* (New York: Harper, 1962); B.S. Bloom, A. Davis, and R. Hess, *Compensatory Education for Cultural Deprivation* (New York: Holt, 1965).

3. C.A. Valentine, *Culture and Poverty: Critique and Counter-Proposals* (Chicago: University of Chicago Press, 1968); S.S. Baratz and J.C. Baratz, "Early Childhood Intervention: The Social Science Base of Institutional Racism," *Harvard Educational Review,* 40 (Winter 1970), 29–50.

4. G. Smitherman, *Talking and Testifying: The Language of Black America* (Boston: Houghton Mifflin, 1977); J. Hale, "Black Children: Their Roots, Culture and Learning Styles," *Young Children,* 36 (January 1981), 37–50; J.L. White, *The Psychology of Blacks* (Englewood Cliffs, N.J.: Prentice-Hall, 1984).

5. M. Ramírez and A. Castañeda, *Cultural Democracy, Bicognitive Development and Education* (New York: Academic Press, 1974); B.J. Shade, "Afro-American Cognitive Style: A Variable in School Success?" *Review of Educational Research,* 52 (Summer, 1982), 219–244; J. Hale-Benson, *Black Children: Their Roots, Culture, and Learning Styles,* rev. ed. (Baltimore: The John Hopkins University Press, 1986).

6. W.J. Wilson, *The Declining Significance of Race: Blacks and Changing American Institutions* (Chicago: University of Chicago Press, 1978); A. Pinkney, *The Myth of Black Progress* (New York: Cambridge University Press, 1984).

7. M. Gordon, *Assimilation in American Life* (New York: Oxford University Press, 1964).

8. Ibid., p. 52.

9. W.L. Warner, *Social Class in America* (Chicago: Science Research Associates, 1949).

10. G.S. Lesser, G. Fifer, and D.H. Clark, "Mental Abilities of Children from Different Social-Class and Cultural Groups," *Monographs of the Society for Research in Child Development,* 30, No. 4 (1965).

11. Cited in S.S. Stodolsky and G. Lesser, "Learning Patterns in the Disadvantaged," *Harvard Educational Review,* 37 (Fall 1967), 546–593; reprinted Series No. 5, *Harvard Educational Review,* 1975, pp. 22–69.

12. K. Burnes "Patterns of WISC Scores for Children of Two Socioeconomic Classes and Races," *Child Development,* 41 (1970), 493–499.

13. M.E. Backman, "Patterns of Mental Abilities: Ethnic, Socioeconomic, and Sex Differences," *American Educational Research Journal,* 9 (Winter 1972), 1–12.

14. I. Siegel, L.M. Anderson, and H. Shapiro, "Categorization Behavior in Lower- and Middle-Class Preschool Children: Differences in Dealing with Representation of Familiar Objects," *Journal of Negro Education,* 35 (1966), 218–229.

15. J. Orasanu, C. Lee, and S. Scribner, "The Development of Category Organization and Free Recall: Ethnic and Economic Group Comparisons," *Child Development,* 50 (1979), 1100–1109.

16. J.F. Rychlak, "Affective Assessment, Intelligence, Social Class, and Racial Learning Style," *Journal of Personality and Social Psychology,* 32 (1975), 989–995.

17. Warner, *Social Class in America.*

18. F.K. Trotman, "Race, IQ, and the Middle Class," *Journal of Educational Psychology,* 69 (1977), 266–273.

19. E.G.J. Moore, "Ethnicity as a Variable in Child Development," in *The Social and Affective Development of Black Children,* ed. M.G. Spencer, G.K. Brookins, and W.R. Allen (Hillsdale, N.J.: Lawrence Erlbaum Associates, 1985), pp. 101–115.

20. C.K. Kamii and N.J. Radin, "Class Differences in Socialization Practices of Negro Mothers." *Journal of Marriage and the Family,* 29 (1967), 302–310; reprinted in *The Black Family: Essays and Studies,* ed. R. Staples (Belmont, Calif.: Wadsworth Publishing Co., 1971), pp. 235–247.

21. Ibid., p. 244.

22. Ramírez and Castañeda, *Cultural Democracy;* A. Hilliard, "Alternatives to IQ Testing: An Approach to the Identification of Gifted Minority Children" (Final report to the California State Department of Education, 1976); White, *The Psychology of Blacks;* and Hale-Benson, *Black Children.*

23. H.A. Witkin, *Psychological Differentiation* (New York: Wiley, 1962); H.A. Witkin and D.R. Goodenough, *Cognitive Styles: Essence and Origins* (New York: International Universities Press, Inc., 1981).

24. H.A. Witkin, "Individual Differences in Ease of Perception of Embedded Figures," *Journal of Personality,* 19 (1950), 1–15.

25. Ramírez and Castañeda, *Cultural Democracy.*

26. Ibid.

27. R.A. Cohen, "Conceptual Styles, Cultural Conflict, and Nonverbal Tests of Intelligence," *American Anthropologist,* 71 (1969), 828–856.

28. M. Ramírez and D.R. Price-Williams, "Cognitive Styles of Children of Three Ethnic Groups in the United States," *Journal of Cross-Cultural Psychology,* 5 (1974), 212–219.

29. M. Ramírez, "Cognitive Styles and Cultural Democracy in Education of Mexican Americans," *Social Science Quarterly,* 53 (1973), 895–904.

30. V.H. Perney, "Effects of Race and Sex on Field Dependence-Independence in Children," *Perceptual and Motor Skills,* 42 (1976), 975–980.

31. H.M. Leftcourt, *Locus of Control: Current Trends in Theory and Research,* 2nd ed. (Hillsdale, N.J.: Lawrence Erlbaum Associates, 1982).

32. Ibid.

33. Ibid.

34. J.A. Vasquez, "Bilingual Education's Needed Third Dimension," *Educational Leadership,* 37 (November 1979), 166–168.

35. C.W. Garner and E.G. Cole, "The Achievement of Students in Low-SES Settings: An Investigation of the Relationship Between Locus of Control and Field Dependence," *Urban Education,* 21 (July 1986), 189–206.

36. E.S. Battle and J.B. Rotter, "Children's Feelings of Personal Control as Related to Social Class and Ethnic Group," *Journal of Personality,* 31 (1963), 482–490.

37. Gordon, *Assimilation in American Life.*

38. H.P. McAdoo and J.L. McAdoo, eds., *Black Children: Social, Educational, and Parental Environments* (Beverly Hills: Sage Publications, 1985).

39. J.E. Blackwell, *The Black Community: Unity and Diversity,* 2nd ed. (New York: Harper and Row, 1985).

40. J.A. Banks, "An Exploratory Study of Assimilation, Pluralism, and Marginality: Black Families in Predominantly White Suburbs," document resume in *Resources in Education.* ERIC document 257–275.

41. E.P. Martin and J.M. Martin, *The Black Extended Family* (Chicago: The University of Chicago Press, 1978).

42. J.W. Moore and H. Pachon, *Mexican Americans,* 2nd ed. (Englewood Cliffs, N.J.: Prentice-Hall, 1976).

43. B.G. Cox and M. Ramírez, "Cognitive Styles: Implications for Multiethnic Education," in *Education in the 80s: Multiethnic Education,* ed. J.A. Banks (Washington, D.C.: National Education Association, 1981), pp. 61–71.

44. R.E. Slavin, *Cooperative Learning* (New York: Longman, 1983); E.G. Cohen, *Designing Groupwork Strategies for the Heterogeneous Classroom* (New York: Teachers College Press, 1986).

45. J.A. Banks, *Teaching Strategies for Ethnic Studies,* 4th ed. (Boston: Allyn and Bacon, 1987).

Contexts of Learning for Minority Students

JAMES A. VASQUEZ

Every classroom has its psychological context, defined in terms of what the student expects as a consequence of contemplated behavior. Such expectations are based on the interactions between the student and the teacher, as well as between the student and his or her peers. How conducive to learning that context is, given the particular set of student traits found in the classroom, has many educational implications.

Studies have found that student perceptions of the classroom environment can have a direct impact not only on achievement of students,[1] but also on their personal-social behaviors. For example, crowding, defined as perceived density, may cause social withdrawal, nervousness among females, and aggressiveness among males.[2] Further, when students hold positive expectations about themselves (which are a product of their perceptions of the psychological context), they are more pleased with how the teacher performs and show more interest in the lesson being taught.[3]

Minority students may perceive what is occurring in the classroom quite differently from majority students. A given classroom atmosphere that nicely fits the majority in relation to their values, learning styles, and reinforcement contingencies may not serve minority students at all since many of them come from different social classes and cultures. Thus, while the majority may be favorably inclined toward the prevailing context (both in terms of *what* is expected and *how* to meet those expectations), minority students may perceive it to be more hostile and less helpful.

Meanwhile, there is some evidence that some minority children may manage to maintain a "foundation of intrinsic self-esteem"[4] in spite of their stigmatized group membership. This suggests that what happens to them in the classroom *as a student,* e.g., poor academic performance, may be held separate from their self-esteem evaluation *as a person,* if attributed to their status as minorities instead of to their basic personhood. A psychological context in which this distinction between self-

From *The Educational Forum,* 52:243–253, 1988. Reprinted by permission of Kappa Delta Pi, An International Honor Society in Education.

as-student and self-as-person is acknowledged would create a freer atmosphere to enable minority youths to think well of themselves irrespective of the level of their academic performance.

This article reviews classroom atmospheres that are commonly found in American schools and examines implications for the instruction of minority students.

Teacher expectations. High expectation levels held by teachers for their students have been a commonly found trait of schools described as effective.[5] There is much evidence to confirm the belief that how a teacher evaluates his or her students' ability to learn, and what the teacher expects from the students by way of performance, are factors closely correlated with the achievement levels of those students. It appears that a simple hint that a student is likely to perform well or poorly is sufficient to bring forth differential behaviors in the teacher.[6] It is generally believed that high expectations are communicated to the student through different types of cues, verbal or nonverbal, and the student's performance is consequently affected. Differences in types of praise offered and in the amount of attention provided to students are among the variables identified as conveyors of expectation. So powerful is the effect of a teacher's expectation on a student that it may be transmitted even when students hold negative expectations about the teacher. Teachers have been rated by outside judges as more adequate when holding positive expectations about their students, and they rate themselves more highly when holding higher expectations of students.[7]

Some research has indicated that minority students, particularly those whose learning style is characterized by field dependence, tend to be more strongly influenced than majority students by adult authority figures in the classroom.[8] Though we expect that the more individualistic student, thought to be field independent, would be somewhat more resistant to the effect of teacher expectations in terms of performance, a teacher must take care not to develop and communicate unrealistic expectations of his or her minority students that may depress their performance levels. Some teachers have been reported to base their expectations on such invalid predictors of performance as type of dress, etiquette, even smell,[9] or dialect.[10]

Feminization of the classroom. Some observers have characterized the school as a place for girls[11]—a place where girls are much more comfortable, where the teacher is far more often than not a female, and where the activities are essentially those that cater to the inclinations of females and turn off males. The prevalent school code is described as one of propriety, obedience, decorum, cleanliness, physical and, too often, mental passivity. An atmosphere of this nature can be a cause of poor performance among males, of their dislike toward school and, eventually, of their dropping out of school.[12] Moreover, such a context governed by women's rules and standards may be problematic for females. While probably related to higher academic performance and social comfort for females, such an atmosphere may also reduce their willingness to take risks and make them more dependent on authority.[13]

One suggestion for defeminization of the classroom is to hire more males as teachers. There is some wisdom in this approach, but it is perhaps not too realistic at this time in view of the actual student population in teacher education programs. A more practical suggestion is that of assisting current teachers to be more aware of the ways to change their classrooms so as to create a better atmosphere for typical male students. It should nevertheless be remembered that a more male-oriented context cannot be created simply by moving in the opposite direction of the so-called feminine traits (obedience, decorum, cleanliness, etc.). It will take careful thought and reflection to determine what needs to be changed, and to what extent, to establish an orientation that is more male in nature.

One must also recognize that in some important ways the typical classroom has also catered to male students, perhaps especially at the secondary level. It is not a secret, for example, that in some content areas, such as mathematics and science, the contexts in which basic concepts have been taught have tended to be much more related to the backgrounds of male students than to those of female students. A more equitable situation, one that serves to enhance more fully participation and learning by all students, would be that which corrected these inequities as well. It would seem that an environment that was accepting of both male and female orientations would indeed be fairer than the present one in which females seem to be favored at the elementary level and males at the secondary level.

This matter of gender orientation is of special importance for those who work with minority students, for research clearly speaks of the presence of more rigidly prescribed sex role behaviors in some minority communities.[14] Thus, we would expect even more resistance by males from these ethnic backgrounds toward a highly feminized classroom.

A cooperative context. There is evidence that classroom activities incorporating cooperation rather than competition promote higher achievement.[15] This situation seems to obtain, perhaps even more clearly, for students of minority background.[16] In heterogeneous classroom settings (i.e., ethnically mixed), a cooperative environment promotes more positive relationships among the students. Once a base for cooperation is established, even intergroup competition becomes a positive factor in promoting good relationships across ethnic lines.[17]

Of course, cooperation may be a variable more closely associated with social class than with culture per se, for the economic needs faced by people who live a day-to-day existence can lead to a certain expectation that one must share with others for the survival of all, and that competition should not be tolerated since the resources are too scarce.[18] The reluctance on the part of some minority students to engage in highly competitive activities in the classroom may also have its root in another interesting dynamic. There is some evidence to suggest that girls prefer to compete in English, while boys prefer to do so in mathematics.[19] If this were indeed the case, it would suggest that individuals prefer competing in areas in which they already hold, or perceive that they hold, some mastery. Many minority students may not feel that they excel consistently in any subject matter area and, hence, they are not inclined toward competition at all.

Anyway, we should not perpetuate a system that is based on the premises that speed is intelligence and success at someone else's expense is acceptable. What is needed is balance. Few would argue that our society is essentially a competitive one and, if school is viewed as a place where our youth are prepared to enter that society successfully, then school must make sure that students acquire this skill of competitive performance as well as others. Nevertheless, learners should not be rushed to attain the skill too early and quickly. Certainly we cannot expect that minority youth, whose early backgrounds have taught them that the way to survive and thrive in the world is to work together for a shared goal, are going to be able to eradicate this deep-seated value with ease. Besides, there are many who see this valuing of cooperation much needed and too important to our society to be discarded. If minority youth are in need of learning competitive skills before leaving school, it is equally true that many majority youth have much to learn in the ways of working with others for a common good. Even in corporate business and industry there have been many efforts to train executives in cooperative skills. The atmosphere most desired in the classroom is one in which there are activities that accommodate both the competitive and cooperative types of students in providing the necessary experiences to learn in the way they prefer but also to learn, in time, in their nonpreferred mode.

Attribution of success and failure. Research has indicated that a difference exists among students in how they explain their successes and failures. On the basis of this notion of locus of control,[20] two contrasting types of students may be identified in our classrooms—those who see themselves as responsible for what happens to them and those who look outside of themselves to explain success or failure. The former group is referred to as the internals, since they generally explain their outcomes by referring to either their own effort or ability. The latter group is called the externals, for they tend to invoke such factors as luck or the lack thereof, ease or difficulty of the task, and the presence of some "powerful others" in their lives. Such traits as self-reliance, expectancy of success, level of aspiration, achievement motivation, skills in taking tests, and responsiveness to reinforcement have all been identified as characteristics more of the internal student than of the external student. In all likelihood it is these traits that account for the superior academic achievement of internal students, even though internals have not been found to be more intelligent than externals.[21]

Minority youth tend to be characterized by an external locus of control.[22] While some hold to the view that culture itself imparts a perception to its adherents, inclining them one way or the other, a more recent view with better explanatory power suggests that the experiences of poverty and failure combine to produce an external person.[23] Poverty, of course, removes decision-making power from people and forces them to live a life that is, at least from their perception, imposed upon them externally. When children from a poor family are also of minority background, the chances of experiencing repeated failure increase once they begin school. This failure experience serves to increase the tendency of the child to become external as he or she seeks to escape the extreme discomfort of blaming self for failure. To blame outside factors is more comfortable, but it is done at great cost academically, since as one comes more and more to align oneself with the external perspective, the traits so necessary to excel as a student begin to diminish.

Fortunately, it is possible to provide assistance to external students and change their perception that nothing they do in the classroom counts for anything. A number of practical activities can help foster internality among external students.[24] Basic to all efforts to foster internality is a series of successful outcomes experienced by the external student in the classroom.[25] While this may appear to be a difficult condition to create, because externals are usually not high achieving students, there are at least some areas in which external students can perform well. The teaching of cause-effect relationships has also been identified as an effective way since external students may not have learned a very basic concept of effort as it is related to outcome. This approach recommends that a series of vignettes be created to help the student see the relationship between cause and effect, first in naturalistic settings, then in the context of human behavior, and finally in terms of the student's own activities in the classroom.

One-on-one counseling has been another aid in helping students to see the relationship between their effort and/or ability and subsequent academic outcomes. Such factors as interest, motivation, concentration, attendance, participation, consistency, and, of course, ability can be pointed out to the student by the teacher to help him or her realize that there is an association between one's behavior and grades. Activities that require an internal attribution are likewise useful in fostering internality. For instance, involvement in peer tutoring and in creative tasks appears to induce an internal attribution upon completion of the task, the former because the external student plays the teacher role, and the latter because creative tasks, by definition, must come from within one's own being. Yet another device for fostering of internality is highly specific instructions, the possible reason being that lack of specificity or ambiguity when assigning a task can be conveniently used by external students to explain a low outcome. It may also be that the act of following highly specific instructions itself helps students to attribute the outcome to their own ability and/or effort. Finally, providing students with various difficulty levels to choose from seems to help them see themselves as responsible for the outcomes. For example, if several mathematical concepts are being taught, the teacher might develop several problems each at, say, three different levels of difficulty, allowing the students to choose the level(s) they will work on. The fact that choice is involved may be the reason for the usefulness of this approach. In one way or another, it is the teacher's responsibility to work toward the creation of an atmosphere in which each student can believe that his or her effort and ability are the primary factors upon which academic outcomes should be based.

Caring of the teacher. Student perceptions of whether the teacher cares for them have meaningful effects on their performance and behavior. It appears that "caring and demanding school environments make kids work hard and learn."[26] For example, when secondary students in London perceived that a caring atmosphere existed, they responded with regular attendance, better behavior, and higher academic achievement.[27] Another study reported that it was the teacher characterized as the "warm demander" who was the most successful with the minority student.[28] Students who perceived that, while teachers would not lower their standards for them, teachers were willing to reach out to them and provide needed assistance in practical ways, were the highest achievers.

It appears that minority students have a tendency not to separate *A* as a person from *A* as teacher as clearly as majority students.[29] In other words, they seem to be unable to say things like: "Mr. Brown is a real bummer, isn't he? But he's a great English teacher." For that reason, some minority students must have a relationship with their teacher that is mutually caring and respectful if they are to learn from her or him. As noted by Bruner, "Public school in its very nature rests on some notion of mutual aid."[30] It is not a good practice for any teacher to say, "They don't have to like me, they just have to learn from me," but it is definitely not recommended for teachers of students of minority background. The fact is, these students not only need to like their teacher, but also must sense that the teacher cares for them as well.[31]

A democratic environment. While a direct relationship between academic achievement and a democratic classroom environment has not yet been clearly established in the literature, it seems probable that such an environment is related to other important student outcomes, including mutual esteem, rapport, and self-esteem.[32] Meanwhile, typical classrooms are middle-class in their orientation, an environment in which lower-class students are unlikely to function freely.[33] An additional adjustment is required of such students in order for them to understand and meet the requirements imposed by middle-class values, perceptions, and expectations. This amounts to a selective burden, by reason of one's socioeconomic status, on many youth from Black, Hispanic, and Native American backgrounds.

In many ways, the prevalence of middle-class orientation among teachers exerts a negative influence on the personality development of lower-class children. This influence is particularly evident in the low self-evaluation and low achievement motivation of these students, resulting in school failure and high dropout rates.[34] One way to bring a more democratic context to the classroom may be the establishment of a bicultural school environment, namely, one in which "both cultures are officially recognized in all aspects of school function and are an integral part of the setting."[35] A study found that, when placed in a bicultural environment, preadolescent Anglo and Latino girls had better self-images than did those in a control group.

Another dimension of the classroom environment is whether the context is a controlling one or not. It appears that the degree of control exerted by the teacher is particularly influential in the area of student motivation. External rewards and punishments predominate in classrooms that are highly controlling, while intrinsic motivation is found in environments where autonomy is supported. There can be "enormous differences" between these two, the first resulting in students who feel less good about themselves and perceive themselves to be less competent, and the second leading to greater conceptual learning.[36] It may be of special importance for teachers of minority students to take pains to establish a setting of autonomy for two additional reasons. The first has to do with the need these students often reveal for structure in the classroom.[37] Given this, some teachers may find justification for exerting an inordinate amount of control. Also, some minority students show unique respect for authority figures in the classroom, the teacher in particular.[38] Again, the temptation for an overly controlling atmosphere should be resisted in the face of such student outlook.

Students function on the basis of what they perceive to be reality, not of what the teacher believes to be reality. For that reason, the teacher must be on the lookout, as a means of identifying those who tend to have difficulties, for (1) seemingly contradictory behavior, that is, behavior that is not consonant with what the classroom environment seems to call for, which may not be clearly perceived by the student; (2) passive, noncommittal behavior, perhaps resulting from mixed signals or uncertain messages; and (3) students who seem to be especially well in tune with the particular psychological context, perhaps due to their backgrounds and characteristics.

The teacher should not seek an *in-between* solution, that is, a psychological context somewhere between the extremes of what students seem to need, because this may miss all students. Likewise, it is not advisable to build a psychological context that is a *best fit* for the majority of students in the classroom, since such a solution may simply disregard the needs of most minority students. What is needed, instead, is an *equitable* context, that is, one that (a) takes into account the psychological needs of all students, (b) gives each type (majority and minority students at the simplest level) the psychological freedom to do their best, and (c) is variable. This suggests that the teacher will have to shift the context from time to time so that it will be now competitive, now cooperative, now structured, now free, and so on. In an equitable context, there will be times when a particular setting is not the preferred one for a given student. But if the student knows and can expect that her or his own preferences will be satisfied in turn, this should help the student by instilling an important value, that of enhancing the learning opportunities of others at one's own (minimal) cost, while learning something about how to achieve in different contexts. Thus, the equitable psychological context is one of balance, and its creation hinges upon the teacher's knowing what is needed by all the types of students in her or his classroom.

ENDNOTES

1. Lee Owens and Jennifer Barnes, "The Relationship between Cooperative, Competitive, and Individualized Learning Preferences and Students' Perceptions of Classroom Learning Atmosphere," *American Educational Research Journal* 19 (No. 2, 1982): 182–200; Paul

E. McGhee and Virginia C. Crandall, "Belief in Internal-External Control of Reinforcement and Academic Performance," *Child Development* 39 (March, 1968): 91–102; James A. Vasquez, *Locus of Control, Social Class, and Learning* (Los Angeles: National Dissemination and Assessment Center, 1978).

2. Carol S. Weinstein, "The Physical Environment of the School: A Review of the Research," *Review of Educational Research* 49 (No. 4, 1979): 577–610.

3. Robert S. Feldman and Andrew J. Theiss, "The Teacher and Student as Pygmalions: Joint Effects of Teacher and Student Expectations," *Journal of Educational Psychology* 74 (No. 2, 1982): 217–223.

4. Ralph Epstein and S.S. Komorita, "Self-esteem, Success-failure, and Locus of Control in Negro Children," *Developmental Psychology* 4 (No. 1, 1971): 2–8. Quoted from p. 7.

5. Stewart C. Purkey and Marshall S. Smith, "Too Soon to Cheer? Synthesis of Research on Effective Schools," *Educational Leadership* 40 (No. 3, 1982): 64–69.

6. Feldman and Theiss, "The Teacher and Student"; Wilbur Brookover, *Creating Effective Schools: An In-Service Program for Enhancing School Learning Climate and Achievement* (Holmes Beach, Florida: Learning Publications, 1982).

7. Feldman and Theiss, "The Teacher and Student."

8. Manuel Ramírez, III, and Alfredo Castañeda, *Cultural Democracy, Bicognitive Development, and Education* (New York: Academic Press, 1974).

9. Ray Rist, "Student Social Class and Teacher Expectation: The Self-fulfilling Prophecy in Ghetto Education," *Harvard Educational Review* 40 (No. 3, 1970): 411–451.

10. Debra K. DeMeis and Ralph R. Turner, "Effects on Students' Race, Physical Attractiveness, and Dialect on Teachers' Evaluations," *Contemporary Educational Psychology* 3 (January, 1978): 77–86.

11. Alan C. Kerckhoff, as cited in Helen A. Moore, "Hispanic Women: Schooling for Conformity in Public Education," *Hispanic Journal of Behavioral Sciences* 4 (No. 1, 1983): 45–63.

12. Beverly Lewis, "Time and Space in Schools," in *Children in Time and Space,* ed. Kaoru Yamamoto (New York: Teachers College Press, 1979), pp. 128–169.

13. Ibid.

14. Moore, "Hispanic Women," *Hispanic Journal of Behavioral Sciences* 5 (No. 1, 1983): 45–63; Sergio Martinez, Joe L. Martinez, Jr., and Esteban L. Olmedo, "Comparative Study of Chicano and Anglo Values Using the Semantic Differential Technique," *Atisbos: Journal of Chicano Research* (Summer 1975): 93–98.

15. David W. Johnson, Roger T. Johnson, and Geoffrey Maruyama, "Interdependence and Interpersonal Attraction among Heterogeneous and Homogeneous Individuals: A Theoretical Formulation and a Meta-analysis of Research," *Review of Educational Research* 53 (No. 1, 1983): 5–54.

16. E.g., Spencer Kagan and Miller Madsen, "Cooperation and Competition of Mexican, Mexican-American, and Anglo American Children of Two Ages under Four Instructional Sets," *Developmental Psychology* 5 (No. 1, 1971): 32–39; Ernest Hilgard, *Theories of Learning* (New York: Appleton-Century-Crofts, 1956).

17. Johnson et al., "Interdependence and Interpersonal Attraction."

18. James A. Vasquez, "Motivation and Chicano Students," *Bilingual Resources* 2 (No. 2, 1979): 2–5.

19. Owens and Barnes, "The Relationship between Learning Preferences."

20. Julian B. Rotter, "Generalized Expectancies for Internal and External Control of Reinforcement," *Psychological Monograph* 80 (No. 1, Whole No. 609, 1966); Richard de Charms, *Personal Causation* (New York: Academic Press, 1968); Herbert M. Lefcourt, *Locus of Control* (Hillsdale, N.J.: Lawrence Erlbaum, 1976); Vasquez, *Locus of Control.*

21. James S. Coleman, Ernest Q. Campbell, Carol J. Hobson, J. McPartland, Alexander M. Mood, Frederick D. Weinfeld, and Robert L. York, *Equality of Educational Opportunity* (Washington, D.C.: U.S. Government Printing Office, 1966); Roger T. Johnson, David W. Johnson, and B. Bryant, "Cooperation and Competition in the Classroom," in *Readings in Educational Psychology: Contemporary Perspectives,* eds. Robert A. Dentler and Bernard J. Shapiro (New York: Harper & Row, 1976–77) pp. 287–290.

22. Vasquez, *Locus of Control.*

23. Herbert H. Lefcourt, "Internal Versus External Control of Reinforcement: A Review," *Psychological Bulletin* 65 (No. 4, 1966): 206–220; Esther S. Battle and Julian B. Rotter, "Children's Feelings of Personal Control as Related to Social Class and Ethnic Group," *Journal of Personality* 31 (December 1961): 482–490.

24. Vasquez, *Locus of Control.*

25. Daniel Bar-Tal, "Attributional Analysis of Achievement-Related Behavior," *Review of Educational Research* 48 (No. 2, 1978): 259–271.

26. Jerome Bruner, as cited in Elizabeth Hall, "Schooling Children in a Nasty Climate," *Psychology Today* 16 (January 1982): 57–63.

27. Michael Rutter, Barbara Maughan, Peter Morimore, Janet Ouston, with Alan Smith, *Fifteen Thousand Hours* (Cambridge, Massachusetts: Harvard University Press, 1982).

28. Judith Kleinfeld, "Effective Teachers of Eskimo and Indian Students," *School Review* 83 (February 1975): 301–344.

29. Ibid.

30. Bruner in Hall, "Schooling Children," p. 58.

31. Ramírez and Castañeda, *Cultural Democracy.*

32. John C. Glidewell, Mildred B. Kantor, Louis M. Smith, and Lorene A. Stringer, as cited in Nancy A. Busch-Rossnagel and Annette K. Vance, "The Impact of the Schools on Social and Emotional Development," in *Handbook of Developmental Psychology,* ed. Benjamin B. Wolman and George Stricker, (Englewood Cliffs, N.J.: Prentice-Hall, 1982, pp. 452–466), pp. 52–53.

33. Martin Maehr, "Culture and Achievement Motivation," *American Psychologist* 29 (December 1974): 887–895.

34. Mavis Hetherington, as cited in Nancy Busch-Rossnagel and Annette K. Vance, "The Impact of the Schools on Social and Emotional Development," in *Handbook of Developmental Psychology,* ed. Benjamin B. Wolman and George Stricker (Englewood Cliffs, N.J.: Prentice-Hall, 1982, pp. 452–466), pp. 84–85.

35. Nancy Busch-Rossnagel and Annette K. Vance, "The Impact of the Schools on Social and Emotional Development," in *Handbook of Developmental Psychology,* ed. Benjamin B. Wolman and George Stricker (Englewood Cliffs, N.J.: Prentice-Hall, 1982), pp. 452–466.

36. Edward L. Deci, "The Well-tempered Classroom," *Psychology Today* 19 (March 1985): 52–53.

37. Katherine Spangler, "Cognitive Styles and the Mexican-American Child." (Anchorage: University of Alaska, 1982: unpublished paper; ERIC Document No. ED 221 285, PS 015 155); Herman Witkin, R.B. Dyk, H.F. Faterson, D.R. Goodenough, and S.A. Karp, *Psychological Differentiation* (New York: John Wiley & Sons, 1962).

38. Ramírez and Castañeda, *Cultural Democracy.*

▶ Part III

Transforming Urban Schools

The context of public schooling in urban settings embodies many problems and possibilities for achieving equality of educational opportunity. Unfortunately, urban education also reflects the inequalities represented in society-at-large, which the concept of equality of educational opportunity was designed to ameliorate. The causes and effects of the inequalities that characterize urban schooling are often hidden beneath the surface level of curriculum, organizational structure, and instructional practice. In order to bring about the conditions necessary for the transformation of urban education, educators must develop a framework in which barriers to equality of educational opportunity can be illuminated and strategies for alternative school practices can be acted on.

Part II of this book illuminates a number of barriers to the realization of equality of educational opportunity and improving urban schools. Many of the barriers identified earlier are part of the "taken for granted" processes that structure schooling. These educational practices, such as tracking, testing, low expectations, and differentiated curriculum and classroom social practices, are often viewed by teachers, students, and parents as a benign part of a neutral process rather than political and ideological in nature. As such, they are often discussed in a language that holds little hope for change. In Part III we provide several articles that present a vision for breaking down some of the barriers to equality of educational opportunity and transforming urban education. This vision makes explicit the political nature of schooling and provides frameworks for acting on that vision.

As political institutions, schools function to legitimate certain interests through the production and reproduction of ideological and cultural formations. These interests are made clear through the way the schooling process functions to train students for different occupational roles or to promote certain types of social characteristics that are inextricably linked to inequitable relations of power (e.g., sexism, racism, class relations). Educators need to investigate how the ideological and cultural forms that are vested in the knowledge and social practices of schooling function to reproduce and legitimate the prevailing or dominant ideologies in society.

If public schooling is the engine of democracy and represents what has been called the "last frontier" for mobility within the social and economic structure of society (Bowles and Gintis, 1976), a large percentage of the population is being systematically excluded from such possibilities. Educators must begin to exploit the contradictory nature of the schooling process with regard to the ideals of equity, social justice, and democracy. These ideals must then be used in the transformation of school structures, which often function to actively silence students, particularly those students representative of groups historically marginalized within dominant society. While schools may now serve the interests of some individuals or groups, they also serve to reproduce the unequal economic, social, and cultural relations of the wider society, particularly around the issues of class, race, ethnicity, and gender.

Any notion of empowerment or efficacy is at risk in urban schools. Teachers must be empowered through a critical examination of educational practice before they can begin to empower students. They must be able to identify the barriers to change and confront the problems that they face in everyday life. This process of transforming urban education can only be realized through the development of frameworks that convey both the complexity of the schooling process and the possibilities for democratic change. Educators must be explicit about what they believe about the purpose of public education and demonstrate the knowledge and courage to act on their beliefs.

In general, teachers are not prepared for urban schools, and many new teachers have little interest in urban education. Teacher preparation programs have most often provided a traditional framework, which reduces teachers to technicians implementing someone else's curriculum. The immense structural problems faced by educators in their daily activities often prevent urban teachers from seriously considering the relationship between educational practices and structural inequalities in the wider society. As such, the organization and structure of urban schools reifies an educational framework that presents significant barriers to the ability of urban educators to critically reflect on what they do.

By challenging this perspective within alternative frameworks, educators can become empowered with the critical tools necessary to confront the structural inequalities that often characterize public schooling, particularly with regard to students marginalized through class-, race-, and gender-based discrimination. Teachers in urban schools must be capable of conceptualizing and implementing curriculum materials and instructional practices that speak to the needs, interests, and experiences that poor and minority students bring to the classroom. They must also be able to reflect on the principles and interests that inform and shape their work as it relates to equality of educational opportunity.

We begin Part III with two articles that address the preparation and practices of urban teachers. Haberman (1991) argues that there is a basic menu of urban teacher functions that appeals to a broad range of constituencies. He identifies the implementation of these functions as a "pedagogy of poverty," which is widely accepted by students, educators, parents, and communities. Fortunately, he also provides an alternative to the pedagogy of poverty by suggesting a set of guiding principles for good teaching that focus more on what students are doing than the traditional focus on teacher-directed behavior. If we take the notion of good teaching seriously, it changes not only student-teacher relationships but can have a profound effect on relationships among teachers. Grant (1989) argues that for schools to change and improve the quality of education for urban students, veteran teachers in urban schools must work with new colleagues to critically analyze their teaching practices and improve the curriculum. By linking these two ideas we can begin to demonstrate the need for developing alternative frameworks for teacher and student empowerment.

The article by Cummins (1986) provides a framework for empowering minority students. He argues that educators and the way they organize, structure, and assess in their classrooms play a key role in whether students are empowered or disabled. For urban educational reform to be successful, the role definitions of individuals and institutions must change to a more deliberate focus on empowerment. Thus, we must rethink the roles of teachers, students, parents, teacher preparation, and schools.

Teachers and students must critically examine the political relationship between schooling and the social inequalities of the dominant society (Villegas, 1988). Creating culturally sensitive curriculum materials and classroom practices alone are not sufficient for urban educational improvement. Parents of poor and minority students must also be active participants in urban educational improvement by working with teachers and other community resources (Ascher, 1988). The links among school, home, and community are too strong to ignore.

We close this book with two articles that specifically point to a framework for empowering urban teachers and students. Erickson (1987) presents the notion of culturally responsive pedagogy as a partial means of transforming urban schools. He argues that students often resist what school teaches because, as an institution, it lacks legitimacy for them. Culturally responsive pedagogy is one way a school can earn legitimacy and reduce miscommunication. This type of pedagogy takes the notion of politics seriously and requires a different approach to teaching. Giroux (1987) complements and extends these arguments by providing us with the framework for teachers as transformative intellectuals. He argues that educators need to develop a language of critique to provide critical forms of analysis and a language of possibility for developing strategies for action that have an explicitly defined political and civic purpose. These are but some of the tools for transforming urban schools. We hope that this is not the end but, instead, the beginning of a constructive and hopeful debate.

REFERENCES

Ascher, Carol. (1988). "Improving the school-home connection for poor and minority urban students." *The Urban Review,* 20:109–123.

Cummins, J. (1986). "Empowering minority students: A framework for intervention." *Harvard Educational Review,* 58(1):18–36.

Erickson, F. (1987). "Transformation and school success: The politics and culture of educational achievement." *Anthropology and Education Quarterly,* 18:335–356.

Giroux, H.A. (1987). "Educational reform and the politics of teacher empowerment." *New Education,* 9:3–13.

Haberman, M. (1991). "The pedagogy of poverty versus good teaching." *Phi Delta Kappan,* 73:290–294.

Villegas, A.M. (1988). "School failure and cultural mismatch: Another view." *The Urban Review,* 20:253–265.

The Pedagogy of Poverty Versus Good Teaching

MARTIN HABERMAN

Why is a "minor" issue like improving the quality of urban teaching generally overlooked by the popular reform and restructuring strategies? There are several possibilities. First, we assume that we know what teaching is, that others know what it is, that we are discussing the same "thing" when we use the word, and that we would all know good teaching if we saw it. Second, we believe that, since most teachers cannot be changed anyway, there must be other, more potent, teacher-proof strategies for change. Third, why bother with teaching if research shows that achievement test scores of poor and minority youngsters are affected primarily by their socioeconomic class; affected somewhat by Head Start, school integration, and having a "strong" principal; and affected almost not at all by the quality of their teachers?

THE PEDAGOGY OF POVERTY

An observer of urban classrooms can find examples of almost every form of pedagogy: direct instruction, cooperative learning, peer tutoring, individualized instruction, computer-assisted learning, behavior modification, the use of student contracts, media-assisted instruction, scientific inquiry, lecture/discussion, tutoring by specialists or volunteers, and even the use of problem-solving units common in progressive education. In spite of this broad range of options, however, there is a typical form of teaching that has become accepted as basic. Indeed, this basic urban style, which encompasses a body of specific teacher acts, seems to have grown stronger each year since I first noted it in 1958. A teacher in an urban school of the

Reprinted from *Phi Delta Kappan,* 73:290–294, 1991, by permission of the author and the publisher.

1990s who did *not* engage in these basic acts as the primary means of instruction would be regarded as deviant. In most urban schools, not performing these acts for most of each day would be considered prima facie evidence of not teaching.

The teaching acts that constitute the core functions of urban teaching are:

- giving information,
- asking questions,
- giving directions,
- making assignments,
- monitoring seatwork,
- reviewing assignments,
- giving tests,
- reviewing tests,
- assigning homework,
- reviewing homework,
- settling disputes,
- punishing noncompliance,
- marking papers, and
- giving grades.

This basic menu of urban teacher functions characterizes all levels and subjects. A primary teacher might "give information" by reading a story to children, while a high school teacher might read to the class from a biology text. (Interestingly, both offer similar reasons: "The students can't read for themselves," and "They enjoy being read to.") Taken separately, there may be nothing wrong with these activities. There are occasions when any one of the 14 acts might have a beneficial effect. Taken together and performed to the systematic exclusion of other acts, they have become the pedagogical coin of the realm in urban schools. They constitute the pedagogy of poverty—not merely what teachers do and what youngsters expect but, for different reasons, what parents, the community, and the general public assume teaching to be.

Ancillary to this system is a set of out-of-class teacher acts that include keeping records, conducting parent conferences, attending staff meetings, and carrying out assorted school duties. While these out-of-class functions are not directly instructional, they are performed in ways that support the pedagogy of poverty. Since this analysis deals with the direct interactions characteristic of urban teachers and their students, I will limit myself to a brief comment about how each of these out-of-class functions is typically conceptualized and performed in urban settings.

- *Record-keeping* is the systematic maintenance of a paper trail to protect the school against any future legal action by its clients. Special classes, referrals, test scores, disciplinary actions, and analyses by specialists must be carefully recorded. This slant is the reason that teachers are commonly prejudiced rather than informed by reading student records; yet the system regards their upkeep as vital. (In teacher preparation, neophytes are actually taught that student records will reveal such valuable information as students' interests!)

- *Parent conferences* give parents who are perceived as poorly educated or otherwise inadequate a chance to have things explained to them.
- *Staff meetings* give administrators opportunities to explain things to teachers.
- *Assorted school duties* are essentially police or monitoring activities that would be better performed by hired guards.

The pedagogy of poverty appeals to several constituencies:

1. It appeals to those who themselves did not do well in schools. People who have been brutalized are usually not rich sources of compassion. And those who have failed or done poorly in school do not typically take personal responsibility for that failure. They generally find it easier to believe that they would have succeeded if only somebody had *forced* them to learn.

2. It appeals to those who rely on common sense rather than on thoughtful analysis. It is easy to criticize humane and developmental teaching aimed at educating a free people as mere "permissiveness," and it is well known that "permissiveness" is the root cause of our nation's educational problems.

3. It appeals to those who fear minorities and the poor. Bigots typically become obsessed with the need for control.

4. It appeals to those who have low expectations for minorities and the poor. People with limited vision frequently see value in limited and limiting forms of pedagogy. They believe that at-risk students are served best by a directive, controlling pedagogy.

5. It appeals to those who do not know the full range of pedagogical options available. This group includes most school administrators, most business and political reformers, and many teachers.

There are essentially four syllogisms that undergird the pedagogy of poverty. Their "logic" runs something like this.

1. Teaching is what teachers do. Learning is what students do. Therefore, students and teachers are engaged in different activities.

2. Teachers are in charge and responsible. Students are those who still need to develop appropriate behavior. Therefore, when students follow teachers' directions, appropriate behavior is being taught and learned.

3. Students represent a wide range of individual differences. Many students have handicapping conditions and lead debilitating home lives. Therefore, ranking of some sort is inevitable; some students will end up at the bottom of the class while others will finish at the top.

4. Basic skills are a prerequisite for learning and living. Students are not necessarily interested in basic skills. Therefore, directive pedagogy must be used to ensure that youngsters are compelled to learn their basic skills.

REFORM AND THE PEDAGOGY OF POVERTY

Unfortunately, the pedagogy of poverty does not work. Youngsters achieve neither minimum levels of life skills nor what they are capable of learning. The classroom atmosphere created by constant teacher direction and student compliance seethes with passive resentment that sometimes bubbles up into overt resistance. Teachers burn out because of the emotional and physical energy that they must expend to maintain their authority every hour of every day. The pedagogy of poverty requires that teachers who begin their careers intending to be helpers, models, guides, stimulators, and caring sources of encouragement transform themselves into directive authoritarians in order to function in urban schools. But people who choose to become teachers do not do so because at some point they decided, "I want to be able to tell people what to do all day and then make them do it!" This gap between expectations and reality that there is a pervasive, fundamental, irreconcilable difference between the motivation of those who select themselves to become teachers and the demands of urban teaching.

For the reformers who seek higher scores on achievement tests, the pedagogy of poverty is a source of continual frustration. The clear-cut need to "make" students learn is so obviously vital to the common good and to the students themselves that surely (it is believed) there must be a way to force students to work hard enough to vindicate the methodology. Simply stated, we act as if it is not the pedagogy that must be fitted to the students but the students who must accept an untouchable method.

In reality, the pedagogy of poverty is not a professional methodology at all. It is not supported by research, by theory, or by the best practice of superior urban teachers. It is actually certain ritualistic acts that, much like the ceremonies performed by religious functionaries, have come to be conducted for their intrinsic value rather than to foster learning.

There are those who contend that the pedagogy of poverty would work if only the youngsters accepted it and worked at it. "Ay, there's the rub!" Students in urban schools overwhelmingly *do* accept the pedagogy of poverty, and they *do* work at it! Indeed, any teacher who believes that he or she can take on an urban teaching assignment and ignore the pedagogy of poverty will be quickly crushed by the students themselves. Examples abound of inexperienced teachers who seek to involve students in genuine learning activities and are met with apathy or bedlam, while older hands who announce, "Take out your dictionaries and start to copy the words that begin with *h*," are rewarded with compliance or silence.

Reformers of urban schools are now raising their expectations beyond an emphasis on basic skills to the teaching of critical thinking, problem solving, and even creativity. But if the pedagogy of poverty will not force the learning of low-level skills, how can it be used to compel genuine thinking? Heretofore, reformers have promulgated change strategies that deal with the level of funding, the role of the principal, parent involvement, decentralization, site-based management, choice, and other organizational and policy reforms. At some point, they must reconsider the issue of pedagogy. If the actual mode of instruction expected by school administrators and teachers and demanded by students and their parents continues to be the present one, then reform will continue to deal with all but the central issue: How and what are students taught?

The pedagogy of poverty is sufficiently powerful to undermine the implementation of any reform effort because it determines the way pupils spend their time, the name of the behaviors they practice, and the bases of their self-concepts as learners. Essentially, it is a pedagogy in which learners can "succeed" without becoming either involved or thoughtful.

THE NATURE OF URBAN CHILDREN AND YOUTH

When he accepted the 1990 New York City Teacher of the Year Award, John Taylor Gatto stated that no school reform will work that does not provide children time to grow up or that simply forces them to deal with abstractions. Without blaming the victims, he described his students as lacking curiosity (having "evanescent attention"), being indifferent to the adult world, and having a poor sense of the future. He further characterized them as ahistorical, cruel and lacking in compassion, uneasy with intimacy and candor, materialistic, dependent, and passive—although they frequently mask the last two traits with a surface bravado.

Anyone who would propose specific forms of teaching as alternatives to the pedagogy of poverty must recognize that Gatto's description of his students is only the starting point. These are the attributes that have been enhanced and elicited by an authoritarian pedagogy and do not represent students' true or ultimate natures. Young people can become more and different, but they must be taught how. This means to me that two conditions must pertain before there can be a serious alternative to the pedagogy of poverty: the whole school faculty and school community— not the individual teacher—must be the unit of change; and there must be patience and persistence of application, since students can be expected to resist changes to a system they can predict and know how to control. Having learned to navigate in urban schools based on the pedagogy of poverty, students will not readily abandon all their know-how to take on willy-nilly some new and uncertain system that they may not be able to control.

For any analysis of pedagogical reform to have meaning in urban schools, it is necessary to understand something of the dynamics of the teacher/student interactions in those schools. The authoritarian and directive nature of the pedagogy of poverty is somewhat deceptive about who is really in charge. Teachers seem to be in charge, in that they direct students to work on particular tasks, allot time, dispense materials, and choose the means of evaluation to be used. It is assumed by many that having control over such factors makes teachers "decision makers" who somehow shape the behavior of their students.

But below this facade of control is another, more powerful level on which students actually control, manage, and shape the behavior of their teachers. Students reward teachers by complying. They punish by resisting. In this way students mislead teachers into believing that some things "work" while other things do not. By this dynamic, urban children and youth effectively negate the values promoted in their teachers' teacher education and undermine the nonauthoritarian predispositions that led their teachers to enter the field. And yet, most teachers are not particularly sensitive to being manipulated by students. They believe they are in control and are responding to "student needs," when, in fact, they are more like hostages responding to students' overt or tacit threats of noncompliance and, ultimately, disruption.

It cannot be emphasized enough that, in the real world, urban teachers are never defined as incompetent because their "deprived," "disadvantaged," "abused," "low-income" students are not learning. Instead, urban teachers are castigated because they cannot elicit compliance. Once schools made teacher competence synonymous with student control, it was inevitable that students would sense who was really in charge.

The students' stake in maintaining the pedagogy of poverty is of the strongest possible kind: it absolves them of responsibility for learning and puts the burden on the teachers, who must be accountable for *making* them learn. In their own unknowing but crafty way, students do not want to trade a system in which they can make their teachers ineffective for one in which they would themselves become accountable and responsible for what they learn. It would be risky for students to swap a "try and make me" system for one that says, "Let's see how well and how much you really can do."

Recognizing the formidable difficulty of institutionalizing other forms of pedagogy, it is still worthwhile to define and describe such alternative forms. The few urban schools that serve as models of student learning have teachers who maintain control by establishing trust and involving their students in meaningful activities rather than by imposing some neat system of classroom discipline. For genuinely effective urban teachers, discipline and control are primarily a *consequence* of their teaching and not a *prerequisite* condition of learning. Control, internal or imposed, is a continuous fact of life in urban classrooms—but, for these teachers, it is completely interrelated with the learning activity at hand.

GOOD TEACHING

Is it possible to describe a teaching approach that can serve as an alternative to the pedagogy of poverty? I believe that there is a core of teacher acts that defines the pedagogy one finds in urban schools that have been recognized as exemplary. Unlike the directive teacher acts that constitute the pedagogy of poverty, however, these tend to be indirect activities that frequently involve the creation of a learning environment. These teaching behaviors tend to be evident more in what the students are doing than in the observable actions of the teacher. Indeed, teachers may appear to be doing little and at times may, to the unsophisticated visitor, seem to be merely observers. Good teaching transcends the particular grade or subject and even the need for lessons with specific purposes.[1]

Whenever students are involved with issues they regard as vital concerns, good teaching is going on. In effective schools, the endless "problems"—the censoring of a school newspaper, an issue of school safety, a racial flare-up, the dress code—are opportunities for important learning. In good schools, problems are not viewed as occasions to impose more rules and tighter management from above. Far from being viewed as obstacles to the "normal" school routine, difficult events and issues are transformed into the very stuff of the curriculum. Schooling is living, not preparation for living. And living is a constant messing with problems that seem to resist solution.

Whenever students are involved with explanations of human differences, good teaching is going on. As students proceed through school, they should be developing ever greater understanding of human differences. Why are there rich people and poor people, abled and disabled, urban and rural, multilingual and monolingual, highly educated and poorly educated? Differences in race, culture, religion, ethnicity, and gender are issues that children and youths reconsider constantly in an effort to make sense of the world, its relationships, and their place in it. This is not "social studies." All aspects of the curriculum should deepen students' basic understandings of these persistent facts of life.

Whenever students are being helped to see major concepts, big ideas, and general principles and are not merely engaged in the pursuit of isolated facts, good teaching is going on. At all levels and in all subjects, key concepts can be made meaningful and relevant. Students cannot be successful graduates without having at some point been exposed to the various forms of knowledge. Historians deal with the nature of sources; artists, with texture, color, and design. A fundamental goal of education is to instill in students the ability to use various and competing ways of understanding the universe. Knowing how to spell is not enough.

Whenever students are involved in planning what they will be doing, it is likely that good teaching is going on. This planning involves real choices and not such simple preferences as what crayon to use or the order in which a set of topics will be discussed. Students may be asked to select a topic for study, to decide what resources they will need, or to plan how they will present their findings to others. People learn to make informed choices by actually making informed choices. Following directions—even perfectly—does not prepare people to make choices and to deal with the consequences of those choices.

Whenever students are involved with applying ideals such as fairness, equity, or justice to their world, it is likely that good teaching is going on. Students of any age can, at some level, try to apply great ideals to their everyday lives. The environment, war, human relationships, and health care are merely a few examples of issues that students can be thinking about. Determining what should be done about particular matters and defending their ideas publicly gives students experience in developing principles to live by. Character is built by students who have had practice at comparing ideals with reality in their own lives and in the lives of those around them.

Whenever students are actively involved, it is likely that good teaching is going on. Doing an experiment is infinitely better than watching one or reading about one. Participating as a reporter, a role player, or an actor can be educational. Constructing things can be a vital activity. We need graduates who have learned to take action in their own behalf and in behalf of others.

Whenever students are directly involved in a real-life experience, it is likely that good teaching is going on. Field trips, interactions with resource people, and work and life experiences are all potentially vital material for analysis. Firsthand experience is potentially more educational than vicarious activity, *provided* it is combined with reflection.

Whenever students are actively involved in heterogeneous groups, it is likely that good teaching is going on. Students benefit from exposure to cultural as well as intellectual heterogeneity, and they learn from one another. Divergent questioning strategies, multiple assignments in the same class, activities that allow for alternative responses and solutions all contribute to learning. Grouping in schools is frequently based on artificial criteria that are not used in life. Grouping can either limit or enhance students' self-concept and self-esteem and thus has a powerful effect on future learning.

Whenever students are asked to think about an idea in a way that questions common sense or a widely accepted assumption, that relates new ideas to ones learned previously, or that applies an idea to the problems of living, then there is a chance that good teaching is going on. Students are taught to compare, analyze, synthesize, evaluate, generalize, and specify in the process of developing thinking skills. The effort to educate thoughtful people should be guided by school activities that involve thought. The acquisition of information—even of skills—without the ability to think is an insufficient foundation for later life.

Whenever students are involved in redoing, polishing, or perfecting their work, it is likely that good teaching is going on. It is in the act of review, particularly review of one's own work, that important learning occurs. This technique may involve an art project or a science experiment as well as a piece of writing. The successful completion of anything worthwhile rarely occurs in a single trial. Students can learn that doing things over is not punishment but an opportunity to excel.

Whenever teachers involve students with the technology of information access, good teaching is going on. Teachers, texts, and libraries as they now exist will not be sufficient in the future. Computer literacy—beyond word processing—is a vital need. As James Mecklenburger points out, "Electronic learning must play a more important part in the mix, even at the expense of customary practices. Today, students and educators alike can create, receive, collect, and share data, text, images, and sounds on myriad topics in ways more stimulating, richer, and more timely than ever before."[2]

Whenever students are involved in reflecting on their own lives and how they have come to believe and feel as they do, good teaching is going on. Autobiography can be the basis of an exceedingly powerful pedagogy—one that is largely discarded after early childhood education. When critics dismiss my characterization of the pedagogy of poverty as an exaggeration, I am reminded of an immense sign hanging in an urban high school that has devoted itself totally to raising test scores: "We dispense knowledge. Bring your own container." This approach is the opposite of good teaching, which is the process of building environments, providing experiences, and then eliciting responses that can be reflected on. Autobiographical activities are readily extended into studies of family, neighborhood, and community. What could be more fundamental to subsequent learning than self-definition? Urban schools, in the way they narrowly structure the role of the teacher and restrict the content to be taught, too frequently repudiate the students and their home lives. The vision of good teaching as a process of "drawing out" rather than "stuffing in" is supported by diverse philosophies, including, most recently, feminist theories of the teaching/learning process.[3]

THE REWARDS OF NOT CHANGING

Taken individually, any of these indicators of good teaching is not a sufficient basis for proposing reform. We all know teachers who have done some of these things—as well as other, better things—for years. Taken together and practiced schoolwide and persistently, however, these suggestions can begin to create an alternative to the pedagogy of poverty.

Unfortunately, we must recognize that it may no longer be possible to give up the present authoritarianism. The incentives for the various constituencies involved may well have conditioned them to derive strong benefits from the pedagogy of poverty and to see only unknown risk in the options.

In the present system, teachers are accountable only for engaging in the limited set of behaviors commonly regarded as acts of teaching in urban schools—that is, the pedagogy of poverty. Students can be held accountable only for complying with precisely what they have specifically and carefully been directed to do. Administrators can be held accountable only for maintaining safe buildings; parents, only for knowing where their children are. Each constituency defines its own responsibilities as narrowly as possible to guarantee itself "success" and leave to others the broad and difficult responsibility for integrating students' total educations.

Who is responsible for seeing that students derive meaning and apply what they have learned from this fragmented, highly specialized, overly directive schooling? It is not an accident that the present system encourages each constituency to blame another for the system's failure. My argument here is that reforms will "take" only if they are supported by a system of pedagogy that has never been tried in any widespread, systematic, long-term way. What prevents its implementation is the resistance of the constituencies involved—constituencies that have a stake in maintaining their present roles, since they are, in effect, unaccountable for educating skilled, thoughtful citizens.

Continuing to define nonthinking, underdeveloped, unemployable youngsters as "adults" or "citizens" simply because they are high school graduates or passers of the General Education Development (GED) examination is irresponsible. Education will be seriously reformed only after we move it from a matter of "importance" to a matter of "life and death," both for society and for the individuals themselves. Graduates who lack basic skills may be unemployable and represent a personal and societal tragedy. However, graduates who possess basic skills but are partially informed, unable to think, and incapable of making moral choices are downright dangerous. Before we can *make* workers, we must first *make* people. But people are not *made*—they are conserved and grown.

ENDNOTES

1. James D. Raths, "Teaching Without Specific Objectives," *Educational Leadership,* April 1971, pp. 714–20.

2. James A. Mecklenburger, "Educational Technology Is Not Enough," *Phi Delta Kappan,* October 1990, p. 108.

3. Madeleine Grumet, *Women and Teaching* (Amherst: University of Massachusetts Press, 1988), p. 99.

Urban Teachers: Their New Colleagues and Curriculum

CARL A. GRANT

It always seems somewhat presumptuous for those of us who are not teaching in urban schools to suggest that *we* know what urban teachers need to know and that *we* understand what they are experiencing as they teach. Many university teachers, social scientists, and school administrators have not taught in an elementary or secondary school for a decade or more.[1] In that time, our understanding and appreciation of the complexities of classroom life may well have faded. Nevertheless, I do believe that educators who regularly study schools and classrooms have information and insights that can help their colleagues in the classroom do a much more effective and personally satisfying job.

It is the research method, in the tradition of Jules Henry and Philip Jackson, that provides these important insights into the dynamics and subtleties of school and classroom life. Researchers have the advantage of being able to observe a number of classrooms over a period of time; to follow up these observations with interviews and discussions with students, parents, and teachers; and then to analyze what they learn in light of related studies of school and classroom life.[2] Although classroom teachers observe many of the same events as the researchers, they are usually unable to analyze these observations in a systematic fashion, partly because of the policies and practices of their schools, partly because of their demanding teaching schedules, and partly because of their lack of training in this area. By contrast, researchers are able to identify trends and patterns and see how they are manifested in other parts of the school system.

Both as a researcher and as a concerned observer, I offer my observations about two areas of school and classroom life that I believe can help urban teachers improve the quality of education for urban students. These areas are the socialization of new colleagues in urban schools and the improvement of the curriculum.

Reprinted from *Phi Delta Kappan,* 70:764–770, 1989, by permission of the author and the publisher.

If it hasn't happened already, urban teachers will soon find that the new teacher across the hall or the new teacher next door will be a white female whose first choice for a teaching assignment was a suburban school.[3] These new colleagues may have some of the knowledge, understandings, and attitudes necessary for teaching urban students, but, for the most part, their backgrounds will be limited and superficial.[4] Their attitudes will have been shaped by a society that is biased along the lines of race, gender, and class. While in college, they probably heard a few lectures on the "minority child," the "at-risk student," and the "second-language student." But they probably didn't take those lectures seriously. They may have found it interesting to hear some (but not too much) information about "those people," and they probably retained enough of the information in those lectures to regurgitate it on subsequent exams.[5]

Their lack of knowledge and understanding and their attitudes (whether benign or negative) toward urban students result, in part, from their lack of interest in urban schools. Many of them would leave immediately if a position were available in the suburbs.

Often, urban teachers will discover that their new colleagues lack an understanding of and have a poor attitude toward urban students for another reason. Many of the lectures that they heard about urban schools, at-risk students, and minority students were delivered by white male professors whose knowledge of these subjects came from secondary and tertiary sources. Many of these professors "teach" about at-risk students and minority students because doing so is in vogue or because state policy requires it of them. For example, a state mandate in Wisconsin sets forth these requirements:

> *Preparation in human relations, including intergroup relations, shall be included in programs leading to initial certification in education. Institutions of higher education shall provide evidence that preparation in human relations, including intergroup relations, is an integral part of programs leading to initial certification in education and [that] members of various racial, cultural and economic groups have participated in the development of such programs.*[6]

While state policies in support of multicultural training for teachers are in place, Walter Secada and I conducted a review of multicultural research and found that very few teacher education programs have a sustained multicultural curriculum.[7] Typical of the findings of the studies that we reviewed is Reynaldo Contreras' description of teacher education programs that explore race, class, and gender diversity. Contreras argues:

> *Teacher educators continue to assume that teacher education students will pick up the necessary knowledge, skills, and attitudes that will help them teach classes of socioculturally diverse students without any direct instruc-*

tion and planned experience. Moreover, teacher educators assume that most of the schools will continue to be monocultural and monosocial; therefore, there is no obligation to commit time and resources to preparing teachers to teach children who are at risk of being miseducated and undereducated.[8]

Like many veteran urban teachers when they first started teaching in an urban school, new urban teachers may experience the "culture shock" that Forrest Parkay describes.

[D]uring my first year at DuSable (an urban high school in Chicago) I was frequently very anxious and frightened. On occasion, I even had nightmares about the place. I despaired of even understanding or accepting the students' behavior and attitudes that were so strange and threatening to me. I experienced what anthropologists and sociologists have termed "culture shock."[9]

Culture shock and low self-esteem from working in an urban school can also be experienced by minority teachers, whose life experiences more closely approximate those of the white middle class. For example, Helen Gouldner found that black teachers grouped and ranked their black urban students according to socioeconomic characteristics, teachability, and adaptability to bureaucratic school norms.

Classroom observation clearly supported the conclusion that teacher favoritism existed and that it is more patterned than capricious. . . . It was regular practice for [the teachers] to select potential high and low achievers early in the term . . . differentiating between those who would make it and those who would not. These were not so much personality traits of the child as they were kinds of behavior displayed in [a] school context. . . . There were three which were the most important, and they were closely interrelated. The first was what we called teachability, the second was adaptability to bureaucratic school norms, and the third was being middle class in attitudes, values, appearances, and goals.[10]

Most urban teachers can recall spending months, even years, learning how to handle this culture shock and learning how to teach urban students effectively. Some never completely get over their culture shock and, therefore, never learn how to work effectively with urban students. For years they have done what they could to maintain order and to appear to know what they are doing. Their new colleagues will be experiencing this culture shock, too, partly because of their white, middle-class backgrounds and partly because their experiences in teacher education, including student teaching, did not place them in settings in which they could work professionally with urban students.

Working *professionally* with urban students means that a teacher must teach an entire class of urban students for at least several months under the guidance of a senior teacher who knows how to teach urban students. It does not mean being a counselor in a summer camp that has a token number of middle-class minority students or even a few poor students from the inner city. Even taking part in practicums in urban schools may not provide professional training, if the cooperating teachers are not prepared to teach prospective teachers how to work with urban students. Under these circumstances, stereotypes and myths about the lives of urban students are only confirmed.[11]

In this regard, it is important to point out that I often encounter prospective teachers who wish to work with urban students but who have an unconscious belief in the cultural superiority of the white middle class. This unconscious attitude becomes a barrier in their teaching relationships with minority students and low-income students. Like all successful urban teachers, they need to be willing to learn about the cultures of urban students and then to use that knowledge in the classroom. This willingness is absent to the degree that these student teachers believe that all will be well if the urban student follows directions and accepts middle-class views and values.

For example, I observed a sixth-grade teacher telling his class of urban students, "I have heard rap music, and I know that rap music is not going to help you learn the English you need in order to get and keep a good job." The students silently tuned out this teacher and whatever instruction he might have offered on topic sentences. Had he introduced the lesson by using a topic sentence from a rap song or by using the words from rap songs to write a paragraph, the students would have remained interested.

Many of the new white teachers in urban schools have had negative experiences with mathematics at a time when career doors are being opened for urban students with solid math backgrounds. Some math educators hypothesize that many teachers are entering the field with a good understanding of teaching basic math facts and computation but a weak understanding of such highly cognitive areas of math as problem solving. If this is so, the new group of urban teachers, like many veterans, will have difficulty explaining math to urban students, who bring with them a wide range of interests, needs, and preferences for learning. Black female students face an additional problem, described by Eloise Scott and Sandra Damico: starting in the very early grades, black girls are academically isolated and are praised for their nurturing behavior, while white girls are praised for their academic behavior.[12]

Many of the new urban teachers will also arrive at their new schools, as many veteran urban teachers did, with weak backgrounds in science that do more to mystify than to clarify scientific concepts. Curricula and teaching methods do not allow urban students to experience the excitement that should be present in science classes. Urban students argue that they are bored by continually reading and answering worksheet questions about experiments that have very little connection to their lives.

For example, I recently observed a teacher giving a lecture on transformers to a sixth-grade science class. The lecture dealt with the purpose and main parts of a transformer. Follow-up activities for students included drawing pictures of step-up and step-down transformers and answering some questions taken from the textbook. The teacher did not show the students transformers in any of the appliances that they might have had in their homes or point out that the power pole clearly visible from the classroom window also had a transformer. Nor were the students informed about how the transformer on the pole outside their home can affect their television viewing and playing of records and tapes.

After class, the teacher expressed pleasure about how well the science lesson had gone and about the quality of the students' drawings. In response to my question about his previous science teaching experience and about his academic background in science, he answered that science was not one of his favorite subjects and that he would be in trouble if he didn't stick to the textbook.

Science teachers who rely on textbooks shortchange their nonwhite students in another way. The "culture" of science is partly taught through the pictures and other displays in textbooks, most of which depict scientific research being performed by white men in white coats, assisted by white women dressed the same way.[13]

Many new teachers in urban classrooms will come with only a textbook understanding of equality and justice. Many were born after—or were only children during—the civil rights movement of the 1960s. Therefore, they have not had to take a stand or test their views on civil rights. Although they may have been raised in households that rejected racism, their sense of history and their knowledge about justice and equality for urban students come, in part, from a biased society.

For example, television and movies often seem to work deliberately to portray blacks and other minorities as pimps and criminals, the dregs of society. Rarely are they shown in leadership or romantic roles.[14]

A similar bias is present in the world of art. About two years ago, two colleagues and I visited the National Women's Museum of the Arts in Washington, D.C. I was dismayed that I could not locate even one painting by an American black woman. Of course, when I mentioned this to the museum staff, I was given a quick rendition of the bureaucratic shuffle. Howardena Pindell, a black female artist, argues:

> *There is a closed circle which links museums, galleries, auction houses, collectors, critics, and art magazines. A statistical study relative to artists of color and art magazine articles and reviews as well as critics' statistical records in terms of reviews, articles, books, and curated exhibitions would also be revealing. The institutions which were open to address the needs of artists of color, because of the racial bias which closed them out of the primary network, are rarely if ever permitted to enter this closed circuit, thus closing access routes to broader documentation of [the] activities and achievements [of artists of color]. This omission creates a false and rather fraudulent impression that only artists of European descent are doing valid work.*[15]

The absence of people of color extends far beyond the arts. Most political, economic, and social institutions, with the exception of some areas of sports and entertainment, regularly fail to portray minorities at all—or else portray them in marginal ways. Although black politicians have been elected to the mayor's office in a number of cities, they are absent at the highest levels of government, such as governorships and the U.S. Senate.

New urban teachers will have entered teaching for the same reasons as the veterans. They love young people, they want to help them, and they want to make a difference in the education system. They will say that they come to their new assignments with "love" and a "desire to help," but they have not analyzed what *love* and *help* mean with regard to children from what has been described as the urban "underclass." Addressing the idea of this underclass, John Kasarda argues that

> *the economic and social plight of a substantial segment of the urban black population is accurately worse now than it was a generation ago as we have witnessed the formation of an immobilized subgroup of spatially isolated, persistently poor, ghetto dwellers characterized by substandard education and high rates of joblessness, mother-only households, welfare dependency, out-of-wedlock births, and crime.*[16]

Thus urban students may come to school hungry and dressed in soiled clothes that are in need of repair. They need a shower or toothpaste or deodorant. The "desire to help" of those teachers who are new to the environment of an urban school will be sorely tested by the human sorrow, the misery, and the oppression that characterize life among the underclass.

Desire to help can lead to teaching decisions that harm. For example, in the urban classroom it is important to teach for the entire class period, but it is not unusual for a portion of teaching time to go unused, because of an unspoken truce negotiated between teachers and students. Teachers let students know—sometimes explicitly, sometimes not—that if they work quietly for 40 minutes of a 55-minute period, they may use the remaining classroom time to talk quietly with their classmates.[17] This arrangement lets teachers feel good for having kept their students on task for a sizable portion of the class period, and it lets students feel good because they have finished their work and thus deserve to be rewarded. The students don't realize that, later in their lives, this wasted time will come back to haunt them. Their knowledge and skills will be inadequate to allow them to take advantage of other educational opportunities. The teachers don't realize that they are unconsciously extending the cycle of poverty and low achievement to another generation of urban students.

Teachers who are new to urban schools need the help of excellent and experienced teachers who understand how to work with urban students. It is crucial that the socialization of new teachers in urban schools include the development of new attitudes and new teaching skills. These are most important because attitudes about urban students and the development of appropriate teaching skills will shape the new teachers' expectations of their students and will establish the school and classroom climate.

In the 1960s and 1970s there was a parade of ideas about the kind of curriculum and teaching methods that urban students need.[18] Many of these ideas derived from a "cultural deficit" model. Teachers were often provided with a so-called "teacher-proof curriculum" in order to make up for their lack of knowledge about teaching urban students and for their lack of skills in teaching content. For example, such reading programs as DISTAR provided explicit instructions for teaching and provided a reading curriculum that assumed that students were culturally deficient and had a particular way of learning.[19] For example, in teaching "opposites," the teacher is given the following instructions regarding how to correct the students.

> *To correct: If the children cannot give the opposite, have them complete a "not" statement. For example: If a dress is not clean, it is (pause) dirty. Then repeat [the original item]. If the children continue to have trouble, repeat the question and give them the answer. Practice this until they give the answer quickly.*[20]

These attempts to design, modify, and supplement the curriculum for urban students have been largely unsuccessful. This is at least partly because curriculum content and teaching methods based on a cultural deficit model of education do not work. Simply stated, the cultural deficit hypothesis is academically and socially flawed: urban students are not culturally deficient.[21]

During the 1960s and 1970s some urban schools also began to include ethnic studies and gender-equity materials in their curricula. In some schools, ethnic and gender studies, such as black history or women in science, became electives. The preparation of curriculum materials for ethnic studies was largely accomplished by giving teachers release time to attend classes at multicultural or ethnic studies centers or by paying them to attend curriculum development workshops in the summer. Because of inadequate support by school administrators and inadequate financial resources, these efforts were short-lived. Usually only a few teachers at a given school were committed enough to sustain the kind of effort that was needed to integrate ethnic and gender studies into the curriculum. Moreover, these new curriculum efforts were often funded with "soft money," and, when the funding ran out, the programs died.

Today, curriculum and instruction are driven by an "economic efficiency" model that ignores the interests and self-empowerment needs of urban students. Curriculum, it seems, has become a "technology for producing predetermined instructional 'output,' defined as skills, test scores, grades, class ranking, etc."[22] Urban teachers have in many ways become shackled by this definition of curriculum and by its corresponding effect on implementation. This meaning of curriculum continues to gain currency through what Henry Giroux has called a "new public philosophy."[23] This philosophy was expressed in *A Nation at Risk* and in several other education reform reports that demanded public support for a more rigorous curriculum and higher standards. *A Nation at Risk* framed this new philosophy by using the catchwords *excellence* and *equity* for all students and by recommending that graduation requirements in English, social studies, mathematics, science, and computer science be increased.[24] Although the call was for excellence *and* equity, many educators believe that equity is not receiving its fair share of attention.[25]

This new philosophy encourages the use of a narrow curriculum for urban schools. Urban teachers argue that, because of the stress on higher standards in this new public philosophy, they don't have time to teach the basics *and* to provide a curriculum that takes into account the cultural needs of urban students. They argue that the new philosophy is degrading to them personally and serves as a barrier to their teaching efforts. They also say that they would like to have a more interesting and meaningful curriculum for urban students but lack the time and knowledge to develop one. Furthermore, they point out that the few workshops that are conducted to help urban teachers develop curriculum materials for their students are usually scheduled at bad times (e.g., late in the school day) and are often poorly organized and poorly conducted.

These arguments are certainly valid. Nevertheless, the teachers rarely ask how, in spite of bureaucratic constraints, *they* themselves contribute to problems with the curriculum. For example, many teachers have abandoned what small efforts they once made to include blacks and other minorities in the curriculum, unless it is a special time of the year, such as Black History Month. And even during these special times, it is rare for teachers to connect the concepts and ideas taught about black history to the traditional curriculum. In fact, the teaching of black history often consists of little more than the creation by teachers of displays for bulletin boards and the reading by students of the same stories about a few noted black heroes and heroines.

Moreover, students are rarely academically challenged to use what they do learn about black history. Black History Month is seen mainly as a time for celebration, rather than as a time for celebration *and* serious reflection on contemporary and historical events and circumstances in the lives of black people, as they fought and continue to fight for equality, recognition, and respect in mainstream society. For example, an eighth-grader may be given the same book on the Rev. Martin Luther King, Jr., that she used in fourth grade. Of course, there is nothing wrong with rereading a book on King; however, it would be more academically challenging and rewarding to make available and to encourage the use of books that probe more deeply into King's ideas. In other words, the teaching of black history during Black History Month (and at any other time during the year) needs to build on what students already know and to challenge them to deeper scholarship on the subject.

Before I continue, I must stress that most educators of color and most parents in urban communities will readily agree that, in order for minority children to be academically successful, they will need to know basic concepts and skills. In fact, educators of color and parents are arguing for more rigor in the curriculum. Even urban students say that their present curriculum is unchallenging and boring and that they want more rigorous courses.[26] However, urban students also argue for a curriculum that pays more attention to their needs, interests, goals, and ambitions.

Some urban students lead lives that make their experiences outside the school more immediately exciting and more financially and socially rewarding than the school curriculum. Others lead lives of such poverty and social disorder that it is difficult for them to concentrate on the school curriculum at all. The new public philosophy is silent on these points. Since the school is the first social institution that urban students deal with on a regular basis, this silence leads them to believe that they are not held in high regard.

Many other urban students, who are struggling to lead lives closer to the mainstream, are put off by what they observe. They witness their classmates struggling with poverty and drugs. For example, several male students who attended a high school in a large city told me that they are afraid as they go to and from school each day. One said, "I really have to keep a low profile and not draw attention to myself both in school and out. I am afraid that if [the gangs] notice me, I will get pressured to join the gangs. If I do that, my parents, especially my father, will kill me. [My parents] intend for me to go to college and not wind up on drugs or in a body bag." Many urban students must contend with living in poverty, grieving over the deaths of friends or relatives in drug-related violence, celebrating the birth of a classmate's baby, or being encouraged by peers to enter (as entrepreneur or user) the drug world.

In order to help as many urban students as possible, the school curriculum must be neither sterile nor remote from the lives of urban students. It must be relevant to their lives, but it must also provide a range of possibilities for the future, if it is to encourage students to pursue positive goals and dreams. It must show that the hundreds of dollars a week earned from trafficking in crack lead to a life of crime and violence and that being a member of the underclass today isn't necessarily a permanent condition. The curriculum must help lead urban students to analyze the circumstances of their own lives, to ask why they and their people are trapped in the barrios and ghettos. It must include information and activities that can help students develop the skills for social action so that they can take charge of their lives.

Perhaps teaching a curriculum that helps urban students learn to empower themselves and take charge of their lives seems too much to ask of teachers. Teachers are directed by and held accountable to a society that espouses the new public philosophy, and they have bosses who demand higher test scores. Teachers are kept busy just trying to maintain their own professional sanity. However, aside from the students and their families, no other group has as much at stake if changes are not made for urban students. In addition, I believe that teachers must realize that, if they don't dare to make a difference, no one else will. Researchers will leave the classrooms and return to their book-lined offices to write their reports; administrators will pursue their career goals and move on to more prestigious jobs; politicians and bureaucrats will flock to the next issue that becomes hot. But the urban teacher will remain and teach.

I have argued that new teachers in urban schools probably need a great deal of help to develop their teaching craft and to acquire attitudes that will enable them to respect, challenge, and hold high expectations for urban students. I now argue that the dedicated professionals at every urban school are the people most able to insure that this socialization into the profession takes place. I have also argued that teachers in urban schools must not be shackled by a curriculum that focuses mainly on raising test scores and that ignores or marginalizes the history, culture, life conditions, and life chances of urban students.

My concerns for the socialization of new teachers and for the improvement of the curriculum may seem insignificant when considered in the context of the larger problems that face urban schools. But such is far from the case. The urban school is the front-line institution in which people who hold the keys to the future success of urban youngsters come into daily contact with these young people. Despite the many socioeconomic problems that the teachers cannot solve, they must nonetheless look for opportunities to make a positive difference in the lives of their students and in their own lives.

The materials for making a positive difference are already at hand. By teaching new colleagues how to analyze critically and then change the narrow and deskilled curriculum, an experienced teacher can turn the "dross" of a poor curriculum into the gold of an enabling curriculum. As any teacher knows, one really learns something only when it becomes necessary to teach it. If experienced teachers have the courage to teach new colleagues how the present curriculum undermines the efforts of urban students to acquire academic skills and self-determination, the experienced teachers themselves will be forced to bring to a conscious level many of the weaknesses in content and in methods of instruction that they know of firsthand. In bringing a critical perspective to bear on the curriculum that the experienced teachers themselves have used—and are in the process of revising—both experienced and new teachers will better understand what their students need. They will learn that many of the problems that their students experience are not the results of an inability to learn or even of a stressful environment; they are the results of a misguided curriculum.

This kind of self-conscious analysis and revision of the curriculum can serve to bring the new and experienced teachers together in an endeavor that can empower both teachers and students. For example, teachers who are involved in school-based management efforts say that, among other reasons, this approach interests them because it gives them some power over the curriculum. Having this power, they argue, is essential to making education better for everyone involved.[27]

Modifying the curriculum would help teachers achieve greater professional and personal satisfaction from their work and would help urban students prepare themselves more effectively to take control of their lives. Teachers who perform high-quality work in urban schools know that, despite reform efforts and endless debates, it is meaningful curricula and dedicated and knowledgeable teachers that make the difference in the education of urban students.

ENDNOTES

1. *Teaching Teachers: Facts and Figures* (Washington, D.C.: American Association of Colleges for Teacher Education, 1987), pp. 22–25.

2. See, for example, Carl A. Grant and Christine E. Sleeter, *After the School Bell Rings* (Philadelphia: Falmer, 1986); Helen Gouldner, *Teachers' Pets, Troublemakers, and Nobodies* (Westport, Conn.: Greenwood Press, 1978); Forrest W. Parkay, *White Teacher, Black School* (New York: Praeger, 1983); and Charles M. Payne, *Getting What We Ask For: The Ambiguity of Success and Failure in Urban Education* (Westport, Conn.: Greenwood Press, 1984).

3. *Teaching Teachers . . .* , pp. 45–46.

4. For a thorough discussion of this point, see Carl A. Grant and Walter G. Secada, "Preparing Teachers for Diversity," in W. Robert Houston, Martin Haberman, and John Sikula, eds., *Handbook of Research on Teacher Education* (New York: Macmillan, 1989).

5. Carl A. Grant, "Education That Is Multicultural and Teacher Preparation: An Examination from the Perspective of Preservice Students," *Journal of Educational Research,* vol. 75, 1981, pp. 95–99; and Carl A. Grant and Ruth Koskela, "Education That is Multicultural and the Relationship Between Preservice Campus and Field Experience," *Journal of Educational Research,* vol. 79, 1985, pp. 197–203.

6. *Human Relations Program* (Madison: School of Education, University of Wisconsin, 1988), p. 1.

7. Grant and Secada, op. cit.

8. A. Reynaldo Contreras, "Multicultural Attitudes and Knowledge of Education Students at Indiana University," paper presented at the annual meeting of the American Educational Research Association, New Orleans, 1988, p. 14.

9. Parkay, p. 18.

10. Gouldner, p. 21.

11. Grant and Sleeter, op. cit.

12. Eloise Scott and Sandra Damico, "Isolation of Black Girls Said to Begin Early," *Education Week,* 21 August 1985, p. 9.

13. Christine E. Sleeter and Carl A. Grant, "Race, Class, Gender, and Disability in Current Textbooks," in Michael Apple and Linda Christian-Smith, eds., *Politics and the Textbook* (New York: Routledge and Chapman, forthcoming).

14. George H. Hill and Sylvia Saverson Hill, *Blacks on Television* (Metuchen, N.J.: Scarecrow Press, 1985).

15. Howardena Pindell, "And World Racism: A Documentation," *New Art Examiner,* March 1989, p. 32.

16. John D. Kasarda, "Urban Industrial Transition and the Underclass," *Annals of the American Academy, AAPSS,* vol. 501, 1989, p. 27. See also, Loïc J. D. Wacquant and William Julius Wilson, "The Cost of Racial and Class Exclusion in the Inner City," *Annals of the American Academy, AAPSS,* vol. 501, 1989, p. 8.

17. Grant and Sleeter, op. cit.

18. See, for example, Stephen S. Baratz and Joan C. Baratz, "Early Childhood Intervention: The Social Science Base of Institutional Racism," *Harvard Educational Review,* Winter 1970, pp. 29–50; Arnold B. Cheyney, *Teaching the Culturally Disadvantaged in the Elementary School* (Columbus, Ohio: Charles E. Merrill, 1967); Frank Riessman, *The Culturally Deprived Child* (New York: Harper & Row, 1962); idem, *The Inner-City Child* (New York: Harper & Row, 1976); Roger R. Woock, *Education and the Urban Crisis* (Scranton, Pa.: International Textbook Co., 1970); and Sidney Trubowitz, *A Handbook for Teaching in the Ghetto School* (Chicago: Quadrangle Books, 1968).

19. Siegfried Engelmann and Jean Osborn, *DISTAR Language II: An Instructional System* (Chicago: Science Research Associates, 1970).

20. Ibid., p. 2.

21. Baratz and Baratz, op. cit.; and Charles A. Valentine, "Deficit, Difference, and Bicultural Models of Afro-American Behavior," *Harvard Educational Review,* May 1971, pp. 137–57.

22. Dennis Carlson, "Curriculum and the School in Work Culture," in Philip G. Altbach, Gail P. Kelly, and Lois Weiss, eds., *Excellence in Education* (Buffalo: Prometheus, 1985), pp. 171–81.

23. Henry Giroux, "Public Philosophy and the Crisis in Education," *Harvard Educational Review,* May 1984, pp. 186–94.

24. National Commission on Excellence in Education, *A Nation at Risk: The Imperative for Educational Reform* (Washington, D.C.: U.S. Government Printing Office, 1983).

25. For a discussion of this point, see the essays in Altbach, Kelly, and Weiss, op. cit.

26. Grant and Sleeter, op. cit.

27. Carl A. Grant and Donald J. McCarty, "Report of a School-Based Management Study for the Milwaukee Public Schools," unpublished paper, Milwaukee Public Schools, 1988.

Empowering Minority Students: A Framework for Intervention

JIM CUMMINS

During the past twenty years educators in the United States have implemented a series of costly reforms aimed at reversing the pattern of school failure among minority students. These have included compensatory programs at the preschool level, myriad forms of bilingual education programs, the hiring of additional aides and remedial personnel, and the institution of safeguards against discriminatory assessment procedures. Yet the dropout rate among Mexican-American and mainland Puerto Rican students remains between 40 and 50 percent compared to 14 percent for whites and 25 percent for blacks (Jusenius & Duarte, 1982). Similarly, almost a decade after the passage of the nondiscriminatory assessment provision of PL94-142,[1] we find Hispanic students in Texas overrepresented by a factor of 300 percent in the "learning disabilities" category (Ortiz & Yates, 1983).

I have suggested that a major reason previous attempts at educational reform have been unsuccessful is that the relationships between teachers and students and between schools and communities have remained essentially unchanged. The required changes involve *personal redefinitions* of the way classroom teachers interact with the children and communities they serve. In other words, legislative and policy reforms may be necessary conditions for effective change, but they are not sufficient. Implementation of change is dependent upon the extent to which educators, both collectively and individually, redefine their roles with respect to minority students and communities.

The purpose of this paper is to propose a theoretical framework for examining the types of personal and institutional redefinitions that are required to reserve the pattern of minority student failure. The framework is based on a series of hypotheses regarding the nature of minority students' educational difficulties. These hypotheses, in turn, lead to predictions regarding the probable effectiveness, or ineffectiveness, of various interventions directed at reversing minority students' school failure.

The framework assigns a central role to three inclusive sets of interactions or power relations: (1) the classroom interactions between teachers and students, (2) relationships between schools and minority communities, and (3) the intergroup power relations within the society as a whole. It assumes that the social organization and bureaucratic constraints within the school reflect not only broader policy and societal factors but also the extent to which *individual educators* accept or challenge the social organization of the school in relation to minority students and communities. Thus, this analysis sketches directions for change for policymakers at all levels of the educational hierarchy and, in particular, for those working directly with minority students and communities.

THE POLICY CONTEXT

Research data from the United States, Canada, and Europe vary on the extent to which minority students experience academic failure (for reviews, see Cummins, 1984; Ogbu, 1978). For example, in the United States, Hispanic (with the exception of some groups of Cuban students), Native American, and black students do poorly in school compared to most groups of Asian-American (and white) students. In Canada, Franco-Ontarian students in English language programs have tended to perform considerably less well academically than immigrant minority groups (Cummins, 1984), while the same pattern characterizes Finnish students in Sweden (Skutnabb-Kangas, 1984).

The major task of theory and policy is to explain the pattern of school success and failure among minority students. This task applies both to students whose home language and culture differ from those of the school and wider society (language minority students) and to students whose home language is a version of English but whose cultural background is significantly different from that of the school and wider society, such as many black and Hispanic students from English language backgrounds. With respect to language-minority students, recent policy changes in the United States have been based on the assumption that a major cause of students' educational difficulty is the switch between the language of the home and the language of the school. Thus, the apparently plausible assumption that students cannot learn in a language they do not understand gave rise in the late sixties and early seventies to bilingual education programs in which students' home language was used in addition to English as an initial medium of school instruction (Schneider, 1976).

Bilingual programs, however, have met with both strong support and vehement opposition. The debate regarding policy has revolved around two intuitively appealing assumptions. Those who favor bilingual education argue that children cannot learn in a language they do not understand, and, therefore, L1 (first language) instruction is necessary to counteract the negative effects of a home/school linguistic mismatch. The opposition contends that bilingual education is illogical in its implication that less English instruction will lead to more English achievement. It makes more sense, the opponents argue, to provide language-minority students with maximum exposure to English.

Despite the apparent plausibility of each assumption, these two conventional wisdoms (the "linguistic mismatch" and "insufficient exposure" hypotheses) are each patently inadequate. The argument that language minority students fail primarily as a result of a home/school language switch is refuted by the success of many minority students whose instruction has been totally through a second language. Similarly, research in Canada has documented the effectiveness of "French immersion programs" in which English background (majority language) students are instructed largely through French in the early grades as a means of developing fluent bilingualism. In spite of the home/school language switch, students' first language (English) skills develop as well as those of students whose instruction has been totally through English. The fact that the first language has high status and is strongly reinforced in the wider society is usually seen as an important factor in the success of these immersion programs.[2]

The opposing "insufficient exposure" hypothesis, however, fares no better with respect to the research evidence. In fact, the results of virtually every bilingual program that has been evaluated during the past 50 years show either no relationship or a negative relationship between amount of school exposure to the majority language and academic achievement in that language (Baker & de Kanter, 1981; Cummins, 1983a, 1984; Skutnabb-Kangas, 1984). Evaluations of immersion programs for majority students show that students perform as well in English academic skills as comparison groups despite considerably less exposure to English in school. Exactly the same result is obtained for minority students. Promotion of the minority language entails no loss in the development of English academic skills. In other words, language minority students instructed through the minority language (for example, Spanish) for all or part of the school day perform as well in English academic skills as comparable students instructed totally through English.

These results have been interpreted in terms of the "interdependence hypothesis," which proposes that to the extent that instruction through a minority language is effective in developing academic proficiency in the minority language, transfer of this proficiency to the majority language will occur given adequate exposure and motivation to learn the majority language (Cummins, 1979, 1983a, 1984). The interdependence hypothesis is supported by a large body of research from bilingual program evaluations, studies of language use in the home, immigrant student language learning, correlational studies of L1–L2 (second language) relationships, and experimental studies of bilingual information processing (for reviews, see Cummins, 1984; McLaughlin, 1985).

It is not surprising that the two conventional wisdoms inadequately account for the research data, since each involves only a one-dimensional linguistic explanation. The variability of minority students' academic performance under different social and educational conditions indicates that many complex, interrelated factors are at work (Ogbu, 1978; Wong-Fillmore, 1983). In particular, sociological and anthropological research suggests that status and power relations between groups are an important part of any comprehensive account of minority students' school failure (Fishman, 1976; Ogbu, 1978; Paulston, 1980). In addition, a variety of factors related to educational quality and cultural mismatch also appear to be important in mediating minority students' academic progress (Wong-Fillmore, 1983). These factors have been integrated into the design of a theoretical framework that suggests the changes required to reverse minority student failure.

A THEORETICAL FRAMEWORK

The central tenet of the framework is that students from "dominated" societal groups are "empowered" or "disabled" as a direct result of their interactions with educators in the schools. These interactions are mediated by the implicit or explicit role definitions that educators assume in relation to four institutional characteristics of schools. These characteristics reflect the extent to which (1) minority students' language and culture are incorporated into the school program; (2) minority community participation is encouraged as an integral component of children's education; (3) the pedagogy promotes intrinsic motivation on the part of students to use language actively in order to generate their own knowledge; and (4) professionals involved in assessment become advocates for minority students rather than legitimizing the location of the "problem" in the students. For each of these dimensions of school organization the role definitions of educators can be described in terms of a continuum, with one end promoting the empowerment of students and the other contributing to the disabling of students.

The three sets of relationships analyzed in the present framework—majority/minority societal group relations, school/minority community relations, educator/minority student relations—are chosen on the basis of hypotheses regarding the relative ineffectiveness of previous educational reforms and the directions required to reverse minority group school failure. Each of these relationships will be discussed in detail.

INTERGROUP POWER RELATIONS

When the patterns of minority student school failure are examined from an international perspective, it becomes evident that power and status relations between minority and majority groups exert a major influence on school performance. An example frequently given is the academic failure of Finnish students in Sweden, where they are a low-status group, compared to their success in Australia, where they are regarded as a high-status group (Troike, 1978). Similarly, Ogbu (1978) reports that the outcast Burakumin perform poorly in Japan but as well as other Japanese students in the United States.

Theorists have explained these findings using several constructs. Cummins (1984), for example, discusses the "bicultural ambivalence" (or lack of cultural identification) of students in relation to both the home and school cultures. Ogbu (1978) discusses the "caste" status of minorities that fail academically and ascribes their failure to economic and social discrimination combined with the internalization of the inferior status attributed to them by the dominant group. Feuerstein (1979) attributes academic failure to the disruption of intergenerational transmission processes caused by the alienation of a group from its own culture. In all three conceptions, widespread school failure does not occur in minority groups that are positively oriented towards both their own and the dominant culture, that do not perceive themselves as inferior to the dominant group, and that are not alienated from their own cultural values.

Within the present framework, the *dominant* group controls the institutions and reward systems within society; the *dominated* group (Mullard, 1985) is regarded as inherently inferior by the dominant group and denied access to high-status positions within the institutional structure of the society. As described by Ogbu (1978), the dominated status of a minority group exposes them to conditions that predispose children to school failure even before they come to school. These conditions include limited parental access to economic and educational resources, ambivalence toward cultural transmission and primary language use in the home, and interactional styles that may not prepare students for typical teacher/student interaction patterns in school (Heath, 1983; Wong-Fillmore, 1983). Bicultural ambivalence and less effective cultural transmission among dominated groups are frequently associated with a historical pattern of colonization and subordination by the dominant group. This pattern, for example, characterizes Franco-Ontarian students in Canada, Finns in Sweden, and Hispanic, Native, and black groups in the United States.

Different patterns among other societal groups can clearly be distinguished (Ogbu & Matute-Bianchi, in press). Detailed analysis of patterns of intergroup relations go beyond the scope of this paper. However, it is important to note that the minority groups characterized by widespread school failure tend overwhelmingly to be in a dominated relationship to the majority group.[3]

Empowerment of Students

Students who are empowered by their school experiences develop the ability, confidence, and motivation to succeed academically. They participate competently in instruction as a result of having developed a confident cultural identity as well as appropriate school-based knowledge and interactional structures (Cummins, 1983b; Tikunoff, 1983). Students who are disempowered or "disabled" by their school experiences do not develop this type of cognitive/academic and social/emotional foundation. Thus, student empowerment is regarded as both a mediating construct influencing academic performance and as an outcome variable itself.[4]

Although conceptually the cognitive/academic and social/emotional (identity-related) factors are distinct, the data suggest that they are extremely difficult to separate in the case of minority students who are "at risk" academically. For example, data from both Sweden and the United States suggest that minority students who immigrate relatively late (about ten years of age) often appear to have better academic prospects that students of similar socioeconomic status born in the host country (Cummins, 1984; Skutnabb-Kangas, 1984). Is this because their L1 cognitive/academic skills on arrival provide a better foundation for L2 cognitive/academic skills acquisition, or alternatively, because they have not experienced devaluation of their identity in the societal institutions, namely schools of the host country, as has been the case of students born in that setting?

Similarly, the most successful bilingual programs appear to be those that emphasize and use the students' L1 (for reviews, see Cummins 1983a, 1984). Is this success due to better promotion of L1 cognitive/academic skills or to the reinforcement of cultural identity provided by an intensive L1 program? By the same token, is the failure of many minority students in English-only immersion programs a function of cognitive/academic difficulties or of students' ambivalence about the value of their cultural identity (Cohen & Swain, 1976)?

These questions are clearly difficult to answer; the point to be made, however, is that for minority students who have traditionally experienced school failure, there is sufficient overlap in the impact of cognitive/academic and identity factors to justify incorporating these two dimensions within the notion of "student empowerment," while recognizing that under some conditions each dimension may be affected in different ways.

Schools and Power

Minority students are disabled or disempowered by schools in very much the same way that their communities are disempowered by interactions with societal institutions. Since equality of opportunity is believed to be a given, it is assumed that individuals are responsible for their own failure and are, therefore, made to feel that they have failed because of their own inferiority, despite the best efforts of dominant-group institutions and individuals to help them (Skutnabb-Kangas, 1984). This analysis implies that minority students will succeed educationally to the extent that the patterns of interaction in school reverse those that prevail in the society at large.

Four structural elements in the organization of schooling contribute to the extent to which minority students are empowered or disabled. As outlined in Figure 7-1, these elements include the incorporation of minority students' culture and language, inclusion of minority communities in the education of their children, pedagogical assumptions and practices operating in the classroom, and the assessment of minority students.

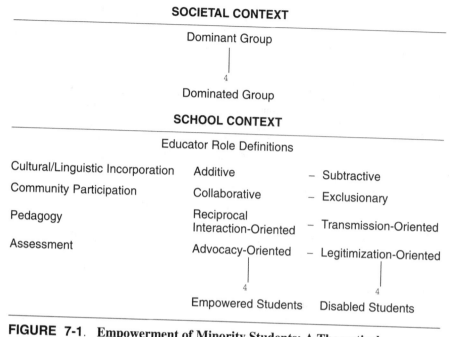

FIGURE 7-1. **Empowerment of Minority Students: A Theoretical Framework**

Cultural/linguistic incorporation. Considerable research data suggest that, for dominated minorities, the extent to which students' language and culture are incorporated into the school program constitutes a significant predictor of academic success (Campos & Keatinge, 1984; Cummins, 1983a; Rosier & Holm, 1980). As outlined earlier, students' school success appears to reflect both the more solid cognitive/academic foundation developed through intensive L1 instruction and the reinforcement of their cultural identity.

Included under incorporation of minority group cultural features is the adjustment of instructional patterns to take account of culturally conditioned learning styles. The Kamehameha Early Education Program in Hawaii provides strong evidence of the importance of this type of cultural incorporation. When reading instruction was changed to permit students to collaborate in discussing and interpreting texts, dramatic improvements were found in both reading and verbal intellectual abilities (Au & Jordan, 1981).

An important issue to consider at this point is why superficially plausible but patently inadequate assumptions, such as the "insufficient exposure" hypothesis, continue to dominate the policy debate when virtually all the evidence suggests that incorporation of minority students' language and culture into the school program will at least not impede academic progress. In other words, what social function do such arguments serve? Within the context of the present framework, it is suggested that a major reason for the vehement resistance to bilingual programs is that the incorporation of minority languages and cultures into the school program confers status and power (jobs, for example) on the minority group. Consequently, such programs contravene the established pattern of dominant/dominated group relations. Within democratic societies, however, contradictions between the rhetoric of equality and the reality of domination must be obscured. Thus, conventional wisdoms such as the insufficient exposure hypothesis become immune from critical scrutiny, and incompatible evidence is either ignored or dismissed.

Educators' role definitions in relation to the incorporation of minority students' language and culture can be characterized along an "additive-subtractive" dimension.[5] Educators who see their role as adding a second language and cultural affiliation to their students' repertoire are likely to empower students more than those who see their role as replacing or subtracting students' primary language and culture. In addition to the personal and future employment advantages of proficiency in two languages, there is considerable, though not conclusive, evidence that subtle educational advantages result from continued development of both languages among bilingual students. Enhanced metalinguistic development, for example, is frequently found in association with additive bilingualism (Hakuta & Diaz, 1985; McLaughlin, 1984).

It should be noted that an additive orientation does not require the actual teaching of the minority language. In many cases a minority language class may not be possible for reasons such as low concentration of particular groups of minority students. Educators, however, communicate to students and parents in a variety of ways the extent to which the minority language and culture are valued within the context of the school. Even within a monolingual school context, powerful messages can be communicated to students regarding the validity and advantages of language development.

Community participation. Students from dominated communities will be empowered in the school context to the extent that the communities themselves are empowered through their interactions with the school. When educators involve minority parents as partners in their children's education, parents appear to develop a sense of efficacy that communicates itself to children, with positive academic consequences.

Although lip service is paid to community involvement through Parent Advisory Committees (PAC)[6] in many education programs, these committees are frequently manipulated through misinformation and intimidation (Curtis, 1984). The result is that parents from dominated groups retain their powerless status, and their internalized inferiority is reinforced. Children's school failure can then be attributed to the combined effects of parental illiteracy and lack of interest in their children's education. In reality, most parents of minority students have high aspirations for their children and want to be involved in promoting their academic progress (Wong-Fillmore, 1983). However, they often do not know how to help their children academically, and they are excluded from participation by the school. In fact, even their interaction through L1 with their children in the home is frequently regarded by educators as contributing to academic difficulties (Cummins, 1984).

Dramatic changes in children's academic progress can be realized when educators take the initiative to change this exclusionary pattern to one of collaboration. The Haringey project in Britain illustrates just how powerful the effects of simple interventions can be (Tizard, Schofield, & Hewison, 1982). In order to assess the effects of parental involvement in the teaching of reading, the researchers established a project in the London borough of Haringey whereby all children in two primary level experimental classes in two different schools read to their parents at home on a regular basis. The reading progress of these children was compared with that of children in two classes in two different schools who were given extra reading instruction in small groups by an experienced and qualified teacher who worked four half-days at each school every week for the two years of the intervention. Both groups were also compared with a control group that received no treatment.

All the schools were in multiethnic areas, and there were many parents who did not read English or use it at home. It was found, nevertheless, to be both feasible and practicable to involve nearly all the parents in educational activities such as listening to their children read, even when the parents were nonliterate and largely non-English-speaking. It was also found that, almost without exception, parents welcomed the project, agreed to hear their children read, and completed a record card showing what had been read.

The researchers report that parental involvement had a pronounced effect on the students' success in school. Children who read to their parents made significantly greater progress in reading than those who did not engage in this type of literacy sharing. Small-group instruction in reading, given by a highly competent specialist, did not produce improvements comparable to those obtained from the collaboration with parents. In contrast to the home collaboration program, the benefits of extra reading instruction were least apparent for initially low-achieving children.

In addition, the collaboration between teachers and parents was effective for children of all initial levels of performance, including those who, at the beginning of the study, were failing in learning to read. Teachers reported that the children showed an increased interest in school learning and were better behaved. Those teachers involved in the home collaboration found the work with parents worthwhile, and they continued to involve parents with subsequent classes after the experiment was concluded. It is interesting to note that teachers of the control classes also adopted the home collaboration program after the two-year experimental period.

The Haringey project is one example of school/community relations; there are others. The essential point, however, is that the teacher's role in such relations can be characterized along a *collaborative-exclusionary* dimension. Teachers operating at the collaborative end of the continuum actively encourage minority parents to participate in promoting their children's academic progress both in the home and through involvement in classroom activities. A collaborative orientation may require a willingness on the part of the teacher to work closely with mother-tongue teachers or aides in order to communicate effectively, in a noncondescending way, with minority parents. Teachers with an exclusionary orientation, on the other hand, tend to regard teaching as *their* job and are likely to view collaboration with minority parents as either irrelevant or detrimental to children's progress.

Pedagogy. Several investigators have suggested that many "learning disabilities" are pedagogically induced in that children designated "at risk" frequently receive intensive instruction which confines them to a passive role and induces a form of "learned helplessness" (Beers & Beers, 1980; Coles, 1978; Cummins, 1984). This process is illustrated in a microethnographic study of fourteen reading lessons given to West Indian Creole-speakers of English in Toronto, Canada (Ramphal, 1983). It was found that teachers' constant correction of students' miscues prevented students from focusing on the meaning of what they were reading. Moreover, the constant corrections fostered dependent behavior because students knew that whenever they paused at a word the teacher would automatically pronounce it for them. One student was interrupted so often in one of the lessons that he was able to read only one sentence, consisting of three words, uninterrupted. In contrast to a pattern of classroom interaction which promotes instructional dependence, teaching that empowers will aim to liberate students from instruction by encouraging them to become active generators of their knowledge. As Graves (1983) has demonstrated, this type of active knowledge generation can occur when, for example, children create and publish their own books within the classroom.

Two major pedagogical orientations can be distinguished. These differ in the extent to which the teacher retains exclusive control over the classroom interaction as opposed to sharing some of this control with students. The dominant instructional model in North American schools has been termed a transmission model (Barnes, 1976; Wells, 1982). This model incorporates essentially the same assumptions about teaching and learning that Freire (1970, 1973) has termed a "banking" model of education. This transmission model will be contrasted with a "reciprocal interaction" model of pedagogy.

The basic premise of the transmission model is that the teacher's task is to impart knowledge or skills that she or he possesses to students who do not yet have these skills. This implies that the teacher initiates and controls the interaction, constantly orienting it towards the achievement of instructional objectives. For example, in first- and second-language programs that stress pattern repetition, the teacher presents the materials, models the language patterns, asks questions, and provides feedback to students about the correctness of their response. The curriculum in these types of programs focuses on the internal structure of the language or subject matter. Consequently, it frequently focuses predominantly on surface features of language or literacy such as handwriting, spelling, and decoding, and emphasizes correct recall of content taught by means of highly structured drills and workbook exercises. It has been argued that a transmission model of teaching contravenes central principles of language and literacy acquisition and that a model allowing for reciprocal interaction among students and teachers represents a more appropriate alternative (Cummins, 1984; Wells, 1982).[7]

A central tenet of the reciprocal interaction model is that "talking and writing are means to learning" (Bullock Report, 1975, p. 50). The use of this model in teaching requires a genuine dialogue between student and teacher in both oral and written modalities, guidance and facilitation rather than control of student learning by the teacher, and the encouragement of student/student talk in a collaborative learning context. This model emphasizes the development of higher level cognitive skills rather than just factual recall, and meaningful language use by students rather than the correction of surface forms. Language use and development are consciously integrated with all curricular content rather than taught as isolated subjects, and tasks are presented to students in ways that generate intrinsic rather than extrinsic motivation. In short, pedagogical approaches that empower students encourage them to assume greater control over setting their own learning goals and to collaborate actively with each other in achieving these goals.

The development of a sense of efficacy and inner direction in the classroom is especially important for students from dominated groups whose experiences so often orient them in the opposite direction. Wong-Fillmore (1983) has reported that Hispanic students learned considerably more English in classrooms that provided opportunities for reciprocal interaction with teachers and peers. Ample opportunities for expressive writing appear to be particularly significant in promoting a sense of academic efficacy among minority students (Cummins, Aguilar, Bascunan, Fiorucci, Sanaoui, & Basman, in press). As expressed by Daiute (1985):

> *Children who learn early that writing is not simply an exercise gain a sense of power that gives them confidence to write—and write a lot. . . . Beginning writers who are confident that they have something to say or that they can find out what they need to know can even overcome some limits of training or development. Writers who don't feel that what they say matters have an additional burden that no skills training can help them overcome. (pp. 5–6)*

The implications for students from dominated groups are obvious. Too often the instruction they receive convinces them that what they have to say is irrelevant or wrong. The failure of this method of instruction is then taken as an indication that the minority student is of low ability, a verdict frequently confirmed by subsequent assessment procedures.

Assessment. Historically, assessment has played the role of legitimizing the disabling of minority students. In some cases assessment itself may play the primary role, but more often it has been used to locate the "problem" within the minority student, thereby screening from critical scrutiny the subtractive nature of the school program, the exclusionary orientation of teachers towards minority communities, and transmission models of teaching that inhibit students from active participation in learning.

This process is virtually inevitable when the conceptual base for assessment is purely psychoeducational. If the psychologist's task is to discover the causes of a minority student's academic difficulties and the only tools at his or her disposal are psychological tests (in either L1 or L2), then it is hardly surprising that the child's difficulties will be attributed to psychological dysfunctions. The myth of bilingual handicaps that still influences educational policy was generated in exactly this way during the 1920s and 1930s.

Recent studies suggest that despite the appearance of change brought about by PL94-142, the underlying structure of assessment processes has remained essentially intact. Mehan, Hertweck, and Meihls (in press), for example, report that psychologists continued to test children until they "found" the disability that could be invoked to "explain" the student's apparent academic difficulties. Diagnosis and placement were influenced frequently by factors related to bureaucratic procedures and funding requirements rather than to students' academic performance in the classroom. Rueda and Mercer (1985) have also shown that designation of minority students as "learning disabled" as compared to "language impaired" was strongly influenced by whether a psychologist or a speech pathologist was on the placement committee. In other words, with respect to students' actual behavior, the label was essentially arbitrary. An analysis of more than four hundred psychological assessments of minority students revealed that although no diagnostic conclusions were logically possible in the majority of assessments, psychologists were most reluctant to admit this fact to teachers and parents (Cummins, 1984). In short, the data suggest that the structure within which psychological assessment takes place orients the psychologist to locate the cause of the academic problem within the minority student.

An alternative role definition for psychologists or special educators can be termed an "advocacy" or "delegitimization" role.[8] In this case, their task must be to delegitimize the traditional function of psychological assessment in the educational disabling of minority students by becoming advocates for the child in scrutinizing critically the societal and educational context within which the child has developed (Cazden, 1985). This involves locating the pathology within the societal power relations between dominant and dominated groups, in the reflection of these power relations between school and communities, and in the mental and cultural disabling of minority students that takes place in classrooms. These conditions are a more probable cause of the 300 percent overrepresentation of Texas Hispanic students in the learning disabled category than any intrinsic processing deficit unique to Hispanic children. The training of psychologists and special educators does not prepare them for this advocacy or delegitimization role. From the present perspective, however, it must be emphasized that discriminatory assessment is carried out by well-intentioned individuals who, rather than challenging a socioeducational system that tends to disable minority students, have accepted a role definition and an educational structure that makes discriminatory assessment virtually inevitable.[9]

EMPOWERING MINORITY STUDENTS: THE CARPINTERIA EXAMPLE

The Spanish-only preschool program of the Carpinteria School District, near Santa Barbara, California, is one of the few programs in the United States that explicitly incorporates the major elements hypothesized in previous sections to empower minority students. Spanish is the exclusive language of instruction, there is a strong community involvement component, and the program is characterized by a coherent philosophy of promoting conceptual development through meaningful linguistic interaction.

The proposal to implement an intensive Spanish-only preschool program in this region was derived from district findings showing that a large majority of the Spanish-speaking students entering kindergarten each year lacked adequate skills to succeed in the kindergarten program. On the School Readiness Inventory, a districtwide screening measure administered to all incoming kindergarten students, Spanish-speaking students tended to average about eight points lower than English-speaking students (approximately 14.5 compared to 23.0, averaged over four years from 1979 to 1982) despite the fact that the test was administered in students' dominant language. A score of 20 or better was viewed by the district as predicting a successful kindergarten year for the child. Prior to the implementation of the experimental program, the Spanish-background children attended a bilingual preschool program—operated either by Head Start or the Community Day Care Center—in which both English and Spanish were used concurrently but with strong emphasis on the development of English skills. According to the district kindergarten teachers, children who had attended these programs often mixed English and Spanish into a "Spanglish."

The major goal of the experimental Spanish-only preschool program was to bring Spanish-dominant children entering kindergarten up to a level of readiness for school similar to that attained by English-speaking children in the community. The project also sought to make parents of the program participants aware of their role as the child's first teacher and to encourage them to provide specific types of experiences for their children in the home.

The preschool program itself involved the integration of language with a large variety of concrete and literacy-related experiences. As summarized in the evaluation report: "The development of language skills in Spanish was foremost in the planning and attention given to every facet of the pre-school day. Language was used constantly for conversing, learning new ideas, concepts and vocabulary, thinking creatively, and problem-solving to give the children the opportunity to develop their language skills in Spanish to as high a degree as possible within the structure of the pre-school day" (Campos & Keatinge, 1984, p. 17).

Participation in the program was on a voluntary basis and students were screened only for age and Spanish-language dominance. Family characteristics of students in the experimental program were typical of other Spanish-speaking families in the community; more than 90 percent were of low socioeconomic status, and the majority worked in agriculture and had an average education level of about sixth grade.

The program proved to be highly successful in developing students' readiness skills, as evidence by the average score of 21.6 obtained by the 1982–83 incoming kindergarten students who had been in the program, compared to the score of 23.2 obtained by English-speaking students. A score of 14.6 was obtained by Spanish-speaking students who experienced the regular bilingual preschool program. In 1983–84 the scores of these groups were 23.3, 23.4, and 16.0, respectively. In other words, the gap between English-background and Spanish-background children in the Spanish-only preschool had disappeared; however, a considerable gap remained for Spanish-background students for whom English was the focus of preschool instruction.

Of special interest is the performance of the experimental program students on the English and Spanish versions of the Bilingual Syntax Measure (BSM), a test or oral syntactic development (Hernandez-Chavez, Burt, & Dulay, 1976). Despite the fact that they experienced an exclusively Spanish preschool program, these students performed better than the other Spanish-speaking students in English (and Spanish) on entry to kindergarten in 1982 and at a similar level in 1983. On entrance to grade one in 1983, the gap had widened considerably, with almost five times as many of the experimental-program students performing at level 5 (fluent English) compared to the other Spanish-background students (47 percent vs. 10 percent) (Campos & Keatinge, 1984).

The evaluation report suggests that

> *although project participants were exposed to less total English, they, because of their enhanced first language skill and concept knowledge were better able to comprehend the English they were exposed to. This seems to be borne out by comments made by kindergarten teachers in the District about project participants. They are making comments like, "Project participants appear more aware of what is happening around them in the classroom," "They are able to focus on the task at hand better" and "They demonstrated greater self-confidence in learning situations." All of these traits would tend to enhance the language acquisition process. (Campos & Keatinge, 1984, p. 41)*

Campos and Keatinge (1984) also emphasize the consequences of the preschool program for parental participation in their children's education. They note that, according to the school officials, "the parents of project participants are much more aware of and involved in their child's school experience than non-participant parents of Spanish speakers. This is seen as having a positive impact on the future success of the project participants—the greater the involvement of parents, the greater the chances of success of the child" (p. 41).

The major relevance of these findings for educators and policymakers derives from their demonstration that educational programs *can* succeed in preventing the academic failure experienced by many minority students. The corollary is that failure to provide this type of program constitutes the disabling of minority students by the school system. For example, among the students who did not experience the experimental preschool program, the typical pattern of low levels of academic readiness and limited proficiency in both languages was observed. These are the students who are likely to be referred for psychological assessment early in their school careers. This assessment will typically legitimize the inadequate educational provision by attributing students' difficulties to some vacuous category, such as learning disability. By contrast, students who experienced a preschool program in which (a) their cultural identity was reinforced, (b) there was active collaboration with parents, and (c) meaningful use of language was integrated into every aspect of daily activities were developing high levels of conceptual and linguistic skills in *both* languages.

CONCLUSION

In this article I have proposed a theoretical framework for examining minority students' academic failure and for predicting the effects of educational interventions. Within this framework the educational failure of minority students is analyzed as a function of the extent to which schools reflect or counteract the power relations that exist within the broader society. Specifically, language-minority students' educational progress is strongly influenced by the extent to which individual educators become advocates for the promotion of students' linguistic talents, actively encourage community participation in developing students' academic and cultural resources, and implement pedagogical approaches that succeed in liberating students from instructional dependence.

The educator/student interactions characteristic of the disabling end of the proposed continua reflect the typical patterns of interaction that dominated societal groups have experienced in relation to dominant groups. The intrinsic value of the group is usually denied, and "objective" evidence is accumulated to demonstrate the group's "inferiority." This inferior status is then used as a justification for excluding the group from activities and occupations that entail societal rewards.

In a similar way, the disabling of students is frequently rationalized on the basis of students' "needs." For example, minority students need maximum exposure to English in both the school and home; thus, parents must be told not to interact with children in the mother tongue. Similarly, minority children need a highly structured drill-oriented program in order to maximize time spent on tasks to compensate for their deficient preschool experiences. Minority students also need a comprehensive diagnostic/prescriptive assessment in order to identify the nature of their "problem" and possible remedial interventions.

This analysis suggests a major reason for the relative lack of success of the various educational bandwagons that have characterized the North American crusade against underachievement during the past twenty years. The individual role definitions of educators and the institutional role definitions of schools have remained largely unchanged despite "new and improved" programs and policies. These programs and policies, despite their cost, have simply added a new veneer to the outward facade of the structure that disables minority students. The lip service paid to initial L1 instruction, community involvement, and nondiscriminatory assessment, together with the emphasis on improved teaching techniques, have succeeded primarily in deflecting attention from the attitudes and orientation of educators who interact on a daily basis with minority students. It is in these interactions that students are disabled. In the absence of individual and collective educator role redefinitions, schools will continue to reproduce, in these interactions, the power relations that characterize the wider society and make minority students' academic failure inevitable.

To educators genuinely concerned about alleviating the educational difficulties of minority students and responding to their needs, this conclusion may appear overly bleak. I believe, however, that it is realistic and optimistic, as directions for change are clearly indicated rather than obscured by the overlay of costly reforms that leave the underlying disabling structure essentially intact. Given the societal commitment to maintaining the dominant/dominated power relationships, we can predict that educational changes threatening this structure will be fiercely resisted. This is in fact the case for each of the four structural dimensions discussed earlier.[10]

In order to reverse the pattern of widespread minority group educational failure, educators and policymakers are faced with both a personal and a political challenge. Personally, they must redefine their roles within the classroom, the community, and the broader society so that these role definitions result in interactions that empower rather than disable students. Politically, they must attempt to persuade colleagues and decisionmakers—such as school boards and the public that elects them—of the importance of redefining institutional goals so that the schools transform society by empowering minority students rather than reflect society by disabling them.

ENDNOTES

1. The Education of All Handicapped Children Act of 1975 (Public Law 94-142) guarantees to all handicapped children in the United States the right to a free public education, to an individualized education program (IEP), to due process, to education in the least

segregated environment, and to assessment procedures that are multidimensional and nonculturally discriminatory.

2. For a discussion of the implications of Canadian French immersion programs for the education of minority students, see California State Department of Education (1984).

3. Ogbu (1978), for example, has distinguished between "caste," "immigrant," and "autonomous" minority groups. Caste groups are similar to what has been termed "dominated" groups in the present framework and are the only category of minority groups that tends to fail academically. Immigrant groups have usually come voluntarily to the host society for economic reasons and, unlike caste minorities, have not internalized negative attributions of the dominant group. Ogbu gives Chinese and Japanese groups as examples of "immigrant" minorities. The cultural resources that permit some minority groups to resist discrimination and internalization of negative attributions are still a matter of debate and speculation (for a recent treatment, see Ogbu & Bianchi, in press). The final category distinguished by Ogbu is that of "autonomous" groups who hold a distinct cultural identity but who are not subordinated economically or politically to the dominant group (for example, Jews and Mormons in the United States).

Failure to take account of these differences among minority groups both in patterns of academic performance and sociohistorical relationships to the dominant group has contributed to the confused state of policymaking with respect to language minority students. The bilingual education policy, for example, has been based on the implicit assumption that the linguistic mismatch hypothesis was valid for all language minority students, and, consequently, the same types of intervention were necessary and appropriate for all students. Clearly, this assumption is open to question.

4. There is no contradiction in postulating student empowerment as both a mediating and an outcome variable. For example, cognitive abilities clearly have the same status in that they contribute to students' school success and can also be regarded as an outcome of schooling.

5. The terms "additive" and "subtractive" bilingualism were coined by Lambert (1975) to refer to the proficient bilingualism associated with positive cognitive outcomes on the one hand, and the limited bilingualism often associated with negative outcomes on the other.

6. PACs were established in some states to provide an institutional structure for minority parent involvement in educational decision making with respect to bilingual programs. In California, for example, a majority of PAC members for any state-funded program was required to be from the program target group. The school plan for use of program funds required signed PAC approval.

7. This "reciprocal interaction" model incorporates proposals about the relation between language and learning made by a variety of investigators, most notably in the Bullock Report (1975), and by Barnes (1976), Lindfors (1980), and Wells (1982). Its application with respect to the promotion of literacy conforms closely to psycholinguistic approaches to reading (Goodman & Goodman, 1977; Holdaway, 1979; Smith, 1978) and to the recent emphasis on encouraging expressive writing from the earliest grades (Chomsky, 1981; Giacobbe, 1982; Graves, 1983; Temple, Nathan, & Burris, 1982). Students' microcomputing networks such as the *Computer Chronicles Newswire* (Mehan, Miller-Souviney, & Riel, 1984) represent a particularly promising application of reciprocal interaction model of pedagogy.

8. See Mullard (1985) for a detailed discussion of delegitimization strategies in antiracist education.

9. Clearly, the presence of processing difficulties that are rooted in neurological causes is not being denied for either monolingual or bilingual children. However, in the case of children from dominated minorities, the proportion of disabilities that are neurological in origin is likely to represent only a small fraction of those that derive from educational and social conditions.

10. Although for pedagogy the resistance to sharing control with students goes beyond majority/minority group relations, the same elements are present. If the curriculum is not predetermined and presequenced, and the students are generating their own knowledge in a critical and creative way, then the reproduction of the societal structure cannot be guaranteed—hence the reluctance to liberate students from instructional dependence.

REFERENCES

Au, K.H., & Jordan, C. (1981). Teaching reading to Hawaiian children: Finding a culturally appropriate solution. In H. Trueba, G.P. Guthrie, & K.H. Au (Eds.) *Culture and the bilingual classroom: Studies in classroom ethnography* (pp. 139–152). Rowley, MA: Newbury House.

Baker, K.A., & de Kanter, A.A. (1981). *Effectiveness of bilingual education: A review of the literature.* Washington, DC: U.S. Department of Education, Office of Planning and Budget.

Barnes, D. (1976). *From communication to curriculum.* New York: Penguin.

Beers, C.S., & Beers, J.W. (1980). Early identification of learning disabilities: Facts and fallacies. *Elementary School Journal, 81,* 67–76.

Bethell, T. (1979, February). Against bilingual education. *Harper's,* pp. 30–33.

Bullock Report. (1975). *A language for life.* [Report of the Committee of Inquiry appointed by the Secretary of State for Education and Science under the Chairmanship of Sir Alan Bullock]. London: HMSO.

California State Department of Education. (1984). *Studies on immersion education: A collection for United States educators.* Sacramento: Author.

Campos, J., & Keatinge, B. (1984). *The Carpinteria preschool program: Title VII second year evaluation report.* Washington, DC: Department of Education.

Cazden, C.B (1985, April). *The ESL teacher as advocate.* Plenary presentation to the TESOL Conference, New York.

Chomsky, C. (1981). Write now, read later. In C. Cazden (Ed.), *Language in Early Childhood Education* (2nd ed., pp. 141–149). Washington, DC: National Association for the Education of Young Children.

Cohen, A.D., & Swain, M. (1976). Bilingual education: The immersion model in the North American context. In J.E. Alatis & K. Twaddell (Eds.), *English as a second language in bilingual education* (pp. 55–64). Washington, DC: TESOL.

Coles, G.S. (1978). The learning disabilities test battery: Empirical and social issues. *Harvard Educational Review, 48,* 313–340.

Cummins, J. (1979). Linguistic interdependence and the educational development of bilingual children. *Review of Educational Research, 49,* 222–251.

Cummins, J. (1983a). *Heritage language education: A literature review.* Toronto: Ministry of Education.

Cummins, J. (1983b). Functional language proficiency in context: Classroom participation as an interactive process. In W.J. Tikunoff (Ed.), *Compatibility of the SBIS features with other research on instruction for LEP students* (pp. 109–131). San Francisco: Far West Laboratory.

Cummins, J. (1984). *Bilingualism and special education: Issues in assessment and pedagogy.* Clevedon, Eng.: Multilingual Matters, and San Diego: College Hill Press.

Cummins, J., Aguilar, M., Bascunan, L., Fiorucci, S., Sanaoui, R., & Basman, S. (in press). *Literacy development in heritage language programs.* Toronto: National Heritage Language Resource Unit.

Curtis, J. (1984). *Bilingual education in Calistoga: Not a happy ending.* Report submitted to the Instituto de Lengua y Cultura, Elmira, NY.

Daiute, C. (1985). *Writing and computers.* Reading, MA: Addison-Wesley.

Feuerstein, R. (1979). *The dynamic assessment of retarded performers: The learning potential assessment device, theory, instrument, and techniques.* Baltimore: University Park Press.

Fishman, J. (1976). *Bilingual education: An international sociological perspective.* Rowley, MA: Newbury House.

Freire, P. (1970). *Pedagogy of the oppressed.* New York: Seabury.

Freire, P. (1973). *Education for critical consciousness.* New York: Seabury.

Giacobbe, M.E. (1982). Who says children can't write the first week?, In R.D. Walshe (Ed.), *Donald Graves in Australia: "Children want to write"* (pp. 99–103). Exeter, NH: Heinemann Educational Books.

Goodman, K.S., & Goodman, Y.M. (1977). Learning about psycholinguistic processes by analyzing oral reading. *Harvard Educational Review, 47,* 317–333.

Graves, D.H. (1983). *Writing: Teachers and children at work.* Exeter, NH: Heinemann Educational Books.

Hakuta, K., & Diaz, R.M. (1985). The relationship between degree of bilingualism and cognitive ability: A critical discussion and some new longitudinal data. In K.E. Nelson (Ed.), *Children's language* (Vol. 5, pp. 319–345). Hillsdale, NJ: Erlbaum.

Heath, S.B. (1983). *Ways with words.* Cambridge: Cambridge University Press.

Hernandez-Chavez, E., Burt, M., & Dulay, H. (1976). *The bilingual syntax measure.* New York: The Psychological Corporation.

Holdaway, D. (1979). *The foundations of literacy.* Sydney, Australia: Ashton Scholastic.

Jusenius, C., & Duarte, V.L. (1982). *Hispanics and jobs: Barriers to progress.* Washington, DC: National Commission for Employment Policy.

Lambert, W.E. (1975). Culture and language as factors in learning and education. In A. Wolfgang (Ed.), *Education of immigrant students* (pp. 55–83). Toronto: O.I.S.E.

Lindfors, J.W. (1980). *Children's language and learning.* (Englewood Cliffs, NJ: Prentice-Hall.

McLaughlin, B. (1984). Early bilingualism: Methodological and theoretical issues. In M. Paradis & Y. Lebrun (Eds.), *Early bilingualism and child development* (pp. 19–46). Lisse: Swets & Zeitlinger.

McLaughlin, B. (1985). *Second language acquisition in childhood: Vol. 2. School-age children.* Hillsdale, NJ: Erlbaum.

Mehan, H., Hertweck, A., & Meihls, J.L. (in press). *Handicapping the handicapped: Decision making in students' educational careers.* Palo Alto: Stanford University.

Mehan, H., Miller-Souviney, B., & Riel, M.M. (1984). Research currents: Knowledge of text editing and control of literacy skills. *Language Arts,* 65, 154–159.

Mullard, C. (1985, January). *The social dynamic of migrant groups: From progressive to transformative policy in education.* Paper presented at the OECD Conference on Educational Policies and the Minority Social Groups, Paris.

Ogbu, J.U. (1978). *Minority education and caste.* New York: Academic Press.

Ogbu, J.U., & Matute-Bianchi, M.E. (in press). Understanding sociocultural factors: Knowledge, identity and school adjustment. In California State Department of Education (Ed.), *Sociocultural factors and minority student achievement.* Sacramento: Author.

Ortiz, A.A., & Yates, J.R. (1983). Incidence of exceptionality among Hispanics: Implications for manpower planning. *NABE Journal,* 7, 41–54.

Paulston, C.B. (1980). *Bilingual education: Theories and issues.* Rowley, MA: Newbury House.

Ramphal, D.K. *An analysis of reading instruction of West Indian Creole-speaking students.* Unpublished doctoral dissertation, Ontario Institute for Studies in Education, 1983.

Rosier, P., & Holm, W. (1980). *The Rock Point experience: A longitudinal study of a Navajo school.* Washington, DC: Center for Applied Linguistics.

Rueda, R., Mercer, J.R. (1985, June). *Predictive analysis of decision making with language-minority handicapped children.* Paper presented at the BUENO Center 3rd Annual Symposium on Bilingual Education, Denver.

Schneider, S.G. (1976). *Revolution, reaction or reform: The 1974 Bilingual Education Act.* New York: Las Americas.

Skutnabb-Kangas, T. (1984). *Bilingualism or not: The education of minorities.* Clevedon, Eng.: Multilingual Matters.

Smith, F. (1978). *Understanding reading* (2nd ed.). New York: Holt, Rinehart & Winston.

Temple, C.A., Nathan, R.G. & Burris, N.A. (1982). *The beginnings of writing.* Boston: Allyn & Bacon.

Tikunoff, W.J. (1983). Five significant bilingual instructional features. In W.J. Tikunoff (Ed.), *Compatibility of the SBIS features with other research on instruction for LEP students* (pp. 5–18). San Francisco: Far West Laboratory.

Tizard, J., Schofield, W.N., & Hewison, J. (1982). Collaboration between teachers and parents in assisting children's reading. *British Journal of Educational Psychology,* 52, 1–15.

Troike, R. (1978). Research evidence for the effectiveness of bilingual education. *NABE Journal,* 3, 13–24.

Wells, G. (1982). Language, learning and the curriculum. In G. Wells, (Ed.). *Language, learning and education* (pp. 205–226). Bristol: Centre for the Study of Language and Communication, University of Bristol.

Wong-Fillmore, L. (1983). The language learner as an individual: Implications of research on individual differences for the ESL teacher. In M.A. Clarke & J. Handscombe (Eds.), *On TESOL '82: Pacific perspectives on language learning and teaching* (pp. 157–171). Washington, DC: TESOL.

School Failure and Cultural Mismatch: Another View

ANA MARIA VILLEGAS

The widely documented poor school performance of minority students in the United States has elicited concern and explanatory efforts. This disturbing problem commands urgent public attention in view of the projected increase in the minority population of the country. Within the next two decades, schools will enroll an increasing proportion of minority students. The change in demographic patterns exerts even more pressure on the school system to develop creative solutions to the academic difficulties of this group of students.

Explanations for the academic failure of minority students abound, but recently the theory of home-school incompatibility has gained credibility among educators. In its broadest expression, this theory attributes the academic problems of minority students to cultural disjunctures between home and school. Several versions of the theory exist, each examining a specific area of disjuncture. Attention has been paid to differences in dialects (Gay and Abrahams, 1972; Labov, 1969; Piedstrup, 1973), and in cognitive style (Cohen, 1969; Ramirez and Castaneda, 1974). More recently, however, the focus of empirical attention has turned to the subtle differences in the ways that language is used at home and in school, and the resulting miscommunication from these differences (Au and Mason, 1981; Cazden, John, and Hymes, 1972; Heath, 1983a; Jordan, 1985; Philips, 1983).

Proponents of this latest version of the theory of incompatibility contend that a better understanding of the use of language across the home and school settings will enable educators to develop culturally sensitive solutions that will remedy the communication problems and improve minority students' poor academic performance. This paper reviews the literature concerning home-school clashes in language use, and examines the theory of incompatibility critically. An argument is made that by reducing the focus of analysis to the home-school link, the theory diverts attention away from the social inequalities that sustain the widespread academic

Reprinted from *The Urban Review*, 20:253–265, 1988, by permission of the publisher.

failure of minority students. Attention is given to the role that the language of the school plays in the reproduction of inequitable social relations. Suggestions are offered for means by which teachers can help minority students improve their future chances.

LANGUAGE USE AT HOME AND IN SCHOOL

Sometimes the things closest to us are the least apparent. Most social activity is conducted through spoken language, yet most of us do not fully understand how language influences our attempts to communicate with others. Spoken language takes on added importance in classrooms because it is the prevalent means by which teachers instruct their students, and students in turn display their knowledge. Those who are interested in teaching and learning cannot ignore how language is used in the classroom.

Students and teachers in a given classroom may speak the same language, but they sometimes have different ways of using it. Sociolinguistic research shows that communities vary in their use of language (Bauman and Sherzer, 1974; Gumperz, 1972; Heath, 1983a; Hymes, 1974; Philips, 1983). Children whose language use at home and in their immediate community corresponds more closely to what is expected in the classroom have an advantage in terms of opportunities for learning. For these students, prior experience transfers to the classroom and facilitates their academic performance. This case seems to be true for white, middle-class, Anglo-American students. In contrast, minority children frequently experience discontinuity between home and school in ways of using language. They are often misunderstood when applying prior knowledge to classroom tasks. Of what use is prior experience to these children if their established ways of using language and making sense of the world are deemed unacceptable or prohibited in the classroom? This discontinuity has often been identified as a source of academic problems for minority children (see Au and Mason, 1981; Cazden, John, and Hymes, 1972; Florio and Shultz, 1979; Genishi, 1979; Heath, 1983a; Jordan, 1985; Philips, 1983).

What We Have Gained from Sociolinguistic Research

During the past two decades, numerous studies have examined sociolinguistic discontinuities between children's home communities and the classroom. Two research approaches are evident in the literature. Some studies compare patterns of language use at home and in school (Heath, 1983a; Philips, 1983). Others focus primarily on the classroom, comparing the communicative strategies of teachers and pupils from different ethnic groups and social classes (Erickson and Mohatt, 1982; Michaels, 1981; Van Ness, 1981). Research conducted by Heath and by Michaels will be used to represent each approach for the purpose of illustrating the sorts of insight gained from these lines of investigation.

Heath (1983a) conducted an extensive study of language use in different communities in the Piedmont Carolinas. She lived and worked in the communities for nine years. Her research was wide in scope, and an important aspect of it was the role of questioning in language and socialization. The proper handling of questions is critical because many teachers structure much of the academic exchange through interrogatives. Heath became interested in why the children from Trackton, a black working-class community, struggled with the questions asked of them in classes. The teachers, who found the children's behavior to be an obstacle to learning, were concerned and perplexed. Trackton parents were frustrated by their children's school difficulties and attributed problems to the fact that "we [at Trackton] don't talk to our children as you folks [in school] do." Findings of the study indicated that the parents were right.

Heath (1982) compared the role of questions in the homes and community of Trackton and in the classrooms that its children attended. She found that questions varied in proportion to other types of utterances across settings, and that questions were used differently at home and in school. In Trackton, adults did not regard children as legitimate sources of information. This cultural assumption about the role of children was reflected in language. Generally, adults did not attempt to engage young children in conversation until they were considered competent conversational partners. Children were immersed in the stream of language, but rarely were they asked questions. Directives occurred with greater frequency. On the rare occasions when questions were asked, these were generally of the unknown information type. That is, the respondent was expected to provide information the questioner lacked.

The classroom represented a very different sociolinguistic environment for Trackton children, in that their teachers expected them to be adept conversational partners. Questions dominated classroom talk, and directives were used far less frequently than in the community. Rather than asking for information, the teachers most often asked display questions, that is, questions that required students to display knowledge. They did this as a way of monitoring what the students knew about the topic being discussed. From the children's perspective, the teachers' questions seemed peculiar. They found it difficult to understand why the teachers asked questions to which they already knew the answers. In brief, Heath showed that the communicative demands placed on the children in the classroom clashed with the rules that guided the use of language in the community. Given the strangeness of the classroom environment to Trackton children, it is no wonder that they were puzzled and frustrated in school, and appeared academically incompetent.

A second example of ethnic differences in language is provided by a study conducted by Sarah Michaels. Michaels (1981) compared the narrative styles of black and white children in a first grade class. She focused on narratives during "sharing time," a recurrent classroom event in which students were expected to tell their classmates and teacher about some past experience. In primary classrooms, where sharing time is used most frequently, it can serve as a bridge between the oral language that pupils bring to the classroom and the literate discourse style of written text, which emphasizes decontextualized language.

Noting that white students did better than their black classmates during sharing time, Michaels set out to discover why. She found that black and white students used different strategies to construct their narratives. Specifically, the accounts produced by the white children were focused on a single topic and organized sequentially. These students were more likely to name objects, and they assumed less shared knowledge on the part of the listener. Michaels provides evidence suggesting that the teacher's criteria for good narratives correspond closely to the white students' "topic-centered" style. She contends that this similarity enabled the teacher to work well with the white students in constructing the stories.

In contrast, the accounts of the black children frequently contained a series of implicitly associated anecdotes. When asked directly by the researcher, the students were able to express a logical connection between the different topics in their narratives, but rarely did they do so during sharing time. The "topic-associating" narrative style of the black children clashed with the teacher's criteria for good stories. Michaels argues that this sociolinguistic mismatch prevented the teacher from collaborating successfully with the black students during sharing time.

Both Heath and Michaels examined the role of language as a medium for accomplishing classroom tasks. Based on their detailed descriptions of questioning strategies and narrative styles, they make a convincing case that the mismatch between home and school environments prevents black children from using their own sociolinguistic competence successfully in the classroom. These studies suggest how well-meaning teachers can contribute unwittingly to the academic difficulties of students. Heath and Michaels make clear to us the intangible yet powerful influence of the use of language in the classroom.

Toward Culturally Sensitive Solutions

After studying language use at home and in school for nearly two decades, we have learned a great deal about the sociolinguistic clashes experienced by many students, particularly those from minority groups. While acknowledging the importance of this line of research, Cazden (1986) maintains that it would be more useful for researchers to join with teachers in bringing about change. She challenges us to go beyond providing explanations of school failure by finding ways to reverse it.

Different approaches to solving the problems associated with sociolinguistic discontinuities between home and school have been tried. One proposed solution calls for teaching strategies to be changed so that they resemble more closely the ways in which language is used in the students' home communities. This approach is exemplified in the Kamehameha Early Education Project (KEEP).

KEEP is a reading program developed in response to the school problems of Polynesian children in Hawaii. The program has been highly successful. Within three years from its inception, the KEEP students improved their scores dramatically on standardized reading tests (Au, 1980). Au believes that the reading lesson is the key to the success of KEEP. The lesson incorporates ways of organizing turns at talk that resemble the rules for participating in the "talk story," a speech event in Hawaiian culture. Students are allowed to build joint responses during story time, either among themselves or together with the teacher. This strategy of collective turn-taking parallels the joint narration of a story by two or more individuals, which is typical of the "talk story." Joint turn-taking contrasts markedly with the one-speaker-at-a-time rule that prevails in mainstream classes. This method constitutes a significant change in the culture of the traditional classroom, and illustrates one way in which the link between home and school can be strengthened.

A second solution to the difficulties resulting from clashes in the communicative requirements of the home and the school entails modeling and explaining to the children how to use the language of the classroom, and giving them early and intensive practice with it. This solution also requires creative changes in teaching strategies. A good example of this approach is found in the work of Shirly Brice Heath. According to Heath (1983b), to succeed in school students must be skilled in producing running narratives or ongoing commentaries on events or objects. White middle-class children are immersed in this type of discourse from infancy. Through interactions with their parents, these children learn to focus on objects and events by giving them labels and describing their features. They are provided with extensive practice in retelling information and connecting their comments within the ongoing stream of interaction. For them, the school experience is an extension of the home experience.

Heath claims that children whose language socialization does not include extensive practice with running narratives generally encounter academic difficulties and find schooling to be a frustrating experience. To remedy this situation, she worked with teachers of minority students to create classroom activities that focused on talk. In these classrooms, the children were given practice in labeling and naming the features of different objects and events. They told stories, narrated skits, put on puppet shows, and gave slide exhibits. On the basis of her research, Heath concludes that even when language is used differently at home and in school, children can learn if they are given guided practice in a variety of ways of expressing themselves in the classroom.

If we reflect upon the current educational literature and bring to mind conversations with colleagues, we would probably agree that the home-school mismatch hypothesis has gained credibility as a valid explanation for the academic difficulties of minority children. From this perspective, it is argued that if we could improve our understanding of the communicative demands of classrooms and the problems that these demands present to students, it would be possible to develop culturally sensitive solutions that will reverse the pattern of academic failure. This position has great appeal in that it offers hope for minority children, and reaffirms the teacher's capacity to influence students' lives in a positive way.

ANOTHER LOOK AT THE
THEORY OF INCOMPATIBILITY

However appealing these culturally sensitive proposals may seem, they are seriously flawed in that they leave unexamined the social inequality underlying the problem, while claiming to offer fundamental solutions to it. It is irresponsible to limit the analysis of minority children's widespread educational failure to the home-school connection and to isolate these two contexts from society at large, as much current sociolinguistic research has done. By ignoring the political nature of schooling and its relation to the dominant society, we help to perpetuate a system of inequality, thus reducing our chances of effecting the change we claim to seek. The remainder of this paper examines these charges in greater detail.

The Role of Schooling in Society

A question seldom asked explicitly in the sociolinguistic literature is to what extent should the language of the home and school be alike for the benefit of the students. Most research studies and pedagogical proposals implicitly assume that school practices should be modified to match the home situation. The call for greater congruence seems pedagogically sound in that it allows students to use background knowledge in their schooling. Additionally, it fosters respect for cultural diversity and affirms the right of communities to be different. While this position is attractive to many, it is questioned by some minority parents who object to the continuity for fear that it will make it more difficult for their children to become integrated into the mainstream of society. For these parents, the proper goal of school is to prepare their children for the Anglo-American way of life.

A second position less commonly advanced in the sociolinguistic literature calls for a break in continuity with the home community. This break is achieved by easing children into the language of the school in order to prepare them for full participation in society. Parents who want their children to develop ethnic pride and maintain their connection with the ethnic community object to this approach. They consider the mainstreaming effect of educational practices to be in opposition to this goal. They want their children to succeed in school and to improve their socioeconomic positions, but they do not want success to come at the expense of personal alienation from, and marginalization within, their own ethnic community. For these parents, the role of school is twofold: to uphold the ways of life of the community and to impart the skills needed to succeed in society.

Embedded in every proposed solution to the educational problems of minority students is a basic question about the purpose of education. Simply stated, should schooling socialize children according to the established ways of mainstream society, or should it promote cultural pluralism? An answer to this question would allow us to decide whether to modify classroom practices significantly by integrating the "different" ways language is used in ethnic communities, or merely to use our knowledge of those differences as a stepping stone to assimilation in the mainstream. However, the role of school in society is rarely discussed in the home-school literature. Consequently, we have developed a number of educational "solutions" that have profound implications for the lives of students, with little attention given to the social implications of those solutions. Perhaps the question about the role of the school is avoided out of fear of social conflict that is likely to result from its discussion. However threatening this fear might be, we must recognize that conflict is unavoidable in socially stratified and ethnically diversified societies. From a more positive perspective, conflict can be viewed as a healthy expression of differences, and it can be used as a means by which members of different communities, especially those from traditionally bypassed minority groups, gain access to participation in our democratic way of life.

We shortchange ethnic communities when we propose "culturally sensitive solutions" to home-school discontinuities without giving their members a say in those decisions. Presently, we pay much lip service to the notion of parental involvement in education, but in practice we continue to rely on "expert solutions" to local problems. What we lack is a process by which problems are identified and possible solutions are considered. Such a process must involve parents as well as educators, and ought to provide opportunities for open debate on the role of schooling in society, and teaching practices that would be appropriate to this role.

The Political Nature of Language in School and Society

There is a fundamental problem with the research on sociolinguistic variation among ethnic and social groups. Generally, it lacks a critique of the social system in which linguistic interaction takes place. It fails to address why differences exist in the first place. This issue is relevant in view of the fact that the language of the white, middle-class, Anglo-American segment of the populace has higher status in our society than do other varieties used by minority groups. To assume that it is natural for there to be variation in language between and among communities, yet not to question why certain varieties have greater or lesser status, serves to perpetuate social inequities. The grave danger of this position is that it masks inequality under the cloak of variety.

Differences in language are not neutral phenomena. Rather, the differences play a major role in the competition for economic and political advantages (Bernstein, 1971; Bourdieu, 1977; Bourdieu and Passeron, 1977). The manipulation of language in the struggle for power is evident in school. We are told that school provides a neutral ground for proving individual talent. We are also told that because everyone has an equal opportunity to prove his or her talent, those who succeed in school will have earned the better positions in society, while those who fail will be denied access to these rewards. However, in spite of our rhetoric about equal opportunity and respect for cultural differences, the educational system continues to evaluate students on the basis of white, middle-class ways of using language. As the home-school literature reveals, the language of the classroom capitalizes on the sociolinguistic competence that middle-class students bring to school, placing minority children at a decided disadvantage in the learning situation. Furthermore, students' progress within the educational system is measured by the results of standardized tests that have been shown to favor those who come to school with middle-class language varieties (Cole, 1977; Gay and Abrahams, 1973; Houts, 1977; Mercer, 1973; Scarr, 1981). In brief, bias toward the language of the middle class is built into our teaching and evaluation practices. This bias legitimates the privileged position of the dominant groups in society, and confirms the inferiority of minority groups.

School is a political institution that contributes to the perpetuation of the existing class structure (Bowles and Gintis, 1976; Bourdieu, 1977; Bourdieu and Passeron, 1977; Collins, 1974; Levitas, 1974). In this conservative process, language serves as an important medium through which dominant and dominated groups compete for power. If dominant groups have the power to impose their own language variety on the educational system, it is to be expected that subordinate groups, whose language varieties are accorded less prestige, will encounter difficulties in school. It is no accident that minority students experience linguistic gaps between home and school, while middle-class students have a smoother transition between the two. The school is not a neutral ground for proving talent, as some would have us believe. As the educational system is currently organized, it functions to maintain the advantage of the socially powerful.

It is simplistic to claim that differences in the languages used at home and in school are the root of the widespread academic problems of minority children. Admittedly, differences do exist, and they can create communication difficulties in the classroom for both teachers and students. Even so, those differences in language must be viewed in the context of a broader struggle for power within a stratified society. To explain the academic failure of minority students in terms of a language mismatch between home and school, without discussing the political nature of language in school and society, is to provide the system with an excuse for institutionalizing inequalities.

School is an instrument of society, and as such, it contributes to the perpetuation of the status quo; however, there is some slack in the system (Bourdieu and Passeron, 1977; Giroux, 1983, 1988). Within the limits of our historical moment, it is possible to work toward social change, if that is what we choose to do. We can proceed by modifying the ways language is used in the classroom. Much can be done to reduce miscommunications with students, and the home-school literature offers numerous suggestions for dealing with this problem. However, we must go beyond the home-school link and assist students to make connections between themselves and society. In this regard, Sleeter and Grant (1988) suggest that teachers need to help students understand how their group's material and political position in society affects its language and culture.

For this process to occur, teachers need support from teacher educators. With the introduction of multicultural education into their curriculum, teacher education programs have generally promoted an appreciation of cultural diversity and have encouraged teachers to use aspects of that diversity in the classroom. But, teacher education must go beyond the acceptance of differences and help teachers analyze the sociopolitical system that gives rise to those differences, and then assign greater or lesser status to them. Additionally, both teachers and teacher educators must become reflective about classroom practices in order to gain insight into how the social relations that we foster in our classrooms serve to perpetuate and/or challenge existing social inequities.

Ultimately, significant social change can be initiated only by those who are most adversely affected by the imbalance of power in society. But as teachers and teacher educators, we can support this process of social change by promoting the development of sociopolitical awareness on the part of our students as well as ourselves. After all, teaching is a political activity.

An Alternative Explanation of "School Failure"

What is lacking in the home-school literature is attention to the relationship between school and the wider society. Ogbu (1985, 1987) has examined this missing link, particularly in efforts to explain the consistent pattern of school failure on the part of certain minority groups. In brief, he argues that the language differences observed in schools are a medium for acting out the political and economic conflict between dominant and dominated groups in society. This alternative explanation sheds new light on the home-school incompatibility theory of academic failure, and merits consideration.

Ogbu calls attention to the wide variation in the school performance of minority students. His research shows that "immigrant" groups—that is, groups that have migrated to the United States more or less voluntarily—tend to do well in school after being given time to settle in. However, "castelike" minorities, or groups that have become part of this country involuntarily through slavery, conquest, or colonization, experience continued academic failure. In this latter category are Native Americans, Black Americans, Mexican Americans, and Puerto Ricans. The differences between immigrant and castelike minorities observed in school led Ogbu to challenge the theory attributing academic failure to language mismatch between home and school. If the explanation is accurate, it should apply to immigrant and castelike minorities alike, as the languages and cultures of both groups often clash with what is expected in school. Why is it, then, that the home-school disjuncture affects castelike minority students more adversely?

According to Ogbu, the poor school performance of castelike minority students is an adaptive response to a history of limited opportunities in society at large. The racist practices they have encountered have led castelike minorities to believe that academic success will not improve their lot in life. Ogbu argues that given their history of oppression, these individuals distrust society and its institutions, including school. The distrust results in "oppositional behavior," that is, active resistance to the white, middle-class ways of the school for fear of loss of their own identity. Stated more broadly, the linguistic and cultural differences that these students bring to the classroom become identity markers to be maintained rather than obstacles to be overcome. Viewed in this manner, the persistence of "differences" represents a political statement against oppression on the part of castelike minority students.

Ogbu's interpretation of school failure has recently attracted much attention. Research conducted by Gibson (1987), Matute-Bianchi (1986), and Suarez-Orozco (1987) provides empirical support for the theory. In light of the growing evidence, questions are raised about the efficacy of "culturally sensitive solutions" that are limited to styles of teaching and learning. The problem of academic failure is much more complex than differences between the language and culture of home and school. The differences that create difficulties for both teacher and pupils stem from the struggle for power in society. In this conflict, both dominant and dominated groups play significant roles. Dominant groups maintain their position by using power to define what is valued in school and society. Conversely, dominated groups exert their power by actively resisting the oppressive authority of the dominant groups. Solutions to the school problems of minority students require political action.

Politically, teachers can help students raise questions not only about the source of their oppositional behavior, but also about its consequences (Giroux, 1983; Sleeter and Grant, 1988). For example while dropping out of school may be a conscious or unconscious form of resistance to oppressive conditions in society, the behavior itself is probably counterproductive in that it can function to disempower minorities further. This issue ought to be raised with the students in order to help them seek ways of converting their resistance into constructive political activity.

CONCLUSIONS

In this country, a person's standing is usually related to his or her performance in school. "Achievers" are promised access to positions of higher status in society, while "nonachievers" are told that they must be satisfied with the lower status positions. As long as school performs this sorting function in society, it must necessarily produce winners and losers. Success and failure are both ingrained in the current organization of education. Furthermore, the criteria for school success continues to favor middle-class students. Therefore, culturally sensitive remedies to the educational problems of oppressed minority students that ignore this political aspect of schooling are doomed to failure. Worse still, they give the illusion of progress while perpetuating the academic problem, and by extension, the social inequities they mask.

I fear that the community of educators is embracing simple solutions to a complex social problem, only to meet with disappointment after these culturally sensitive remedies undergo a trial period. When this trial period passes, I suspect that we will once again place the onus of failure upon minorities rather than on the institutional structure where it rightly belongs.

REFERENCES

Au, Kathryn H. (1980). Participation structures in a reading lesson with Hawaiian children: Analysis of a culturally appropriate instructional event. *Anthropology and Education Quarterly* 11: 91–115.

Au, Kathryn H., and Mason, Jana M. (1981). Social organizational factors in learning to read: The balance of rights hypothesis. *Reading Research Quarterly* 1: 115–151.

Bauman, Richard, and Sherzer, Joel (eds.) (1974). *Exploration in the Ethnography of Speaking.* London: Cambridge University Press.

Bernstein, Basil (1971). *Class, Codes, and Control.* New York: Schocken Books.

Bourdieu, Pierre (1977). Cultural reproduction and social reproduction. In Jerome Karabel and A. H. Halsey (eds.), *Power and Ideology in Education,* pp. 487–510. New York: Oxford University Press.

Bourdieu, Pierre, and Passeron, Jean-Claude (1977). *Reproduction in Education, Society and Culture.* Beverly Hills: Sage Publication.

Bowles, Samuel, and Gintis, Herbert (1976). *Schooling in Capitalist America.* New York: Basic Books.

Cazden, Courtney (1986). Classroom discourse. In C. Wittrock (ed.), *Handbook of Research and Teaching,* pp. 432–463. New York: Macmillan Publishing Company.

Cazden, Courtney B., John, Vera P., and Hymes, Dell (eds.) (1972). *Functions of Language in the Classroom.* New York: Teachers College Press.

Cohen, R.A. (1969). Conceptual styles, cultural conflict, and nonverbal tests of intelligence. *American Anthropologist* 71: 824–856.

Cole, Michael (1977). Culture, and IQ testing. In P.L. Houts (ed.), *The Myth of Measurability,* pp. 116–123. New York: Hart Publishing Company.

Collins, Randall (1974). Where are educational requirements for employment highest? *Sociology of Education* 47: 429–442.

Erickson, Frederick (1987). Transformation and school success: The politics and culture of educational achievement. *Anthropology and Education Quarterly* 18: 335–356.

Erickson, Frederick, and Mohatt, Gerald (1982). Cultural organization of participation structures in two classrooms of Indian children. In George Spindler (ed.), *Doing the Ethnography of Schooling,* pp. 132–175. New York: Holt, Rinehart and Winston.

Florio, Susan, and Shultz, Jeffrey (1979). Social competence at home and at school. *Theory into Practice* 18: 234–243.

Gay, G., and Abrahams, R. (1973). Does the pot melt, boil, or brew? Black children and white assessment procedures. *Journal of School Psychology* 11: 330–349.

Gay, G., and Abrahams, R.D. (1972). Talking black in the classroom. In R.D. Abrahams and Rudolph Troike (eds.), *Language and Cultural Diversity in Education,* pp. 200–208. Englewood Cliffs, NJ: Prentice-Hall.

Genishi, Celia (1979). Young children communicating in the classroom: Selected research. *Theory Into Practice* 18: 244–250.

Gibson, Margaret A. (1987). The school performance of immigrant minorities: A comparative view. *Anthropology and Education Quarterly* 18: 262–275.

Giroux, Henry A. (1988). *Teachers as Intellectuals.* Granby, MA: Bergin & Garvey Publishers, Inc.

Giroux, Henry A. 1983). Theories of reproduction and resistance in the new sociology of education. *Harvard Educational Review* 53: 257–293.

Gumperz, John J. (1972). The speech community. In P.P. Giglioli (ed.), *Language and Social Context,* pp. 219–231. Middlesex, England: Penguin Education.

Heath, Shirley B. (1983a). *Ways with Words.* Cambridge University Press.

Heath, Shirley B. (1983b). A lot of talk about nothing. *Language Arts* 60: 999–1007.

Heath, Shirley B. (1982). Questioning at home and at school: A comparative study. In George Spindler (ed.), *Doing the Ethnography of Schooling,* pp. 102–131. New York: Holt, Rinehart and Winston.

Houts, P.L. (1977). A conversation with Banesh Hoffmann. In P.L. Houts (ed.), *The Myth of Measurability,* pp. 194–217. New York: Hart Publishing Company.

Hymes, Dell H. (1974). On ways of speaking. In Richard Bauman and Joel Sherzer (eds.), *Explorations in the Ethnography of Speaking,* pp. 433–452. New York: Cambridge University Press.

Jordan, Cathie (1985). Translating culture: From ethnographic information to educational program. *Anthropology and Education Quarterly* 16: 105–123.

Labov, William (1969). The logic of non-standard Negro English. In James E. Alatis (ed.), *Linguistics and the Teaching of Standard English.* Monograph Series on Language and Linguistics, No. 22. Washington, DC: Georgetown University Press.

Levitas, Maurice (1974). *Marxist Perspective in the Sociology of Education.* London: Routledge and Kegan Paul.

Matute-Bianchi, Maria E. (1986). Ethnic identities and patterns of school success and failure among Mexican-descent and Japanese-American students in a California high school: An ethnographic analysis. *American Journal of Education* 95: 233–255.

McDermott, Ray, and Gospodinoff, Kenneth (1981). Social contexts for ethnic borders and school failure. In Henry Trueba, Grace Guthrie, and Kathryn Au (eds.), *Culture and the Bilingual Classroom,* pp. 212–230. New York: Newberry House.

Mercer, J.R. (1973). Implications of current assessment procedures for Mexican American children. *Journal of the Association of Educators* 1: 25–33.

Michaels, Sarah (1981). Sharing time: Children's narrative styles and differential access to literacy. *Language in Society* 10: 30–34.

Ogbu, John U. (197). Variability in minority school performance: A problem in search of an explanation. *Anthropology and Education Quarterly* 18: 312–324.

Ogbu, John U. (1985). Cultural-ecological influence on minority school learning. *Language Arts* 62: 212–219.

Philips, Susan U. (1983). *The Invisible Culture.* New York: Longman.

Piedstrup, Ann (1973). *Black Dialect Interference and Accommodation of Reading Instruction in First Grade* (Monograph No. 4). Berkeley, CA: Language Behavior Research Laboratory.

Ramirez, Manuel, and Castaneda, Amado (1974). *Cultural Democracy, Bicognitive Development, and Education.* New York: Academic Press.

Scarr, S. (1981). Testing minority children: Why, how, and with what effect? In S. Scarr (ed.), *Race, Social Class, and Individual Differences in IQ.* Hillsdale, NJ: Lawrence Erlbaum Associate.

Sleeter, Christine E., and Grant, Carl A. (1988). *Making Choices for Multicultural Education.* Columbus, OH: Merrill Publishing Company.

Suarez-Orozco, Marcelo M. (1987). "Becoming somebody": Central American Immigrants in U.S. inner city schools. *Anthropology and Education Quarterly* 18: 287–299.

Van Ness, Howard (1981). Social control and social organization in an Alaskan Athabaskan classroom: A microethnography of getting "ready" for reading. In Henry Trueba, Grace Guthrie, and Kathryn Au (eds.), *Culture and the Bilingual Classroom,* pp. 120–138. New York: Newbury House.

Improving the School-Home Connection for Poor and Minority Urban Students

CAROL ASCHER

Of all education issues, parent involvement is one of the vaguest and most shifting in its meanings. Parent involvement may easily mean quite different things to different people. It can mean advocacy: parents sitting on councils and committees, participating in the decisions and operation of schools. It can mean parents serving as classroom aides, accompanying a class on an outing, or assisting teachers in a variety of other ways, either as volunteers or for wages. It can also conjure up images of teachers sending home notes to parents, or of parents working on bake sales and other projects that bring schools much needed support. Increasingly, parent involvement means parents initiating learning activities at home to improve their children's performance in school: reading to them, helping them with homework, playing educational games, discussing current events, and so on.

Sometimes, too, parent involvement is used most broadly to include all the ways in which home life socializes children for school. Here, it means the assumed effect, good or bad, of family background on children's achievement. Related to this definition is the finding that, because books, magazines, a corner for study, good nutrition, and other factors conducive to learning are often absent in low-income homes, disadvantaged children generally have more difficulty in school than do those of more advantaged families; and the controversial belief that having a single parent negatively affects achievement.

Contained in all these meanings of parent involvement is a need that both concerned parents and educators have always sensed: for continuity between the

Reprinted from *The Urban Review,* 20:109–123, 1988, by permission of the publisher.

home and the school. Traditionally, both American public schools and middle-class parents have taken this continuity for granted. Just as middle-class parents have trusted that the public schools would educate their children for successful roles in mainstream society, educators have relied on middle-class parents to take an active role in socializing their children for school: to convey to their children the importance of education, to back up teachers by making school attendance, homework, and good grades a priority; and generally to be willing to participate in a wide variety of school activities from signing report cards, observing classes, and chaperoning trips and dances to attending PTA meetings and sitting on school boards. To put it another way, while public schools have assumed the support of these middle-class parents, the parents have taken for granted that the schools will act as extensions of their desires and values in educating their children. Although this mutuality has begun to break down in some urban areas, where middle-class families have run from the declining test scores, increased violence, and the growing preponderance of poor and minority children in the schools, it is likely that most middle-class parents still feel that their values and goals and those of public school staff are congruent, and that there is a continuity between school and home.

In contrast, the fragile links that have long existed between the schools and poor and minority parents have also been made more tenuous by periodic suspicion and misunderstanding on both sides—with school staff often overwhelmed by bouts of futility, and parents equally often filled with resentment. While school administrators and teachers have often seen these parents as failing to provide their children with the intellectual and motivational prerequisites for successful learning, the parents (themselves often undereducated by prevailing standards) have viewed teachers and schools with a mix of awe and anger: for teaching subjects whose importance they do not understand; or, more commonly, for cheating their children of the same quality of education that they believe middle-class children receive. At the same time as poor and minority parents have complained that the schools are not run to benefit their children, and that teachers do not welcome them, educators have lamented that exactly those parents, whose children tend to be lower achievers and who most need extra help to achieve, have tended to be so burdened by their own lives that they are the hardest to reach.

TODAY'S INNER-CITY FAMILY

In the past, when researchers focused on family background, they usually did so in order to point out the relationship between social class and achievement. However, knowledge of the changing urban family can also explain the difficulty of generating active parent involvement, and may enable educators to plan more effectively for increasing this involvement. Although no characterization can include fully the wide range of family types, there are general trends in the urban minority family that will likely make parent involvement increasingly difficult.

As prospects for industrial employment, jobs once held by black men, have declined, the rate of marriage among black men has dropped sharply (Edelman, 1987). Among poor blacks and Hispanics living in poor urban neighborhoods, the proportion of female-head families is higher than among whites in comparable areas: 74% among blacks and 55% among Hispanics, compared with 49% among whites (Nathan, 1986). Of the nation's 4.6 million black families with children, 2.6 million, or over half, are now headed by a single woman—and in some ghetto areas it may be close to 90% ("Today's Native Sons," 1986). The great majority of poor children in these urban neighborhoods live in single-parent, female-headed households; households that, because of low wages and unemployment, have typically become poorer since 1980. In 1985, the after-tax income of the typical female-headed household with children was 39.9% of the income of the typical U.S. household with children (Center on Budget and Policy Priorities, 1987).

Of all areas of society, our cities are now the poorest. As the black middle-class has moved out of the central city ghettos, these areas have become increasingly populated by what is now called the "underclass"—people who are under- or unemployed, and who, given current conditions, have little prospect of improving their lot. Crime, drug addiction, welfare dependency, poor housing and homelessness, and, understandably, bitterness and resentment toward the rest of society are all too common. In these inner-city areas, the daily struggle to survive may at times make it impossible for parents to reach out to an educational institution that cannot provide relief for immediate needs. A welfare client may have the time to come to school, but may not have the emotional or spiritual resources to do so.

Even among those urban families for whom poverty is not a problem, time is nevertheless a luxury, and the opportunity to reach out for school contacts is increasingly limited. The "traditional family," comprised of a stable couple who are biological parents to the children, and where the father has a job and the mother is available in the home for the care of her children, exists in a very small minority of households—one estimate is as low as 7% (Brice Heath and McLaughlin, 1987). Increasingly, families are also comprised of children of more than one relationship. With 64% of all American mothers of school-age children in the work force (Swap, 1987), "latchkey" children are becoming increasingly common, and mothers' and fathers' time increasingly constrained (Bastian et al., 1987). Moreover, it is becoming more and more difficult for schools to remain in touch with those most concerned for any child's care. Now grandparents, stepmothers, custodial mothers, and a variety of paid helpers are all part of the complicated and imperfect patchwork of child care that, to some observers, may at times verge on neglect.

Demographic studies suggest that these trends will accelerate over the next years. More families will be urban and more of these urban families will be minority, poor, and headed by women. This means that there will be more poor and minority children for urban schools to teach and care for, and more overburdened grandparents, stepparents, custodial parents, and single parents to involve in schools and schooling.

THE EFFECT OF PARENT INVOLVEMENT ON LOW-INCOME URBAN CHILDREN

Several serious obstacles stand in the way of saying anything with clarity about the effect of parent involvement, no matter what the economic circumstances of the students. First, researchers are seldom evaluating the same thing in the same way. Studies of parent involvement may be based on questionnaires posed to school principals about whether or not the school involves parents in decision making, offers community-oriented events, holds meetings and workshops for parents to work with teachers, etc. Or parents may be asked about a different set of activities. Still other analyses are based on teachers' reports of parent involvement, and yet another set of possible activities (or some of the same possibilities, but with different meanings) comprises the list. Given these variables, the findings reported here repeat the specific terms used in the research.

A second limitation in discussing the effects of parent involvement stems from the fact that studies of parent involvement have almost uniformly linked the success of various strategies and programs with the achievement of the children as measured by grades and, even more commonly, standardized test scores. This should not be surprising, given the hegemony of achievement tests in evaluating schooling. However, it is likely that most teachers and administrators seek parent involvement as much for the changes in children's citizenship, social values, attitudes, and behaviors, as for their increased achievement. In fact, a few studies have measured far more wide-ranging effects of parent involvement, including effects on children's sense of well-being, and even on the empowerment of parents themselves (Cochran, 1987). A famous exception to the narrow focus on achievement is the complex analysis of the Perry Preschool, a program that included parent involvement among a number of enrichments. The Preschools' graduates, who were studied longitudinally, have shown better school attendance, decreased delinquency, and lower pregnancy rates, among other positive qualities (Berreuta-Clement et al., 1984). However, the effectiveness of parent involvement can obviously not be separated out from the other enrichments the program offered. Nevertheless, while, at best, the meaning of parent involvement shifts from study to study, and at worst is left open to a wide latitude of interpretation, it is generally studied in its narrowest effects: on the academic achievement of those children involved. Thus, while recommending a wider vision of how to evaluate schooling, this review necessarily follows the confines of the research.

A third problem in discussing the involvement of low-income parents is isolating the effect of social class on both this involvement and the achievement of their children. That is, schools serving high socioeconomic families tend to have both high parent participation and high student achievement, while the reverse is true for schools serving low socioeconomic families. Thus findings that do not control for class may well confuse the effects of parental background on achievement with those of parent participation. In fact, research evidence suggests that, somewhat linked to social class, family size and parent education are also related to parent involvement (Revicki, 1981; Dornbusch, 1986).

Fourth, the total body of research on parent participation is relatively small, and the populations studied are demarcated in very different ways (some by grade level or grade bands, others by whole schools, or even by district policies). There are extremely few studies of the involvement of parents of middle and secondary school students. Thus it is nearly impossible to say anything about the possibly different effects of various kinds of parent involvement as children age and move through school.

Finally, it is not clear how strong a value various kinds of parent involvement have in comparison with other types of intervention: compensatory education programs, tutorials, or even school lunch programs, for instance. Parent participation in school meetings or even in learning projects at home may have relatively weak value in comparison with other interventions and family background and socialization.

Fortunately, some studies, using preschool and elementary school populations, either compare a variety of in-school parent participation activities in low- and high-achieving, low-income schools, or isolate the effects of ethnicity and/or socio-economic status in other ways. These generally find that the more parents participate in a sustained way, at every level—in advocacy, decision-making and oversight roles, as fund raisers and boosters, as volunteers and paraprofessionals, and as home tutors—the better for student achievement. That parent involvement is reasonably well-planned, comprehensive, and long-lasting is apparently more important than the form it takes (Gordon, 1978). On the other hand, public relations campaigns, one-way communications devices, and "dog and pony shows" are not effective (Henderson, 1987).

Two syntheses of the research attempt to make some analytical statements about findings for different types of parent involvement. One, by Gordon (1978), finds that most of the research on parents and the home to improve the child's learning has been done on programs at the preschool level, where the evidence for the positive effects is consistent. Although such parent impact programs for school-aged children have not been as thoroughly researched, home visits by teachers appear to be an important aspect of these programs. Gordon finds little research on the effect of direct parent involvement in the school, from volunteering to serving on governance councils. As for a more active parent involvement both in the home and in a range of community affairs, Gordon finds its effect on achievement to be strong and positive: children whose parents are directly involved over a period of years, beginning in preschool, score higher on achievement tests than other children, and the effect seems to be greater on second children than on first children.

Taking a somewhat different approach, Leler (1983) categorizes approximately 65 studies (often of low-income and minority communities) according to whether the parent involvement was largely one-directional from the school to the home, or whether the line of influence was to and from the home and school and included the larger community. Seventy percent of the research on programs in which school-to-home influence predominated showed positive effects on student achievement. Best among these were somewhat structured programs that trained parents to tutor their own children. On the other hand, all of the programs stressing mutual influence had positive results. In fact, "the fuller the participation of parents, the more effective were the results obtained" (Leler, p. 173). Unlike Gordon, who found little research on direct parent involvement in school decision making, Leler finds sufficient research to argue with confidence that the most powerful approaches are those in which parents have a definite role in decision making.

In fact, not all researchers focusing on parents' role in decision making arrive at Leler's enthusiastic conclusion. Rather, there are significant disagreements on the effectiveness of this politically volatile type of involvement for enhancing student achievement. For example, in a study of low-income minority sixth graders, efforts to involve parents and the community played an important role in increasing achievement in the black community, but not in the Mexican-American neighborhoods studied (Armor et al., 1976). The researchers speculate that this may be partly because of differences in the content of the schools' outreach, and partly because of language barriers in the Hispanic communities. Another study, this time of second and third graders, indicates the importance of parents' *perceptions* of being involved in decision making, though the authors claim only its indirect effects on student achievement. Participation (it is not clear in what) made parents feel more positive both about their influence on school decision making and about the quality of their relations with teachers; it also made teachers feel more positively about their relationships with parents, and this general satisfaction directly influenced students' achievement (Herman and Yeh, 1983). Finally, a survey of 135 Midwestern elementary principals showed that schools with higher achievement were more open to parent and community involvement, while more "closed" schools had lower achievement levels and community support. However, not all types of involvement made a difference: while community support, fund raising, and attendance at school meetings were all highly correlated with achievement, citizen participation in policy decision making was not related to achievement (Wagenaar, 1977).

Less controversial than parent involvement in decision making, both politically and in terms of its effects on achievement, is the effect of parent participation through meeting formally with teachers and attending open school nights. In fact, the few studies of high school students and their parents focus on this type of activity; they show that such middle-range participation in school-based activities is, indeed, effective in raising student achievement (Dornbusch, 1986; McDill, Rigsby, and Meyers, 1969).

MAKING THE INVOLVEMENT OF LOW-INCOME PARENTS EASIER

Given the many problems urban parents face daily, as well as the increasing pressure on teachers' and administrators' time, several questions concerning the school's expectations for parent involvement must be considered. In what ways can single or working parents be expected to participate? What responsibility do schools have to engage parents who may be particularly busy, whose households may be chaotic, or who, for other reasons, are more difficult to reach? What should be done for the increasing number of parents whose native language is not English, and whose cultural background may remove them from the goals and workings of the school?

Whatever their potential for becoming involved, research indicates that single and working parents may be discriminated against by school personnel, who tend to decide in advance that these parents cannot be approached or relied on (Epstein, 1984a). While concern does not necessarily lead to action, a recent survey showed that single working parents as well as dual working parent families are especially likely to want more contact and consultation with teachers. Although teachers see these parents as hard to reach, the parents themselves are often equally dissatisfied about any loss of contact (The Metropolitan Life Survey, 1987).

In both dual working parent and single working parent families, parents' involvement in school activities is usually related to the flexibility of leave policies on the job. Unfortunately, most employers are still rigid about the time and hours they demand of their workers. However, one research project found that employers can be encouraged to allow flextime for working parents, as well as to extend short leaves beyond emergencies, so that parents can observe their children in the classroom or attend meetings (Espinosa et al., 1985). Where a corporation employs a large number of parents, times can actually be arranged with the employer for parent-teacher conferences and school meetings. It is important to point out to companies that increased employer-school collaboration humanizes the work place and increases productivity along with employee morale, at the same time as the organization is making clear its commitment to the next generation of workers.

The increasing number of parents whose native language is not English raises additional problems for schools trying to generate parent involvement. Recently, several studies have been conducted on involving Asian/Pacific American parents, including new refugees from Southeast Asia. Not only is language a barrier, making communication between parents and school personnel difficult, but few Asians parents initially want to participate in the American educational system. For Asians, the concept of citizen participation is alien; instead, Asians tend to believe that schools have the expertise and right to make all decisions. Because these parents come from poorer countries where shortages in educational resources far exceed those in American schools, "few parents can see that the American schools are not equally equipped and staffed, and that children are not treated equally according to their cultural, linguistic, and socioeconomic backgrounds" (Tran, 1982, p. 18).

Obviously, some families are too burdened by personal troubles or the struggle for survival to be easily reachable, and schools may be justified in considering the time and resources necessary too great. However, these few families should not be used as an excuse to give up on all outreach efforts. There is a substantial urban working class whose connection with the schools can be strengthened with a little extra effort. Although schools can become overwhelmed by the tasks that are clearly inside their own doors, they should not give up trying to coordinate parent involvement efforts. A variety of methods have been tried around the country to generate better communication between schools and single and working parents. These offer a number of directions in which schools can choose to move (Rich, 1985):

1. Increasing the awareness and sensitivity of the school staff to parents' real time constraints, and announcing meetings and other events long enough in advance for parents to arrange for time off from work if necessary;

2. Creating a more accepting environment for working and single parents, as well as those undergoing separation, divorce, or remarriage, or acting as a custodial parent;

3. Creating evening meetings, with child care, so that parents can talk to teachers and counselors;

4. Allowing open enrollment so that children can attend school near their parents' places of work;

5. Providing before-school and after-school care, as well as some supervision for older children;

6. Being more careful about cancelling school at the last minute due to weather conditions, thus leaving single and working parents with no resources for the care of their children;

7. Acting as a facilitator for teen-, single-, working-, and custodial-parent peer support groups;

8. Providing both legal and custodial parents with regular information on what is going on in the child's classroom, as well as the help they may need to help.

PARENT INVOLVEMENT IN HOME LEARNING AND THE ACHIEVEMENT OF LOW-INCOME STUDENTS

According to the current wisdom, when parents' time is limited, becoming involved in home learning is one of the most efficient uses of their time (Walberg, 1984a). "What parents do to help their children learn is more important to academic success than how well-off the family is" (U.S. Dept. Of Ed., 1986, p. 7) epitomizes this point of view. And Walberg (1984, May) argues that homework, when it is graded or commented upon by the teacher, has three times the effect of socioeconomic status (SES). Although a number of studies support the effectiveness of home learning, for some, the effects of social class may be so great that not even parent involvement in various educational experiences at home can substantially change their children's school achievement. These are the findings of a study of the effects of parents' use of time in different SES groups (Benson, 1979; Benson, Buckley, and Medrick, 1980). In the high SES group, the children did well in school regardless of their parents' attention, although cultural and family group activities helped them to do better. In the middle SES group, family activities, parent control, and parent involvement made a substantial difference in student achievement. In the low SES group, however, parent time and activities were not related to achievement, although family activities, parent control, and helping with homework counted a little. The authors speculate that class, neighborhood, and social environments are strong counterweights to individual family influence: low SES children, even those with strong, positive families, must surmount many negative influences around the home and the school.

Only one study has tried to compare directly school-based parent involvement with home-based parent involvement among low-income families. In this study, programs offering home visits were more successful in involving disadvantaged parents than were programs requiring parents to visit the school, although programs requiring visits produced greater reading gains. The author speculates that this discrepancy is caused by bias: teachers favor parents who are willing to come to school, and those who do come are more self-confident and committed to the program. A cycle of positive reinforcement thus leads to gains for those children whose parents come to school and shuts out parents who are afraid or unable to do so. Thus, according to the author, the normal operation of home-school relations, which asks that parents come to school, may actually increase the tendency of teachers to favor parents who are already involved (Toomey, 1986).

According to another study, single and working parents often *can* and *do* spend as much time helping their children as do parents with more leisure (Epstein, 1984a). At times, it is the teachers who hesitate to give these children work to take home, wrongly fearing that the parents will not be available to help. However, Epstein found that when teachers reached out to parents, these parents were generally more than willing to help. More impressive is Epstein's finding that, when teachers *help parents to help their children,* these parents can be as effective with their children as those parents with more education and leisure whom teachers expect to help their children (Epstein, 1984b).

Recent research on methods to increase parent involvement in home learning can be viewed as divided according to the amount of mutuality worked for between the home and school. For instance, some researchers, while paying lip service to mutuality, would work to reform what goes on in the low-income or minority home in order to create learning situations that are more consistent with school learning. Walberg speaks of "the alterable curriculum of the home" and argues for cooperative efforts by parents and educators to "modify these alterable academic conditions" (1984b, p. 25). The Committee for Economic Development notes that good programs "should teach parents how to provide a home environment that encourages learning" (1987, p. 42).

Others focus more on what can be done to increase teachers' understanding of the "natural" learning that goes on in any low-income home, or even to help these families help each other (Brice Heath, 1983; Cochran, 1987). As Brice Heath's work makes clear, *all* families participate in extensive literacy practices at home. She argues that, just as parents can be helped in their parenting functions, teachers' effectiveness can be enhanced by learning from parents how they teach. This can help make teachers' instructional styles more harmonious with those the children have grown up with (Brice Heath, 1983; Lareau and Benson, 1984). Cochran, for example, suggests that home visits allow teachers to see what activities are already being carried out and enable them to write up summaries of useful parent activities so that parents can learn from other parents (ibid). Summarizing the evidence from a number of studies, Cole and Griffin note that the "school-to-home pathway . . . is more likely to be effective if the two-way nature of the path is explicitly recognized by educators" (1987, p. 78).

CONVINCING PARENTS TO BECOME INVOLVED

Virtually all parents want to help their children, but, for a variety of reasons, many who are not already involved feel helpless to do so. A number of schools have found ways of letting parents know that there are simple, time-efficient ways to help their children (Rich, 1985). These include:

- Bilingual media campaigns on the important role of the home in educating children;
- Stress by ministers and other respected leaders of the importance of this route;
- Family learning centers in schools, store fronts and churches that offer help (that is bilingual, when necessary) to parents wanting to help their children learn;
- Bilingual hot-lines for parents who need help in helping their children with their homework;
- Learning activities created by the schools that parents can use at home with their children.

Although schools may choose different ways to help parents enhance their children's learning, it is important to keep in mind that the greater the continuity and contact between the school and the home, the better it is for the child's learning. Moreover, the mutuality of that contact appears to be an important key to its success.

CREATING OTHER SCHOOL PARTNERSHIPS

Despite a nearly universal current acceptance of the importance of involving parents in some aspects of schooling, urban educators often point out that many parents can no longer perform the traditional home-care functions the schools once expected of them. Thus a question as important as what kinds of parent involvement schools should ask for has become: Should schools compensate for and assume the socialization and caretaking roles of the absent family and torn community? As Coleman (1987) notes, the historic division of labor between the family and the school no longer pertains, largely because even the middle-class family has given up many of its traditional roles. But, as urban educators are only too aware, their agendas are already overburdened. Should schools, then, be the institution to provide what many families cannot offer, or should other urban institutions join in helping families assume their traditional responsibilities?

To provide a framework for viewing the current discussion about the changing responsibilities of home and schools, Coleman and Hoffer note that American schools have always fluctuated between acting as extensions of the family and emancipators of individuals from the family. "Schools complement the family and the immediate community as agents of socialization, which means as the role and functioning of the family changes in modern society, different problems are posed for the school. It means also that the role and functioning of the school must change if it is to constitute an effective complement to the changing institutions of the family and the community" (1987, p. 27). However, because schools have traditionally provided the kind of learning that Coleman loosely characterizes as "opportunities and demands," while relegating what he calls "attitudes and effort" to the family, he argues that schools, no matter what their quality, are more effective for children from strong family backgrounds than for children from weak ones. According to Coleman, when families are weak (and the human capital from the family is scarce), schools are more effective if they can draw on the *social capital* of the surrounding community, that is, on a network of people and a community of shared values that most often goes along with religiously homogeneous schools (but not necessarily independent private schools) (Coleman and Hoffer, 1987; Coleman, 1987).

Although Coleman and Hoffer suggest policy changes that might make it easier for public schools to draw on the resources of churches and religious institutions, their framework is based largely on the traditional notion of "complementarity" between the home and the school. This model of complementarity has recently been rejected by many educational thinkers, who argue that both the school and the family have become too frail for the enormous tasks at hand. Instead, they suggest an expanded vision of those who should be called on to participate in the task of educating our nation's students. The Committee for Economic Development, for example, urges the combined efforts of many institutions: public schools, businesses, foundations, community agencies, and every level of government. The CED advocates a particularly strong role for business, both as a pacesetter in educational change and an advocate in support of educational programming and funding (1987). This view of the school working in tandem, or "as partners," with other urban institutions is increasingly expressed by urban superintendents. The Urban Superintendents' Network has recently argued that, "To intervene in the vicious cycle of failure for many urban and minority youth, schools need to join with community institutions and agencies," and the group suggests joint school and business connections as a major strategy (Ascher and Flaxman, 1987, pp. 11).

Pointing out that "only 7 percent of families could be described as the 'typical family' . . . of the mid 1960s," Brice Heath and McLaughlin argue that the old role of the school as the "deliverer" of educational services no longer can pertain. They speak of "moving beyond the dependence on school and family" and call for a new view of the school as a "broker" of the multiple services that can be used to achieve the functions previously filled by families or by families and schools acting together (1987, p. 579).

CONCLUSIONS

The resurgence of interest in parent involvement in education has numerous social and educational sources. Most obviously, this new interest has come at a time when the schools are under serious criticism, particularly for failing to educate low-income and minority school children; and the traditional two-parent family, where one parent works and the other cares for the children, has all but disappeared among the urban and minority poor. Thus the resources of both schools and families are stretched, and each is overwhelmed by its traditional tasks.

While parent involvement once conjured images of parents sitting on advisory councils and participating in a range of school activities, for most educators and researchers, the meaning of parent involvement in this new era has shifted from the affairs of the school to the home site. The term parent involvement now is largely used to suggest parents' efforts to socialize their children at home both in informal and in school-directed learning tasks. One might say that the aim of educators is now to increase school effectiveness by improving the assistance they receive from parents at home. As with research on parent participation in school-based activities, the research on parent involvement in home-based learning shows generally positive effects on students' achievement—though nothing so dramatic as to suggest a revolution in the educational process. It should be said, however, that measuring the effectiveness of parent involvement either at home or in the school by student achievement outcomes is extremely narrow: parent involvement may have much wider effects, such as on student citizenship and social values.

The issue of the fragile connection between low-income minority parents and the schools is a serious one. Efforts are needed to make it more smooth and secure, and to decrease parents' alienation. For however parent involvement is found to directly and indirectly effect student achievement, it is also clear that, for the schools' sake, schools cannot proceed in a vacuum, without parental support. However, although the problem for schools in the next period will be to give some priority to parent involvement efforts, educators should not demand more from this strategy than it can deliver. Nothing would be gained in subjecting parents to another round of blame when home-learning does not yield hope for improvements.

As some analysts suggest, the home and the school may no longer be a sufficient unit: wider collaborative arrangements may be necessary. What these will be is not yet clear. When problems are serious and change is rapid, as is the case in the education of low-income and minority students, there can be ultimately no simple analysis or strategy for change. Yet one thing is clear: whichever institutions join in the schooling endeavor, parents must be retained as an active participant in the partnership.

REFERENCES

Armor, D., Conny-Osegura, P., Cox, M., King, N., McDonnell, L., Pascal, A., Pauly, E., and Zellman, G. (1976). Analysis of the school preferred reading program in selected Los Angeles minority schools. Santa Monica, CA: The Rand Corporation. ED 130–243.

Ascher, C., and Flaxman, E. (1987). Lowering the dropout rate: The experience of urban superintendents. Prepared for the OERI Urban Superintendents Network. New York: ERIC Clearinghouse on Urban Education, Teachers College, Columbia University. March. ED 286 966.

Bastian, A., Fruchter, N., Gittell, M., Green, C., and Haskins, K. (1987). *Choosing Equality.* Philadelphia: Temple University Press.

Benson, C.S. (1979). Household production of human capital: Time uses of parents and children as inputs. Paper prepared for a National Symposium on Efficacy and Equity in Educational Finance, University of Illinois, May.

Benson, C.S., Buckley, S., and Medrick, E.A. (1980). Families as educators: Time use contributions to school achievement. In J. Guthrie (ed.), *School Finance Policy in the 1980s: A Decade of Conflict.* Cambridge, MA: Ballinger.

Berreuta-Clement, J.R., Schweinhart, L.J., Barnett, W.S., Epstein, A.S., and Weikart, D.P. (1984). Changed lives: The effects of the Perry Preschool Program on youths through age 19. Ypsilanti, MI: High/Scope Educational Research Foundation, Number eight.

Brice Heath, S., and McLaughlin, M. (1987). A child resource policy: Moving beyond dependence on school and family. *Phi Delta Kappan* (April), 579.

Brice Heath, S. (1983). *Way with Words.* New York: Cambridge University Press.

Center on Budget and Policy Priorities (1987). After-tax income of female-headed households lower in 1985 than in 1980, as gap widens between rich and poor Americans. Washington, D.C. July.

Cochran, M. (1987). The parental empowerment process: Building on family strengths. *Equity and Choice* 4(1): 9–24.

Cole, M., and Griffin, P., eds. (1987). Contextual factors in education: Improving science and mathematics education for minorities and women. Madison, WI: Committee on Research on Mathematics, Science, and Technology Education, Wisconsin Center for Educational Research.

Coleman, J.S. (1987). Families and schools. Paper presented at the 1987 Annual Meeting of the American Educational Research Association, Washington, D.C. April.

Coleman, J.S., and Hoffer, T. (1987). *Public and Private High Schools: The Impact of Communities.* New York: Basic Books.

Committee for Economic Development, Research and Policy Committee (1987). Children in need: Investment strategies for the educationally disadvantaged. New York.

Dornbusch, S. (1986). Helping your kid make the grade. *The Stanford Magazine* (summer). Palo Alto, CA.

Edelman, M.W. (1987). *Children's Time.* Washington, D.C.: Children's Defense Fund.

Epstein, J. (1984a). Single parents and the schools: The effect of marital status on parent and teacher evaluations. Baltimore: The Johns Hopkins University, Center for Social Organization of Schools, March.

Epstein, J. (1984b). Effects of teacher practices of parental involvement on change in student achievement in reading and math. Paper presented at the 1984 Annual Meeting of the American Educational Research Association, April. ED 256–863.

Espinosa, R., et al. (1985). Working parents project. Final report (December 1, 1984–November 30, 1985). Austin, TX: Southwest Educational Development Lab. ED 266–871.

Gordon, I. (1978). What does research say about the effects of parent involvement on schooling? Paper presented at the Annual Meeting of the Association for Supervision and Curriculum Development.

Grau, M.E., Weinstein, T., and Walberg, H.J. (1983). School-based home instruction and learning: A quantitative synthesis. *Journal of Educational Research* 76: 351–360.

Henderson, A.T. (1987). The evidence continues to grow: Parent involvement improves student achievement. Columbia, MD: National Committee for Citizens in Education.

Herman, J.L., and Yeh, J.P. (1983). Some effects of parent involvement in schools. *The Urban Review* 15(1): 11–17.

Lareau, A., & Benson, C. (1984). The economics of home/school relationships: A cautionary note. *Phi Delta Kappan* 65(6): 401–404.

Leler, H. (1983). Parent education and involvement in relation to the schools and to parents of school-aged children. In R. Haskins and D. Adamson (eds.), *Parent education and Public Policy.* Norwood, N.J.: Ablex.

McDill, E.L., Rigsby, L., and Meyers, E. (1969). Educational climates of high schools: Their effects and sources. Baltimore: Johns Hopkins University Center for the Study of Social Organization of Schools. April. ED 030–205.

The Metropolitan Life Survey (1987). The American teacher, 1987: Strengthening links between home and school. New York: Louis Harris and Associates, Inc.

Nathan, R.P. (1986). The concentration of poor people in poverty areas in the nation's 100 largest cities. New York: New School for Social Research.

Revicki, E.A. (1981). The relationship among socioeconomic status, home environment, parent involvement, child self-concept, and child achievement. ED 206–645.

Rich, D. (1985). The forgotten factor in school success: The family—A policymaker's guide. Washington, D.C.: The Home and School Institute.

Swap, M.S. (1987). *Enhancing Parent Involvement in Schools.* New York: Teachers College Press.

Today's native sons: Inner-city black males are America's newest lost generation. (1986). *Time Magazine,* Dec. 1, 26–32.

Toomey, D. (1986). Home-school relations and inequality in education. School of Education, La Trobe University, Melbourne, Australia. Address given to a Conference on Education and the Family, Brigham Young University.

Tran, X.C. (1982). The factors hindering Indochinese parent participation in school activities. San Diego, CA: San Diego State University, Institute for Cultural Pluralism. ED 245–018.

U.S. Department of Education (1986). What works: Research about teaching and learning. Washington, D.C.: Office of Educational Research and Improvement, U.S. Department of Education.

Wagenaar, T.C. (1977). School achievement level vis-a-vis community involvement and support: An empirical assessment. Columbus, OH: Ohio State University, Hershon Center. Paper presented at the 1987 Annual Meeting of the American Sociological Association, Chicago, September. ED 146–111.

Walberg, H.J. (1984a, February). Families as partners in educational productivity. *Phi Delta Kappan* 65(6): 397–400.

Walberg, H.J. (1984b). Improving the productivity of America's schools. *Educational Leadership* (May), 19–27.

Transformation and School Success: The Politics and Culture of Educational Achievement

FREDERICK ERICKSON

There are numerous explanations for the generally low school achievement of minority students and working-class students in schools in the United States and other developed societies. A common explanation has been that of genetic deficit—poor children of color or of minority cultural or language background have been seen as inherently inferior, intellectually and morally, to the children of the middle class. In the 1960's, among professional educators, cultural deficit explanations began to replace the genetic deficit explanation. Nurture replaced nature as the main reason for school failure. Minority children, it was argued, did not achieve because they did not experience a cognitively stimulating environment (Bereiter and Engelmann 1966; Deutsch et al. 1967; Hess and Shipman 1965). Their language and lifestyle were intellectually impoverished. They were "culturally deprived" or "socially disadvantaged."

As the anthropology of education became a distinct field in the mid-1960s, its members were generally appalled by the ethnocentrism of the cultural deficit explanation. It was not literally racist, in the sense of a genetic deficit explanation. Yet it seemed culturally biased. The poor were still being characterized invidiously as not only deprived but depraved. The cultural deficit explanation seemed especially reprehensible to many because its ethnocentrism was cloaked in the legitimacy of social science. Various critiques were presented (e.g., Baratz and Baratz 1970; Valentine 1968). These did not receive much attention within the community of professional educators; perhaps because the cultural deficit explanation was so

Reproduced by permission of the American Anthropological Association from *Anthropology & Education Quarterly* 18:4, December 1987. Not for sale or further reproduction.

attractive it enabled educators, frustrated by their difficulties in working with minority children, to place the responsibility for school failure outside the school.

In the late 1960s, sociolinguistically oriented anthropologists identified a factor inside the school as playing an important role in the low school achievement and morale of minority students. This was the factor of cultural difference in communication style between teachers and their students. This was a culturally relativist position. It blamed neither the children of the poor nor the school staff. Rather, it provided a way of seeing classroom troubles as inadvertent misunderstanding—teachers and students playing into each other's cultural blind spots.

In the middle 1970s the sociolinguistic position began to be criticized strongly by Ogbu (1978a, 1982). He identified a cause of school failure outside the school itself. Inequity in access to employment, he argued, had over many generations made minority people cynical about their life chances in American society. They communicated this cynicism to their children, and that accounted for the children's school failure.

In this article I will review the sociolinguistically oriented position and that of Ogbu. I will characterize the sociolinguistic position as a "communication process explanation" and Ogbu's position as a "perceived labor market explanation." I will then discuss both explanations in terms of a more comprehensive frame of reference, within which the two lines of explanation can be seen to be complementary in some ways although contradictory in others. I will also consider the nature of school failure and success. *School failure* in this discussion is used in two senses. It refers to the reflexive ways in which schools "work at" failing their students and students "work at" failing to achieve in school. School success is used in a similarly reflexive sense, as something the school does as well as what the student does. I will conclude by arguing that, whatever the reasons for school failure may be in schools, it is necessary for educators to transform routine practice and symbol systems in their own school settings as well as to work for change in the larger society. Changing society is a big order, and changing school societies is also a big order, in that it involves reorienting the daily struggles of doing school from collective work at failure toward collective work at success.

THESIS: THE COMMUNICATION PROCESS EXPLANATION

This position emphasizes the role of culturally learned verbal and nonverbal communication styles in explaining the high rates of school failure by students of low socioeconomic status and minority ethnic and cultural background. The argument is that, especially in the early grades, when teachers and students differ in implicit expectations of appropriateness in behavior, they act in ways that misinterprets. Their expectations are derived from their experience outside school in what sociolinguists have called *speech communities* (Gumperz 1972) or, more recently, *speech networks*. The networks are sets of people who associate closely and who come to share similar assumptions about the appropriate uses and styles of communication. Culturally distinctive *ways of speaking* (Hymes 1974) differ from one speech network to the next. Boundaries between networks tend to run along the lines of major social divisions in modern mass societies, such as class, race or ethnicity, and first language background. Thus while many people in the United States belong to the same language community (i.e., they know the sound system, grammar, and vocabulary of English), they are members of differing speech networks (i.e., they have differing assumptions about ways of communicating that show functional intentions such as irony, sincerity, approval and positive concern, rapt attention, disinterest, disapproval, and the like). In addition, other subtle cultural differences obtain across networks—differences in assumptions regarding how much emotion should be displayed or felt, how social control should be exercised. There are differences in preferred room arrangements, body ornaments, and clothing styles. However, since it is the verbal and nonverbal aspects of interactional style that have been most intensively studied in recent sociolinguistically oriented educational anthropology, it is these differences that are mainly addressed here.

Cultural differences in ways of speaking and listening between the child's speech network and the teacher's speech network, according to the communication process explanation, lead to systematic and recurrent miscommunication in the classroom (Hymes 1972; xix–xxv). For example, if a child comes from a speech network in which direct questions are avoided because they are regarded as intrusive, when a teacher routinely asks that child a direct question in the classroom the child may be puzzled by the teacher's strange behavior, and assume the teacher is angry. If the teacher comes from a speech network in which it is expected that listeners will show attention by direct eye contact while listening, and a child comes from a speech network in which it is considered impolite to look directly at a speaker, the teacher may infer that the child who is listening with averted eyes may be bored, confused, or angry.

To the extent that either party in these routine interactional engagements reflects on the situation, cultural explanations for what is happening do not occur to them. The teacher tends to use clinical labels and to attribute internal traits to students (e.g., "unmotivated") rather than seeing what is happening in terms of invisible cultural differences. Nor does the teacher see student behavior as interactionally generated—a dialectical relation in which the teacher is inadvertently coproducing with students the very behavior that he or she is taking as evidence of an individual characteristic of the student. Given the power difference between teacher and student, what could be seen as an interactional phenomenon to which teacher and student both contribute ends up institutionalized as an official diagnosis of student deficiency (Mehan 1978, 1980, 1987).

There is considerable empirical support for the communication process explanation. Numerous studies have documented interactional difficulty in elementary classrooms that is related to cultural differences in communication style (e.g., Barnhardt 1982, Erickson and Mohatt 1982, and Philips 1982, reporting studies of Native Americans in Alaska, Northern Ontario, and Oregon; and Heath 1983,

Michaels and Collins 1984 and Piestrup 1973, reporting studies of urban and rural black Americans). In addition, Barnhardt and Heath, among others, have gone beyond documenting the existence of trouble that is related to cultural difference. They have also claimed that culturally responsive pedagogy resulted in higher school achievement and morale than was typical of Native American and black students in most schools. It should be emphasized, however, that the relationship between cultural difference in communication and actual school achievement is not clear, since most of the research that has been done on cultural differences in communication style between home and school was not designed to test directly a cause and effect relationship with school achievement. (Indeed, many ethnographers would argue that such inference is not possible in social science.)

One set of studies (Au and Mason 1981) comes as close as one can get toward demonstrating a causal connection between the cultural communication patterns of classroom discourse and academic achievement. This work was part of the research and development effort at the Kamehameha Early Education Project in Hawaii (see the discussion in Jordan 1985). In controlled experiments, two culturally differing ways of teaching reading were done with native Hawaiian first graders. In one way of teaching, the students followed mainstream Anglo patterns for the conduct of turn-taking while discussing reading stories. Those patterns required that only one child speak at a time. The other way of teaching was to allow students to overlap in speaking while others were speaking. This allowed students to comment and build on each other's comments. Overlapping talk of this kind was characteristic of certain kinds of speech situations that were common in students' experience in family and community life, especially in a named speech event, "talk-story." The way of teaching that incorporated talk-storylike ways of speaking can be called a culturally responsive pedagogy because it accommodated to community cultural norms for conversation.

When conversation in reading lessons was organized in a talk-storylike way the students' participation was manifestly more enthusiastic than it was when overlapping turns at speaking were prohibited. Moreover, the students' understanding of the reading texts, as measured by tests given immediately after each lesson, was markedly greater when the talk-storylike conversational format was used by the teachers.

Why might so seemingly simple an adaptation as altering the structure of conversational turn-taking in a lesson enhance the school achievement of minority students? One line of explanation comes from anthropology—the cultural adaptation may reduce culture shock in the classroom, enabling students to feel conversationally competent in familiar ways in an otherwise unfamiliar setting. In addition, the school's acceptance of ways of acting that the children employ in a mode of interaction that is positively regarded in their community may, even for young children, be perceived by them at some level as a symbolic affirmation of themselves and their community by the school. There may be a chance to feel a bit at home, to feel you know what you are doing, that what others do makes sense. You can feel that there is some safety in this new world, and that the teacher likes you.

Another line of explanation comes from cognitive psychology and cognitively oriented theories of reading instruction. By using a familiar conversational organization to approach the practice of unfamiliar concepts and skills (those of reading a text) the overall cognitive task structure is made simpler than it would be if both the social organizational aspects of the task and the academic subject matter organizational aspects of the task were unfamiliar. Thus students are able to concentrate mental effort on the reading rather than on the reading and the talking simultaneously. Moreover, the nature of talk-storylike conversation, in which conversational partners repeat and amplify each other's ideas, makes for a conversational environment appropriate for the kind of reading that was being asked of the children—"comprehension" of full sentences and of even larger discourse units in the written text, as contrasted to "decoding" of smaller text units, such as letter/sound combinations, morphemes, and words. When students talk overlappingly about the sense of the story, echoing each other and adding ideas in a conversational "Dagwood sandwich" of many layers, they may, by the very repetition and overlapping in their talk, provide mutually constructed cognitive scaffolding for each other. This form of conversation may make it easier for students to grasp the idea of the story than if those ideas were strung out one by one, in more linear fashion, with less repetition.

In sum, the communication process explanation seems reasonable. It is warranted by theory in anthropology and psychology and empirical evidence. Let us now turn to what has been presented as a competing explanation for school failure and success.

ANTITHESIS: THE PERCEIVED LABOR MARKET EXPLANATION

This position, as articulated by its chief proponent, John Ogbu (1974, 1978a, 1982, 1987b), argues that the main reason for the low school achievement of many minority students in the United States is that those students (and their parents and peers) are convinced that school success will not help them break out of a cycle of poverty that they attribute to racism that is endemic in American society. Such minority students are members of what Ogbu calls "castelike" minority groups (e.g., blacks, Chicanos, Puerto Ricans) who have resided for generations in the United States in situations of oppression. Such groups are distinguished from immigrant minority groups who have not yet experienced oppression across many generations (e.g., Punjabis, Southeast Asians). In the castelike minority group, according to Ogbu, members share a fatalistic perspective—there will never be jobs (because of racism), so why try hard to succeed at school? Ogbu sees the members of immigrant minority groups as much more optimistic about their life chances in American society. Things may be bad here, but not as bad as in the old country. Immigrant minority people in the United States may still be committed to their ethnic heritage yet also see the United States in a basically positive light. Since conditions in the United States are better than the extremely negative conditions they left when departing their home countries, the immigrants experience America, despite its flaws, as being a land of opportunity for them. Consequently, immigrant minority students and their parents believe that effort devoted to school success is likely to pay off in future employment. Students persist in their school work, encouraged in this by their parents, and this persistence accounts for their school success.

The labor market explanation has much to recommend it. First, there appears to be empirical support for it. In cross-cultural demographic and school achievement data (Ogbu 1978b), it appears that domestic minority students fare less well in school than do immigrant minority students. Indeed, immigrant minority students who come from groups that were in the position of being a domestic minority group in their country of origin in some cases seem to have done better in school in the United States than did comparable students from that ethnic group in the home country.

There seems also to be evidence that goes beyond that of formal research. The recent dramatic success in American schools of many students who were refugees from Southeast Asia is being mentioned in the press and in political debate as evidence that culturally differing students whose first language is not English can succeed in school without the special assistance of bilingual or multicultural education programs. Asian-American students represent an ever-increasing proportion of the graduate student population in American universities. This is also pointed to as evidence that cultural difference is not necessarily a barrier to school success.

Ogbu's demographic evidence appears to be borne out in ethnographic case studies of immigrant minority groups. For example, a study of Punjabi immigrants in a California town (Gibson 1987b, this volume) reports that despite linguistic and cultural differences between home and school and despite overt stigmatizing of Punjabi students in high school, those students showed higher graduation rates and academic performance than did domestic minority students within the same school system. Analogous case studies have been conducted in other immigrant ethnic communities.

The labor market explanation can also be justified because of its theoretical force. It is comprehensive in scope, linking phenomena across diverse levels of social organization. Ogbu's analysis shows how labor market conditions can be related to the local decisions of individuals in everyday life, as mediated by socially shared perceptions derived from experience as members of a social group that is either a domestic or an immigrant minority ethnic community. The explanation connects individual thought and action with the situation of individuals at the local school and community level and in the wider society and political economy.

In sum, on both theoretical and empirical grounds, it would seem that the perceived labor market explanation for school failure had much to recommend it. Yet so does the communication process explanation. The two positions are not mutually exclusive. Ogbu has repeatedly claimed that they are, however, arguing that the labor market explanation is the far more powerful factor (Ogbu 1982). He has distinguished between primary and secondary cultural differences—those characterizing domestic and immigrant minority groups, respectively. Using this distinction, he has argued that the cultural differences between speech networks in a mass society are so slight as to be trivial (Ogbu 1982, 1987b:276). This seems too extreme a claim. It is necessary to reexamine the two positions in relation to each other.

SYNTHESIS: THE POLITICS AND CULTURE OF SCHOOL FAILURE AND SUCCESS

One way to reconcile the two positions is to consider school motivation and achievement as a political process in which issues of institutional and personal legitimacy, identity, and economic interest are central. To do this we must also consider as well the nature of the symbolic discourse through which issues of legitimacy, identity, and interest are apprehended and framed by individual students and teachers in local communities and schools. Social theory as related to pedagogical theory—more especially, implications of resistance theory—provides a framework within which the alternative explanations can be reconsidered (see Giroux 1983; see also Apple and Weis 1983; Everhart 1983). I will begin the synthesis with a negative critique of the two positions as originally stated. Within that critique some facets of resistance theory will be mentioned. These will be elaborated later in the discussion.

Both the communication process explanation and the labor market explanation have some inadequacies. The first type of inadequacy involves accounting for certain kinds of school success. The kinds of school success that go unaccounted for differ for the two explanations. First I will consider the communication process explanation. That explanation can account for the success of strategies for teaching castelike minority students that involve culturally responsive pedagogy. But some teaching strategies have been successful that do not involve culturally responsive pedagogy—at least the strategies do not involve use of communication styles found in children's homes.

We can find instances of teaching domestic minority students (Obgu's "castelike" minority students) in which teachers go to great lengths not to have classroom interaction resemble interaction patterns found in the students' homes and communities. One thinks immediately of Black Muslim schools, of Roman Catholic parochial schools with white teachers, of special nonsectarian schools such as that of Marva Collins in Chicago (in which a curriculum is built on classic literature of Western Europe), and of special programs designed for minority populations, such as the intense drill and practice sessions conducted according to predetermined scripts in the DISTAR model for early grades education. One thinks as well of the countless cases of individual teachers who are unusually effective with domestic minority students but who know very little about the students' home cultural communication patterns and who do not teach by making use of those patterns instructionally. There are the cases, already discussed, of immigrant minority students who achieve in school without special bilingual instruction or culturally responsive pedagogy. These are very different kinds of instances. At some level, however, each does "work," in that students rise to the challenge, put forth effort, and appear to be doing well academically, in terms of achievement as measured by standardized test scores. (That such measurements can be criticized as too narrow and too literal a way of defining achievement is an issue beyond the scope of this article.) How is such school success possible, if the instructional processes violate the expectations of students regarding communicative routines and norms? The communication process explanation as presented above cannot account for any school success save that attributed to culturally responsive pedagogy. This reveals the communication process explanation, taken literally and read narrowly, as an implicitly cultural determinist position in which cultural difference is seen as necessarily leading to trouble and conflict and cultural similarity is seen (implicitly at least) as necessarily leading to rapport and the absence of conflict.

The perceived labor market explanation can account for the school success of immigrant minority students in school. It does not account for the success of domestic minority students, whether the conditions of that success involve culturally responsive pedagogy or not. Yet instances of school success by domestic minority students and their teachers do occur. Even though, in the majority of cases, domestic minority students do not show high rates of school success, enough exceptions to that general pattern can be found so as to raise serious questions about the adequacy of the perceived labor market explanation as it has been articulated presently.

The perceived labor market argument has two chief weaknesses, in my judgment. First and fundamentally, if taken literally and read narrowly it is an economic determinist argument. It appears to presume a strictly functionalist social theory in the manner of Comte and Durkheim or of the later writings of Marx or Althusser—an organic or mechanical view of society in which there are tight and invariant causal connections across subsystems so that the general social structure drives the actions, perceptions, and sentiments of particular actors in local scenes of action. In such a view there is no room for human agency. Such a social theory, when applied to education, implies that neither the domestic minority students nor their teachers can do anything positive together educationally.

The second major weakness in the labor market explanation is less fundamental, yet also serious. This has to do with the empirical validity of the work. The very comprehensiveness of the causal argument, for all that it satisfies one theoretically, makes the argument very shaky on empirical grounds. Causal linkages across system levels are asserted in the models that Ogbu has published, but those causal relationships are merely asserted, not demonstrated directly. Where empirical quantitative evidence bears on the assertions it is entirely correlational, and no amount of correlational evidence can demonstrate cause. Where empirical ethnographic evidence is presented, as in the case studies of high-achieving immigrant minority students, causal relationships are also not shown. Moreover, these case studies cannot tell us how immigrant minority students might fare in less culturally alien school environments than the ones they usually encounter in the United States. Perhaps the immigrant minority students would do even better than they do already if they were educated in a more culturally responsive learning environment.

It seems necessary to consider the nature of school success or failure from points of view not directly covered by either of the alternative explanations as I have presented them in summary fashion. To speak of school success or failure is to speak of learning or not learning what is deliberately taught there.[1] Learning is ubiquitous in human experience throughout the life cycle, and humans are very good at it. They are also good at fostering learning through deliberate instruction (Poirier and Hussey 1982). Yet in schools, deliberately taught learning seems to be a problem. It is differentially distributed along lines of class, race, ethnicity, and language background.

Students in school, like other humans, learn constantly. When we say they are "not learning" what we mean is that they are not learning what school authorities, teachers, and administrators intend for them to learn as the result of intentional instruction (Gearing and Sangree 1979). Learning what is deliberately taught can be seen as a form of political assent. Not learning can be seen as a form of political resistance.

Assent to the exercise of authority involves trust that its exercise will be benign. This involves a leap of faith—trust in the legitimacy of the authority and in the good intentions of those exercising it, trust that one's own identity will be maintained positively in relation to the authority, and trust that one's own interests will be advanced by compliance with the exercise of authority. In taking such a leap of faith one faces risk. If there is no risk, trust is unnecessary. (I should note here that I do not mean in this discussion to imply that the existential choices to be made are necessarily considered in reflective awareness. They may well be made intuitively. But however apprehended, a sense of trust entails a sense of risk.)

In pedagogy it is essential that the teacher and students establish and maintain trust in each other at the edge of risk (Howard van Ness, personal communication). To learn is to entertain risk, since learning involves moving just past the level of competence, what is already mastered, to the nearest region of incompetence, what has not yet been mastered. As learning takes place, the leading edge of the region of incompetence is continually moving. A useful analogy is that of riding a surfboard—in learning, one must lean forward into a constantly shifting relationship with the crest of the wave. In teacher/learner interaction, the learner places himself or herself at the edge of incompetence and is drawn slightly beyond it with the assistance of this teacher and/or other students. Vygotsky (1978:84–91) refers to this as the "zone of proximal development"—that region within which the learner can function with the assistance of another more competent partner. As the learner's bottom threshold of competence rises (that level at which the learner can function unassisted) so does the top threshold (the level beyond which the student cannot function effectively even with the aid of a teacher). Thus the zone of proximal development can be thought of as constantly moving upward. However, as new learning takes place with a teacher, the student again engages risk because the student reenters the zone within which the student cannot function successfully alone. If the teacher is not trustworthy the student cannot count on effective assistance from the teacher; there is high risk of being revealed (to self and to others) as incompetent (see Shultz 1985). Risk is also involved for the teacher. If the teacher engages a student with the genuine intention to foster the student's learning and the student then fails to learn what the teacher intended, the teacher is revealed, at best, as less than consummately competent pedagogically.

Risk is exciting, yet dangerous. Both for the student and for the teacher, risk in the form of a potential threat to positive social identity seems inherent in the process of learning. Consequently the legitimacy of the school and its teachers, affirmed at the existential level as trust by individual students, is essential if deliberate instruction is to succeed in its aims. School success must be earned by the school staff as well as the students in a process of political rhetoric by which the subordinates in the institution are persuaded to assent to the authority of the superordinates.

Legitimacy, trust, and interest are phenomena that are both institutional and existential. As institutional phenomena, they are located in the social structure and in patterns of role relationships that recur over long spans and are differentially allocated according to access to monetary capital and cultural capital. But legitimacy, trust, and interest are also existential and emergent phenomena that are continually negotiated within the intimate circumstances and short time scale of everyday encounters between individual teachers, students, and parents. The institutional legitimacy of the school is affirmed existentially as trust in face-to-face encounters between school staff and students and their parents.[2]

Labor market inequity, as perceived by members of a domestic minority community, and conflictual teacher/student interaction that derives in part from culturally differing communicative styles can both be seen as impediments to the trust that constitutes an existential foundation for school legitimacy. It is appropriate therefore to look outside the school, into the local community and the broader social order, as well as inside the school, within classroom interaction, to identify the roots of educational failure or success, trust or mistrust, assent or dissent.

I want now to amend the previous discussion of the communication process explanation. We can apply the notion of resistance—withholding of assent—to the progressive development of conflict that occurs between teachers and some domestic minority students. In considering relationships between minority group cultures and student resistance in intercultural learning environments, we can make an important and useful distinction. This is the distinction between cultural boundaries and cultural borders.

Cultural boundaries can be thought of as behavioral evidence of culturally differing standards of appropriateness—in this instance, two subculturally differing ways of pronouncing final consonants. Boundaries—the manifest presence of cultural difference—are politically neutral phenomena; no difference in rights and obligations accrues to persons who act in either of the culturally differing ways. In situations of intergroup conflict, however, cultural boundaries can be treated as cultural borders, that is, the features of culture differences are no longer politically neutral phenomena; rights and obligations are allocated differently, depending on whether a person is revealed as possessing one kind of cultural knowledge rather than another.[3]

Different groups with different interests at stake can treat the existence of behaviorally similar items politically as opportunities for cultural boundary work or border work. This was dramatically apparent in my own research on ethnic and racial cultural differences in communication style in the United States (Erickson 1975; Erickson and Shultz 1982). In detailed analysis of filmed interviews between college counselors or job interviewers and students or job applicants, it was apparent that sometimes subtle cultural differences in communication style made a big difference for rapport and understanding, and sometimes the cultural differences did not seem to impede rapport and understanding. In the absence of special positive motivation to communicate, cultural difference did seem to make interaction difficult. But this was not always true, and it varied from occasion to occasion for the same individual. Distinguishing between cultural boundaries and borders enables one to consider cultural differences as significant in intergroup relations without falling into the trap of a cultural determinist argument. As Bekker and I noted recently,

> *cultural difference can be thought of as a risk factor in the school experience of students and teachers; it need not cause trouble but it usually provides opportunities for trouble. . . . Those opportunities can serve as resources for escalating conflict that might already exist for other reasons, such as conflict between social classes, genders, or races. [Erickson and Bekker 1986:175, 177]*

To understand this rather abstract argument more fully let us turn to an instance of classroom research by Piestrup (1973). She studied desegregated first grade classrooms in which predominantly working-class black children were taught with predominantly middle-class white children. We will first look at a single point in time in the school year; a moment in a reading lesson. Then we will consider what Piestrup reports as patterns of resistance that developed across the course of the whole year.

We can consider an example from Piestrup's study of working-class black and middle-class white children and their teachers (Piestrup 1973:96–97). In this example of a first grade reading lesson, all the children are black. (*CC* in the transcript means *children reading aloud in chorus*):

1 *T:* All right, class, read that and remember your endings.

2 *CC:* "What did Little Duck see?" (final *t* of "what" deleted)

3 *T: What.*

4 *CC:* What (final *t* deleted, as in turn 2)

5 *T:* I still don't hear this sad little *"t."*

6 *CC:* "What did—What did—What—(final *t*'s deleted)

7 *T:* What.

8 *T&CC:* "What did Little Duck see?" (final *t* spoken)

9 *T:* OK, very good.

By saying "What" (line 3) with special emphasis on the final /t/ the teacher has adopted a midcourse correction in order to emphasize and correct a particular detail of oral performance. In so doing the teacher departed from the aim of the initial question, which focused on the general content of the utterance being read. Fostering standard English pronunciation in reading aloud is one pedagogical aim, while fostering comprehension of the text being read is another pedagogical aim. What indeed was it that Little Duck saw? We don't know. If the transcription were to continue we could see whether or not the comprehension point got lost entirely as the teacher went on after having sidetracked the students for their nonstandard pronunciation style.

The teacher's emphasis on the final /t/ is not necessary in terms of the aim of teaching comprehension. We can infer that this is not just a matter of simple miscommunication—the teacher not understanding the children's answers. We can assume that he or she could hear the children saying "wha" (in turns 2 and 4) as standing for "what," with the final /t/ pronounced. Rather, we can see this as a deliberate lesson in pronunciation (in turn 1 the teacher said " . . . and remember your endings"). This was to make a special point of the cultural communication style of the black children and to do so in a negative way.

This cultural border work—making cultural communication style a negative phenomenon in the classroom—seems to have stimulated student resistance that was manifested linguistically. In some of the classrooms the teacher was white, in others the teacher was black. Piestrup monitored the speech style of the working-class black children across the whole school year. In those classrooms in which the teacher, whether black or white, negatively sanctioned the children's use of black English vernacular, by the end of the year the children spoke a more exaggerated form of that dialect than they had done at the beginning of the year. The opposite was true in the classrooms in which the teacher, whether black or white, did not negatively sanction the black English vernacular spoken by the black students. In those classrooms by the end of the year the black children were speaking in the classroom in ways that more closely approximated standard English than did their ways of speaking at the beginning of the year. Consider the implications of this. The culturally distinctive oral performance of working-class black children was initially present in both kinds of classrooms. In the latter kind of classroom the speech style of the students did not become an occasion for stigma and resistance. In the former kind of classroom, however, the use of black English vernacular became an occasion for stigmatizing border work by the teachers and for resistance by the children. As that happened, and as the year progressed, the speech style of the children became more and more different from that of the teacher. This meant that cultural difference was increasing in a situation of cross-cultural contact. This is an instance of a more general phenomenon—progressive cultural differentiation across time as a means of symbolic distancing between competing groups that are subsystems of a larger system. That phenomenon has been called *complementary schismogenesis* by Bateson (1975), who sees it as a basic process of culture change.[4]

By amending the sociolinguistic communication process explanation for school failure and considering a case of a reading lesson, we can see that cultural difference can, for a variety of reasons, be an initial source of trouble between teachers and students. But apparently the story does not stop there. What may have begun as simple misinterpretation of intent and literal meaning can develop across time into entrenched, emotionally intense conflict between teacher and student. The cycle can repeat from year to year during elementary school (see McDermott and Gospodinoff 1979).

Teachers and students in such regressive relationships do not bond with each other. Mutual trust is sacrificed. Over time the students become increasingly alienated from school. It is no longer a matter of difference between teacher and student that derives from intergenerationally transmitted communicative traditions. It is also a matter of cultural invention as a medium of resistance in a situation of political conflict. As students grow older and experience repeated failure and repeated negative encounters with teachers, they develop oppositional cultural patterns as a symbol of their disaffiliation with what they experience (not necessarily within full reflective awareness) as an illegitimate and oppressive system. The more alienated the students become, the less they persist in doing schoolwork. Thus they fall farther and farther behind in academic achievement. The student becomes either actively resistant—seen as salient and incorrigible—or passively resistant—fading into the woodwork as an anonymous well-behaved, low-achieving student.

Bekker and I further observed:

Why would it be a punishable offense for a young black man in an urban American high school to wear a black leather coat in the school hallway? . . . If a principal can suspend an adolescent for wearing a leather coat, some kind of interactional process of evaluation is happening in which judgments of social identity change in negative directions. If students are dressing in such ways then perhaps the problem is not just a matter of cultural patterns that do not fit. Rather it would seem that struggle is going on—struggle that is mutually constructed by teachers and students who, as conflict escalates over time and their forbearance for one another runs out, become locked in regressive social relationships to which all parties in the local social system contribute, as in pathological interaction systems in families. McDermott and Tylbor (1983) use the term collusion when describing this cycle of progressively intense conflict. [Erickson and Bekker 1986:177]

Some of Ogbu's recent research suggests that by the time American black students are of high school age, cultural differentiation through resistance has developed to the point that a sharp distinction is made between "acting black" and "acting white." The political definition of school instruction as legitimate or illegitimate is caught up in this symbolic opposition.

In a recent chapter, Ogbu has noted this phenomenon, citing DeVos (1982) on the development of oppositional identity by domestic minority students. Ogbu observes that

minority students who adopt the school style in communication, interaction, or learning may be accused of "acting white." Even more serious a problem is that castelike minority students may define academic effort or success as a part of the white cultural frame of reference or white way of behavior. [1987b:268]

Ogbu refers here to research of Signithia Fordham (Fordham and Ogbu 1986). Her findings were reported recently on National Public Radio ("All Things Considered," 12 June 1987). Phyllis Crockett, an NPR reporter, interviewed two high-achieving black adolescents from the study:

Reporter: Black (high school) students who spend reasonable amounts of time studying and who speak Standard English can be accused by their peers of acting white . . . . This student, we'll call him Eric, attends an inner-city school in Washington, D.C.

Eric: People are afraid to show that they can speak grammatically correct English. When I do, my friends in my neighborhood will say "You nerd!" or "Talk English! Talk to us like we talk to you."

Reporter: High school students, like this student we'll call Paula, who take college prep courses, often are called "oreos"—like the cookie, black on the outside, white on the inside.

Paula: I've been *per se* called an oreo because black as I am and bright, everybody thinks I'm too proper and talk white . . . and people tend to *tease* me.

Notice that Eric's and Paula's peers focus on their speech style as a badge of group identity. Two points are especially relevant here—the subtlety of the cultural judgments involved and the process of oppositional identity maintenance that is revealed. As evidenced by their recorded speech while addressing the NPR reporter, Eric and Paula do not, in fact, speak fully Standard English. Their grammar is standard but in pronunciation, in voice pitch and stress patterns, and in word choice (i.e., Paula's interpolation of a "fancy" term, *per se*), Eric's and Paula's speech is characteristic of nonstandard black English. Thus Eric's and Paula's peers are making a big issue of slight divergence from a cultural norm. Fine nuances of cultural performance are being attended to as salient, not large cultural differences, such as those between immigrant students and American students. These are secondary cultural differences, according to Ogbu's taxonomy (1982). The cultural differences are small, but they are not trivial as Ogbu has claimed (1987b) because they are not being treated as trivial by the actors themselves. On the contrary, Eric's and Paula's friends seem to be treating such cultural differences as a powerful political symbol.

The peers of the high-achieving students use strong sanctions to enforce a stringent cultural standard that symbolizes group membership. This is border maintenance work. It is significant that the students do not invoke the inequity of the labor market. They do not say, "You can't get a job in white America." Rather, their message is much more indirect. Their immediate focus is on the maintenance of oppositional identity within everyday life in school.

In the example of Eric and Paula, the vehemence of the exercise of sanctions and the focus on subtle features of cultural distinctiveness recall the earlier classroom example in which the teacher made a big issue of a final consonant ("What did Little Duck see?"). The first grade teacher was forcing working-class black children to speak Standard English. In mirror image, Eric's and Paula's working-class black adolescent friends are forcing them to speak nonstandard English. Identity definition is involved in both cases. It is the voice and locus of authority and definition that has changed; from the teacher's voice as an individual institutional officer doing border work on white culture to the students' voices doing collective and institutionally illegitimate border work on black culture.[5] In both examples culturally patterned speech performance becomes a symbolic medium within which a student is forced to take sides between "us" and "them."

The situation reported for American black students is reminiscent of the resistance to school achievement among working-class English high school males reported by Willis (1977). It is also reminiscent of a speculation by Scollon and Scollon (1981) that many Native American school students in Koyukon Athabascan villages of the Alaskan interior associate the acquisition of literacy with betrayal of ethnic identity. Since the students see so many members of their communities as nonliterate (including their parents), to learn to read and write fluently would seem metaphorically to be leaving the community and to be no longer Koyukon.

To summarize, consistent patterns of refusal to learn in school can be seen as a form of resistance to a stigmatized ethnic or social class identity that is being assigned by the school. Students can refuse to accept that negative identity by refusing to learn. Yet the sensitivity and salience of stigmatized ethnic identity among teenagers who are members of domestic minority groups (and of working-class identity more generally) is not a phenomenon that derives exclusively from within a school. Students' school experiences may contribute to their need to resist acceptance of a stigmatized identity, but the sources of such an identity lie in part outside the school, in the conditions of access to the labor market and in the general assumptions of nonstigmatized members of society regarding the members of stigmatized groups.

This is why, within the perspective of resistance theory, both the communication process and the labor market explanations of school failure can be seen as complementary. Influences from outside the immediate school experience of students and teachers, including labor market opportunity as perceived by parents and other members of the minority community, are clearly important to consider, especially among older students for whom issues of future employment become more and more salient. But it is also important to consider the immediate school experience of students and teachers, including the culturally differing communication styles of students and teachers, especially as young children encounter school initially in the early grades and as they continue through high school. Perception of the labor market and cultural style difference both appear to be involved in the development by domestic minority students of oppositional identity in school.

I have argued that both the perceived labor market explanation and the communication process explanation when read literally have serious limitations. Each can be seen as at least implicitly determinist, leaving little room for human agency. Each has trouble accounting for certain kinds of school success. It is therefore appropriate to attach a coda considering some of the reasons why school success might happen with populations of students for whom such success seems demographically unlikely. Let us say that we wanted to try to transform school struggle from working at failure to something more productive. Where then might we look to start?

CODA

If education can be no more than an epiphenomenon tied directly to the requirements of an economy, then little can be done within education itself. It is a totally determined institution. However, if schools (and people) are not passive mirrors of an economy, but instead are active agents in the processes of reproduction and contestation of dominant social relations, then understanding what they do and acting upon them becomes of no small moment. For if schools are part of a "contested terrain," . . . then the hard and continuous day-to-day struggles at the level of curriculum and teaching practice is part of these larger conflicts as well. The key is linking these day-to-day struggles within the school to other action for a more progressive society in that wider arena. [Apple and Weis 1983:22]

As an educator I cannot accept the premise that there is nothing we can do to improve the educational situation of domestic minority students in the United States. I am not simply willing to wait for a revolution in the general society. As Apple and Weis have pointed out, there are progressive choices people can make in their own immediate circumstances while they also work for social change in the wider society. The task is not only to analyze the structural conditions by which inequity is reproduced in society but to search out every possible site in which the struggle for progressive transformation can take place.

Schools are one of the arenas in which people can work to change the existing distributions of power and knowledge in our society. When school practice is conducted according to the existing conventional wisdom, minority students—especially domestic minority students—usually do not fare well. The conventional wisdom involves assumptions that are part of the cultural hegemony of established classes in society. Hegemony refers to the ubiquitous and taken-for-granted status of a dominant culture within a culturally plural and class-stratified society such as the United States. Because of the ubiquity of the dominant culture and of the institutional arrangements that are consonant with its assumptions, it is not necessary for dominant groups to use overt means, i.e., naked force, to maintain their position of advantage. Rather as members of the society, dominant and subordinate alike, act routinely in concert with the cultural assumptions and interests of the dominant group, existing power relationships can be maintained, as it were, by an invisible hand. This is the essential element in Gramsci's notion of hegemony (Bluci-Glucksmann 1982); through influence, leadership, and by consent from the masses themselves, domination comes to appear as reasonable.[6]

Hegemonic practices are routine actions and unexamined beliefs that are consonant with the cultural system of meaning and ontology within which it makes sense to take certain actions, entirely without malevolent intent, that nonetheless systematically limit the life chances of members of stigmatized groups. Were it not for the regularity of hegemonic practices, resistance by the stigmatized would not be necessary. Were it not for the capacity of the established to regard hegemonic practices as reasonable and just, resistance could be more overt. Resistance could be informed by an explicit social analysis that unmasks the practices as oppressive. Yet currently neither the oppressors nor the oppressed face squarely the character of their situation, and resistance is often inchoate just as oppression is not deliberately intended.[7]

Hegemonic practices are not only ramified throughout the general society and in the local community outside the school, they are also alive and well inside the classroom. They permeate and frame the school experience of students who are members of stigmatized social groups. These practices are enacted by particular social actors. Domination and alienation of the oppressed does not simply happen by the anonymous workings of social structural forces. People do it. It is the result of choice (not necessarily deliberate) to cooperate with the reigning ideological definitions of what minority students are, what curriculum is, what good teaching is.

Yet if hegemonic practices are the result of human choice, they are not inevitable. Particular individuals can scrutinize the options enjoined by the conventional wisdom of practice. They can decide which aspects of that conventional wisdom to adopt and which to reject, creating learning environments that not only do not stigmatize minority students, but stimulate them to achieve.

Reconsider what Piestrup's teacher did in the reading lesson. She insisted that the children pronounce the final /t/ in the word "what," while reading the sentence, "What did Little Duck see?" This can be seen as an instance of hegemonic practice (James Collins, personal communication). What makes it so is that the teacher's exercise of a particular pedagogical option at a certain point in the lesson is consonant with a widely held theory or philosophy of reading instruction. According to one well-established view of good reading teaching, drill on isolated subskills, such as recognition and pronunciation of a final /t/, and mastery of that subskill must necessarily precede moving on to mastering the so-called higher order skills of comprehension.

According to another well-established view, the "whole language" or "language experience" approach, comprehension of larger semantic units in written discourse takes precedence over drill on isolated subskills. The teacher in this example was not, we can infer, deliberately choosing to make salient in a negative way the culturally patterned pronunciation the children have learned in their homes. Rather, the teacher was acting on a strongly supported belief about good reading teaching. Yet entailed in the choice of one pedagogical strategy rather than another is the opportunity to make a culture trait negatively salient or not. If the teacher had emphasized the sense of the text, focusing on what in fact Little Duck had seen, the children's pronunciation style would not have become visible in the lesson interaction as a stigmatizing badge of racial and social class identity.

We could simply write off the reading lesson example as one in which the teacher produced contradiction and cognitive confusion by beginning one way and then going off on another instructional tack. But I think the example shows more than that, since the new option that was followed—pronunciation correction—made salient the children's home cultural style and negatively evaluated that style. Thus we would not just want to say to this teacher, "Be consistent." We would want the teacher to learn to reflect on his or her practice and say, "What are the consequences of my being consistent in following one pedagogical aim or another?" From the point of view of culturally responsive pedagogy as informed by resistance theory, the teacher could conclude that to choose to fight and temporarily win a small battle over the pronunciation of a final consonant is to risk losing the war, by setting off a long-term process of schismogenetic cultural conflict. The threat to trust inherent in engaging in the pronunciation battle may simply not be worth it in the long run.[8]

In the cultural politics of pedagogy in the early grades one route to maintaining trust and earning the learner's assent to learn is to adapt instruction in the direction of the students' home cultural communication style. We saw this in adaptation to Hawaiian conversational turn-taking patterns, and we considered a hypothetical strategy for avoiding needless conflict over black American children's pronunciation while reading aloud.

Culturally responsive pedagogy is not the only route to establishing and maintaining trust and legitimacy between teacher and students, however. If children and their parents believe very strongly in the legitimacy of school staff and in the content and aims of a school program, as in the case of a black Muslim school (or in the case of some immigrant minority students and their parents as they encounter an arbitrary American public school), then even if the cultural style of classroom interaction is very discontinuous with that of the children's early childhood experience, they may well learn the new cultural styles without setting off a chain reaction of resistance and cultural schismogenesis. The same could hold for the models of "direct instruction" currently mooted. If instructional patterns are very clear and consistent (unlike the reading lesson about Little Duck), the teacher believes strongly in what he or she is doing, and children and parents can recognize the teacher's unambivalently authoritative style as a sincere attempt to foster minority children's learning, then the children may trust the teacher and assent to learn, even though the interaction style of instruction violates the minority community's norms regarding appropriate communication style.

To conclude, the politics of legitimacy, trust, and assent seem to be the most fundamental factors in school success. For cultural minority students, whether immigrant or domestic, the role of culture and of cultural difference varies in relation to school success. In some exceptional circumstances, because of high motivation to succeed in school, cultural difference does not seem to prevent students from persisting and achieving. A much more prevalent pattern, I have argued, is for cultural differences to make a negative difference, (1) because they contribute to miscommunication in the early grades and (2) because those initial problems of miscommunication escalate into student distrust and resistance in later grades. Moreover, it is important to note that for typical public schools (as distinct from special schools or alternative programs), it appears that in dealing with the majority of domestic minority students, school personnel cannot count on being perceived as highly legitimate, nor can they count on high motivation to learn when they try to teach in learning environments that are culturally alien to the students. Rather, if the ordinary public school is to be perceived as legitimate, the school must earn that perception by its local minority community. This involves a profound shift in the direction of daily practice and its symbolism, away from hegemonic practice and toward transformative practice. In the absence of special effort by the school, the deep distrust of its legitimacy that increases among students as they grow older and the resources for resisting by developing oppositional identity that the school provides (in the cultural hegemony that inheres in its routine ways of doing daily business) pose serious threats to the school's perceived legitimacy. On the other hand, it appears that immigrant minority students may tend to be likely to trust the legitimacy of the school as it currently exists and to hope to benefit by participating in the American labor market.

Culturally responsive pedagogy is one kind of special effort by the school that can reduce miscommunication by teachers and students, foster trust, and prevent the genesis of conflict that moves rapidly beyond intercultural misunderstanding to bitter struggles of negative identity exchange between some students and their teachers. In the light of the preceding discussion, culturally responsive pedagogy seems most appropriate and important in the early grades. It may be especially important for domestic minority students and less important for first generation immigrant minority students. It is only one piece in a large puzzle, yet it provides a positive option for educators who wish, through critically reflective practice, to improve the chances for learning by their students and to improve their own work life as well. Culturally responsive pedagogy is not a total solution. It can, however, be seen as part of a total solution that also includes work to transform the general society within which schooling takes place.

NOTES

Acknowledgments. I wish to thank Cathie Jordan, Evelyn Jacob, Rosemary Henze, and Marge Murray for editorial suggestions. The contributions from Howard van Ness and James Collins are acknowledged in the text itself. Defects in the interpretation presented are my own responsibility.

1. Admittedly it is also important to school success that students learn, or at least appear to comply with, what is nondeliberately taught (i.e., the "hidden curriculum"). Yet what seems to me crucial to school success is that students appear to comply with what school staff think they are trying to teach (i.e., the manifest curriculum of academic and social skills and knowledge).

2. The distinction between institutional and existential aspects of legitimacy, and the distinction and connection between the long and short term patterns by which we can see connections between general history and social order and specific, concrete history and social order, is made in a recent essay on social theory by Giddens (1984). A related notion is found in the approach to intellectual history taken by Foucault (1979), and in the literary theory of Bakhtin (1981).

3. The distinction between cultural borders and boundaries was made initially by Barth (1969), and has been elaborated in terms of its implications for education by McDermott and Gospodinoff (1979) and by Erickson and Bekker (1986).

4. Piestrup's is a single study, to be sure, and some could argue that too much weight should not rest on it in the line of explanation set forth here. But the phenomenon Piestrup reports has been found more generally. The phenomenon is increasing speech style differentiation between speakers across time in situations of conflict. This has been reported in shorter and longer time spans than the single school year studied by Piestrup. Giles and Powesland (1975) showed that social class and regional dialect styles diverged across half-hour conversations in which conflict was experimentally induced. Reporting naturalistic research, Labov (1963) has shown how, across a generation, certain features of the dialect of

islanders from Martha's Vineyard have become more marked. Thus the speech of the island- ers has become progressively more and more distinct from that of the tourists who visit the island in the summer.

5. On the significance of the collective nature of the students' actions, see Everhart 1983: 186–187.

6. Considered in this light, Gramsci looks like an anthropologist. He can be seen as presenting a cultural analysis of the plausibility of domination.

7. For further discussion, see Giroux 1983.

8. We could argue that such pronunciation battles always make bad sense in reading instruction—indeed, that reading aloud itself is unnecessary in reading lessons, but these are matters beyond the scope of this article.

Educational Reform and the Politics of Teacher Empowerment*

HENRY A. GIROUX

I want to begin with the issue of teacher empowerment and what I think that means for making schools public places where students can learn the languages of history, critique and possibility. In this case, languages that both dignify teacher work and provide a democratic vision for public schooling. In one sense, I want to recover and reaffirm the ideological sentiments of George S. Counts who writing in 1932 argued that if "education is to be genuinely progressive, it must . . . face squarely and courageously every social issue, come to grips with life in all of its stark reality, establish an organic relation with the community, develop a realistic and comprehensive theory of welfare, and fashion a compelling and challenging vision of human destiny."[1]

The significance of Counts' message is as important today as it was when first delivered. And yet, such a vision is decidedly at odds with the current appeal to develop public education around increased forms of elaborate accountability schemes; it is important to note that the central assumptions of Counts' vision are in direct opposition to the policies of the current United States federal administration which defines excellence at the expense of equity, while simultaneously devaluing both teaching and learning as a process of self and social formation. Such a vision would also have difficulty developing within many schools of education that more often than not treat teachers primarily as technicians and learning itself as hardly more than the mastering of disparate facts and methodologies suitable to trivialized forms of measurement.[2] The point, of course, is not to embrace despair but to recognize that much of what passes for educational reform is generally not about empowerment at all but actually about teacher disempowerment. Moreover, the ideological vision that sustains such reforms has little to do with democracy and,

---

*This paper was first given as a speech in the Schooling and American Dreams Conference held at Indiana University of Pennsylvania in October of 1986.

Reprinted from *New Education*, 9:3–13, 1987, by permission of the publisher.

in my mind, represents a powerful force for turning schools into "dead zones," places in which the politics of social adjustment and the ideology of technique come together to often produce classroom settings where there is little of much complexity or relevance to learn regarding how one is to function as an agent of progressive change, vision and compassion.[3] It is my hope that this essay will make a small contribution toward legitimizing the need for teachers and educators to fight for schools as public places, as living spaces where dialogue, difference, knowledge, and social relations co-exist in order to affirm and strengthen the possibilities inherent in human life. With that in mind, let me get to the specifics of my concerns.

It is worth noting that since the 1980s there has been a major ideological shift both in the schools and in the wider society around the language of schooling, citizenship and democracy. This shift is most evident in the gathering momentum of the current reform period to redefine the purpose of education so as to eliminate its citizenship function in favor of a narrowly-defined labor market perspective. Most obviously, the thrust of many of the new reforms along with the ideological position advocated by the Reagan Administration have moved away from defining public education within its historically sanctioned utopian mission of nurturing a critical and committed citizenry, one that is capable of extending the workings of political and social democracy. Academic success is defined almost exclusively in terms of the accumulation of capital and the logic of the marketplace.[4] Consequently, the new reformers provide a limited vision of political and social possibilities. In part, this is exemplified by the fact that the hero of the times is Lee Iaccocca, rather than such figures as a Martin Luther King or John Dewey. In this case, the concept of educator collapses into the notion of manager. Nor do such reformers celebrate a politics of social and cultural difference and tolerance; instead, they are performing ideological surgery on the public schools both by cutting away the language of equity and social justice and by implanting a technical and instrumental logic that redefines teacher work in terms that often contribute to the deskilling of teachers and to a sterile standardization of learning. Similarly, Reagan and his cohorts would like to turn public schools into institutions approximating a mixture of the local Sunday School, the company store, and the old west museum. Industrial psychology, religious sectarianism, and cultural uniformity provide the basis for reconstructing the public schools in the political image of the Reagan policy-makers.

It is also important to stress that in the current educational reform movement a version of schooling and pedagogy has emerged in which students rarely find themselves exposed to modes of knowledge that celebrate democratic forms of public life or that provide them with the skills they will need to engage in a critical examination of the society in which they live and work. Underlying the dominant trend in teaching and in learning, one that increasingly structures the form and content of most public school curricula, are the principles of mastery, efficiency, and control. Under the rubric of excellence the greatest challenge facing educational reform appears to be developing more stringent forms of graded assessment, the value of which seems more appropriate for measuring the heights of trees than for evaluating students and teachers. The language that informs this perspective is a direct descendant of the social efficiency movement of the 1920s. It is the language of means and techniques, a language without a substantive vision and politics, one that subverts the ethical force of education and has little to do with the concept of empowerment.

Moreover, within the dominant view, public schooling is no longer structured around interests that promote the development of citizens who possess the social and critical attributes to improve the quality of public life. For instance, there is no talk of conflict within the dominant discourse of schooling, no mention of the messy social relations of sexism, racism, and class discrimination that underlie many school and classroom social practices. It is the discourse of uneasy harmony, one that smooths over the conflicts and contradictions of everyday life with an appeal to teaching tradition and character development. Underlying this call to harmony and tradition is the illusion of technique and a politics of silence. One current consequence of this approach is a pedagogy of chauvinism dressed up in the lingo of the Great Books, which presents a view of culture and history as if they were a seamless web, a warehouse of great cultural artefacts. There is no politics of democratic difference at work here. For within this vision cultural and social difference quickly becomes labelled as a deficit, as the other, deviancy in need of psychological tending and control. In the meantime, the languages, cultures, histori- cal legacies of minorities, women, blacks, and other subordinate groups are actively silenced under the rubric of teaching the dominant version of American culture and history as an act of patriotism. Within this language, the appeal to old-fashioned virtues is matched only by a similar appeal to old-fashioned pedagogy.[5] Teachers simply have to teach a narrowly defined warehouse of cultural wealth, students have to be regularly monitored, scrutinized, and measured in order to make sure they are succeeding, and school achievement is assessed and displayed in a dizzying array of numerical scores posted monthly in the local newspaper. Of course, nothing will be said about the 44 percent dropout rate for Puerto Rican students in the urban centres or the 48 percent dropout rate for Blacks, or the 65 percent dropout rate for Native Americans in our urban schools. Nor will anything be said about the more than 30 per cent of potential graduates who leave high school before their senior year.[6] In addition, the dominant discourse will remain silent about those teachers overburdened by deplorable working conditions, students silenced by administra- tors and teachers who believe they don't count, or those parents from subordinate groups who are ignored by school administrations because they lack the "right" cultural currency.

In this context, students learn little about the language of community and public association, or how to create and affirm their own memories and stories along with those of others who inhabit different cultural, racial and social positions, or how to balance their own individualistic interests with those of the public good. Justice stands outside the critical range of this new conservatism and its attendant peda- gogical formulations. In fact, the new conservatism has little to do with civic or minority education in the emancipatory sense of the practice; instead, under the notions of character development and moral regulation, it provides the basis for curricula and pedagogy that enshrine the virtues of possessive individualism, the struggle for advantage, and the legitimation of forms of knowledge that restrict the possibility for political understanding and action. When the language of moral responsibility is invoked, as, for instance, by Mr. Bennett, it is often trivialized or used as a weapon to admonish those ideological tendencies with which he disagrees.[7] In this case, moral practice becomes important in addressing the drug problems in our nation's schools, or for berating liberal faculties in such bastions of "radicalism" as Harvard University. At the same time, moral practice is exorcized as a basis for addressing the instances of suffering and despair that often turn schools into lifeless places, if you will, for minorities of race and class. The current federal administration invokes the language of morality in order to disempower it, to silence critics of society, to admonish critical intellectual practice, and to reduce teachers and educators to the moral gatekeepers of a Reagan-like evangelicalism. It should be noted that this is not the language of character development but of *character underdevelopment,* nor is this the practice of moral development as much as it is the practice of moral infantilism. What are we to make of an administration, for example, that detains and prevents a noted Columbian journalist who has been critical of United States policy in Latin America from entering the US on the grounds she might "engage in subversive activities in the US". Patricia Lara's detention provides an important signal as to how this administration treats intellectuals—people who teach, work with ideas, and provide a social function essential to any free society. This seemingly insignificant act is one that should not be taken lightly by teachers who believe that the best of learning takes place amidst the free flow of ideas, and that democracy itself is central to such an exchange.[8]

The ideological shift that characterizes the current reform period is also evident in the ways in which teacher preparation and classroom pedagogy are currently being defined. With few exceptions, the major reform proposals point to a definition of teacher work that seriously exacerbates conditions which are presently eroding the authority and intellectual integrity of teachers. In fact, the most compelling aspect of the influential reports, especially the widely publicized *A Nation at Risk, Action for Excellence,* and *A Nation Prepared,* is their studious refusal to address the ideological, social, and economic conditions underlying poor teacher and student performance.[9] For example, little is said regarding the fact that public school teachers constantly confront conditions such as the overwhelming emphasis on quantifying tasks, the growing lack of control over curriculum, little or no input into the decisions that critically affect their work, isolation from their peers, and the often condescending treatment they receive from school by administrators.[10]

Instead of addressing these issues many of the reforms taking place at the state level further consolidate administrative structures and prevent teachers from collectively and creatively shaping the conditions under which they work. For instance, at both the local and federal levels, the new educational discourse has influenced a number of policy recommendations, such as competency-based testing for teachers, a lockstep sequencing of materials, mastery learning techniques, systematized evaluation schemes, standardized curricula, and the implementation of mandated 'basics'. The consequences of these reforms are evident not only in their substantively narrow view of the purpose of education, but also in the definitions of teaching, learning and literacy that are championed by the new management-oriented policy-makers. In place of developing critical understanding, engaging student experience, and fostering active and critical citizenship, schools are redefined through a language that emphasizes sterile forms of standardization, competency, and narrowly defined performance skills. Linda Darling-Hammond is instructive on this issue:

> *In a Rand study of teachers views' on the effect of educational policies on their classroom practices, we learned from teachers that in response to policies that prescribe teaching practices and outcomes, they spend less time on untested subjects, such as science and social studies; they use less writing in their classrooms in order to gear assignments to the format of standardized tests; they resort to lectures rather than classroom discussions in order to cover the prescribed behavioral objectives without getting "off the track;" they are precluded from using teaching materials that are not on prescribed textbooks lists, even when they think these materials are essential to meet the needs or some of their students; and they feel constrained from following up on expressed student interests that lie outside the bounds of mandated curricula. We also heard the frustration that results from the dual-accountability dilemma experienced by teachers when they must follow strictures from above that collide with their view of what they should responsibly do to meet the needs of their students. And 45 percent of the teachers in this study told us that the single thing that would make them leave teaching was the increased prescriptiveness of teaching content and methods—in short, the continuing deprofessionalization of teaching.*[11]

Within this paradigm, the development of curricula is increasingly left to administrative experts or simply adopted from publishers, many of whom are under siege from right-wing political and religious groups, with few, if any, contributions from teachers who are expected to implement the new programs. In its most ideologically offensive form, this type of prepackaged curriculum is rationalized as teacher-proof and designed to be applied to any classroom context regardless of the historical, cultural, and socioeconomic differences that define various schools and students. What is important to note is that the deskilling of teachers is related to the ways in which a particular form of technocratic rationality is used to inform state educational policy, to consolidate the power of school administrators, and to redefine teacher work. This type of rationality increasingly takes place within a social division of labor in which thinking is removed from implementation and the model of the teacher becomes that of the technician or white-collar clerk. Likewise, for students, learning is often reduced to time on task skills, the exercise of lifeless paperwork, the "mastery" of knowledge that has little to do with their own experiences, and the organization of classroom social relations based on the military model of discipline.

Within this language, democracy loses its one dynamic nature and is reduced to a set of inherited principles and institutional arrangements that teach students how to adapt rather than question the basic precepts of society. What we are left with in the new reform proposals is often a view of authority constructed around a national mandate to follow and implement predetermined rules, to transmit an unquestioned version of cultural tradition, and to sanctify industrial discipline. Couple these problems with large classes, excessive paperwork, fragmented work periods, low salaries, and it comes as no surprise that teachers are increasingly leaving the field.

In effect, the ideological shift at work here points to a restricted definition of schooling, one that almost completely strips education of a democratic vision, one in which citizenship and the politics of possibility are given serious consideration. In arguing that the recent conservative or "blue-ribbon" reform recommendations lack a politics of possibility and citizenship, I mean that primacy is either given to the celebration of techniques of learning or to education as economic investment, that is, to pedagogical practices designed to create a school-business partnership and make the American economic system more competitive in world markets. A politics of possibility and citizenship, by contrast, refers to a conception of schooling in which classrooms are seen as active sites of public intervention, where students and teachers learn to redefine the nature of critical learning and practice outside of the narrow imperatives of the corporate marketplace or the reductive logic of means and methods.

If we are to develop modes of teaching informed by the politics of possibility, imagination, and commitment, it is imperative that existing and prospective teachers learn how to develop pedagogical approaches that combine the language of critique with the language of possibility. In doing so, teachers need a language that can provide forms of analyses that acknowledge the spaces, tensions, and opportunities for democratic struggles and reforms within the day-to-day workings of schools. Similarly, there is the need to provide a language that allows teachers and others to view and experience schooling in a critical and potentially transformative way. Some elements of such a discourse that I believe are important for such a project might focus around defining schools as democratic public spheres and viewing teachers as transformative intellectuals. In what follows I want to sketch some of the broader pedagogical implications of these categories and the practices they suggest.

Central to developing a language of possibility is the need to make the political and civic project of public schooling clear. This means regarding schools as democratic sites dedicated to forms of self and social empowerment. Understood in these terms, schools are viewed as public places where students learn the knowledge and skills necessary to live in a critical democracy. Instead of defining schools as extensions of the workplace or as front-line institutions in the battle for international markets and foreign competition, schools as democratic public spheres can be constructed around forms of critical inquiry that dignify meaningful dialogue and human agency. Students are given the opportunity to learn the discourse of public association and social responsibility, and to engage in public dialogue that would encourage moral leadership and responsibility. Such a discourse seeks to recapture the idea of critical democracy as a social movement grounded in a set of practices that embody a fundamental respect for individual freedom and social justice. Moreover, viewing schools as democratic public spheres provides a rationale for defending them, along with progressive forms of pedagogy and teacher work as institutions that perform a public service essential to the construction of the democratic state.[12]

There is another important and related issue at work in defining schools as democratic public spheres. By politicizing the notion of schooling, it becomes possible to illuminate the role that educators play as intellectuals who operate under specific conditions of work and who in doing so perform a particular social, ethical, and political function. The category of intellectual is useful in a number of ways for describing the nature and practice of teacher work. First, it provides a theoretical basis for examining teacher work as a form of intellectual labor, as opposed to defining it in purely instrumental and technical terms. In other words, it points to the interrelation of conception and practice, thinking and doing, and producing and implementing as integrated activities that give teaching its dialectical meaning. Within this perspective there is a critical foundation for rejecting those philosophies and management pedagogies that separate conceptualization, planning, and design from the nature of teacher work itself. Second, the concept of teacher as intellectual carries with it the imperative to critique and reject those approaches to teacher work that reinforce a technical and social division of labor that disempowers teachers by deskilling them. Third, the category highlights the political and ideological interests that structure teacher work and illuminates the various social functions that intellectuals perform. Fourth, the notion of teacher as intellectual also makes problematic the ideological and practical conditions teachers need to function in their capacity as intellectuals.[13]

In this case, teachers need to analyze and change when necessary the fundamental nature of the conditions under which they work. That is, teachers must be able to shape collectively the ways in which time, space and knowledge organize everyday life in schools. More specifically, in order to function as intellectuals, teachers must struggle to create the ideological and structural conditions necessary for them to write, research, and work with each other in producing curricula and sharing power. But in the final analysis, to take this logic further, teachers need to develop a discourse and set of assumptions that allow them to function as transformative intellectuals.[14] Such intellectuals are not merely concerned with promoting individual achievement or advancing students along career ladders, that is creating good yuppies with MBA degrees and Commodore computers, they are concerned, instead, with empowering students through a project of possibility, one that enables students to read the world critically in order to change it through the power of struggle and community. I want to elaborate on some of the concerns that are central to assuming the role of a transformative intellectual before I address the more specific issue of what it means to develop a critical pedagogy consistent with the role teachers assume as transformative intellectuals.

To speak of teachers as transformative intellectuals means that such educators are not merely concerned with forms of empowerment that promote individual achievement and traditional forms of academic success. Instead, they should also be concerned in their teaching with linking empowerment—the ability to think and act critically—to the concept of social transformation. Teaching for social transformation means educating students to take risks and to struggle within ongoing relations of power in order to be able to alter the grounds upon which life is lived. Acting as a transformative intellectual means, as John Dewey has argued, helping students acquire critical knowledge about basic societal structures, such as the economy, the state, the workplace, and mass culture so that such institutions can be open to critical examination and potential transformation. A transformation, in this case, aimed at the progressive humanization of the social order.

As transformative intellectuals, teachers need to make clear the political and moral referents for the authority they assume in teaching particular forms of knowledge, taking a stand against forms of oppression, and treating students as if they ought also to be concerned about the issues of social justice and political action. In my view, the most important referent for this particular view of authority rests in a commitment to an ethics of solidarity and resistance that addresses the many instances of suffering that are both a growing and threatening part of everyday life in America and abroad. Such an ethic embodies a particular kind of commitment and practice. As a commitment, it suggests, as Sharon Welch has pointed out, a recognition and identification with "the perspective of those people and groups who are marginal and exploited."[15] As a form of practice, it represents a break from the bonds of isolated individuality and the need to engage for and with other groups in political struggles that challenge those aspects of the existing order of society that are institutionally repressive and unjust. The pedagogical rationality at work here is one that defines transformative intellectuals as bearers of "dangerous memory," intellectuals who keep alive the memory of human suffering along with the forms of knowledge and struggles in which such suffering was shaped and contested.[16] Dangerous memory has two dimensions: first, it recounts the history of the marginal, the vanquished, and the oppressed; in other words, it points to those forms of knowledge and history that often become part of what Michelle Fine calls the politics of "not naming," a curious culture of silence that maps out of existence knowledge that is critical, that challenges, that raises alternative possibilities.[17] Second, dangerous memory posits the need for a new kind of subjectivity and community in which the conditions that create such suffering can be eliminated. Michel Foucault describes the political project that is central to the meaning of dangerous memory as an affirmation of the insurrection of subjugated knowledge—those forms of historical and popular knowledge that have been suppressed or ignored, and through which it becomes possible to discover the ruptural effects of conflict and struggle.[18] Underlying this view of dangerous memory and subjugated knowledge is a logic that provides the basis upon which transformative intellectuals can advance both the language of critique and the language of possibility and hope. I believe that it is in this combination of critique, the historical reconstruction of the relationship between knowledge and power, and the commitment to an ethic of risk and resistance that the basis exists for a pedagogy that is both empowering and transformative. Of course, developing a rationale for assuming the role of a transformative intellectual does not guarantee that a critical pedagogy will follow. But it does point to principles for making such a pedagogy possible. Furthermore, it establishes the criteria for organizing curricula and classroom social relations around goals designed to prepare students to understand and value the relation between an existentially lived public space and their own practical learning. By public space, I mean as Hannah Arendt did, a concrete set of learning conditions where people come together to speak, to dialogue, to share their stories, and to struggle together within social relations that strengthen rather than weaken the possibility for active citizenship.[19]

Central to developing a critical pedagogy consistent with the practice of a transformative intellectual is the need to give the categories of voice and student experience a major place in our school curricula and classroom practices. In other words, teachers have to redefine curriculum not as a warehouse of knowledge and techniques merely to be passed on to waiting consumers but, more importantly, as a configuration of knowledge, social relations and values that represents an introduction to and affirmation of a particular way of life. This means that the issue of student experience will have to be analyzed as part of a wider relationship between culture and power. Let me be more specific. Schools are not merely instructional sites designed to transmit knowledge, they are also cultural sites. As cultural sites, they generate and embody support for particular forms of culture as is evident in the school's support for specific ways of speaking, the legitimating of distinct forms of knowledge, the privileging of certain histories and patterns of authority, and the confirmation of particular ways of experiencing and seeing the world. Schools often give the appearance of transmitting a common culture. More often than not schools legitimate what can be called a dominant culture. Moreover, schools are not uniform places simply catering democratically to the needs of different students; they are characterized by the presence of students from both dominant and subordinate cultures, with the dominant culture often sanctioning the voices of White, middle-class students, while simultaneously disconfirming or ignoring the voices of students from subordinate groups, whether they be Black, working class, Hispanic, or other minority groups.[20]

Crucial to this argument is the recognition that it is not enough for teachers to merely dignify the grounds on which students learn to speak, imagine, and give meaning to their world. This is important but it is also crucial for teachers to understand how schools as part of the wider dominant culture often function to marginalize, disconfirm, and delegitimate the experiences, histories, and categories that students use in mediating their lives. This means understanding how texts, classroom relations, teacher talk, and other aspects of the formal and hidden curricula of schooling often function to actively silence students.

At issue here is understanding that student experience has to be understood as part of an interlocking web of power relations in which some groups of students are often privileged over others. But if we are to view this insight in an important way we must understand that it is imperative for teachers to critically examine the cultural backgrounds and social formations out of which their students produce the categories they use to give meaning to the world. For teachers are not merely dealing with students who have individual interests, they are dealing primarily with individuals whose stories, memories, narratives and reading of the world are inextricably related to wider social and cultural formations and categories. The issue here is not merely one of relevance but one of voice and power. Schools produce not only subjects but also subjectivities and in doing so often function to disempower students by tracking them into classes with lowered expectations, or by refusing to provide them with knowledge that speaks affirmatively and critically to the context of their everyday lives.[21] We know, for example, that many educators view different languages and backgrounds in students as deficits to be corrected, rather than as strengths to build upon. We also know that Black, working class, and other minority children are vastly over-represented in special education classes and that they make up a large share of the dropout statistics in our nation's schools.[22] I believe that teachers add an important theoretical dimension to their teaching when they incorporate a more critical understanding of how experience is named, produced, sustained, and rewarded in schools. When they begin to take seriously the notion that children learn best from their strengths rather than their weaknesses. That is, teachers need a critical language that allows them to understand how school knowledge and classroom social relations are constructed, disseminated, and legitimated in everyday instruction and how the underlying interests they embody function so as to both enable and/or disable student learning.

I also believe that developing a pedagogy that takes the notion of student experience seriously means developing a critically affirmative language, one that dialectically engages the experiences that students bring to the classroom. This means not only taking seriously and confirming the language forms, modes of reasoning, dispositions, and histories that give students an active voice in defining the world, it also means working on the experiences of such students in order for them to examine both their strengths and weaknesses. Student experience, like the culture and society of which it is a part, is not all of one piece, and it is important to sort through its contradictions and to give students the chance to not only confirm themselves but also to raise the question: *what is it this society has made of me that I no longer want to be?* Similarly, this means teaching students how to critically appropriate the codes and vocabularies of different cultural experiences so as to provide the skills they will need in order to define and shape, rather than simply serve, in the modern world. In other words, students need to understand the richness and strengths of other cultural traditions, other voices, particularly as these point to forms of self and social empowerment.

Developing a critical pedagogy that takes the notion of student experience seriously also involves rethinking the very nature of curriculum discourse. At the outset this demands understanding curriculum as representative of a set of underlying interests that structure how a particular story is told through the organization of knowledge, social relations, values and forms of assessment. In short, curriculum itself represents a narrative or voice, one that is multi-layered and often contradictory but also situated within relations of power that more often than not favor White, middle-class, English-speaking students. What this suggests for a critical theory of schooling and pedagogy is that curriculum must be seen as an introduction to a particular form of life, and as such must be questioned regarding the issue of whose knowledge, history, visions, language, culture, and authority will prevail as a legitimate object of learning and analysis.

In addition to legitimating student experiences and treating curriculum as a narrative whose guiding interests must be uncovered and critically interrogated, progressive teachers must develop conditions in their classrooms that allow different student voices to be heard and legitimated. In other words, as transformative intellectuals, teachers must create classroom social relations that allow students to speak and to appreciate the nature of difference as both a basis for democratic tolerance and as a fundamental condition for critical dialogue and the development of forms of solidarity rooted in the principles of trust, sharing and a commitment to improving the quality of human life. In this case, the notion of voice is developed around a politics of difference and community that is not rooted in simply a celebration of plurality, but in a particular form of human community that allows and dignifies plurality as part of an ongoing effort to develop social relations in which all voices in their differences become unified in their efforts to identify and recall moments of human suffering and the need to overcome the conditions that perpetuate such suffering.[23]

Second, teachers should provide students with the opportunity to interrogate different languages or ideological discourses as they are developed in an assortment of texts and curriculum materials. This is important because it provides the basis for students to critically analyze the forms of intelligibility, interests, and moral and political considerations that different voices embody in both their immediate and wider contexts. Examining such discourses must be done not only as a form of ideology-critique intended to uncover and demystify how knowledge claims distort reality, but also as an attempt to recover and reconstruct knowledge that embodies interests which allows students to more fully understand their own histories in order to be able to analyze and question the dominant forms of history as they are presented against the histories that actually construct their everyday lives. In this case, all aspects of curriculum knowledge and pedagogy can be examined as historical constructions that embody particular interests that not only shape the content and forms of curriculum knowledge, but also produce and legitimate particular forms of subjectivity and experience.[24]

Third, a critical pedagogy must take seriously the articulation of a morality that posits a language of public life, emancipatory community, and individual and social commitment. In other words, students need to be introduced to a language of morality that allows them to think about how community life should be constructed around the question of how one ought to live one's life. Fundamental here is what it means to be human and to recognize those ideological and material constraints that also restrict human possibilities. But also those that function to improve the quality of human life for all. A discourse of morality is important both because it points to the need to educate students to fight and struggle in order to advance the discourse and principles of a critical democracy, and because it provides a referent against which students can decide what forms of life and conduct are most morally appropriate amidst the welter of knowledge claims and interests they confront in making choices in a world of competing and diverse ideologies.

Fourth, essential to the creation of a critical pedagogy is the development of what my colleague Roger Simon has called a project of possibility and a moment of transformation. That is, as transformative intellectuals, teachers need to educate students not only to make choices and to think critically but also to believe that they can make a difference in the world. In this case, a project of possibility is one that can be developed around forms of community work, through curriculum practices that address concrete instances of suffering, or through school projects aimed at addressing public issues with which students are familiar. I want to conclude by re-emphasizing the importance of empowering teachers as a central precondition for the success of any learning process.

If teachers are to take an active role in raising serious questions about what they teach, how they are to teach, and the larger goals for which they are striving, it means they must take a more critical role in defining the nature of their work as well as in shaping the conditions under which they work.[25] In summary, teachers need to view themselves as intellectuals who combine conception and implementation, thinking and practice. The category of intellectual is important here for analyzing the particular practices in which teachers engage. For it provides a referent for criticizing those forms of management pedagogies, accountability schemes, and teacher-proof curricula, that would define teachers merely as technicians. Moreover, it provides the theoretical and political basis for teachers to engage in a critical dialogue among themselves and others in order to fight for the conditions they need that will allow them to reflect, read, share their work with others, and to produce curriculum materials. At the present time teachers in the United States generally labor under organizational constraints and ideological conditions that leave them little room for collective work and critical pursuits. Their teaching hours are too long, they are generally isolated in cellular structures and have few opportunities to work with their peers; moreover, they generally have little to say over the selection, organization, and distribution of teaching materials. Furthermore, they operate under class loads and within an industrial timetable that is oppressive. Their salaries are a scandal and only now is this being recognized by the American public.

The issue is, of course, that intellectual work that operates in the interest of critical pedagogies needs to be supported by practical conditions, and that by fighting for conditions that support joint teaching, collective writing and research, and democratic planning, teachers will make inroads into opening new spaces for creative and reflective discourse and action. The importance of such a discourse cannot be overemphasized. For within such a discourse teachers can develop an emancipatory pedagogy that relates language and power, takes popular experiences seriously as part of the learning process, combats mystification and helps students to reorder critically the raw experiences of their lives.

I want to end by arguing that all those concerned with the issue of how schools can empower both teachers and students need to re-establish a concern for the political and moral purposes of education. We need to fight against those who would simply make schools an adjunct of the corporation or local church. Schools, after all, are more than "company stores" and Sunday Schools, and need to be seen as vital sites for the development of democracy. Schools need to be defended as an important public service that educates students to be critical citizens capable of exhibiting civic courage. Democracy requires citizens who can think, challenge, take risks, and believe that their actions will make a difference in the larger society. This means that public schools need to become places that provide the opportunity for literate occasions, that is, opportunities for students to share their experiences, work in social relations that emphasize care and concern for others, and be introduced to forms of knowledge that provide them with the opportunity to fight for a quality of life in which all human beings benefit.

In short, I want to re-emphasize that teachers as transformative intellectuals must concern themselves with the business of moral and political education and not be a party to the ideologically transparent argument that they become more like experts and professionals. As educators, we need to become empowered, and the route to that goal is not through definitions of professionalism that take as their first concern the testing of teachers. The goal for us as teachers is to take seriously a view of collective power that provides the ideological and material conditions to work with dignity, and to expand the possibilities that all humans have to make democracy a reality and the world a better place in which to live. The real issue for teachers and for public schooling in general is to reclaim the notions of struggle, solidarity and hope around forms of pedagogy and social action that expand rather than restrict the notions of democracy and public life. If we are to prevent democracy from collapsing into a new form of barbarism, we will have to fight hard both in and out of schools to rescue the language of tradition, morality, and possibility from the militarists, cold-war warriors, evangelists, and corporate technocrats who are more aggressive then ever in squelching out voices that don't represent their own interests, who threaten the quality of life and civil liberties that need to be preserved and extended in this country. This means we will have to struggle collectively as transformative intellectuals, as educators who have a social vision and commitment to make public schools democratic public spheres, where all children, regardless of race, class, gender, and age, can learn what it means to be able to fully participate in the ongoing struggle to make democracy the medium through which they extend the potential and possibilities of what it means to be human and to live in a just society.

ENDNOTES

1. George S. Counts, "Dare Progressive Education Be Progressive?", *Progressive Education* 9:4 (April 1932), p. 259.

2. Henry A. Giroux and Peter McLaren, "Teacher Education and the Politics of Engagement: The Case for Democratic Schooling," *Harvard Educational Review* 56:3 (August 1986), pp. 213–238.

3. Richard Sennett, "Living and Dead Space," unpublished paper.

4. Edward H. Berman, "The Improbability of Meaningful Educational Reform," *Issues in Education* 3 (1985), pp. 99–112; Barbara Finkelstein, "Education and the Retreat from Democracy in the United States, 1979-198?", *Teachers College Record,* 86 (Winter, 1984), pp. 280–281.

5. See, for instance, U.S. Department of Education, *What Works: Research About Teaching and Learning* (U.S. Government Printing Office, 1986).

6. National Coalition of Advocates for Students, *Barriers to Excellence: Our Children at Risk* (Boston: The National Coalition of Advocates for Students, 1986).

7. See, for example, the text of Secretary Bennett's Address at Harvard University 350th Anniversary in *The Chronicle of Higher Education,* 33:7 (October 15, 1986), pp. 27–30.

8. *New York Times,* October 17, 1986.

9. I am using the term "influential" to refer to those reports that have played a major role in shaping educational policy at both the national and local levels. These include: The National Commission on Excellence in Education, *A Nation at Risk: The Imperative for Educational Reform* (Washington, D.C.: Government Printing Office, 1983); Task force on Education for Economic Growth, Education Commission of the States, *Action for Excellence: A Comprehensive Plan to Improve our Nation's Schools* (Denver: Education Commission of the States, 1983); The Twentieth Century Fund Task Force on Federal Elementary and Secondary Education Policy, *Making the Grade* (New York: The Twentieth Century Fund, 1983); Carnegie Corporation, *Education and Economic Progress: Toward a National Policy* (New York: Carnegie Corporation, 1983); Carnegie Forum on Education and the Economy, *A Nation Prepared: Teachers for the 21st Century* (Hyattsville, MD, Carnegie Forum, 1986).

10. Marilyn Frankenstein and Louis Kampf, "Preface" to "The Other End of the Corridor: The Effect of Teaching on Teachers," by the Boston Women Teachers' Group. *Radical Teacher,* No. 23 (1983), p. 1.

11. Linda Darling-Hammond: "Valuing Teachers: The Making of a Profession," *Teachers College Record* 87:2 (Winter 1985), p. 210.

12. Stanley Aronowitz and Henry A. Giroux, *Education Under Siege* (South Hadley, Mass.: Bergin and Garvey Publishers, 1985).

13. Ibid, pp. 23–45.

14. Ibid.

15. Sharon Welch, *Communities of Resistance and Solidarity* (New York: Orbis Press, 1985), p. 31.

16. See Rebecca S. Chopp, *The Praxis of Suffering: An Interpretation of Liberation and Political Theologies* (New York: Orbis Press, 1986).

17. Michelle Fine, "Silencing in Public Schools," *Language Arts* (forthcoming).

18. Michel Foucault, "Two Lectures," in *Power/Knowledge: Selected Interviews and Other Writings, 1972–1977*, edited by Colin Gordin (New York: Pantheon Press, 1980), pp. 31–32.

19. Hannah Arendt, *The Human Condition* (Chicago: University of Chicago Press, 1958).

20. Henry A. Giroux, "Radical Pedagogy and the Politics of Student Voice," *Interchange* 17:1 (1986), pp. 48–69.

21. Valerie Walkerdine, "On the Regulation of Speaking and Silence: Subjectivity, Class and Gender in Contemporary Schooling," in *Language, Gender, and Childhood*, eds. Carolyn Steedman, Cathy Urwin, and Valerie Walkerdine (London: Routledge and Kegan Paul, 1985). pp. 203–241.

22. Michelle Fine, "Why Urban Adolescents Drop Into and Out of Public High School," *Teachers College Record* 87:3 (1986), pp. 393–409.

23. Agnes Heller, "The Basic Question of Moral Philosophy," *Philosophy and Social Criticism* 1:11 (1985), pp. 35–61.

24. Roger Simon, "Empowerment as a Pedagogy of Possibility," an invited paper delivered at The American Dreams Symposium: The National Debate About the Future of Education, Indiana. Pennsylvania, October 23–25, 1986.

25. Aronowitz and Giroux, op. cit.

26. Henry A. Giroux, "Citizenship, Public Philosophy, and the Struggle for Democracy," *Educational Theory* (forthcoming).

Index